REGNUM EDINBURGH 2010 SERIES

Evangelical and Frontier Mission Perspectives on the Global Progress of the Gospel

REGNUM EDINBURGH 2010 SERIES

The Centenary of the World Missionary Conference of 1910, held in Edinburgh, was a suggestive moment for many people seeking direction for Christian mission in the twenty-first century. Several different constituencies within world Christianity held significant events around 2010. From 2005, an international group worked collaboratively to develop an intercontinental and multi-denominational project, known as Edinburgh 2010, and based at New College, University of Edinburgh. This initiative brought together representatives of twenty different global Christian bodies, representing all major Christian denominations and confessions, and many different strands of mission and church life, to mark the Centenary.

Essential to the work of the Edinburgh 1910 Conference, and of abiding value, were the findings of the eight think-tanks or 'commissions'. These inspired the idea of a new round of collaborative reflection on Christian mission – but now focused on nine themes identified as being key to mission in the twenty-first century. The study process was polycentric, open-ended, and as inclusive as possible of the different genders, regions of the world, and theological and confessional perspectives in today's church. It was overseen by the Study Process Monitoring Group: Miss Maria Aranzazu Aguado (Spain, The Vatican), Dr Daryl Balia (South Africa, Edinburgh 2010), Mrs Rosemary Dowsett (UK, World Evangelical Alliance), Dr Knud Jørgensen (Norway, Areopagos), Rev. John Kafwanka (Zambia, Anglican Communion), Rev. Dr Jooseop Keum (Korea, World Council of Churches), Dr Wonsuk Ma (Korea, Oxford Centre for Mission Studies), Rev. Dr Kenneth R. Ross (UK, Church of Scotland), Dr Petros Vassiliadis (Greece, Aristotle University of Thessalonikki), and coordinated by Dr Kirsteen Kim (UK, Edinburgh 2010).

These publications reflect the ethos of Edinburgh 2010 and will make a significant contribution to ongoing studies in mission. It should be clear that material published in this series will inevitably reflect a diverse range of views and positions. These will not necessarily represent those of the series' editors or of the Edinburgh 2010 General Council, but in publishing them the leadership of Edinburgh 2010 hopes to encourage conversation between Christians and collaboration in mission. All the series' volumes are commended for study and reflection in both church and academy.

Series Editors

Knud Jørgensen	Areopagos Foundation, Norway, MF Norwegian School of Theology & the Lutheran School of Theology, Hong Kong. Chair of Edinburgh 2010 Study Process Monitoring Group
Kirsteen Kim	Leeds Trinity University College and Edinburgh 2010 Research Coordinator, UK
Wonsuk Ma	Oxford Centre for Mission Studies, Oxford, UK
Tony Gray	Words by Design, Bicester, UK

REGNUM EDINBURGH 2010 SERIES

Evangelical and Frontier Mission Perspectives on the Global Progress of the Gospel

Edited by Beth Snodderly and A. Scott Moreau

First published 2011 by Regnum Books International

Regnum is an imprint of the Oxford Centre for Mission Studies
St. Philip and St. James Church
Woodstock Road
Oxford OX2 6HR, UK
www.ocms.ac.uk/regnum

09 08 07 06 05 04 03 7 6 5 4 3 2 1

British Library Cataloguing in Publication Data
A catalogue record for this book is available from the British Library

ISBN: 978-1-506476-00-1

Typeset by Words by Design

Distributed by 1517 Media in the US and Canada

CONTENTS

Foreword

The centennial celebrations of the Edinburgh 1910 conference offered Christians of all stripes multiple opportunities to reflect on the past century of mission. Dynamic growth in many sectors of the church in almost every corner of the world might not have surprised the Edinburgh delegates, but the flavor and consistency of the present world church might well have.

Over the course of the twentieth century one of the stories of the church that has moved towards center stage is the growth of evangelicalism around the world. While certainly until the late 1980s this went largely unnoticed among the academic elite of the world, even so by then the vast majority of the missionaries serving to and from every corner of the globe were be framed in some way by this evangelical surge (see Moreau).

As we reflect on the past century, then, the stories of the evangelical world church deserve to be heard. In this volume, we do not have space to even begin to scratch the surface. Being forced to choose an orientation, we collected stories and thinking related to the way evangelicals have idealized, operationalized and organized in light of the remaining frontiers of mission.

Is it appropriate to talk about frontiers when there are literally Christians in every country of the world, and almost every country is sending out missionaries in some form or another? Evangelicals resoundingly say "Yes!" The frontiers, as evidenced by the authors found herein, are not identified in terms of national identity, but people groups. Evangelicals, characterized as activists, have actively pursued an emerging set of goals developed in relation to "peoples" of the world. While there is not yet unanimity in how a "people group" is to be defined, there is large agreement that cultural and linguistic boundaries are front and center in our understanding of the frontiers that remain.

It is appropriate, then, to consider this book as a collection of case studies in evangelical reflection and praxis in relation to what we see as the continuing frontiers in mission. This means that the collection is not intended to give a full picture of evangelicals and all of our efforts. Rather, it is a picture highlighting elements of what we as editors consider the most central of the numerous evangelical missional trajectories.

As reading through the chapters will make clear, while there are numerous "cooperative" efforts among evangelicals, there is no overarching organization orchestrating us. Instead, there are Edinburgh 1980 (Taylor) and Tokyo 2010 conference (Higgins) follow-up organizations (Cho and Taylor; Wan). Pentecostal mission movements dot almost every nook and cranny of the globe (Johnson), the Lausanne Movement empowers multiple networks (Moreau; Lorance; Wan), associations of agencies research and count "unreached" peoples (Haney). This does not even include the World Evangelical Alliance, the nearest evangelical equivalent to the World Council of Churches (the WEA is not the complete focus of any chapter, but the story of the Missions Commission is outlined by Moreau).

This does not even take into account the unnumbered organizations and movements springing up around the world, from Francophone Africa (Bongoyok) to Korea (Park) to China (Xin). Nor does it consider the leavening influence among evangelical mission by institutions that promoted frontier mission thinking, including Fuller School of Intercultural Studies (Parsons), the US Center for World Mission (Winter) and the Perspectives course (Huneycutt). Each of these organizations and associations operate independently and will continue to do so for the foreseeable future, a natural outgrowth of the 'sodalities' as 'corporate kingdoms' (Blincoe).

Despite the numerical success of evangelicals globally over the twentieth century, there are also significant challenges ahead. In the final section we are oriented to some of these challenges. For example, evangelicals have been characterized as too "soul" focused and not genuinely holistic, charges leveled not only without but also within. For decades Rene Padilla has been one such voice challenging fellow evangelicals towards integral mission. Before his death in 2009, Ralph D. Winter stated, "The most important trend in missions today is a recovery from a gospel of merely personal salvation to a restoration of kingdom thinking." Gregory Boyd reminds us that our enemies are not people, but a spiritual army arrayed against the advance of God's Kingdom; this challenge is unavoidable and is foundational to biblically-framed mission. Robert Priest concludes the volume by pulling together multiple strands to weave an outlook on this new globalized mission from everywhere to everywhere.

The vast majority of today's evangelicals are completely unaware that in ecumenical circles by the early 1960s the reality of mission on six continents was already recognized. While it is true that we have only lately come to this recognition, it is also true that the framing of today's "from everywhere to everywhere" is not the same vision as "Mission on Six Continents" promoted at the 1963 WMC gathering in Mexico City. Perhaps that is the clearest message emanating from the chapters collected in this volume. That it highlights evangelical perspectives and priorities on global mission is a reminder of just how significant the differences are.

A. SCOTT MOREAU

HISTORICAL OVERVIEW

EVANGELICAL MISSIONS DEVELOPMENT 1910 TO 2010 IN THE NORTH AMERICAN SETTING: REACTION AND EMERGENCE

A. Scott Moreau

***Editors' Note**: The following article was developed for the 9th International Symposium, 'Reflection on 20th Century Church and Theology and 21st Century Outlook on Mission of Korean Church', sponsored by the Presbyterian College and Theological Seminary. The Symposium was designed to help Koreans better understand the relationship of the Lausanne Movement to the World Council of Churches in light of the separate conferences that were held in 2010 celebrating the centenary of the 1910 World Missionary Conference held in Edinburgh. Thus this chapter is intended to highlight the Lausanne Movement rather than evangelical mission as a whole.*

Historical Antecedents: (1600s to 1800s)

A good student of history understands that it is wise to see the century of mission from 1910 on in light of the context of the centuries that directly preceded it. While time and space requires that we do little more than gloss over very important issues in the prior centuries, each of those issues had a strong impact on what took place beginning in 1910.

In the World

The Scientific Revolution, starting in the 16th century, brought massive changes in thinking in Western circles which two centuries later culminated in the Industrial Revolution. Throughout these periods, thinking in the West shifted and many Westerners steadily lost their inherently religious worldview as their beliefs were challenged in ever increasing ways. For example, most of the best scientific thinkers of the 16th through 18th centuries were committed Christians whose belief in God motivated them to explore his creation through increasingly powerful tools of mathematics and reason. However, by the 19th and 20th centuries many of the best of the scientists were those who challenged religious faith and the Bible with scientific and rational reasoning. While the Romanticism of the 19th century in the West sought to re-capture intuition, especially in art and literature, this was not a return to faith as previously practiced. It is understandable then that by the late 19th and early 20th centuries, proponents of Modernism proclaimed traditional forms of living, thinking, and working as outdated and in need of replacement to keep up with the massive technological and industrial changes that were sweeping the Western world. Ultimately the modernist replacement of traditions had greatest impact on the Church in the period we are considering in this presentation.

In the Church

The Lausanne Movement as we know it today had its origins in the evangelicalism of the West, and the United States in particular. This is not to deny the concurrent massive shifts in the world church, and especially in the Majority World, which will come to the front in the later parts of this discussion.

Despite changes in thinking in the sciences that ultimately brought in Modernism, the extraordinary impact of the Protestant Reformation continued during these centuries. So too did the impact of the influence of Pietism. Together these were powerful prompts for many Europeans to migrate to the United States, and for such developments in the US as First Amendment of the US Constitution, which separated church from state, allowing American churches to be untethered and establishing them as voluntary organizations, which dramatically affected the era we consider in this presentation (Beuttler 2008, 113-14). They were also the foundation for many of the values embedded within today's American forms of evangelicalism such as the centrality of the Bible, that we are saved by grace through faith, personal piety, the priesthood of believers, and focus on preaching the gospel everywhere in the world.

The first Great Awakening (1730s to 1740s), precipitated by George Whitefield's arrival in the new world, touched people of all classes. The revivals incorporated emotion as a significant element in religious experience, which sharply contrasted with the focus on reason in the scientific worldview. Near the end of the 18th century, William Carey's *An Enquiry into the Obligations of Christians to use Means for the Conversion of the Heathens* (1792) made the case both for the relevancy of the Great Commission for contemporary Christians and for the development of missionary societies. The Second Great Awakening (1790s to 1840s) further stimulated religious devotion in the Americas. During this time, the word 'evangelical' was a negative one. It was applied especially to those coming to faith through the Second Great Awakening, used by detractors to indicate fanaticism in religious devotion and condemnation of the pleasures that society most enjoyed (*Oxford English Dictionary*).

Over the course of the nineteenth century, travelers – including missionaries – encountered new religions and new cultures and were challenged by lack of response in many parts of the world. Missionaries in particular hoped to spread Christianity, civilization and commerce (the famous 'Three C's' of the colonial era) across the world, though not always in that order. At the same time, the continued shifts towards Modernism challenged Christians and eventuated in the beginnings of liberal Christianity.

The intermingling of Carey's vision and the various revivals, built on the foundation of the Reformation and Pietism, and together with advances in transportation, yielded what has been termed the Great Century of Mission, even though at the time this was primarily due to British and European – rather than American – missionary efforts. The Americans were too busy taming their own country – especially the so-called Wild West – to have much extra energy for international missions! However, by the end of the 19th century, this had changed.

Thus, by 1900, rival forces were influencing European and American churches and pulling them in multiple directions simultaneously. The American missional enterprise was set for splits in multiple directions during the century to follow. In what follows we present the story of evangelical mission in four time periods: 1) 1910 to 1945; 2) 1946 to 1974; 3) 1975 to 2000; and 4) 2001 to the present. For each period we will 1) sketch out major events in the world that shaped missions as a whole, 2) identify evangelical perspectives on selected issues of the growing ecumenical movement and 3) survey developments within evangelical mission practice and thinking. By this we hope to give a better understanding of the Lausanne Movement and the reasons Lausanne chose to celebrate the centenary of the 1910 Edinburgh Conference separately from the Ecumenical Movement.

Evangelical Missions 1910–1945: Shaken Foundations

World Context

Tumultuous is too mild of a word to describe the world events between the Edinburgh World Missionary conference and the end of World War II. Participants at Edinburgh, including Samuel A. Moffett, founder of PCTS, who came as the Korean Presbyterian representative, could have hardly imagined that in the next 36 years 1) a great world war which would kill some 15 million soldiers would be started within 4 years between 'Christian' countries, 2) Russia would become a communist nation, 3) a massive influenza pandemic would strike one-third of the world's population and take the lives of some 50 million people, 4) the US stock market would crash resulting in a decade-long unprecedented economic depression and 5) this would be followed by an even greater world war in which as many as 72 million would die (including 6 million Jews) and atomic weapons would be developed and deployed. It was a tumultuous period indeed!

The Ecumenical World from an Evangelical Perspective

Kyo Seong Ahn, a graduate of PCTS and missionary in Mongolia, noted of the participants at the Edinburgh conference:

> ... To put it bluntly, most of the participants of the Edinburgh Conference could be labeled as 'ecumenical evangelicals'. While they were open to the ideal of the ecumenism, their basic stance of mission was of traditional evangelicalism. In their understanding of mission, mission and evangelism (or church-planting) were nearly interchangeable. (2003, 4)

Following Latourette, Samuel Escobar agrees, noting that the Edinburgh 1910 participants reflected the 'evangelical-pietistic-puritan spirit that marked world Protestantism' at the time (2006, 3). While it was originally to be called the 'Third Ecumenical Missionary Conference' the word 'ecumenical' in the title was intended to convey 'the whole human race in its scope' (Stanley 2006, 171) rather than the meaning of the term as used today.

Unfortunately, as far as evangelicals have been concerned, over the thirty-six years encompassed in this period a confluence of events shifted the mainline denominations in an ever-more modernist (or liberal) direction. While evangelicals participated less frequently as the years went by, they still closely watched and grew increasingly concerned at the theological trajectories evidenced in the writings and conferences that followed.

Starting in 1910 among Presbyterians, the fundamentalist-modernist controversy raged over more than two decades, with Modernism gaining increasing influence (see Beuttler 2008, 113-15). The positions of liberal preacher Harry Emerson Fosdick and the financially significant Rockefeller family gained increasing influence among mainline churches, colleges and seminaries. Wilbert Shenk summarizes:

> The lines of division between liberal and fundamentalist were increasingly drawn with liberals embracing the 'civilizing' vision of modernity and fundamentalists reacting by emphasizing what they felt the liberals had abandoned of orthodox faith. (1992, 74)

Evangelical missionaries typically lived abroad for years between home furloughs. Each time they came home, they saw modernist shifts in home churches, denominations, and schools. At the same time, the International Missionary Council (IMC), founded in 1921 at Lake Mohonk as a result of Edinburgh 1910 meetings – and despite strong evangelical voices within its ranks – also drifted in the modernist direction, seen through articles in *International Review of Missions (IRM)* (founded 1912) and books such as *Rethinking Missions* (1933; the Hocking Report; see Pierson 2003, 70). Just as alarming to evangelicals was the decline of evangelistic vigor of important mission-focused organizations such as the YMCA, YWCA, Student Volunteer Movement and World Student Christian Federation, which were co-opted by Woodrow Wilson's concept of 'internationalization', which predisposed them to focus on human efforts to establish world peace and unity as the coming of the Kingdom of God (see Robert 2002).

It needs to be recognized that many (if not most) of the missionaries who had been on the field prior to 1910 were far more conservative than their church leaders at home. Over this span, they felt increasingly ignored (at best) and ridiculed (at worst) in the public eye. They lost control of almost every mainline denomination and mission organization and felt that reversing those losses an insurmountable task. Though strong conservative voices remained in the ecumenical missions world (e.g., Hendrik Kraemer 1938), many conservatives perceived them to be fighting a losing battle. Adding to their alarm was the influence of the increasingly liberal colleges on the next generation of well-educated missionaries and denominational leaders.

Evangelical Missions

Considering the total effect of these perceptions, and putting it terms and Koreans well understand, evangelicals in the mainline denominations and mission structures experienced a great loss of face. They began questioning whether they should stay with their eroding organizations or leave. Those who stayed had to decide whether to remain quietly faithful to what God had called them to do or to join the fight to turn their organizations around. Throughout this period, the terms 'evangelical', 'fundamentalist', and 'conservative' were all developing but generally could be applied to the same group of people (Bassett 1991) who were distinguished primarily by the commitments to the five fundamentals (see below).

Those who left their mainline organizations also had to choose between joining the more conservative faith missions movement, such as China Inland Mission, and starting their own evangelical mission organizations, denominations, and Bible colleges. The separation of church and state in the US Constitution, as noted earlier, granted to every individual the right and freedom to choose which direction he or she would go. Even though many new organizations appeared during this time, perhaps what is more difficult for Asian and other international audiences to appreciate is the priority Americans placed then and now on individual freedom and the ability to make their decisions on what to do largely as individuals rather than as collective groups. In light of the stress on the individual in American culture, and the voluntary nature of churches and mission organizations, it is not surprising that the pattern of splintering of American denominations and mission structures, which started during this period of 1910–1945, has not stopped since then.

The flashpoint for the fundamentalist-modernist controversy came in 1909 with the ordination of three pastors in the Presbyterian Church in the USA who refused to affirm the virgin birth of Jesus. In the following 1910 General Assembly, the Presbyterians decided to accept five doctrines as fundamental to the Christian faith: 1) The inspiration of the Bible by the Holy Spirit and the inerrancy of Scripture as a result of this; 2) The virgin birth of Christ; 3) The belief that Christ's death was an atonement for sin; 4) The bodily resurrection of Christ; and 5) The historical reality of Christ's miracles (see Marsden, 1991,

117). Proponents called these teachings the fundamentals, and those who promoted them were fundamentalists. Evangelicals, committed to these beliefs, were thus identified as fundamentalists. Initially the evangelical-fundamentalists did not insist on separating from the mainline denominations. Rather, they stayed within them and struggled for continued acceptance of their views.

Preachers like Dwight Moody and Billy Sunday were part of the fundamentalist movement, and were largely disdained by intellectual mainline church leaders and members. As more US denominations engaged in their own versions of the fundamentalist-modernist controversy, and as prominent denominational universities – most notably Princeton – publicly fought theological battles, many evangelical-fundamentalists felt that becoming educated was equivalent to becoming liberal, and this attitude carried to the end of this period. Bible institutes were started, but without the intention of becoming colleges or universities.

Because mainline church organizations and leaders so thoroughly dominated mission leadership and structures, the more conservative missionaries also eventually had to decide their own response. Many who stayed within their mainline missions did so at least in part because of the strong evangelical voices that still were part of the IMC. It is easy to understand, however, that people on both sides closely watched everything the IMC did.

In 1917, when nondenominational agencies lost their vote in the Foreign Mission Conference of North America (FMCNA, the founder of the National Council of Churches in the USA), they banded together to found the Interdenominational Foreign Missions Association (IFMA). The splintering of mission over the modernist-fundamentalist divide was evident, in that at least fifty-six new agencies were founded from 1918 to 1945, the vast bulk of them nondenominational faith agencies founded by conservatives. In a parallel development, at least in part due to the shocks of WW I and the increasingly secular vision of the mainline Christian internationalists, fundamentalists increasingly identified with Premillennial eschatology (a requirement for agencies affiliated with the IFMA). They judged the promotion of building the Kingdom of God through human efforts and commitment to the social gospel as non-biblical wasting of resources.

By and large mainline leaders ignored or ridiculed the fundamentalists during this time. Some fundamentalists fought back. Others decided to withdraw and found new organizations, including Bible colleges and other educational institutions, which eventually became the evangelical Christian colleges, universities, and seminaries of today and served at the time as the seedbeds of early evangelical intellectualism. By the 1930s those who most explicitly identified themselves as fundamentalists – eventually called separatists – were demanding separation from every organization that had compromised at any level. Not all fundamentalists agreed, and by the end of WW II a more cooperative type of evangelical – initially called neo-evangelicals – began to surface which maintained fundamental doctrines but chose to engage the mainline church and culture rather than separate from it. With the founding of the National Association of Evangelicals (1942) and a commission within the NEA called the Evangelical Foreign Mission Association (EFMA) which was to 'serve common interests of members in government relations (domestic and foreign); use of communication channels; cooperative purchasing/travel; and relations between each other' (Billy Graham Center), evangelical denominations and mission agencies both had means to associate under a non-separatist organizational umbrella.

Finally, we must mention that during this period a third stream of the church was born and began to grow rapidly. Pentecostals, growing from the holiness denominations, and experiencing God's presence in tongues and other signs and wonders, were disdained by both mainliners and fundamentalists. Pentecostals felt the sting of rejection from their very beginnings and knew that they had to grow their own missionaries and mission organizations from within. For example, in 1910 the Church of God (Cleveland) began missions efforts in the Bahamas, Egypt and Cuba (http://churchofgod.org/centennial-of-church-of-god-world-missions). By the end of WW II, Pentecostals had started numerous denominations, many with vibrant international missions.

Evangelical Missions 1946–1974: New Opportunities

World Context

Tension, turmoil and wonder are all terms that apply to this era of world history. One poignant symbol of the *tension* was the 'doomsday clock'. Started in 1947, the minute hand of the clock was moved closer or farther away from midnight depending on the military tensions in the world, and especially during the Cold War between the United States (and Western democratic nations) and the Soviet Union (and its allies).

'Winds of Change' is perhaps the best symbol of the *turmoil* in which the 400 years of European political imperialism drew to a close (at least politically; see Winter 1970, 3). These winds – of hurricane force – blew across the colonial empires resulting in most of the former colonies in Asia and Africa emerging as independent nations. The turmoil was also seen as Russia and the United States fought proxy wars in Asia (e.g., Korea, Vietnam) and wrangled for the allegiance of Africa's new nations (e.g., Congo, Mozambique, Uganda).

Internally, the US and many Western countries experienced other types of turmoil during the 1960s, including the US civil rights battles, student militancy over the war in Vietnam, fascination with drugs and new forms of music. Europe and Japan began the long process of rebuilding after the war; Korea, finally free from Japanese control, was divided by outside forces into two nations; Mao's Cultural Revolution (1966 to 1976) left China in shambles; Cambodia became known for its killing fields and the Czech uprising (1968) foreshadowed things to come. From the evangelical perspective, it is vitally important to bear in mind that during this period the newly formed nations – while physically more accessible than ever – were able to make their own decisions on closing their borders to overt missionary work.

Wonder does not even begin to describe the changes seen in the communication explosion of the dawn of television and satellite and the leaps in transportation ranging from the emergence of commercial airlines to the space race and first steps of a human on the moon. Suddenly everywhere in the world was far more accessible than ever before, opening doors to relief and development aid – as well as military intervention – in any location on the globe. The day of global communication, travel, and real-time interaction had dawned.

The Ecumenical World from an Evangelical Perspective

The initial swelling of American mainline churches in the 1950s stalled in the late 1960s and began to reverse in the 1970s. By 1975 the mainline denominations as a whole were losing members, whether to evangelical churches or to no church at all. Even so, it was arguably the strongest period of the century for the whole ecumenical movement.

The creation of the World Council of Churches (WCC) in 1948 formalized one of the dreams of institutional ecumenism. Over the next decade, IMC members debated whether to join the WCC or remain separate. Those who argued for separation feared that the concerns of the WCC would marginalize the IMC once it became one of several administrative units within in the WCC. The current organigram of the WCC shows that the expressed concerns were well-founded [1] (e.g., see Pierson 2003, 72, 76-77)

With the merger accomplished in 1961, the IMC became the Division on World Missions and Evangelism (DWME) and in 1973 the Commission on World Mission and Evangelism (CWME). As a result of the merger, a number of evangelicals left the IMC, depriving it of energy and passionate commitment to mission (Pierson 2003, 76). Now within the WCC orbit, during this phase, the DWME focused on ideas such as evangelism as presence (versus proclamation), interreligious dialogue, and seeing mission as what God is doing in the world rather than what the church does (coined in the term *missio Dei*, generally framed as the struggle for justice, and expressed with the motto 'Let the world set the agenda'). By the end of the 1960s, ecumenists had dropped the final 's' in missions and debated whether non-Christian religious adherents were 'anonymous Christians' or not (see Yates, 175-76). While evangelicals would wrestle with all of these ideas in the coming decades, the one with arguably the greatest impact was *contextualization*. First used in 1972, by the end of that decade the term would find a home in ecumenical and evangelical discussion and thinking. Many also heeded the call to a moratorium on mission

---

[1] www.oikoumene.org/en/who-are-we/organization-structure/organigram.html.

in 1973, and the decline of mainline missionaries in the 1950s eventuated in a drought by the end of the century (from 8,800 in 1952 to 2,900 in 1996 [Pierson 2003, 80]). As evangelicals interpreted it, further evidence of the erosion that was to come was seen in three mainline Protestant institutions ending formal missions training programs by 1973 (see Horner 1984, 121). South African missiologist David Bosch noted:

> Whereas evangelicals seek to apply Scripture deductively – in other words, make Scripture their point of departure from which they draw the line(s) to the present situation – ecumenicals follow the inductive method; the situation in which they find themselves becomes the hermeneutical key. Their thesis is: we determine God's will *from* a specific situation rather than *in* it. The nature and purpose of the Christian mission therefore has to be reformulated from time to time so as to keep pace with events. In the words of the Uppsala Assembly: 'The world provides the agenda'. (1980, 38)

With few exceptions (such as Anglican evangelical John Stott), evangelicals watched these shifts either from the margins of the WCC or completely outside of it. One largely unrecognized area in which mainline ecumenists, conservative evangelicals, and Roman Catholic missiologists found common ground during this time was in the American Society for Missiology (ASM; founded 1973). An outgrowth of the American Professors of Missions (APM; founded 1952), from its inception the ASM incorporated an ingenious structure of rotating the leadership among conciliars, evangelicals and Catholics, that ensured that none could gain control of the society. However, not all evangelicals were interested in taking part.

While it was not an ecumenical event, we must mention the Second Vatican Council (1962-65) because it impacted both the WCC and evangelicals through the unprecedented Catholic recognition of Protestants as separated brethren and the sweeping *aggiornamento* (updating) reforms that came (Yates 1994, 172).

Evangelical Missions

From the explosion of new evangelical mission agencies in the immediate aftermath of WW II to the Congress on World Evangelization in Lausanne in 1974, evangelicals were the most active proponents of mission through this period (Robert 1994; 50; see also Anderson 2000, 276-97). In the 1950s neo-evangelicals lost the 'neo' and became mainstream evangelicals. In the meantime, from the evangelical perspective, the fundamentalists had withdrawn from everyone but themselves.

Both the 1945 call of Douglas MacArthur for 10,000 missionaries to come to Japan and the organizational skills learned by many lay Christians in the military around the world contributed to the explosion of new evangelical organizations formed after WW II. From student organizations to newly formed missions agencies, they built up evangelical missions in ways never before seen.

Over the 1950s the ecumenical movement reached its peak, but by the 1960s had begun to decline. Evangelicals, however, continually gathered personnel, organizational, and financial strength. The newly formed NAE and EFMA grew consistently after 1945, the latter becoming an umbrella for the new student ministries and mission agencies. Important highlights include evangelicals founding Fuller Theological Seminary (1947), Billy Graham holding numerous successful and well-publicized evangelistic crusades starting in Los Angeles (1951), the founding of the World Evangelical Fellowship (re-organized from The Evangelical Alliance in 1951) with four commissions (Evangelism, Missionary, Literature and Christian Action), Campus Crusade for Christ starting on the UCLA campus (1951), the Billy Graham Evangelistic Association (BGEA) being formed and in turn launching *Christianity Today* (1956), the IFMA and EFMA jointly launching *Evangelical Missions Quarterly* (1964) and Donald McGavran starting the Fuller School of World Missions (1965). Evangelicals founded at least 126 new missions agencies by the end of 1974, clearly demonstrating mission vitality. As early as 1963 an ecumenical observer pointed to the explosive growth of evangelical missions and comparatively slow growth of mainline missions:

> The number of foreign missionaries of all agencies related to the Division of Foreign Missions of the National Council increased from 1952 to 1960 by 4.5%; those of the conservative evangelicals by 149.5%; the income for 'foreign missions' of the former by 50.5% ; of the latter by 167.3%. (Smith 1963, 182; see also Anderson 2000, 277)

Further evidences of evangelical vitality were the numerous mission conferences and congresses organized by and for evangelicals from the end of WW II to 1974. In 1936, evangelicals within the increasingly liberal Student Volunteer Movement formed the Student Foreign Mission Fellowship (SFMF). InterVarsity Christian Fellowship (IVCF) traces its origin to 1877 when a group of Cambridge students organized to pray and study the Bible together. The resulting organization came to the United States in 1938. In 1945, SFMF merged into ICF, becoming its mission department (Beuttler 2008, 124). In 1946 InterVarsity organized a missions conference for college students which, in spite of an ice storm on the first day, was attended by 576 students – 300 of whom pledged to serve Christ overseas (Rice 2006). This blossomed into the much-anticipated triennial Urbana conferences. The last Urbana of this period took place in 1973 and welcomed 14,158 delegates.[2] In 1947, ICF became one of the founding members of the International Fellowship of Evangelical Students (now in 143 countries.[3]

In early 1966, the IFMA and EFMA jointly sponsored the Congress on the Church's Worldwide Mission (Wheaton 1966). The 938 registered delegates

---

[2] www.urbana.org.

[3] http://www.intervarsity.org/aboutus/history.php.

represented over 258 evangelical mission-focused organizations. The two associations at that time represented more missionaries than the entire WCC, and the Congress redressed the fact that no explicitly evangelical mission conference had been held since Edinburgh 1910 (Moreau 2000). By 1972, Clyde Taylor, chair of the WEF Missionary Commission since 1951, reported:

> There are only 9 evangelical missions associations in the world.... The total missionary staff of these 9 fellowships approximates 20,000 overseas missionaries. For a total picture ... there are at least 30,000 evangelical missionaries on active duty now. Of these two-thirds are directly or indirectly related to WEF. (Howard 1986, 173)

The same year, concern on the part of Billy Graham and Carl Henry (then editor of *Christianity Today*) over the radical shift in Western theology – and the WCC in particular – framed the need for an international conference to unite evangelicals and clearly articulate and promote the evangelistic task of the Church. The result was the World Congress on Evangelism, held in Berlin (1966) with the theme 'One Race, One Gospel, One Task' attended by nearly 1,200 delegates from 100 countries. This was followed by four regional conferences (in Europe, North America, Asia, and Latin America) from 1968 to 1971. With a total of just over 8,000 delegates, they were geared to ensure that evangelicals would remain focused on the primacy of evangelism and to generate sustained momentum for the anticipated Congress on World Evangelization held in Lausanne in 1974, the evangelical capstone of this period. In the same span and independently of Lausanne, Campus Crusade organized Explo '72 (Dallas) with 80,000 participants and Explo '74 (Seoul) in which 300,000 receiving training in evangelism and discipleship.

We chose 1974 as the final year of this period because it was the year of the Congress on World Evangelization held in Lausanne. Lausanne focused on evangelization (by which the organizers meant the whole task of the church) rather than evangelism (by which they meant the proclamation of the Gospel). Over 2,700 delegates came from 150 nations; including observers, media, and guests, more than 4,000 were present. With almost one-half of the delegates from the Majority World, it was clear that evangelicals were not just Westerners. The report in *TIME* magazine noted that Lausanne '74 was 'a formidable forum, possibly the widest-ranging meeting of Christians ever held'.[4]

The Lausanne gathering had an immediate impact in at least two significant ways for evangelical mission. First was the Lausanne Covenant, ratified by all delegates. In the decades ahead the Covenant became the statement of faith adopted by literally hundreds of organizations and institutions. Second, the energy generated at Lausanne for reaching people groups rather than nation states provided a significant shift in the way evangelicals thought about the

[4] http://www.lausanne.org/about.html.

fulfillment of the Great Commission. Further impact will be seen in the discussion of the next period (1975–2000).

While the Lausanne Congress clearly deserves to be the capstone of this period, the vitality of evangelical mission-focused organizations outside of the Lausanne orbit clearly demonstrate healthy growth both in breadth across the world and in depth of theological commitment and missiological sophistication. Having felt sidelined and marginalized by ecumenical organizations through much of the first half of the twentieth century, by the end of 1974 evangelicals realized that they had significant people, organizational and financial resources. The age of the modern evangelical as a significant part of the world Church was dawning.

In the context of this dawning momentum, new foci were added to the evangelical missions agenda during this time period, 1946–1974. Bible translation was galvanized through the development of Wycliffe Bible Translators. Israel was born as a nation, generating intense interest in biblical prophecy and fueling conferences, political support, and financial support for missionary efforts. Evangelicals gained national prominence when five missionaries lost their lives while trying to reach an indigenous Indian group in Ecuador in 1956. The rise of communism and the blockade of missionary efforts behind the Iron Curtain eventuated in the development of Bible smuggling, made famous in evangelical circles by Brother Andrew. In 1963 the Theological Education by Extension (TEE) movement was launched in Guatemala by Ralph Winter and James Emery.

The development of people group thinking started with Donald McGavran's *Bridges of God* (1955) and was brought to the forefront by Ralph Winter's Lausanne 1974 address in which he demonstrated that more than two billion people were not only not yet reached, but would never be reached without important changes in missionary strategy and deployment (1975). At the same time, however, at Lausanne a significant number of evangelicals insisted that social concerns had a significant role in mission (Anderson 2000, 281-893), an issue that would grow and mature in the coming years. Finally, a new word – contextualization – appeared in the mission lexicon in 1972. While initial evangelical reaction was mixed in no small measure because it was coined in ecumenical circles and framed in terms of justice, this term would be incorporated – with shifts in its definition – into evangelical missiology by the end of the decade (Moreau 2005).

Pentecostal Missions

As with the prior period, we cannot neglect the remarkable growth of the Pentecostal movement and the developing growth of charismatics within mainline as well as evangelical denominations and organizations. Prior to the 1960s, despite their shared passion for Scripture and evangelism, evangelicals had largely dismissed the Pentecostal doctrines that evangelicals considered aberrant and the practices they had considered excessive. In the 1960s, when the Pentecostal and charismatic movements were gaining in numbers and momentum, their challenges to evangelical pneumatology in both doctrine and practice could no longer be ignored.

At least in part because of disdain for perceived Pentecostal abuses, many evangelical organizations either dismissed or even banned specific Pentecostal and charismatic practices, especially speaking in tongues. Some were more willing to accommodate Pentecostal distinctives, but not many (see Wagner 1973). By 1974, the general attitude of evangelicals towards their Spirit-oriented fellow believers was that of tension and, in too many cases, outright hostility.

As the evangelicals had felt about the ecumenical movement, so many Pentecostals felt about evangelicals. Marginalized (e.g., the IFMA did not allow Pentecostal organizations to join) and attacked (numerous evangelical books and articles criticizing Pentecostal doctrines were published from the 1960s on) some responded in kind. Most, however, simply continued to be faithful to their understanding of God's call to being Spirit-filled and doing what the Spirit led them to do. Essentially left to their own devices, Pentecostals built their own organizations and associations largely without evangelical participation. Charismatics, on the other hand, stayed in evangelical and mainline denominations and mission organizations, initiated renewal movements from within and generated both interest and anxiety primarily because they wanted others to experience what God had given to them.

Evangelical Missions 1975–2000: New Partners

World Context

Surprise is a good word to characterize the world context from 1975 to the end of the century. If you told almost anyone in 1975 that by the turn of the century the Soviet Union would have collapsed and fragmented into some fifteen countries and that the former Soviet Bloc nations in eastern Europe would be determining their own political destiny they would think of you as an unrealistic dreamer. If you added that China would finish the cultural revolution and become an economic powerhouse by pursuing capitalist economic policies, they would wonder if you could ever be taken seriously.

They would have been equally unconvinced if you predicted a rise in Islamic fundamentalism, the first Gulf War over Iraq's invasion of Kuwait; the massive failure of numerous expensive aid and development efforts (Easterly 2006), long-term civil wars in Africa, and the HIV/AIDS pandemic.

Even science fiction aficionados would find it difficult to imagine that the exponential growth of a world-wide computer network called the Internet would impact every type of media that existed in 1975 – from newspapers to television to movies – by putting instant, de-centralized world-wide communication and publication into the hands of ordinary people in most countries of the world. To imagine the impact of this development on things ranging from everyday vocabulary ('surf the Web' or 'browsing' or using 'Just Google it!' would not make sense to anyone prior to 1990) and to the world's economy would simply not be imaginable. Surprise is perhaps too mild a word; astonishment may be more accurate!

The Ecumenical World from an Evangelical Perspective

From the perspectives of many evangelicals, the WCC continued to follow the path of significant theological, religious and missiological compromises, even though evangelical voices were given space in WCC circles in new and significant ways. For example, the Commission on World Mission and Evangelism (CWME) issued statements that appeared to be intended to satisfy evangelical criticisms. Evangelical missiologists began to feel that they were being listened to, something they had not previously experienced. The fact that in an *International Review of Mission* (*IRM*) article (the *IRM* is the missiological quarterly of the WCC), an ecumenical brought together the 'stream' of the WCC conferences and assemblies with the Lausanne congresses (see Figure 1), indicated that Lausanne evangelicals were on the 'map' of ecumenical consideration. (However, the WEF general assemblies and its Mission Commission global consultations, which are better parallels to the WCC and the CWME, were conspicuously absent in this article.)

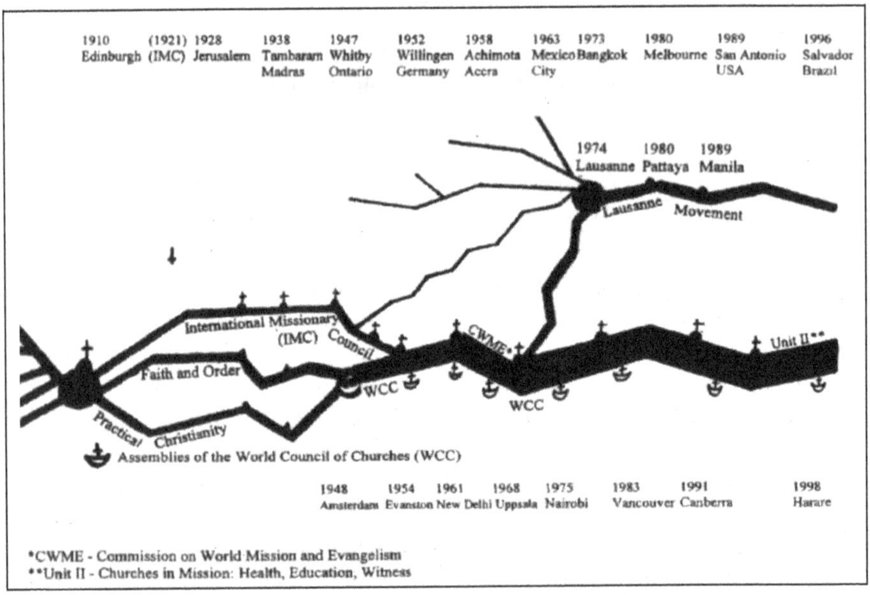

Conferences of the 20th Century from an Ecumenical Perspective (Günther 2003)

At the same time, however, events such as the incorporation of traditional religious rituals at WCC assemblies and CWME events was particularly troubling to evangelicals, and was all the evidence some needed to conclude that no real changes had been made. During the course of this phase, the commitment to Marxism as a framework for bringing justice was initially strengthened, but, with collapse of Communism, appeared to evangelicals to have lost significant momentum by the turn of the millennium.

Perhaps the biggest change – from an evangelical perspective – was that by the year 2000 many evangelical missiologists simply thought of the WCC and CWME as irrelevant to the world mission scene, which was an almost total reversal from the previous periods under consideration. Reflecting on the ecumenical streams of mission, Wilbert Shenk wrote in 1992, 'Every sign points to the fact that with the end of the modern period in world history has also come the end of modern missions' (75).

Evangelical Missions Developments

The vitality and energy of evangelical missions from the US grew almost exponentially from 1975 to 2000 (see, e.g., Crawley 2001) so that by 1991, for example, 'overseas missionary personnel of evangelical agencies outnumber those in mainline agencies by a ratio of 10 to 1' (Coote 1991). The growth was so significant that American secular intellectuals could no longer ignore evangelicals, eventuating in a shift in the historiography of mission in the 1980s (Robert 1994). Prior to then, secular intellectuals conceived of mission as nothing more than an ecumenical effort and the extension of American culture (and foreign imperialism). When they even bothered to portray evangelical missions, they did so as schismatic and ideologically driven. The massive changes in mission demographics together with the reluctant recognition of evangelical scholarship were such that secular religious historians began to disengage missions from American cultural extension and to acknowledge that evangelicals played significant roles in the story of American missional history (see Robert 1994). Within this shift, in 1989 four key distinctives that characterized evangelicals were proposed: 1) conversion and a changed life; 2) activism (especially evangelism and missionary work); 3) being Bible-centered; and 4) being Christ-centered (especially on Christ's work on the cross on our behalf) (Bebbington 1989). In 1997, Klaus Fielder noted:

> In spite of the pluriform expressions of the evangelical theology of mission, ... the evangelical theology of mission is distinguished by certain common features: (a) a close relationship to holy scripture, which is regarded as inspired and all-sufficient for life and doctrine; (b) emphasis on the atoning and redemptive work of Christ; (c) emphasis on the necessity of a personal decision of faith (conversion); and (d) the priority of evangelization and the building up of

> congregations over all other work (e.g., social justice and interreligious dialogue) in the field of mission. (1997)

In addition, it is important to note that in 1997 the definition of evangelicalism also included what evangelicals rejected, namely:

> It could not follow liberal Protestantism in embracing *(a)* the kinds of biblical criticism which undermined the deity of Christ and the authority of scripture, (*b*) evolutionary theory, or *(c)* a social gospel separated from the life-changing power of the proclaimed gospel. (Scherer *et al*., 1997)

In this section, our overview of evangelical missions will focus on the more important developments as portrayed in four confluent 'streams'. First, because they represent the evangelical parachurch and church worlds respectively, we focus on the co-sponsors of the Capetown 2010 conference. The growth and development of evangelical mission agencies was also significant during this time, and we touch on those next. This was an era in which regional and international gatherings of evangelicals virtually exploded, and in the third section we survey some of the meetings that took place outside of the LCWE and WEA orbits. While all of this was happening, a parallel set of developments in evangelical academic missiology also grew vibrantly, so we give some attention to this development as well. Throughout this period, and in each of the streams discussed, there were issues that evangelical missions discussed, analyzed, prayed about and debated. The final section of our discussion on evangelical missions is a brief presentation of those issues.

THE LAUSANNE MOVEMENT AND WEF

The Lausanne Movement blossomed with the founding of the Lausanne Committee for World Evangelization (1976), which sponsored two major gatherings and at least 47 other conferences and consultations. Regional meetings included the Chinese Congress on World Evangelization (CCOWE; 1976, 1981, 1986, 1991, 1996), the Asia Lausanne Conferences on Evangelism (1978, 1988, 1992), and Latin American Congresses on Evangelism (1969, 1979). A sampling of the national conferences held from 1975 to 1980 includes those in Kenya (1975), Nigeria (1975), India (1977), Ghana (1977), Norway (1978), Malaysia and Singapore (1978), Venezuela (1979), Germany (1980) and Guatemala (1980). Ongoing topical conferences included the International Conferences on Jewish Evangelization (1983, 1986, 1991, 1995, 1999) and the International Researchers Conferences (1987, 1996). Additionally, there were individual conferences geared to address particularly relevant issues, such as the consultations on the Homogenous Unit Principle (1977), Gospel and culture (1978), Muslim evangelization (1978), simple lifestyle (1980), evangelism and social responsibility (1982), prayer (1984), faith and modernity (1993), contextualization (1997), nominalism (1998) and spiritual warfare (2000).

The most important LCWE *consultation* of this period was the Conference on World Evangelization, held in Pattaya (Thailand) in 1980. Organized as seventeen simultaneous mini-consultations, the 650 delegates met to study theological and strategic issues related to world evangelization and to develop specific evangelistic strategies for unreached people groups (marginalized, ethnic, religious, and city peoples) as well as nominal Christian peoples. The categories indicated a lack of unanimity over the concept of 'peoples' within evangelicalism at that time. Though the conference issued a statement, its greatest legacy was the publication of the Lausanne Occasional Papers,[5] which guided evangelical mission thinking for years to come.

The most important Lausanne *congress* was the International Congress for World Evangelization II, known as 'Manila 1989'. Some 4,300 from 173 countries attended, and the organizers made a conscious effort to include more women as well as Pentecostals and charismatics in both attendance and platform participation. The primary document that came from Manila 1989 was the Manila Manifesto. It consisted of 21 affirmations followed by longer discussion under three headings (The Whole Gospel, The Whole Church, and The Whole World) and a concluding challenge. It was not intended to replace the Lausanne Covenant, but to affirm and supplement it.

The WEF held four major congresses from 1974 to 2000: 1980 (England); 1986 (Singapore), 1992 (Philippines), and 1997 (Canada). Solid growth for the WEF did not come until David Howard took over as General Secretary in 1982. Over the following decade Howard tirelessly invigorated the WEF and enabled its development as an umbrella for the global evangelical church.

WEF missional focus came initially in the development of the Theological Commission (TC), which published the journal *Evangelical Review of Theology* (1977), intended as a digest of international evangelical theology. Under Bruce Nicholls' leadership (1974 to 1986), the TC provided significant evangelical reflection on contextualization (e.g., Nicholls 1979) as well as social components of the gospel (Parker). It was his proposal which led to the 1983 conference convened by the WEF (and jointly sponsored by the LCWE, among others), 'The Church in Response to Human Need'. Known as Wheaton '83, a significant focus was to consider ways in which evangelism and social concern are both part of mission. It ultimately resulted in the publication of a book by the same title (Samuel and Sugden 1987) and the journal *Transformation* (1984).

The WEF long term impetus for mission, however, has come from the Missions Commission (MC). Re-formed in 1974, just after Lausanne congress, the MC has these goals:

1. To provide coordination, services, and exchange of information to member associations;

---

[5] http://www.lausanne.org/documents.html.

2. To offer assistance and resources for seminars, study conferences and international meetings as desired;
3. To provide mutual assistance in developing missions, education, and exchange of personnel; and,
4. To encourage the establishment of national committees where none exist. (Howard 1986, 174)

By 1975, Waldron Scott (then General Director), added that the WEF had the responsibility to 'keep the missionary task of the Church before the evangelical churches throughout the world' and that the WEF needed the MC to 'stimulate and provide guidance on strategy for mission in various forms'. Additionally, the MC would be a 'bridge-building body between the new Third World Missions and the traditional Western Missions so that help can travel in both directions in the furtherance of the Lord's work worldwide' (Howard 1986, 175).

The MC held several consultations from 1977 to 2000. The first had twelve representatives meeting in India in 1977. At the consultation on Unreached Peoples (Badenzell 1979), 27 mission leaders attended resulting in the first MC publication *World Mission: Building Bridges or Barriers?* (Williams 1979). Leaders met again under the theme, Together in Mission (Bangalore 1982). Just as David Howard had energized the WEF, Bill Taylor energized the MC after his 1986 appointment as Executive Director. Because of his background and connections, the MC played a significant role in the first COMIBAM conference in Brazil in 1987, and then organized their own major conference on Missionary Training (Manila 1989), producing *Internationalizing Missionary Training: A Global Perspective* (Taylor 1991). This was followed by the consultation on Strategic Partnerships (Manila, 1992) from which came *Kingdom Partnerships for Synergy in Missions* (Taylor 1994). Beginning in 1993, the MC turned its attention to attrition, developing the Reducing Missionary Attrition Projects (REMAP I and II) and holding an international consultation on Missionary Attrition (England, 1996) and publishing *Too Valuable to Lose: Exploring the Causes and Cures of Missionary Attrition* (Taylor 1997) as well as ongoing articles in a variety of missions journals. In 1997, attention once again was turned to National Mission Movements (Canada). The final MC consultation in this period was on Global Missiology, held in Brazil (1999); which resulted in *Global Missiology for the 21st Century: The Iguassu Dialogue* (Taylor 2000). In addition, WEF developed the widely observed International Day of Prayer for the Persecuted Church, in which millions participate around the world.

After Manila 1989, the Lausanne Movement lost energy and support from European evangelicals during the 1990s. While it is true that the 1976 formation of the Lausanne Committee for World Evangelization (LCWE) served as a launching pad for notable evangelical alliances and movements at local, national, regional and international levels (Moreau 2006), its formation was also a source of tension. The World Evangelical Fellowship (WEF) had struggled from its founding in 1951, facing such challenges as funding and tensions over American domination. Prior to the Lausanne meeting, it had requested that Lausanne allow it to handle follow-up from the 1974 consultation, but the formation of the LCWE confirmed that this would not happen. Added to the mix was the formation of the AD 2000 and Beyond Movement shortly after Manila 1989, which also drew energy and support away from Lausanne. To deal with these issues, Norwegian mission leaders from Lausanne, the WEF, and the AD 2000 Movement, together with other missions associations, met together in 1999 in Norway to reconcile and band together in what was called the Great Commission Roundtable to enable all to benefit from mutual encouragement and partnership on mission issues.

Finally, we note that in 1989 the LCWE, WEF and WCC representatives meet in an consultation on evangelism. Robert Coote, writing for the *Dictionary of the Ecumenical Movement*, noted, 'Divergent stances on the uniqueness and finality of Jesus Christ for salvation, on the role of interfaith dialogue, and on the doctrine of inspiration continue to be sources of tension between the WEF and the WCC' (1991a).

Agency Growth and Development

American evangelicals formed at least 210 mission agencies or organizations from 1975 to 2000 (derived from Moreau 2000c). By 1980 evangelicals comprised as much as 90% of the missionaries on the field (derived from Beuttler 2008, 119), and by 1999 US Protestant mission agencies which specifically defined themselves as 'ecumenical' in ecclesiastical stance comprised only 1.1% of the US Protestant mission force (though their reported budget for overseas missions work was 9.1% of the Protestant agency total [Moreau 2000c, 42]).

From 1975 to 2000, US evangelical agencies developed numerous initiatives for recruiting new missionaries, being more effective in mass outreach and the managing of tasks of missions, including the 10/40 Window, people group thinking, and coming of AD 2000.

The 10/40 Window (coined in 1989) captured the imagination of evangelical missions and became a major focus (though not without debate) for missiologists, mission agencies and mission-minded churches ('10/40 Window'). The people group thinking that came onto the public stage at Lausanne became an organizing agenda for new missions efforts among people who had no access to the gospel in their own language or cultural frames of reference. The coming of the turn of the millennium was seen by evangelicals as a challenging target date for completing the task of the Great Commission now defined in people group categories, and they developed, announced and deployed literally hundreds of plans focused on AD 2000 (Barrett and Reapsome 1988; Johnson and Barrett 1994), using tools such as the Jesus Film (developed in 1979; Eshleman 2002), SAT-7 satellite broadcasting, and Internet-based evangelism.

At the same time countries that had achieved their independence during the 'winds of change' of the second era no longer welcomed overt missionary presence, and new strategies (e.g., non-residential missionaries; Garrison 1990) and terminology (e.g., creative-access) were developed to describe and deploy people in such settings. While some doors closed in the 1950s and 1960s, others opened in the 1990s when the Soviet Union split into multiple independent countries. Such a massive missionary influx resulted that many agencies banded together to ensure better cooperation and less competition for their work in Russia (Bahler 1992).

By the end of the century, however, evangelicals began discussing changes in the younger generation that would impact the entire evangelical missions enterprise. They urged mission agencies to change if they wanted to meet the new challenges in the coming century (e.g., Engel and Dyrness 2000; Gibbs 2000; Hunter 2000; Sweet 1999).

GATHERINGS

The work of Lausanne and the WEA in this period, while significant, is in some respects only the tip of the iceberg of the whole of evangelical missions. Other movements have perhaps been less visible in the larger public eye, but were the engines that drove evangelical missions to the end of the millennium. In this section we will catalog some of the more significant gatherings and events not organized by LCWE or WEF that took place from 1975 to 2000.

In what the organizers called the only parallel to Edinburgh 1910 during the century, the First World Consultation on Frontier Missions was held in Edinburgh in 1980 and brought together 270 people representing 194 evangelical mission structures to focus on anticipated mission issues prior to the turn of the century (Winter 1980). A follow up conference took place in 1989.

The BGEA sponsored three International Conferences of Itinerant Evangelists before the turn of the century (1983, 1986 and 2000), each of which had some 10,000 participants. The Billy Graham Center (established at Wheaton College in 1980) sponsored more than 100 mission conferences and consultations between its founding in 1976 and 2000 (Billy Graham Center N.d.), including A Century of World Evangelization: North American Evangelical Missions, 1886–1986 (1986), Conference on Evangelizing World Class Cities (1986), Evangelicalism in Transatlantic Perspective (1992), Evangelism Consultation 2000 (1995), Consultation on Support of Indigenous Christian Ministries in the Majority World (1996) and Internet Evangelism Conference (1999).

The AD 2000 and Beyond Movement, formed immediately after the LCWE Manila 1989 congress, sponsored three major Global Consultation on World Evangelization (GCOWE) meetings Singapore (1989), Seoul, Korea (1995), and Pretoria, South Africa (1997). Their planned consultation for 2000 was cancelled, and they disbanded (by constitutional provision) in 2001.

InterVarsity continued the Urbana Student Mission conferences every three years, which grew from 17,112 delegates in 1976 to 18,818 in 2000, with further growth hampered by the size of the facilities. Campus Crusade organized the largest international conference linking 95 locations in 55 countries around the world by satellite feeds (Explo' 85; Barrett and Johnson 2001, 177) and later brought together delegates from 102 countries in 2000 to evangelize Manila. Over a six-month span, participants shared the gospel with more than 3.2 million people (DeMoss NewsPond.com). In addition to the conferences and consultations, evangelicals gathered to publicly demonstrate their faith in Marches for Jesus (started in 1987) (Moreau 2000).

Evangelical Academics

Observers of the vigor of evangelical missions noticed not only the missions activities mentioned, they also saw growth in academic institutions and publications supporting the entire enterprise. By 2000, the perspective that evangelical missionaries were not well-trained or educated, though still widely held in some non-evangelical circles, was no longer valid.

In the broader scheme of evangelicalism, it was people like Carl Henry, Kenneth Kantzer, and Francis Schaeffer who propelled nascent evangelical intellectualism during much of the 1960s and 1970s. In missiological circles, it was faculty at institutions such as Fuller Theological Seminary, Gordon Conwell, and Trinity Evangelical Divinity School who were active contributors in evangelical and ecumenical journals and academic societies. On a far more popular level, the US Center for World Missions developed the course, 'Perspectives on the World Christian Movement', which thousands of lay evangelicals across the United States took. Perhaps more than any institution, Perspectives championed evangelical mission thinking, mobilized new energy, and generated significant enthusiasm among missions-interested evangelical laity. (See the chapter in this volume by Yvonne Wood about this history of this movement.)

Evangelical mission journals that started between 1975 and 2000 include *Gospel in Context* (1978; ended 1979), *Mission Frontiers* (1979), *Urban Mission* (1983; ended 1998), *International Journal for* Frontier *Missions* (*IJFM*; 1984), *Transformation* (1984), *Journal of Applied Missiology* (1990; ended 1996), *Taiwan Mission Quarterly* (1991; ended 2000), *Missio Apostolica* (1999) and *Journal of Asian Missions* (1999).

Academic associations initiated during the same period include The US Society for Frontier Missions (1986; later changed to the International Society of Frontier Missiology) and the Association of Evangelical Professors of Missions (1968, reorganized as the Evangelical Missiological Society – EMS – in 1990). Both have regular publications (the *EMS Bulletin* and the *Evangelical Missiological Society Series*; *International Journal for Frontier Missiology*) and hold annual regional and national conferences typically co-hosted with the IFMA, the EFMA, or the Evangelical Theological Society (ETS). Additionally, many evangelicals continue to be active members in the American Missiological Society, the International Association for Mission Studies, and they publish articles in journals such as *Missiology* and *International Bulletin of Missionary Research (IBMR),* and *International Review of Mission (IRM)*.

In addition to uncounted journal articles, evangelical missiologists, missionaries, and mission leaders produced significant research tools for understanding mission as a whole (Moreau 2000) and missional statistics for prayerful consideration (Johnstone 1993). It is not surprising that evangelicals produced solid biblical studies on mission (e.g., O'Brien 1995; Köstenberger 1998; Larkin and Williams 1998) and theological texts on the missionary nature of the biblical narrative (Piper 1993; Kaiser). However, it would not have been anticipated in the early 1900s that they would also write significant books on anthropology (Conn 1984; Hiebert 1994), communication (Kraft 1983), cross-cultural ethics (Adeney 1995), culture (Stott and Coote 1979), intercultural communication (Hesselgrave 1978), history (Walls 1996) and sociology (Grunal and Reimer, 1982). They also produced resources on the globalizing of theology (Dyrness 1990, 1992, 1994), newer ways of theologizing (Van Engen, Thomas and Gallagher 1999), contextualization (Kraft 1979) and the challenges of the world's religions (Parshall 1980; Mangalwadi 1998), and wrestled over church growth (Shenk 1983), holism (Padilla 1985), justice (Escobar and Driver 1983), money (Bonk 1991), transformation (Samuel and Sugden 1999), and transformational development (Myers 1999).

In the applied frame, they produced grounded books for practitioners on a wide range of topics including church growth (Wagner 1981), church planting movements (Garrison 1999), cross-cultural church planting (Hesselgrave 1980), cross-cultural conflict (Elmer 1993), cross-cultural evangelism (Mayers 1974), cross-cultural ministry (Lingenfelter and Mayers 1986), folk religions (Hiebert, Shaw and Tienou 2000); planning and strategy (Dayton and Fraser 1990), trends (Guthrie 2000), urban dynamics (Greenway and Monsma, 1989) and women in mission (Tucker 1988). And this cursory listing does not even begin to account for the numerous and very popular mission-focused books published, such as *Peace Child* (Richardson 1974) and *For This Cross I'll Kill You* (later re-titled *Bruchko,* Olson 1978).

One of the more fascinating developments of this period was the gradual introduction into evangelical thinking and terminology the common use of terms and ideas first seen in ecumenical circles though articulated and reshaped within a frame of evangelical convictions (e.g., *missio Dei*, justice, mission from everywhere to everywhere), typically twenty years or more after it first appeared in ecumenical circles.

TRENDS AND CONTENTIOUS ISSUES

Across the spectrum of the four streams identified in this period it is easy to recognize significant trends and issues over which evangelical struggled to resolve. While evangelicals wrote a host of journal articles, books, and statements, such as those we mention here, space permits only brief acknowledgement of each.

The Church Growth Movement (pioneered by Donald McGarvan and his colleagues at Fuller Theological Seminary in the prior phase) helped missionaries understand the dynamics of church growth (McGavran 1980; Wagner 2000). While the movement as a whole peaked and began to decline during this time, it generated huge energy over two core issues (see, e.g., Shenk 1983), namely 1) To what extent was 'growth' definable in terms of quantity rather than quality? and 2) Is 'people group' thinking (which dominated evangelical agencies) as biblical as proponents believed?

Evangelicals also wrestled with issues related to holistic (or integral) mission. Significant impetus came from evangelicals outside of US settings who critiqued the position of many American evangelicals who promoted mission exclusively as evangelism and church planting (e.g., Stott 1975). Though evangelicals produced statements on the need for evangelism and social concerns in mission, the fact that discussions and publications over this issue continue today is clear evidence that evangelicals have not yet come to a settled conclusion (see, e.g., Hiebert and Cox 2000). It also is a reminder of the long-standing concern among US evangelicals to avoid an uncritical acceptance of the social gospel. However, the generation that most directly experienced that conflict is no longer with us, and the next generation of US evangelical missionaries and missiologists do not share the same concerns as their predecessors.

By the 1990s, international short-term missions trips (typically one to three weeks long) organized within evangelical churches of all sizes began to explode, all without significant input from the agencies and well before evangelical scholars began any serious study of the phenomenon. Evangelical entrepreneurs, on the other hand, founded a host of new agencies with an exclusive focus on short-term missions trips (see Peterson and Peterson 1991).

Evangelical concerns over Pentecostal or charismatic emphases reached a peak among missions in the 1970s. By the 1990s, however, many (though not all) of the same organizations were far less concerned with this as a doctrinal issue. Those evangelicals who did not become charismatic or Pentecostal during this period but who still recognized the continuation of the miraculous gifts in operation today were labeled 'Third Wave' (Wagner 1988), and many simply continued within their institutions and agencies. They took analytic approaches to their concerns (e.,g., the 'flaw of the excluded middle' [Hiebert 1982]) as justification for what they had experienced. Some engaged in energetic spiritual warfare (Kraft 1989 1992; Wagner 1991, 1996), though not without controversy (Smedes 1987; Rommen 1995; Moreau, *et al.*, 2002).

At the very end of this period questions were being raised about evangelical contextualization practices with the concern that some were going so far that they were in danger of syncretism (e.g., Parshall 1998; Travis 1998). There were also evangelical reflections on how to respond to the religions of the world, noting that some evangelicals were shifting in a direction of inclusivism or universalism (Netland 1991).

The final trend we note is the incredible advent of the Internet and the way it enabled wholly new forms of instant communication that evangelical missionaries and organizations were quick to grasp. From e-mail to Web sites such as *Brigada* (1995), Mission Network News (1999), MisLinks (1997), evangelicals explored ways to utilize this tool for missional purposes.

Majority World Evangelical Missions

Missiologists such as David Barrett (1982; 2001), Kwame Bediako (1995) and Andrew Walls (1996) had carefully pointed out that the majority of the world evangelical church was not in the West, but in the rest of the world. Evangelical missiologists had been discussing and debating related issues at least since Lausanne, but this reality remained largely unknown outside of missiological circles by the close of the century.

Once the Chinese cultural revolution ground to a halt, reports began to trickle in of a massive influx of new Christians into house churches across China. The one million known Chinese Christians when the missionaries left in 1952 grew to somewhere between 30 to 100 million or more believers. Churches across Africa grew spectacularly, especially those churches that started by splitting off from mission churches, and some 340 million African Christians inhabited every corner of the continent by 2000. In Latin America the grass roots Protestant churches – and particularly the Pentecostal ones – grew in rates that drew attention from a host of secular researchers (see Berg and Pretiz 1996). While missionaries were certainly involved in these stories of growth, and perhaps it was the translation of the Bible that was the most important thing they did (Sanneh 1989), it was the indigenous Christians on every continent who carried the vast bulk of the load (see, e.g., Kalu 2008).

As the Majority World church eclipsed the Western church by the end of the century, Majority World missionaries and mission agencies cropped up everywhere on the planet (see, for example, Keyes 1983). By one estimate, Majority World evangelical missionaries rose from comprising less than ten percent of the total evangelical missionary force in 1972 to more than forty percent by 2001, an astonishing growth rate (Ekström 2006). As they grew, evangelical voices emerged from Majority World settings critiquing evangelical missions (Wakatama 1976; Escobar and Driver 1983; Padilla 1985; Samuel and Sugden 1987; Yohannen 1989).

In 1987 Dr. David J. Cho invited other Majority World mission leaders (Patrick Sookhdeo, Luis Bush, Panya Baba, Petros Octavianus, and Minoru Okuyama) to gather in Seoul, Korea and plan the Consultation on Third World

Missions Advance, which took place in Portland Oregon in 1988 to consider how to advance Majority World missions. The Third World Missions Association was inaugurated in 1989 at a consultation in Portland (http://www.strategicnetwork.org/index.php?loc=kb&view=v&id=4673&fto=541&). They issued the Millennial Manifesto,[6] which they wanted to affirm at the Celebrate Messiah 2000 consultation planned to take place in Israel but cancelled due to Israeli government actions. The Manifesto affirms eight foundational values in light of twelve contemporary realities which include the poor and needy, the role of women, emerging leaders, unreached peoples, community transformation, and global partnership. Mission is one of the foundational values, and they state:

> God wants all persons to have the opportunity to become true disciples of Jesus within their own social, cultural, and language context. Therefore, as the Church enters the new millennium, we covenant to work together for a worldwide mission movement that will give every person in every segment of the human mosaic an opportunity to hear, understand and respond to the gospel during his or her lifetime; to be incorporated into the life of a local congregation, to grow in ongoing intimacy with God, to manifest the life of Christ and exhibit the fruit of the Spirit as salt and light in the world; and to be empowered to minister effectively both in the Church and in the world. (Mt 5:13-14; Ro 16:26; 1 Co 12:13; Gal 2:20, 5:22-23; Col 1:28; 2 Pe 3:18; Rev 5:9-10). [7] Given the growth rates as well as the strength and vitality of Majority World mission agencies, it is not surprising that Western evangelical agencies scrambled to develop partnerships in a bewildering variety of ways. New coalitions were established to help member agencies think through the issues and share resources together (e.g., the Coalition for the Support of Indigenous Ministries; COSIM). During this period we also see evangelical voices from the Majority World take their rightful place in the Western academic discussions (e.g., Nuñez 1985; Bediako 1992, 1995, 2000; Hwa 1997).

Pentecostals

Pentecostalism expanded at an almost exponential rate, and initially evangelicals maintained the antagonism of the prior period. However, they slowly thawed as they realized that the Pentecostals were not going to go away and were not interested in power games. By the end of the century, Barrett and Johnson estimated that there were 400 to 500 million Pentecostals/charismatics in the world (2000, 24-25) and Pentecostal scholars began to publish important works (e.g., Yong 2000). Even so, by the turn of the century a Pentecostal assessment of their own mission reflection was that they had little focused mission theology (Kärkkäinen 2000, 210-11). They also recognized that they shared the following implicit values in their missional focus:

---

[6] http://www.ad2000.org/celebrate/manifesto.htm.

[7] http://www.ad2000.org/celebrate/manifesto.htm.

> (1) a high value placed on experience and participation; (2) a preference for oral communication; (3) spontaneity; (4) otherworldliness with the sense of eschatological urgency; (5) biblical authority; (6) openness to the Spirit; and (7) lay participation. (Kärkkäinen 2000, 212)

An increasing number of evangelicals recognized that Pentecostals and charismatics were very evangelical in their convictions on Scripture, the need for evangelism, their eschatology and their energy for mission. Some evangelical missiologists such as Charles Kraft, C. Peter Wagner and Tim Warner promoted spiritual warfare and power ministries. It is therefore not altogether surprising, then, that some evangelical mission organizations took a more pragmatic stance of cooperation rather than competition or avoidance (see McGee 2000). Even so, by the end of the century some of the evangelical missions associations (e.g., the IFMA) still did not offer membership to mission agencies that did not repudiate Pentecostal doctrines, let alone those that promoted them.

Evangelical Missions 2001–2010

World Context

While some components of our world today would have been imaginable to a person in 1910, others would have been far more difficult to comprehend. Table 1 indicates a few of the more significant areas that reflect this reality, and provides a brief summary of the world context faced by both ecumenical and evangelical Christians.

2010 Reality That Was Imaginable in 1910	*2010 Reality That Was Unimaginable in 1910*
The population growth of Asian nations	The economic prowess of Asian nations in today's globalized world and the real-time economic interconnectedness of global markets
The possibility of massive development aid around the world	The massive failure of such projects over the past fifty years as well as the AIDS pandemic
Wars of 'Christian' nations against 'Muslim' nations	The frightening ability of terrorists to develop and deploy weapons of mass destruction
The struggle for equality of all people	Fights within mainline Western denominations over gay ordination and marriage

Fast electronic communication around the world	The incredible power of today's personal computers and the use of the Internet

Table 1: The Realities of 2010 in the Imaginations of People in 1910

The Ecumenical World from a Conservative Evangelical Perspective

Before 2001, many evangelicals felt that by and large the ecumenical movement had lost momentum and no longer represented the majority of the non-Catholic Christians in the world. Those in the ecumenical movement were referring to it as the 'post-missionary era' and were looking for new images to depict cross-cultural mission (George 2002). For those who had been around in the 1950s, it was startling how little the ecumenical world was even on the cognitive map of most mission-minded evangelicals.

Evangelicals no longer felt themselves belittled or demeaned. Instead, they realized that a major shift had happened in terms of finances, personnel, and churches. To many it no longer even mattered what the ecumenical world was doing, because (if they even took the time to think about it) they perceived that the WCC had lost any metaphorical battle as having an influential Protestant Christian missional voice. Evangelical missiologists and mission leaders observed their numerical domination at mixed missiological society meetings (such as APM and ASM). They received invitations to participate in a variety of WCC events and processes in significant ways, something they had not seen previously.

While a number of American evangelical missiologists chose to participate in some fashion (for example, many of the authors of papers preparing for the 2010 WCC consultation were written by evangelicals,[8] many missionaries and mission leaders (along with their core constituencies) declined for two major reasons: 1) They did not trust that there was a genuine possibility of the ecumenical movement truly embracing core evangelical values and 2) They anticipated that their own constituencies would react negatively to such participation.

Evangelical Missions

By the 1990s the term 'evangelical' in the American context had significantly broadened. Evangelicals of all stripes may be found, but our focus will continue on those who most closely identify with the Bebbington criteria mentioned above (1989). The biggest change is not in the evangelicals themselves, but in the larger public perception of them. This did not come through evangelical missiological discussions, but largely as a result of scholars in the 1990s such as Harvey Cox (1995), Peter Berger (1999) and, after the turn of the century,

---

8 http://www.towards2010.org.uk/papers.htm; http://www.edinburgh2010.org/en/resources/papersdocuments.html.

Philip Jenkins (Jenkins 2002, 2006) and mainstream media correspondents such as David Aikman (2003). Each in their own way brought out important reflections on the massive growth of the Majority World church and its conservative characteristics.

THE LAUSANNE MOVEMENT AND WORLD EVANGELICAL FELLOWSHIP

The conferences and congresses that have become so familiar to evangelicals continued in this decade. Lausanne returned to Pattaya, Thailand to host the World Forum in 2004, which paralleled the 1980 Pattaya consultation and through which the 1,500 participants produced 32 additional Lausanne Occasional Papers. The World Inquiry, led by Luis Bush, helped in the process of identifying specific topics for discussion through a comprehensive world-wide effort gathering input from a diverse group of evangelical Church leaders on every continent (Lausanne Connecting Point 2003; Birdsall 2005).

The WEF changed its name to the World Evangelical Alliance (WEA) at the Kuala Lumpur 2001 General Assembly, and currently represents 420 million evangelical Christians around the world. The 2008 General Assembly met in Thailand; 500 evangelical leaders attended, including Doug Birdsall of the LCWE. They reaffirmed their commitment to evangelism and called the evangelical church to frame practical responses to issues such as poverty, human trafficking, persecution and HIV/AIDS.

The WEA Mission Commission (MC) held three international meetings, including the Globalization and World Evangelism Consultation (Canada 2003), Global Issues Summit III (South Africa 2006), and the Missions Consultation (Thailand 2008). The MC launched *Connections* in 2002 and is available online.[9] In 2004 they launched REMAP II as a follow-up of their first missionary retention study. At the 2006 Global Issues Summit Bertil Ekström replaced Bill Taylor as the MC administrative leader. At the 2008 Thailand meeting the MC launched four new initiatives: 1) the Continuum (of younger reflective practitioners); 2) the Mission & Art Task Force; 3) the Pastors and Church in Mission Task Force; and 4) the Global Dialogue (focused on current mission leader North-South dialogue).

The LCWE and the WEA were joint sponsors of Capetown 2010. The WEA Theological Commission and The LCWE Theological Working Group met four times (Kenya [2007], Thailand [2008] and Panama City [2009]) and Beirut [early 2010]) in preparation for the 2010 congress.

AGENCY GROWTH AND CHALLENGES

In the 2007 edition of the *Mission Handbook* Scott Moreau analyzed the data from 700 US Protestant mission agencies (2007). More than 82% were not denominationally oriented, and even among the denominational agencies many were evangelical. Thus, it is fair to say that the results identified among the 700

---

[9] http://www.weaconnections.com.

agencies will largely reflect the changes that took place among the evangelical agencies. Moreau distinguished the findings by identifying as *trends* changes that were consistent over ten years or more and *shifts* as changes that happened for less than ten years (in this case, between 2001 and 2005).

The *trends* for the US Protestant agencies (2007) were increases in the number of US citizens working for US agencies, non-US citizens working for US agencies, non-residential fully-supported missionaries, tentmakers, US agency home staff. Additionally, there was an increase in the budgets used for overseas ministries, though this was concentrated in the largest agencies whose primary activities focused on relief and development.

The *shifts* were decreases in the number of long term US missionaries, middle-term US missionaries, and short-term missionaries and number of agencies reporting primary activities in mass evangelism and national church nurture/support; together with an increase in the number of agencies reporting activities in the areas of discipleship, community development, short-term missions coordination, personal and small group evangelism, partnership, childcare/orphanage and member care; as well as an increase in the extent of financial and human resources shifted *away* from agencies reporting primary activities in the evangelism/discipleship category and *towards* agencies reporting primary activities in the relief and development category.

In other words, *long term* changes were more US citizens working for mission agencies as expenditures for overseas ministries increased. *Short term* changes included fewer US missionaries on the field and shift in resources and activities away from evangelism towards relief and development. Challenges for US evangelical mission agencies include 1) mobilizing more US citizens to serve as full-time residential missionaries, 2) the appropriate care and support of the burgeoning non-US citizens serving under US agencies, 3) deeper reflection and attention on the short-term missions and its long-term impact on US agencies, 4) ensuring that the increasing ranks of tentmakers are appropriately supported, and 5) ensuring that agencies whose primary activities are in evangelism and discipleship are adequately staffed and financed so that this remains a central focus for US Protestant evangelical mission agencies.

It is still too recent to determine the number of agencies founded since the turn of the millennium. Many are small and specialty focused (on short-term work, focused projects or specialized emphases). For example, The Berean Way (Portland, Oregon) was founded in 2005 having arisen from multiple short-term missions projects from a single megachurch. To date, all of its work has been in two countries (India and Uganda) based on newly developed connections with leadership in the two countries. It is named after the Bereans in Acts 17:11 (who confirmed Paul's teaching from the scriptures), and self-described as a recognized missionary organization of Rolling Hills Community Church in Tualatin, Oregon; a member of the Next Generation Alliance; a ministry of Luis Palau Association and part of the teaching arm of the Reid

Saunders Association.[10] Only one of the Board members has formal theological training, and none have missiological backgrounds. It is likely that many of the next generation of mission agencies will parallel The Berean Way. Others framed themselves around such things as highly focused ministries[11] (ministry to street kids)[12] or ways of living (the new monasticism)[13] (Moll 2005; Rice, 2006; Bessenecker 2006]). It is possible that, given the American ideals of entrepreneurial individualism seen among evangelicals over the course of the century, a host of virtual agencies and missionally-framed social network sites or twitter groups will also spring up, having an Internet presence but no offices or central locations or even ministries.

The numerous megachurches have now developed their own approaches to mission that are tailored to their particular philosophy of ministry so that they the money given by their members is used in ways that gives them a greater sense of ownership. Evangelical mission agencies founded thirty or more years prior to this period are scrambling to develop viable and healthy partnerships with churches that no longer think of the agency first, but think of the people they know in the agency.

One of the more significant changes today is the global financial meltdown and its impact on evangelical missions. At that same time, the agencies are facing the retirement (and expiration) of a generation of donors who were more financially committed than the generation replacing them. With the transfer of wealth to this newer generation, reputed to be known for its greed rather than its generosity, evangelical mission agencies will be challenged financially in ways they have never before seen. Finally, a whole generation of post WW II missionaries is now retiring and meeting their needs is becoming a significant issue for American evangelical agencies (Corwin 2007a).

GATHERINGS

In addition to the consultations of the LCWE and WEA, the Urbana conferences moved to St. Louis in 2006 to take advantage of more space at lower cost, enabling almost 23,000 delegates to attend the 2006 convention. The Micah Network (founded in 1999) held three global consultations on Integral (or holistic) mission [14] with themes of Integral Mission and the Poor (140 participants; England, 2001), Globalisation and the Poor (185 participants; Mexico, 2003), and Integral Mission in a World of Conflict (330 participants; Thailand, September 2006). By October 2008, there were 320 member organizations and some 220 associate members (Micah Network 2009).

---

[10] http://www.thebereanway.com/about.htm.
[11] http://www.micahcentral.org http://www.newmonasticism.org/;
[12] http://www.micahcentral.org.
[13] http://www.newmonasticism.org/.
[14] www.micahnetwork.org.

EVANGELICAL ACADEMICS

Evangelical mission programs proliferated with degrees offered through the PhD. While these were in place in the 1990s, they have expanded in significance and scope since the turn of the millennium. This is putting in place a whole generation of scholarship among evangelicals that did not exist twenty years previously, and the impact will be felt for generations to come.

Several new evangelical mission print journals were launched, *Connections* [2002] and *Acta Missiologiae* [2009]. Entrepreneurs also founded a new spate of Internet-only journals such as *Global Missiology* [2004], *Momentum* [2005], and *The Cauldron* [2008]), and collections of journals in online databases greatly expanded (especially the Network for Strategic Missions KnowledgeBase, which grew to more than 18,000 articles by 2009).

Topics being subjected to rigorous academic study are short term missions (Priest 2008), evangelical mission theology (Wright 2006) and the globalizing of theology (Sanneh 2003, 2008; Vanhoozer 2005; Ott and Netland 2006; Wright 2006; Tennent 2007;), the emergent church and its impact on mission (Gibbs and Bolger 2005), 'at risk' populations (e.g., street kids, trafficking, orphans; Pocock, McConnell and VanRheenen 2005) and transformational development (e.g., Nabie 2005; Phiri 2007) – to name a few.

Contextualization practices continued stretching traditional boundaries in such areas as translation (Dixon 2007; Brown 2007) ecclesiology (e.g., 'churchless' Christianity; Hoefer 2001; Tennent 2005), and insider movements (Corwin 2006, 2007; Garrison 2004; Higgins 2004; 2007; Richard 2007).

CONTENDING ISSUES

It should be noted that each of the contending issues from the previous period continue to be issues for evangelical missions. In addition, however, perhaps the most significant for evangelical missions in the future has been the increasing splintering and broadening of what the term 'evangelical' means. Bebbington's four-fold depiction has stood well for twenty years, but a parallel study done today may come to very different conclusions. Voices such as Brian McLaren challenge evangelical orthodoxy (McLaren 2001; 2004; see also Hesselgrave 2007); many in the mainline speak of themselves as evangelical but do not necessarily share the same orientation to the Bible that characterized evangelicals over the past century. Inerrancy, for example, is not the centerpiece for evangelicals it was several decades ago, and in the United States the emergent church challenges Modernist evangelical views on multiple fronts (e.g., Sweet 2002).

In the meantime, the massive growth seen prior to 2000 in short-term missions accelerated, with an estimated 1.6 million Americans Christians of all theological persuasions going on international short term missions trips through American churches (Livermore 2006, Fortunak and Moreau 2008, Moreau 2007 and 2008b).

The 'shrinking' of our world has brought evangelicals face to face with the great religious traditions of the world, and issues of pluralism, universalism, proselytism, and fundamentalism are going to increase rather than decrease.

Technological advancements, together with shifts in conceptualizing the task of missions, also enable the development of a more accurate picture of the task remaining as well as the possibility of updating that picture in real time. See for example the websites for joshuaproject.net and worldmap.org. Such technology can be harnessed for good and ill in the task of reaching the world for Christ. Missionaries have found that blogs, twitters, and Facebook all enhance mission networking effectiveness even as they clog up time constraints. Missionary news and prayer letters are available online, but they can expose missionaries in sensitive areas to discovery through Internet searches.

One of the more fascinating developments within evangelical missions has been the recognition of the value of previous WCC reflections and ideas. Evangelicals are currently wrestling with new approaches to the world's religions (e.g., Muck and Adeney 2009), discussing the theology of *missio Dei* (Wright 2006) in ways ecumenical missiologists were twenty to fifty years ago.

Majority World Evangelical Missions

David Lee notes 'The emergence of the missionary movement from the Two Thirds World ... was probably the most significant development in mission during the latter half of the twentieth century' (2007). It was not until the publication of Philip Jenkins' *The Next Christendom* (2002) that the American public grasped the reality of the size and vigor of the Majority World churches (called the Global South). Jenkins' *The New Faces of Christianity* (2006) extended the argument of their conservative nature in specific categories. While evangelical missiologists had been aware of this, suddenly it became a topic of discussion in far more than evangelical circles. Andrew Walls succinctly summarizes:

> The fact remains that, by a huge reversal of the position in 1910, the majority of Christians now live in Africa, Asia, Latin America or the Pacific, and that the proportion is rising. ... The map of the Christian Church, its demographic and cultural make-up, changed more dramatically during the twentieth century than (probably) in any other since the first. (2002a, 6)

Part of the story is the Majority World missionaries working under US agencies. In 2005, almost 65.7 percent of the missionaries under the employ of US Protestant mission agencies were not US nationals – a jump from 58.1 percent in 2001 (Moreau 2007, 14). Clearly US evangelical agencies are hiring non-US nationals to work. Of those non-US nationals, 6.3 percent worked in countries other than their own as missionaries (up by 186 percent since 1996; ibid., 13).

The more significant part of the story, however, is the growth and maturation of Majority World agencies. Davie Lee notes several characteristics of Majority World missionaries and their agencies: 1) most of the missionaries serve in their own countries; 2) they do not have the unfavorable image that comes with the colonial history of the West; 3) they have much simpler mission structures than Western agencies; 4) mission costs less for them; 5) they are more creative in finding ways to have a viable presence in another country, and 6) they are more used to living in a harsh environment (2007).

Another important part is the more recent development of the birth and growth of Majority World missions associations (see the website mislinks.org). For example, the Nigerian Evangelical Missions Association (NEMA), founded in 1982, has almost 100 mission agency members. The Philippine Missions Association (PMA), founded in 1983, and currently has 118 agencies as members. The India Missions Association (IMA), founded in 1977, has 220 agency members, and is the largest national mission association in the world. The Brazil Association of Cross-Cultural Missions (AMTB), was founded in 1982 and now has 40 member organizations. The Korean World Mission Association (KWMA) was founded in 1990 and has 130 mission agency members.

In addition, evangelicals from Majority World settings do not have the same agenda as those from the West. For example, Majority World evangelical theologians tend to be 1) intentionally contextual (rather than universal) – they have a deep appreciation of cultural, social, and historical dimensions of what they do; 2) intentionally occasional (they recognize that what they do, say, and write is limited in time and place); 3) aware of the missiological nature of all theology (they do not think of theology as a purely academic project); 4) careful to consider *who* interprets as just as important as *how* interpretation takes place (they are sensitive to issues of empowerment in neo-colonial settings); and 5) very serious about the questions of non-Christian religions (since they are often minority people in the midst of other major religions) (see, e.g., Escobar 2003; Sanneh 2003, 2008). Each of these areas shapes not only theology, but also missiology and missions practice.

Pentecostal Missions

With the core of Pentecostal-Charismatic pneumatology focused on empowerment for witness (Ma 2006) it is natural that Pentecostal energy flows into mission. During the past decade this has been increasingly subjected to study (e.g., Anderson 2007; Yong 2003, 2008). A large online database of Pentecostal scholarship was launched (Pentecostal-Charismatic Theological Inquiry International (www.pctii.org); and has some six hundred scholars who are members. Pentecostal missiological scholars such as Allen Anderson offered significant studies of Pentecostal missions (artsweb.bham.ac.uk/aanderson), adding rigor to the energy that has always characterized Pentecostal work. From the annual World Pentecostal Conferences to various regional

Pentecostal society meetings, Pentecostal scholars have met to raise and discuss issues of mission scholarship throughout the past decade (see www.pctii.org/schedule.html for a list of the international meetings). While there are no academic Pentecostal journals devoted exclusively to mission, a body of research is growing and it would be expected that more journals and books focused on mission will be developed in the coming years.

Conclusion

It is appropriate to return to Kyo Seong Ahn, who as we previously noted spoke of the people who attended Edinburgh 1910 as 'ecumenical evangelicals'. He continued after that observation to state:

> ... The meaning of mission, however, has been stretched out to the extent that it seems to cover almost every ministry of the church, so finally Stephen Neill had to declare that 'if everything is mission, nothing is mission'. Anyway, we are still not quite sure how different the holistic mission (ecumenical) and whole mission (evangelical) are from each other, at face value. By the time of 1970s, the approachment between two groups seemed to symbolize the coming of a new era in the Christian missionary relations. But the leftism of the ecumenical group and the rightism of the evangelical group after 1980s have been so accelerated that the prospects of gathering together of these two groups are discouraging. (2003, 4)

For the first fifty years after the Edinburgh 1910 meetings, we can only understand evangelical missions in light of their antithetic relationship with ecumenical missions. The strong ecumenical movement tended to not see or understand evangelicals as part of the missional efforts coming from the West. American intellectuals almost completely overlooked them, and when they bothered to portray evangelicals, they presented them as schismatic legalists who refused to keep up with the times. As a result, evangelicals defined themselves as an opposition set to the ecumenicals, whom they characterized as despised compromisers of God's word and uncaring about the unsaved peoples of the world. Thus, for some six to seven decades, evangelicals perceived themselves with such words as faithfulness, fidelity, obedience, evangelistic, and uncompromising.

Even though by 1960 the demographics were reversed, most evangelicals and ecumenicals were not aware of this. Evangelicals continued to see ecumenicals as power-brokers who compromised the Word of God. They did not trust overtures to participate meaningfully in ecumenical events (with some exceptions, such as the ASM) and felt that the ecumenical movement was so taken with Modernism (and now Post-modernism) that they would never return to their biblical roots. It took another three decades before this was acknowledged by the press or in the public sphere, and now for the past twenty years or so evangelicals have been recognized as being far more significant in missionary energy, missionary work, and missionary personnel.

Bibliography

'10/40 Window'. Online: http://en.wikipedia.org/wiki/10/40_Window [cited 18 March 2009].

Adeney, Bernard. *Strange Virtues: Ethics in a Multi-Cultural World.* Downers Grove: InterVarsity, 1995.

Ahn, Kyo Seong. 'In Search of an Authentic Missiology: From Orthodoxy to Orthopraxis to Orthopathy'. Online: http://www.towards2010.org.uk/downloads/t2010paper06escobar.pdf [accessed 2 April 2009].

Aikman, David. *Jesus in Beijing: How Christianity Is Transforming China and Changing the Global Balance of Power.* Washington, D.C.: Regnery Publishing, 2003.

Anderson, Allen. *Spreading Fires: The Missionary Nature of Early Pentecostalism.* Maryknoll: Orbis, 2007.

Anderson, Gerald H. 'Christian Mission in AD 2000: A Glance Backward'. *Missiology* 28 (July, 2000), 275-88.

Arnold, Clinton. *Three Crucial Questions about Spiritual Warfare.* Grand Rapids: Baker, 1997.

Bahler, Donna. 'The Co-Mission'. *Mission Frontiers* 14 (March-April, 1992), 3-4.

Bebbington, David. *Evangelicals in Modern Britain: A History from the 1730s to the 1980s.* London: Unwin, 1989.

Barrett, David B. (ed.). *World Christian Encyclopedia: A Comparative Survey of Churches and Religions in the Modern World, AD 1900–2000.* New York: Oxford University Press, 1982.

Barrett, David B. and James W. Reapsome. *Seven Hundred Plans to Evangelize the World: The Rise of a Global Evangelization Movement.* Birmingham, AL: New Hope, 1988.

Barrett, David B., George T. Kurian and Todd M. Johnson (eds.). *World Christian Encyclopedia: A Comparative Survey of Churches and Religions in the Modern World, 2nd edition,.* 2 vols. Oxford: Oxford University Press, 2001.

Barrett, David B. and Todd Johnson (eds.). *World Christian Trends AD 230–AD 2200: Interpreting the Annual Christian Megacensus.* Pasadena: William Carey Library, 2001.

Bassett, Paul Merritt. 'Evangelicals'. *Dictionary of the Ecumenical Movement.* Nicholas Lossky *et al.*, Eds. Grand Rapids: Eerdmans, 1991.

Bediako, Kwame. *Christianity in Africa: The Renewal of a Non-Western Religion.* Edinburgh: Edinburgh University Press, 1995.

– *Jesus in Africa: The Christian Gospel in African History and Experience.* Yaounde, Cameroun: Editions Cle., 2000.

– *Theology and Identity: The Impact of Culture upon Christian Thought in the Second Century and Modern Africa.* Regnum Studies in Mission. Oxford: Regnum Books, 1992.

Berg, Clayton L. Jr. and Paul Pretiz. *Spontaneous Combustion: Grass-Roots Christianity, Latin American Style.* Pasadena: William Carey Library, 1996.

Berger, Peter L. (ed.). *The Desecularization of the World: Resurgent Religion and World Politics.* Grand Rapids: Eerdmans, 1999.

Bessenecker, Scott. *The New Friars: The Emerging Movement Serving the World's Poor.* Downers Grove: InterVarsity, 2006.

Beuttler, Fred W. 'Evangelical Missions in Modern America'. In Martin I. Klauber and Scott M. Manetsch (eds). *The Great Commission: Evangelicals and the History of World Missions.* Nashville: B&H Academic, 2008, 108-32.

Billy Graham Center. 'Records of Billy Graham Center (BGC) – Collection 3'. Online: http://www.wheaton.edu/bgc/archives/GUIDES/003.htm#501 [accessed 30 March 2009].

– 'Records of the Evangelical Fellowship of Mission Agencies (EFMA) – Collection 165'. Online: http://www.wheaton.edu/bgc/archives/GUIDES/165.htm [accessed 24 March 2009].

Bonk, Jonathan J. *Missions and Money: Affluence as a Western Missionary Problem.* Maryknoll: Orbis, 1991.

Borthwick, Paul. *Six Dangerous Questions to Transform Your View of the World.* Downers Grove: InterVarsity Press, 1996.

Bosch, David J. Witness to the World: The Christian Mission in Theological Perspective. Atlanta: John Knox Press, 1980.

Brown, Rick. 'Why Muslims Are Repelled by the Term 'Son of God'. *Evangelical Missions Quarterly* 43 (October, 2007): 422-29.

Carpenter, Joel A. 'Appendix: The Evangelical Missionary Force in the 1930s'. In Joel A. Carpenter and Wilbert R. Shenk (eds). *Earthen Vessels: American Evangelicals and Foreign Missions 1880–1980.* Grand Rapids: Eerdmans, 1990, 335-42.

– *Revive Us Again: The Reawakening of American Fundamentalism.* New York: Oxford University Press, 1997.

Conn, Harvie M. *Eternal Word and Changing Worlds: Theology, Anthropology, and Mission in Trialogue*. Phillipsburg, NJ: P&R Publishing, 1984.

Coote, Robert T. 'Evangelical Missions'. *Dictionary of the Ecumenical Movement.* Nicholas Lossky, *et al.*, Eds. Grand Rapids: Eerdmans, 1991.

– 'World Evangelical Fellowship'. *Dictionary of the Ecumenical Movement.* Nicholas Lossky, *et al.*, Eds. Grand Rapids: Eerdmans, 1991.

Corwin, Gary. 'A Humble Appeal to C5/Insider Movement Muslim Ministry Advocates to Consider Ten Questions'. *International Journal of Frontier Missions* 24 (January, 2007), 5-20.

– 'A Second Look: Insider Movements and Outsider Missiology'. *Evangelical Missions Quarterly* 42 (January, 2006), 10-11.

– 'A Second Look: Retiring and Shy'. *Evangelical Missions Quarterly* 43:1 (2007), 8-9.

Cox, Harvey Gallagher. *Fire from Heaven: The Rise of Pentecostal Spirituality and the Reshaping of Religion in the Twenty-First Century.* Reading, Mass.: Addison-Wesley, 2005.

Crawley, Winston. *World Christianity 1970–2000: Toward a New Millennium.* Pasadena: William Carey Library, 2001.

Dayton Edward R. and David A. Fraser. *Planning Strategies for World Evangelization.* Rev. ed. Monrovia, CA: MARC, 1990.

DeMoss NewsPond. 'Campus Crusade for Christ, International Historical Fact Sheet'. Online: http://www.demossnewspond.com/ccci/press_kit/campus_crusade_for_christ_international_historical_fact_sheet [accessed 12 March 2009].

Dixon, Roger. 'Identity Theft: Retheologizing the Son of God'. *Evangelical Missions Quarterly* 43 (April, 2007): 220-26.

Dyrness, William A. (ed.). *Emerging Voices in Global Christian Theology.* Grand Rapids: Zondervan, 1994.

– *Invitation to Cross-Cultural Theology.* Grand Rapids: Zondervan, 1992.

– *Learning about Theology from the Third World.* Grand Rapids: Zondervan, 1990.

Ekström, Bertil. 'From Seoul to Capetown: A Missionary Journey'. Unpublished paper delivered at the Global Issues Summit III of the World Evangelical Alliance Mission Commission. Capetown, South Africa, 2006.

Elmer, Duane. *Cross-Cultural Conflict: Building Relationships for Effective Ministry.* Downers Grove: InterVarsity Press, 1993.

Engel, James and William Dyrness. *Changing the Mind of Missions: Where Have We Gone Wrong?* Downers Grove, Illinois: InterVarsity, 2000.

Eshleman, Paul A. 'The 'Jesus' Film: A Contribution to World Evangelism'. *International Bulletin of Missionary Research* 26 (April, 2002): 66-73.

Escobar, Samuel. *The New Global Mission: The Gospel from Everywhere to Everyone.* Downers Grove: InterVarsity, 2003.

Escobar, Samuel and John Driver. *Christian Mission and Social Justice.* Scottdale, Penn.: Herald, 1978.

Escobar, Samuel. 'Mission From Everywhere to Everyone: The Home Base in a New Century'. Online: http://www.towards2010.org.uk/downloads/t2010paper06escobar.pdf [accessed 2 April 2009].

'Evangelical church'. *Encyclopædia Britannica,* from Encyclopædia Britannica Online: http://search.eb.com/eb/article-9033320 [retrieved February 28, 2009].

Fielder, Klaus. 'Evangelical Mission Theology I'. *Dictionary of Mission: Theology, History, Perspective*. Karl Müller *et al*, Eds. Maryknoll: Orbis, 1997.

Fortunak, Laurie and A. Scott Moreau (eds.). *Engaging the Church: Analyzing the Canvas of Short Term Missions*. Wheaton: Evangelism and Missions Information Service, 2008.

Garrison, David. *The Nonresidential Missionary*. Monrovia, Calif.: MARC, 1990.

Garrison, David. *Church Planting Movements*. Richmond: International Mission Board of Southern Baptist Convention, 1999.

– 'Church Planting Movements Vs. Insider Movements: Missiological Realities Vs. Mythiological Speculations'. *International Journal of Frontier Missions* 21 (October, 2004), 151-54.

George, Sherron K. 'The Quest for Images of Missionaries in a 'Post-Missionary' Era'. *Missiology* 30 (January, 2002), 51-65.

Gibbs, Eddie. *Church Next: Quantum Changes in Christian Ministry.* Downers Grove: InterVarsity, 2000.

Gibbs, Eddie and Ryan K. Bolger. *Emerging Churches: Creating Christian Community in Postmodern Cultures*. Grand Rapids: Baker, 2005.

Gnanakan, Ken R. *Kingdom Concerns: A Biblical Exploration Towards a Theology of Mission.* Bangalore: Theological Book Trust, 1989.

Greenway, Roger S. and Timothy M. Monsma. *Cities: Mission's New Frontier*. Grand Rapids: Baker, 1989.

Günther, Wolfgang. 'The History and Significance of World Mission Conferences in the 20th Century'. *International Review of Mission* (October, 2003.), 521-37.

Guthrie, Stan. *Missions in the Third Millennium: 21 Key Trends for the 21st Century.* Waynesboro, Georgia: Paternoster, 2000.

Hesselgrave, David M. 'Brian McLaren's Contextualization of the Gospel'. *Evangelical Missions Quarterly* 43:1 (January, 2007): 92-100.

– *Communicating Christ Cross-Culturally: An Introduction to Missionary Communication*. Grand Rapids: Zondervan, 1978.

– *Planting Churches Cross-Culturally.* Grand Rapids: Baker, 1980.

Hiebert, Paul G. *Anthropological Reflection on Missiological Issues.* Grand Rapids: Baker, 1994.

– 'Critical Contextualization'. *Missiology: An International Review* 12 (July, 1984), 287-96.
– 'The Flaw of the Excluded Middle'. *Missiology: An International Review* 10:1 (January, 1982), 35-47.
Hiebert, Paul G., Daniel Shaw and Tite Tienou. *Understanding Folk Religions.* Grand Rapids, Baker, 2000.
Hiebert, Paul G. and Monty Cox. 'Evangelism and Social Responsibility'. *Evangelical Dictionary of World Missions*. A. Scott Moreau *et al.*, Eds. Grand Rapids: Baker, 2000.
Higgins, Kevin. 'The Key to Insider Movements: The 'Devoted's of Acts''. *International Journal of Frontier Missions* 21 (October, 2004), 155-65.
– 'Acts 15 and Insider Movements among Muslims: Questions, Process and Conclusions'. *International Journal of Frontier Missions* 24 (January, 2007): 29-40.
Hoefer, Herbert. *Churchless Christianity*. Pasadena: William Carey Library, 2001.
Horner, Norman A. 'The Association of Professors of Mission'. *International Bulletin of Missionary Research* 11:3 (July, 1987), 120-24.
Howard, David. *The Dream That Would Not Die: The Birth and Growth of the World Evangelical Fellowship, 1846–1986*. Exeter, England: Paternoster, 1986.
Hunter, George R. III. *The Celtic Way of Evangelism: How Christianity Can Reach the West Again.* Nashville: Abingdon, 2000.
Hwa, Yung. *Mangoes or Bananas?: The Quest for an Authentic Asian Christian Theology. Regnum Studies in Mission.* Oxford, England; Regnum International, 1997.
Jenkins, Philip. *The Next Christendom: The Coming of Global Christianity*. New York: Oxford University Press, 2002.
– *The New Faces of Christianity: Believing the Bible in the Global South.* New York: Oxford University Press, 2006.
Johnson, Todd M. and David B. Barrett (eds.). *AD 2000 Global Monitor: Keeping Track of World Evangelization 1990–1994*. Pasadena: William Carey Library, 1995.
Johnstone, Patrick. *Operation World.* Grand Rapids: Zondervan, 1993.
Kaiser, Walter C. *Mission in the Old Testament: Israel as a Light to the Nations*. Grand Rapids: Baker, 2000.
Kalu, Ogbu. *African Pentecostalism: An Introduction*. Oxford: Oxford University Press, 2008.
Kärkkäinen, Veli-Matti. 'One Hundred Years of Pentecostal Missions: A Report on the European Pentecostal/Charismatic Research Association's 1999 Meeting'. *Mission Studies* 17 (2000), 207-16.
Keyes, Lawrence E. *The Last Age of Missions: A Study of Third World Missionary Societies*. Pasadena: William Carey Library, n.d.
Köstenberger, Andreas J. *The Missions of Jesus and the Disciples According to the Fourth Gospel.* Grand Rapids: Eerdmans, 1998.
Kraemer, Hendrik. *The Christian Message in a Non-Christian World.* New York: Harper and Brothers, 1938.
Kraft, Charles H. *Christianity in Culture: A Study in Dynamic Biblical Theologizing in Cross-Cultural Perspective*. Maryknoll: Orbis, 1979.
– *Christianity with Power: Your Worldview and Your Experience of the Supernatural.* Ann Arbor, Michigan: Vine Books, 1989.
– *Communication Theory for Christian Witness*. Nashville: Abingdon Press, 1983.
– *Defeating Dark Angels: Breaking Demonic Oppression in the Believer's Life*. Ann Arbor, Michigan: Vine Books, 1992.

Larkin, William J. and Joel F. Williams (eds.). *Mission in the New Testament: An Evangelical Approach*. Maryknoll, New York: Orbis, 1998.

Lausanne Committee for World Evangelization. 'The Willowbank Report: Consultation on Gospel and Culture'. Online: http: //www.lausanne.org/willowbank-1978/lop-2.html [cited 27 February 2009].

– 'World Inquiry Enters Second Stage: Final Results to be Presented at 2004 Forum'. *Lausanne Connecting Point* (February). Online: http://www.lausanne.org/lausanne-connecting-point/2003-february.html [cited 31 March 2009].

Lee, David Tai-Woong. 'Two-Thirds World Missionary Movement'. *Dictionary of Mission Theology: Evangelical Foundations*. John Corrie, *et al.*, Eds. Downers Grove: InterVarsity, 2007.

Lewis, Donald M. *Christianity Reborn: The Global Expansion of Evangelicalism in the Twentieth Century*. Grand Rapids: Eerdmans, 2004.

Lingenfelter, Sherwood G. and Marvin K. Mayers. *Ministering Cross-Culturally: An Incarnational Model for Personal Relationships*. Grand Rapids: Baker Book House, 1986.

Livermore, David A. *Serving with Eyes Wide Open: Doing Short-Term Missions with Cultural Intelligence*. Grand Rapids: Baker, 2006.

Marsden, George. *Fundamentalism in American Culture: The Shaping of Twentieth-Century Evangelicalism, 1870–1925*. Grand Rapids: Eerdmans, 1991.

Ma, Wonsuk ''When the Poor Are Fired Up': The Role of Pneumatology in Pentecostal-Charismatic Mission'. *Cyberjournal for Pentecostal-Charismatic Research* 15 (February). Online: http://www.pctii.org/cyberj/cyberj15/Ma.html [cited 31 March 2009].

McGavran, Donald Anderson. *The Bridges of God: A Study in the Strategy of Missions*. New York: Friendship Press, 1955.

– *Understanding Church Growth*. Grand Rapids: Eerdmans, 1970.

McGee, Cary B. 'Pentecostal Movement'. *Evangelical Dictionary of World Missions*. A. Scott Moreau, *et al.*, Eds. Grand Rapids: Baker, 2000.

McQuilkin, Robertson. *The Great Omission: A Biblical Basis for World Evangelism*. Grand Rapids: Baker Book House, 1984.

Mangalwadi, Vishal. *Missionary Conspiracy: Letters to a Postmodern Hindu*. Carlisle, Cumbria, UK: OM Publishing, 1998.

Mayers, Marvin K. *Christianity Confronts Culture: A Strategy for Cross-Cultural Evangelism*. Grand Rapids: Zondervan Publishing House, 1974.

Micah Network 'History'. Online: http://www.micahnetwork.org/en/about-us/history [cited 29 March 2009].

'Modernism'. Online: http://en.wikipedia.org/wiki/Modernism [accessed March 10, 2009].

Moffett, Samuel H. *A History of Christianity in Asia*. San Francisco, California: Harper San Francisco, 1992.

Moll, Rob. 'The New Monasticism: A Fresh Crop of Christian Communities is Blossoming in Blighted Urban Settings All over America'. Christianity Today (September). Online: http://www.christianitytoday.com/ct/2005/september/16.38.html [cited 31 March 2009].

Moreau, A. Scott. 'Congress on the Church's Worldwide Mission'. *Evangelical Dictionary of World Missions*. A. Scott Moreau, *et al.*, Eds. Grand Rapids: Baker, 2000.

– 'Contextualization'. In Michael Pocock, Gailyn VanRheenen and Douglas McConnell (eds) and A. Scott Moreau (gen. ed.). *The Changing Face of World*

Missions: Engaging Contemporary Issues and Trends. Grand Rapids: Baker Book House, 2005, 321-48.

– 'The Lausanne Movement'. In A. Scott Moreau (ed.). *Lausanne Movement Resources Disk, CD-ROM*. Wheaton: Lausanne Committee for World Evangelization, 2006.

– 'March for Jesus'. *Evangelical Dictionary of World Missions*, A. Scott Moreau, *et al.*, Eds. Grand Rapids: Baker, 2000.

– 'Putting the Survey in Perspective'. In John A. Siewert and Dotsey Welliver (eds). *Missions Handbook: US and Canadian Christian Ministries Overseas 2001–2003,* 18th ed. Wheaton: Evangelism and Missions Information Service, 2000, 33-80.

– 'Putting the Survey in Perspective'. In Linda Weber (ed.). *Handbook of North American Protestant Missions 2007–2009*. Wheaton: Evangelism and Missions Information Service. 2007, 11-75.

– 'Short Term Missions in the Context of Missions Inc.'. In Robert J. Priest (ed.). *Effective Engagement in Short-Term Missions: Doing it Right!* Evangelical Missiological Association Series Volume 16. Pasadena: William Carey Library, 2008, 1-34.

Moreau, A. Scott, Tokunboh Adeyemo, David Burnett, Bryant Myers and Hwa Yung (eds.). *Deliver Us From Evil: An Uneasy Frontier in Christian Mission*. Monrovia, CA: World Vision, 2002.

Muck, Terry and Frances S. Adeney. *Christianity Encountering World Religions: The Practice of Mission in the Twenty-First Century*. Grand Rapids: Baker, 2009.

Myers, Bryant L. *Walking with the Poor: Principles and Practices of Transformational Development*. Maryknoll: Orbis, 1999.

Nabie, Solomon. 'The Challenge of the Poor to Christians: IcFEM's Experience in Integrating Christian Mission and Transformational Development in Kenya'. *Transformation* 22 (April, 2005), 115-20.

Netland, Harold. *Dissonant Voices: Religious Pluralism and the Question of Truth*. Grand Rapids: Eerdmans, 1991.

Nicholls, Bruce J. *Contextualization: A Theology of Gospel and Culture*. Downers Grove: InterVarsity, 1979.

Nuñez, Emilio A. *Liberation Theology*. Translated by Paul E. Sywulka. Chicago: Moody Press, 1985.

O'Brien, Peter T. *Gospel and Mission in the Writings of Paul*. Grand Rapids: Baker, 1995.

Olson, Bruce. *Bruchko*. Altamonte Springs, Florida: Creation House, 1978.

Otis, George. *The Twilight Labyrinth: Why Does Spiritual Darkness Linger Where It Does?* Grand Rapids: Chosen Books, 1997.

Ott, Craig and Harold A. Netland. *Globalizing Theology: Belief and Practice in an Era of World Christianity*. Grand Rapids: Baker, 2006.

Padilla, C. René. *Mission Between the Times*. Grand Rapids: Eerdmans, 1985.

Parker, David. 'World Evangelical Alliance Theological Commission'. Online: http://en.wikipedia.org/wiki/World_Evangelical_Alliance_Theological_Commission [cited 30 March 2009].

Parshall, Phil. *New Paths in Muslim Evangelism: Evangelical Approaches to Contextualization*. Grand Rapids: Baker, 1980.

– 'Danger! New Directions in Muslim Contextualization'. *Evangelical Missions Quarterly* 34 (October, 1998), 404-10.

Peterson, Roger P. and Timothy D. Peterson. *Is Short-term Mission Really Worth the Time and Money? Advancing God's Kingdom through Short-term Mission.* Minneapolis: STEM, 1991.

Phiri, Isaac. 'From Hand out to Hand up: Three Arkansas Entrepreneurs Are Helping Build Rwanda's Largest Bank for the Poorest of the Poor'. *Christianity Today* 51 (October, 2007), 86-90, 92, 94-95.

Pierson, Paul. 'Lessons in Mission from the Twentieth Century: Conciliar Misisons'. In Jonathan J. Bonk (ed.). *Between Past and Future: Evangelical Mission Entering the Twenty-First Century.* EMS series 10. Pasadena: William Carey Library, 2003, 67-84.

Piper, John. *Let the Nations Be Glad! The Supremacy of God in Missions.* Grand Rapids: Baker Book House, 1993.

Pocock, Michael, Gailyn Van Rheenen and Douglas McConnell. *The Changing Face of World Missions.* Grand Rapids: Baker, 2005.

Priest Robert J., ed. *Effective Engagement in Short-Term Missions: Doing it Right*! Evangelical Missiological Association Series Volume 16. Pasadena: William Carey Library, 2008.

Ranson, Charles W. 'The Theological Education Fund'. *International Review of Missions* 47:188 (October, 1958), 432-38.

Rice, Jonathon. 'The New Missions Generation'. *Christianity Today* 50:9 (September, 2006), 100-104.

Richard, H. L. 'India: Debating Global Missiological Flashpoints: Community Dynamics in India and the Praxis of 'Church''. *International Journal of Frontier Missions* 24 (October, 2007), 185-94.

Richardson, Don. *Peace Child.* Glendale, California: G/L Regal Books, 1974.

Robert, Dana L. ''The Crisis of Missions': Premillennial Mission Theory and the Origins of Independent Evangelical Missions'. In Joel A. Carpenter and Wilbert R. Shenk (eds). *Earthen Vessels: American Evangelicals and Foreign Missions 1880–1980.* Grand Rapids: Eerdmans, 1990, 29-46.

– 'The First Globalization: The Internationalization of the Protestant Missionary Movement between the World Wars'. *International Bulletin of Missionary Research* 26 (April, 2002), 50.

– 'From Missions to Mission to Beyond Missions: The Historiography of American Protestant Foreign Missions since World War II'. *International Bulletin of Missionary Research* 18 (October, 1994), 146.

Rommen, Edward, ed. *Spiritual Power and Missions: Raising the Issues.* Pasadena, California: William Carey Library, 1995.

Russell, Mark. 'Christian Mission Today: Are We on a Slippery Slope? Christian Mission Is Holistic'. *International Journal of Frontier Missiology* 25 (2008), 93-98.

Samuel, Vinay and Chris Sugden (eds.). *The Church in Response to Human Need. Papers from the Consultation on the Church in Response to Human Need, held in Wheaton, Ill., in June 1983 and sponsored by the World Evangelical Fellowship.* Grand Rapids: Eerdmans, 1987.

– *Mission as Transformation: A Theology of the Whole Gospel.* Oxford: Regnum, 1999.

Sanneh, Lamin. *Translating the Message: The Missionary Impact on Culture.* Maryknoll, New York: Orbis, 1989.

– *Whose Religion is Christianity? The Gospel beyond the West.* Grand Rapids: Eerdmans, 2003.

– *Disciples of All Nations: Pillars of World Christianity*. New York: Oxford University, 2008.

Scherer, James A., Richard H. Bliese, and John Nyquist. 'Evangelical Mission Theology II (Lausanne Movement)'. *Dictionary of Mission: Theology, History, Perspective*. Karl Müller *et al.*, (eds). Maryknoll: Orbis, 1997.

Schnabel, Eckhard J. *Early Christian Mission,* 2 vols. Downers Grove: InterVarsity, 2004.

– *Paul the Missionary: Realities, Strategies and Methods.* Downers Grove: InterVarsity, 2008.

Shea, Nina. *In the Lion's Den: A Shocking Account of Persecution and Martyrdom of Christians Today and How We Should Respond.* Nashville: Broadman & Holman Publishers, 1997.

Shenk, Wilbert R. (ed.). *Exploring Church Growth.* Grand Rapids: Eerdmans, 1983.

– 'Reflections on the Modern Missionary Movement: 1792–1992'. *Mission Studies* 9 (January, 1992), 62-78.

Smedes, Lewis B. (ed.). *Ministry and the Miraculous: A Case Study of Fuller Theological Seminary*. Pasadena: Fuller Theological Seminary, 1987.

Smith, Eugene L. 'The Conservative Evangelicals and the World Council of Churches'. *Ecumenical Review* 15:2 (January, 1963), 182-91.

Snow, Donald B. *English Teaching as Christian Mission: An Applied Theology.* Scottdale: PA: Herald Press, 2001.

Stanley, Brian. 'Where Have Our Mission Structures Come From?' *Transformation* 20 (January, 2003), 39-46.

– 'Defining the Boundaries of Christendom: The Two Worlds of the World Missionary Conference, 1910'. *International Bulletin of Missionary Research* 30:4 (October, 2006), 171-76.

Steffen, Tom. *Passing the Baton Church Planting that Empowers*. LaHabra, California: Center for Organizational and Ministry Development, 1993.

Stott, John. *Christian Mission in Today's World.* Downers Grove: InterVarsity Press, 1975.

Sweet, Leonard I. *Soul Tsunami.* Grand Rapids: Zondervan, 1999.

Taylor, William D. (ed.). *Global Missiology for the 21st Century: The Iguassu Dialogue*. Grand Rapids: Baker, 2000.

– *Internationalizing Missionary Training: A Global Perspective.* Grand Rapids: Baker Book House, 1991.

– *Kingdom Partnerships for Synergy in Missions.* Pasadena: William Carey Library, *1994.*

– *Too Valuable to Lose: Exploring the Causes and Cures of Missionary Attrition.* Pasadena: William Carey Library, 1997.

Tennent, Timothy C. *Theology in the Context of World Christianity.* Grand Rapids: Zondervan, 2007.

Travis, John. 'The C1 to C6 Spectrum'. *Evangelical Missions Quarterly* 34 (October, 1998), 407-408.

Tucker, Ruth A. *Guardians of the Great Commission: The Story of Women in Modern Missions*. Grand Rapids: Zondervan Publishing House, 1988.

Van Engen, Charles. *Mission on the Way: Issues in Mission Theology*. Grand Rapids: Baker Book House, 1996.

Van Engen, Charles, Nancy Thomas and Robert Gallagher (eds.). *Footprints of God: A Narrative Theology of Mission*. Monrovia, California: MARC Publications, 1999.

Vanhoozer, Kevin J. *The Drama of Doctrine: a Canonical-linguistic Approach to Christian Theology.* Louisville: Westminster John Knox, 2005.

Van Rheenen, Gailyn. *Communicating Christ in Animistic Contexts*. Grand Rapids: Baker Book House, 1991.

Wagner, C. Peter. *Apostles and Prophets: The Foundation of the Church*. Ventura, California: Regal Books, 2000.

– *Church Growth and The Whole Gospel: A Biblical Mandate*. New York: Harper and Row, 1981.

– *Confronting the Powers: How the New Testament Church Experienced the Power of Strategic-level Spiritual Warfare*. Ventura, California: Regal Books, 1996.

– *Engaging the Enemy: How to Fight and Defeat Territorial Spirits*. Ventura, California: Regal Books, 1991.

– *Look Out! The Pentecostals Are Coming*. Carol Stream, Ill.: Creation House, 1973.

– (ed.). *The Third Wave of the Holy Spirit: Encountering the Power of Signs and Wonders Today*. Ann Arbor, Mich.: Servant Publications, 1988.

Wakatama, Pius. *Independence for the Third World Church: An African's Perspective on Missionary Work*. Downers Grove: InterVarsity Press, 1976.

Walls, Andrew F. *The Cross-Cultural Process in Christian History*. Maryknoll: Orbis, 2002.

– 'The Great Commission 1910-2010'. Online: http://www.towards2010.org.uk/downloads/t2010paper01walls.pdf [accessed 2 April 2009].

– *The Missionary Movement in Christian History: Studies in the Transmission of Faith*. Maryknoll: Orbis, 1996.

Ward, Ted. *Living Overseas: A Book of Preparations*. New York: The Free Press, 1984.

Winter, Ralph and Kenneth Scott Latourette. *The Twenty-Five Unbelievable Years, 1945 to 1969*. Pasadena: William Carey Library, 1970.

Winter, Ralph. 'Edinburgh 1980 Reports: World Consultation on Frontier Missions'. *Mission Frontiers* 2:12 (December, 1980), 1, 4.

– 'The Highest Priority: Cross-Cultural Evangelism'. In J. D. Douglas (ed.). *Let the Earth Hear His Voice: Official Reference Volume, Papers and Responses. International Congress on World Evangelization, Lausanne, Switzerland*. Minneapolis: World Wide Publications, 226-41.

– 'Is It Possible? Global Cross-Cultural Mission Collaboration: 1910 to 2010'. *Mission Frontiers* (January-February, 2009), 9-11.

World Evangelical Alliance. 'World Evangelical Alliance'. Online: http://www.worldevangelicals.org/aboutwea/history.htm [cited 29 March 2009].

Williams, Theodore (ed.). *World Mission: Building Bridges or Barriers?: Papers Presented at the Missions Commission Conference of the World Evangelical Fellowship Held at Bad Liebenzell, Germany*. Bangalore, India: World Evangelical Fellowship, 1979.

Wright, Christopher J. H. *The Mission of God: Unlocking the Bible's Grand Narrative*. Downers Grove: InterVarsity, 2006.

Yates, Timothy. *Christian Mission in the Twentieth Century*. Cambridge: Cambridge University Press, 1994.

Yohannen, K. P. *The Coming Revolution in World Missions*. Altamonte Springs, Florida: Creation House, 1986.

Yong, Amos. *Beyond the Impasse: Toward a Pneumatological Theology of Religions*. Grand Rapids: Baker, 2003.

– *Discerning the Spirit(s)*. Sheffield: Sheffield Academic, 2000.

– *Hospitality and the Other*. Maryknoll: Orbis, 2008.

Additional Resources

Anderson, Gerald H., James M. Phillips, and Robert T. Coote. *Toward the Twenty-First Century in Christian Mission: Essays in Honor of Gerald H. Anderson.* Grand Rapids: Eerdmans, 1993.

Carpenter, Joel A., Wilbert R. Shenk. *Earthen Vessels: American Evangelicals and Foreign Missions, 1880–1980.* Grand Rapids: Eerdmans, 1990.

Dowsett, Rose. 'An Evangelical Perspective'. Online: http://www.towards2010.org.uk/downloads/t2010paper08dowsett.pdf [accessed 2 April 2009].

Hastings, Adrian. *The Clash of Nationalism and Universalism within Twentieth-Century Missionary Christianity.* Cambridge: Currents in World Christianity Project, 2000.

Lewis, Donald M. *Christianity Reborn: The Global Expansion of Evangelicalism in the Twentieth Century*. Grand Rapids: Eerdmans, 2004.

Ross, Kenneth R. 'The Centenary of Edinburgh 1910: Its Possibilities'. *International Bulletin of Missionary Research* 30:4 (October, 2006), 177-79.

Stanley, Brian, North. *Twentieth Century World Christianity: A Perspective from the History of Missions.* Cambridge: Currents in World Christianity Project, 1999.

The Progress of the Frontier Mission Movement: A Thirty-Year Glance from Edinburgh 1980 through Tokyo 2010

David Taylor

Editors' Note*: The vast bulk of the mission world links "Edinburgh" to the World Missionary Congress of 1910. Evangelicals who focus on frontier missions, however, also point to the gathering in 1980 at Edinburgh as a significant event in generating the energy directed towards frontier missions by evangelicals today.*

Although it is difficult to pinpoint exact moments and fixed dates in time when historical movements begin, it is probably roughly accurate to say that the modern 'frontier mission movement' began to gather significant momentum around 40 years ago, in the early 1970s. It is around this time that the first lists of unreached peoples began to be compiled, building on the research conducted by Wycliffe Bible Translators in their pursuit of identifying the world's 'Bibleless' peoples. David Barrett's comprehensive study of church growth among all the peoples in Africa (introduced at the world's first frontier mission consultation held in 1972) became a model for research around the world.[1] He later expanded his research to include a global list of 13,000 'ethnolinguistic' peoples, which became the foundation for many people group databases over the next two decades.[2]

The first estimates of the number of unreached peoples were prepared for the 1974 Lausanne conference on evangelism by Ralph Winter and the missiology team at the Fuller School of World Mission.[3] Leading up to this conference, the first global survey of unreached peoples was also conducted, involving 2,200 questionnaires sent out around the world to mission organizations and field offices.[4] Six years later, the Edinburgh 1980 conference launched the

[1] Pierce Beaver, *The Gospel and Frontier Peoples* (Pasadena: William Carey Library), 1972.

[2] David Barrett. *World Christian Encyclopedia*, (Oxford: Oxford University Press), 2001. See the chapter in this volume by Jim Haney comparing the three major research databases on the world's peoples.

[3] Ralph Winter, 'Penetrating the New Frontiers', in C.P. Wagner and E.R. Dayton (eds), *Unreached Peoples '79* (Elgin, IL, David C. Cook, 1979), 37-77.

[4] Edward Dayton, *Unreached Peoples Directory* (Monrovia: MARC, 1974).

watchword, "A Church for Every People By the Year 2000!" which gave inspiration to the Adopt-A-People campaign (the first inter-mission cooperative effort to reach all peoples) and the AD2000 movement (the first global network focused on frontier missions). These initiatives resulted in more attention given to unreached peoples around the world, both among mission agencies as well as local churches, than any other mission mobilization effort in history.[5] Here at Edinburgh 1980, which was organized by a number of leading Evangelical mission organizations from around the world, the frontier mission movement finally leaped beyond the realm of missiologists and researchers and into the realm of missionary sending societies which had the capacity to act on the facts being unearthed by strategists such as Barrett and Winter.

The progress of the gospel among formerly unreached peoples has been significant as a result of the research and mobilization initiated over the last forty years. These decades witnessed more Muslims, Buddhists and Hindus coming to know Christ than in all previous centuries of missionary endeavour combined. Dozens of church planting movements have been initiated among the world's major unreached mega-peoples (those over one million in population),[6] where just two decades before the ground remained untilled for literally centuries.

The first major breakthrough in the Muslim bloc came in South Asia, where at least half a million Muslim background believers have come to faith among the Bengali. This breakthrough proved the effectiveness of a contextualized approach for winning Muslims and became a model for many church planting movements around the world. Next door to South Asia, in Iran, a strong underground church movement continues to emerge with thousands of house fellowships multiplying throughout the country. Surveys in the country indicate that Christian satellite broadcasting in Farsi, which began in the year 2000, is being viewed by well over half the population.[7] One satellite broadcasting ministry in the Arab world, SAT7, has a regular audience of 8.5 million people.[8] In North Africa, the Berbers are responding to the gospel in massive numbers, with one movement among the Kabyle estimated to encompass several hundred thousand believers.[9]

In the Buddhist world, two significant breakthroughs occurred among the Khmer and the Mongolians. In Cambodia the church grew exponentially from

---

[5] Ralph Winter, 'Seeking Closure: The Story of a Movement from William Carey to Tokyo 2010', *Mission Frontiers* (September–October, 2009).

[6] The International Mission Board of the Southern Baptist Convention is tracking over 200 Church Planting Movements as they are developing among the world's least-reached peoples.

[7] Krikor Markarian, 'Today's Iranian Revolution', *Mission Frontiers* (September–October, 2008).

[8] Estimate from SAT7. www.sat7.org.

[9] Estimate from the Global Mission Database, US Center for World Mission, Research Dept.

just a handful of believers twenty years ago to an estimated 400,000 today.[10] In Mongolia, the church grew from a few isolated believers, to over 70,000 in 200 established fellowships in the same period.[11] Amongst Hindus a movement has emerged, quite distinct from any form of western Christianity, estimated to involve at least 10 million devotees of Jesus, also known as *Krista-bhaktas*.[12] Additionally, fast growing house-church movements are expanding throughout India, which are intersecting multiple spheres of Hindu and Muslim society, and giving rise to the possibility that the caste system in South Asia is not as formidable a challenge to the spread of the gospel as once thought.

In the last decade, missionary deployment among unreached peoples has increased at a rapid pace, effectively doubling the number of missionaries among the least-reached. In 1980, the ratio of missionaries to Muslims was one per million. It is now only one per hundred-thousand.[13] Most of these missionaries are not western, and many are from nearby or related peoples.[14] Although much work remains to be done, the significance of an increasing number of believers among the world's non-Christian peoples cannot be underestimated. What this means is that the cultural distances dividing unreached peoples from the gospel are shrinking. Momentum is gaining. For the first time in history, the very real possibility of reaching all peoples with the gospel in one generation is well within sight.

Looking Forward: What Might Happen in the Next Decade?

The AD2000 and Beyond movement gave birth to many significant frontier mission networks and movements in the last decade with the years 2020 and 2025 as milestones. Three of the more prominent of these global initiatives focusing on missionary deployment among the 'unengaged' are Finishing the Task, Vision 5:9, and the Global Network of Mission Structures. (The term, 'unengaged', is being used to refer to those unreached groups which have no long-term church-planting efforts currently among them.) The Finishing the Task (FTT) network, which was launched in the year 2003, is focusing on those unreached groups over 100,000 in population which are unengaged. At the time the network was launched, there were 639 groups in this category. By the year

[10] Estimate from the Global Mission Database.
[11] Estimate from the Global Mission Database.
[12] Barrett, *World Christian Encyclopedia*, 368-71. One movement among the Bhojpuri is reported by the International Mission Board (IMB) to have at least 4 million members now.
[13] Bruce Koch and Ralph Winter, 'Finishing the Task', in Ralph D. Winter and Steven C. Hawthorne (eds), *Perspectives on the World Christian Movement: A Reader* (Pasadena: William Carey Library, 2009), 541.
[14] Patrick Johnstone, *Operation World* (Waynesboro: Paternoster, 2001), 747.

2010, all but 95 had been engaged. The network is now expanding its efforts to those unengaged peoples which are 50,000 in population or greater.[15]

Another important and similar group, Vision 5:9, has become the primary network for those agencies working among Muslim people groups. Their goal is to see all Muslim peoples engaged by at least one missionary team by the year 2025. The network has grown to include every major mission sending agency working among Muslim peoples around the world. As a result, Vision 5:9 has become a valuable global forum to discuss strategy issues relating to reaching Muslim peoples, advocating a standard of best-practices in Muslim evangelism, discipleship and church planting. This is in contrast with the FTT network which focuses exclusively on mobilizing agencies to make commitments to 'adopt' one of the unengaged peoples for future outreach.

The third network, which was founded by Ralph D. Winter is the Global Network of Mission Structures (GNMS). The purpose of this network is to build an alliance of 2,000 mission agencies around a global strategy to see all peoples reached with church planting and discipleship movements. Part of this strategy is to organize regional, national, and people-cluster engagement task forces that will bring together field leaders of participating agencies to assess the progress being made in their area, and propose plans to deploy additional personnel as needed. These task forces will tackle the 'under-engaged' issue, which has been largely unaddressed. The under-engaged issue relates to those large groups which have an inadequate number of missionaries distributed throughout their population. The GNMS research efforts will identify every strategic population segment among the least-reached peoples requiring church-planting coordination, and then encourage member agencies to deploy church-planting coordinators among each one in the next ten to fifteen years.

Over the next ten years, many additional missionaries will be deployed by mission agencies around the world. The Korean mission movement alone, which is becoming increasingly frontier mission focused, has made a national commitment to send out 100,000 missionaries in the next twenty years. The Philippine church and the Chinese church both have similar goals.[16] All three of these mission sending movements have distinctly frontier mission DNA. The issue then of reaching the remaining least reached peoples is not so much a lack of personnel and resources but that of coordination. There is a growing understanding of this, and the result of this increased awareness is that the next ten years may see some of the most significant cooperative efforts to finish the task in the history of the Great Commission. Should world conditions hold stable, there is no compelling reason why the vision of Revelation 5:9 could not be fulfilled in our generation. In terms of the ethnic and geographic dimensions of the Great Commission mandate, this would represent a significant milestone

[15] Paul Eshleman, 'The State of the Unfinished Task', Tokyo 2010 Global Mission Consultation (Seoul: Tokyo 2010 GMC, 2010), 46-47.

[16] Yong Cho, 'Challenge and Opportunity for the Global Network of Mission Structures', *Mission Frontiers* (July–August, 2010).

in the history of God's redemptive plan announced to Abraham 4,000 years ago, "through you all the families of the earth will be blessed" (Genesis 12:3).

Bibliography

Beaver, Pierce. *The Gospel and Frontier Peoples*. Pasadena: William Carey Library, 1972.

Barrett, David, George T. Kurian, and Todd M. Johnson (eds.). *World Christian Encyclopedia: a Comparative Survey of Churches and Religions in the Modern World*. Oxford: Oxford University Press, 2001.

Cho, Yong. 'Challenge and Opportunity for the Global Network of Mission Structures'. *Mission Frontiers* (July–August, 2010).

Dayton, Edward. *Unreached Peoples Directory*. Monrovia: MARC, 1974.

Eshleman, Paul. 'The State of the Unfinished Task'. *Tokyo 2010 Global Mission Consultation*. Seoul: Tokyo 2010 GMC (2010), 46-47.

Johnstone, Patrick. *Operation World*. Waynesboro: Paternoster, 2001.

Markarian, Krikor. 'Today's Iranian Revolution'. *Mission Frontiers* (September–October, 2008).

Winter, Ralph. 'Penetrating the New Frontiers'. In C.P. Wagner and E.R. Dayton (eds.). *Unreached Peoples '79*. Elgin, IL, David C. Cook, 1979.

Winter, Ralph. 'Seeking Closure: The Story of a Movement from William Carey to Tokyo 2010'. *Mission Frontiers* (September–October, 2009).

Winter, Ralph and Bruce Koch. 'Finishing the Task'. In Ralph D. Winter and Steven C. Hawthorne (eds.). *Perspectives on the World Christian Movement: A Reader*. Pasadena: William Carey Library, 2009, 531-46.

Unreached Peoples Insights

History and Impact of the Fuller School of World Mission

Greg Parsons

Editors' Note: *Among conservative missionaries and missiologists, Fuller Theological Seminary's School of Intercultural Studies (SIS) is arguably the most widely recognized missiological training institution in the world. Because the evangelical focus on frontier missions was framed by faculty serving at Fuller, the history of the SIS provides a significant case study for those who would understand American evangelicals and frontier mission.*

Following World War II, growing in part out of the experiences of soldiers, an increasing number of global ministries were founded. From 1900 through 1945, there were a total of 113 mission organizations founded in North America, 36 of which were denominationally affiliated.[1] From 1945 until 1976 [2] there were 426 new organizations founded, 28 of which were denominationally affiliated. This reflects, in part, not only growing differences within evangelicalism in theology and practice, but perhaps more importantly, a desire to advance God's purposes.[3] In the West in particular, major streams within evangelicalism took different approaches to engaging the culture around them. Some were called new or neo-evangelical. One of those was Fuller Theological Seminary (FTS) founded in the fall of 1947.

The path FTS took, seeking to be a voice both to the evangelical movement and to the world, has had a wide-ranging impact and produced many results, interpreted by conservative evangelicals as a failure and weakness, but those seeking reform within parts of evangelicalism saw it as success and strength.

An Idea: A School of Evangelism

Charles E. Fuller was well known in conservative Christian circles. In 1942 and 1943 his nationwide radio broadcasts, The Pilgrim Hour and especially The Old

---

[1] Denominational affiliation means they are either the mission arm of the denomination or the have a denominational name in the organization name. Many of the groups founded mid-century were break-off groups from a larger 'parent' denomination.

[2] This is when Ralph Winter left Fuller's SWM and founded the US Center for World Mission.

[3] It may also reflect American independence and/or entrepreneurialism.

Fashioned Revival Hour, were on the Mutual Broadcasting System, and had audiences surpassing in size those of the most popular secular shows, including Bob Hope and Charlie McCarthy.[4] He believed there was a need for a high quality seminary on the west coast. Since he was an evangelist, Fuller's original vision was for a place to train evangelists and missionaries with the 'tools' necessary to spread the faith. Reflecting back fifty years later, on the founding of what was initially called the School of World Mission and Institute of Church Growth, Ralph D. Winter believed that when the School of World Mission was established in 1965, it was a 'mid-course correction' to get back to what Charles Fuller originally had in mind.[5]

Charles Fuller's son, Dan Fuller, wrote explaining the school to Eugene Nida, whom he wished to be on the Steering Committee:

> We are impressed by the great need for such a school as the Christian church faces a variety of complex tasks in attempting to carry out the Great Commission. ... There is a need for a school to serve as a center for grappling with the issues that confront Christians as they seek to establish churches throughout the world. Here research into these problems can be pursued and the results made available not only to the students but also to the Church at large.[6]

In the 1960s, the idea of an evangelical graduate school of world mission was something that hadn't been tried, at least in the West. At that time and over the next few years, seminaries that had any faculty in missions usually had only one, often with experience in only one field or culture. As the founding dean of the Fuller School of World Mission, Donald A. McGavran brought an unusually broad range and depth of experience.

Donald A. McGavran

Vernon Middleton, McGavran's biographer, summarized McGavran's life:

> McGavran's life has been one long search for effective evangelism. He is a missiologist with a rich and varied background of experience and research in virtually every aspect of missionary endeavor. [7]

McGavran's missionary career grew out of his varied experiences growing up and serving in India as the son and grandson of missionaries. He was able to build upon his family's history in the country and became interested churches that were growing and multiplying throughout India. When McGavran visited some of these 'mass movements to Christ' his whole perspective changed.

---

[4] Daniel P. Fuller, *Give the Winds a Mighty Voice: the Story of Charles E. Fuller* (Waco, TX: Word Books, 1972), 149-52.

[5] Personal communication to author.

[6] Letter from Daniel P. Fuller to Eugene Nida, December 17, 1964, 1.

[7] Vernon J. Middleton, 'The Development of a Missiologist: The Life and Thought of Donald Anderson McGavran, 1897–1965' (PhD dissertation, Fuller Theological Seminary,1990) , ix.

> Many people have been involved in the discovery of church growth. While God has granted me a part in the process, I neither invented church growth nor am solely responsible for it. Indeed, I owe my interest in church growth to a great Methodist bishop, Jerrell Waskom Pickett. In 1934, he kindled my concern that the Church grow. I lit my candle at Pickett's fire. [8]

As McGavran continued to work with Pickett, he did his own studies of these movements, checking to see if they could be verified. After studying and working on this with Pickett for twenty years he documented the principles behind these 'people movements', as he preferred to call them, in the book Bridges *of God.* That book played a large part in increasing his influence outside of India and his own denomination. Central to McGavran's thinking was his definition of mission, found in the first edition of *Understanding Church Growth*, 'an enterprise devoted to proclaiming the Good News of Jesus Christ and persuading men to become his disciples and dependable members of His Church'. [9]

The core idea in *Bridges of God* was that people prefer to come to Christ with people who are similar to them in cultural background. McGavran's thesis in *Understanding Church Growth* is summarized by Middleton:

> The normal way in which peoples are Christianized is by group action. The individual acceptance of Jesus Christ as Lord and Savior, which is what the individualistic western Church now believes is the only correct, orthodox, and meaningful way, is not the way in which peoples, societies, races, castes, and clans turn to Christ. Peoples (as opposed to individuals) turn to Christ in group action, by consultation among themselves, by following some convinced leaders, by religious migration, so to speak. After that, sanctification can proceed through individual conversion and meaningful dedication by individuals. [10]

What some termed, 'evangelistic opportunity' grew from McGavran's idea of working with those who were open to the gospel. [11] The reverse idea, the concept of resistance to the gospel, was raised in McGavran's observations and comparisons between church growth in India and Africa. It became a larger issue when McGavran traveled through Africa on his way home for a furlough.[12] Why, he wondered, did the church grow amazingly in places in

---

[8] Donald A. McGavran and George G. Hunter, *Church Growth: Strategies That Work* (Nashville: Abingdon, 1980), 14.

[9] Donald A. McGavran, *Understanding Church Growth* (Grand Rapids: Eerdmans, 1978), 26.

[10] Middleton, 'Development', 371.

[11] Wilbert R. Shenk, 'Church Growth Studies: A Bibliography Review', in W.R. Shenk (ed.), *The Challenge of Church Growth: A Symposium* (Elkhart, IN: Institute of Mennonite Studies,1973), 16.

[12] Middleton, 'Development', 150.

African south of the Sahara? Why did it fail to grow similarly in India, or only in select people groups?

The core idea undergirding McGavran's Church Growth ideas was what became know as the Homogeneous Unit Principle or HUP. McGavran used the phrases, 'people movements to Christ' and 'Christward movements'. McGavran defined homogeneous units as, 'a section of society in which all members have some characteristics in common'.

When McGavran returned from India at age 57, he was intent on passing on his wisdom and insights any way he could, through writing, speaking and especially through more in-depth missionary training. After establishing the Institute of Church Growth (ICG) in Oregon, he was invited at age 65 to the School of World Mission (SWM) at Fuller as its founding dean.

In March of 1965, after the SWM was established, F. Carlton Booth wrote to Eugene A. Nida about the aspects of the school that could be highlighted on Charles Fuller's radio program. These included the high priority of church planting, field experienced faculty and visiting lecturers, and providing advanced training for missionaries home on furlough.[13]

There were many who characterized the Church Growth Movement as being focused mainly on numerical growth without regard to discipleship and depth. They believed church growth promoters such as McGavran and later C. Peter Wagner were just trying to build bigger churches or church movements, and were willing to justify anything that worked. Most of that perspective seems to have grown from the application of McGavran's church growth principles to established churches in the North America as well as places such as Korea, where Church Growth became popular and effective in its application. [14]

In McGavran's book, *Crucial Issues in Missions Tomorrow*, Ralph Winter wrote a chapter dealing with those who suggested the Church Growth Movement was only, or even mainly, interested in numbers. He wrote:

> Those who emphasize 'church growth' are sometimes accused of being more interested in quantities of church members than in their quality. This is despite the fact that the very phrase church growth implies an additional dimension of emphasis beyond conversation, since it focuses not on how many raise their hands at an evangelistic service but on the incorporation of the new believer into church life. Other religions may consist of individuals worshiping at shrines, but the essence of Christianity goes beyond individual experience. Thus, the very concept of church growth is an attempt to emphasize the quality of corporate life beyond the quantity of individual decisions. [15]

---

[13] Letter from F. Carlton Booth to Eugene A. Nida, March 15, 1965, 1. Billy Graham had recorded a message about Fuller starting the SWM. Booth was asking Nida to make a similar audio recording to be played on the Old Fashioned Revival Hour as the SWM was launched.

[14] For examples of various views on this, see Gary McIntosh (ed.), *Evaluating the Church Growth Movement: 5 Views* (Grand Rapids: Zondervan, 2004).

[15] Ralph D. Winter, 'Church Growth Calculations: Facts and Fallacies, No. 1', *Church*

There were also those who disagreed with the Homogeneous Unit Principle, which was foundational to the church growth movement. In the extreme, some felt the HUP was racist. Although the HUP has been used by some to forward or support essentially racist agendas, it is not inherently racist [16] The misunderstanding or misinterpretation of McGavran's core idea often grows from those who desire an integrated church fellowship sooner than the new believers may be ready for it. [17] As early as *The Bridges of God* in 1955, McGavran hinted at the idea of spreading Christ to those groups that were on the fringe of an existing church, not merely spreading the message through more 'effective evangelism'[18] (however helpful and necessary that is). Embedded in the title, *The Bridges of God*, was the idea that a person who was from another culture, who expressed interest in the gospel and the things of God, could be a bridge of God back to that people.

The element of pioneering or frontiers is core to what McGavran was seeing in India's people movements as well as the Church Growth idea. He saw his mission in India and after his retirement to help the church advance to where it had not been. He wanted to help others understand how people movements could be encouraged and nurtured. [19] Serving as the founding dean of Fuller's SWM was an opportunity for him to fulfill this mission.

An announcement in the *Church Growth Bulletin* noted that, 'The School of World Mission at Fuller envisages ultimately a faculty of six and a student body made up of missionaries on furlough and missionary candidates under appointment. Graduate fellows from younger Churches in Asia, Africa, and Latin America will strengthen the research arm of the School'. [20]

Fuller's Bulletin listed the following purposes of the 'Graduate School of World Mission':

1. Prepare men to fulfill the Great Commission in the midst of change peculiar to our age.
2. Provide a theology of missions for all seminary students looking toward a pastorate.
3. Bring Christian nationals to the school as students and teachers to provide opportunities for mutual exchange.
4. Develop a team of research specialists to study and provide a center of thought

---

Growth Bulletin 6:4 (March, 1970), 175-76.

[16] In a dissertation, Bruce W. Fong evaluates the Homogeneous Unit Principle and suggests that, 'It is clear that neither McGavran or Wagner are perpetuating a racist ideal. Neither are racists. Also, their concern is not 'number' for numbers sake. Neither of these criticisms are legitimate'. (Bruce W. Fong, *Racial Equality in the Church: A Critique of the Homogeneous Unit Principle in Light of a Practical Theology Perspective* [Lanham, MD: University Press of America, 1996], 180.)

[17] McIntosh, *Evaluating*.

[18] This is the title of one of McGavran's later books, *Effective Evangelism: A Theological Mandate*.

[19] Donald A. McGavran, *The Bridges of God: A Study in the Strategy of Missions* (New York: Friendship Press, 1955), 109.

[20] Donald A. McGavran, *Church Growth Bulletin Volume 2* (South Pasadena: William Carey Library, 1977), 70.

and information regarding World Mission.[21]

Expanding the School

McGavran and Alan Tippett started the SWM together and Tippett brought an anthropological perspective and solid scholarship to missions the program. McGavran also saw the need for training for leaders in the Church Growth Movement. Ken Mulholland tied Winter's being asked to come to Fuller SWM as a sign of McGavran's sense 'that TEE [Theological Education by Extension] was a vital instrument for church growth'.[22] McGavran also saw research as a vital part of missions strategy. This grew naturally from his experiences with Pickett in India.[23] Accordingly, McGavran was ready to accept the position of dean of the Fuller School of World Mission and was inaugurated on September 27, 1966, although first class had been held on September 28, 1965.[24]

There was a lot of informal 'learning' in the early days of the Fuller SWM. The students were called 'associates' and they were almost all field-experienced missionaries. Faculty and associates would meet regularly just to discuss ideas, often totally unconnected to any particular assignment. When asked by professors at other institutions how many students the SWM had, Ralph Winter, half joking, would say 'four to five ... but we have 100 teachers.' He would add that he was not sure what the students learned, but he and the other faculty learned a great deal about the world where the students had served as missionaries.

The first three full-time faculty members (McGavran, Tippett and Winter) were close and worked well together. McGavran was very practical and fairly private. He was the diplomat, the activist. Tippett was the scholar, the academic. Winter brought an emphasis on church history, or 'the expansion of Christianity', as he preferred, favoring Kenneth Scott Latourette's approach.

Winter also added the dimension of promotion of McGavran's Church Growth ideas as well as those of Theological Education by Extension. In a dissertation on the missiology of McGavran, Donald M Wodarz, Priest of the Society of Saint Columban, wrote:

> Dr. Winter's projects have had a large influence on the promotion of Dr McGavran's ideas. Winter's work with the systems of extension education led to his publishing *Theological Education by Extension*, which is a method whereby church leaders can be training in their own communities. But the most important

---

[21] *The Bulletin of Fuller Theological Seminary* 1 (Spring, 1965), 3.

[22] Kenneth B. Mulholland, 'Donald McGavran's Legacy to Evangelical Missions', *Evangelical Missions Quarterly* 27:1 (January, 1991), 67.

[23] Mulholland, 'Legacy', 66-70.

[24] In the early days, the SWM was called the School of World Missions and Institute for Church Growth. Middleton's PhD dissertation on McGavran, finished in 1990, had that full name on the cover page, perhaps in part to honor McGavran's desire and the original agreement with FTS. 'Institute for Church Growth' was dropped at some point.

> contribution by Ralph Winter to the School of World Mission was the establishment of William Carey Library. …which handles low volume publications at reasonable prices and quickly makes available the publication of research carried on at the School of World Mission.[25]

William Carey Library

The faculty was fully aware that the work of their students would be helpful to others in mission work because the students were all experienced field workers. At first, the influence of McGavran and others convinced Eerdmans Publishing Company to publish some of the theses coming out of the SWM. A sampling of titles includes:

1. Church Growth in Mexico by Donald McGavran, John Huegel, and Jack Taylor (c. 1963)
2. Wildfire – Church Growth in Korea by Roy E. Shearer (c. 1966)
3. New Patterns of Church Growth in Brazil by William R. Read (c. 1965)
4. Church Growth in Central an Southern Nigeria by John B. Grimley and Gordon E. Robinson (c 1966)
5. God's Impatience in Liberia by Joseph Conrad Wold (c. 1968)
6. Tinder in Tabasco by Charles Bennett (c. 1968)
7. Latin American Church Growth by William R. Read, Victor M. Menterroso and Harmon A. Johnson (c.1969)

The SWM faculty discussed the idea of publishing the work of the students and urged Winter to try to implement this. To this end, William Carey Library (WCL) was established in 1969. WCL produced and published the work of the students and faculty but Winter also continued to enlist other publishers to take on some of the books to give the key thinking of SWM faculty and students a wider market to which WCL did not have access.

Winter's innovative bent benefitted Fuller's SWM in other ways as well. When McGavran was first in negotiations to move the Institute of Church Growth to Fuller, he was promised that they would be able to offer a PhD through the SWM. But President Hubbard argued that two things were preventing FTS from offering the PhD degree: a scholarly society that was engaging the community of scholars on the subject of missiology (at the time this was considered to be an inter-disciplinary subject), and a scholarly journal. [26] Winter and others set about to solve that problem since the degrees given at that time in Seminaries were not understood by the rest of the world. Degrees such as D.Min. or D.Miss. did not make sense to some governments when deciding to give a visa for someone to come and help teach or serve, for

---

[25] Donald M. Wodarz, *Church Growth: The Missiology of Donald Anderson McGavran* (PhD dissertation, Pontificia Universitas Gregoriana, 1979), 124, 297.

[26] Roberta Winter, 'Winter Initiatives', Pasadena, September 31, 2000, 33.

instance. So, Winter reasoned, why not give degrees that could be respected and understood, such as an MA or a PhD? [27]

Seedbed for New Ideas and Structures

There were a number of new things that grew out of the Fuller SWM. One of those was the American Society of Missiology and *Missiology: An International Review*. Winter and George Peters of Dallas Theological Seminary convened a meeting to discuss the idea of having a broad group that could draw from evangelical, ecumenical and Roman Catholic scholarship. They wrote to a select group of well-known missiologists for their input, and announced a meeting for June 9-10 at Anderson's Scarritt College in Nashville, Tennessee. Their proposal suggested that the new society:

1. Be comprehensive by including members (a) from all Christian traditions, (b) from all missions related scholarly fields, and, (c) open to mission executives and missionaries, along with the scholars.
2. Be a professional society, to counteract the 'bad press' that had plagued mission studies.
3. Produce a scholarly journal as well as high caliber monographs. [28]

In 1972 the society was established, with Gerald Anderson, Winter and Donald M. Wodarz SSC authorized to help run it until the next meeting. With that, the American Society of Missiology (ASM) began a pattern it has continued until this day: having representatives from each of the three major Christian traditions: Roman Catholic, ecumenical, and evangelical.

FOUNDING OF MISSIOLOGY: AN INTERNATIONAL REVIEW

In 1972, with a growing publishing background, Winter heard that the small, quality journal *Practical Anthropology* was reconsidering its role and audience. Winter negotiated transfer of it to the ASM and continued as the business manager of the new journal for the first six years. [29] The new journal, *Missiology: An International Review*, produced its first issue in January 1973. [30] Over those first years, various Fuller SWM faculty were editors, starting with Tippett as well as Glasser. Tippett was a perfect choice for the first three years,

---

[27] Interview with Ralph D. Winter by the author on October 18, 2006, 1.

[28] Wilbert R. Shenk and George R. Hunsberger, *American Society of Missiology: The First Quarter Century* (Decatur, GA: The American Society of Missiology, 1998), 12.

[29] This is a situation in which Winter's accounting experience came in handy, as *Practical Anthropology* was some $4000 in debt, not realizing they had already spent money 'due' to subscribers for future issues.

[30] Interview with Ralph Winter by the author, August 30, 2006, 14-15. *Missiology* started on the base of the journal, *Practical Anthropology*, which had run out of money. Alan Tippett was the first editor of *Missiology* and Winter was the secretary/business manager.

because of the respect he had in anthropological circles, providing a transition for the readership of the former Practical Anthropology journal.

These initiatives to found a scholarly society and journal, by Winter and other SWM faculty, eventually persuaded the leadership of Fuller Theological Seminary to offer the PhD degree through the School of World Mission, an upgrade from the Doctor of Missiology.

Unreached Areas of the World

As time went by, Winter began to focus on the places around the world from which the faculty of the SWM was not getting any information, or at least not very much. Western missions and the national church seemed to be overlooking certain religious or cultural segments. When later describing what he had experienced during those days, Winter often said, 'I was sitting there and realized that I could have 1,000 more missionaries come through my classroom and I would never have a missionary from a place where no missionary had ever gone'. [31]

School of World Mission Input into Lausanne '74

In his typical innovative way, Winter gathered the faculty and students of the SWM to collect data and produce charts to document the parts of the world where no missionary had ever gone. Their immediate motivation was to give a presentation at Billy Graham's International Congress on Evangelism, to be held in Lausanne, Switzerland in 1974. The agenda of the congress was well planned ahead of time, including Graham's hope:

> ... that the Congress would (1) 'frame a biblical declaration on evangelism', (2) challenge the church 'to compete the task of world evangelization', (3) 'state what the relationship is between evangelism and social responsibility', and (4) help to develop 'a new 'koinonia' or fellowship among evangelicals of all persuasions.[32]

The Lausanne Congress was a watershed in many ways. Certainly the Lausanne movement itself, which grew out of the '74 meeting, was productive. There were six consultations from 1977–1982 instigated by the Theology and Education Group and the Strategy Working Group. One of those was on the Homogeneous Unit Principle, discussed earlier.[33] A number of other results of

---

[31] Interview with Ralph Winter by the author, August 30, 2006.

[32] John Stott summarized these five points under 'basic beliefs': a commitment to the authority of Scripture, the lostness of men and women apart from Christ, salvation in Christ alone, the need to witness in both word and actions, and the necessity of evangelism for salvation. (John R. W. Stott, *Making Christ Known: Historic Mission Documents from the Lausanne Movement, 1974–1989* (Grand Rapids: Eerdmans, 1997), xiv.

[33] Other consultations included topics such as: the Willowbank meeting in Bermuda on Gospel and Culture; a consultation on Muslim evangelization; a consultation on Simple

Lausanne can be found and evaluated in the PhD thesis, by Klas Ingvar Lundström, 'Gospel and Culture in the World Council of Churches and the Lausanne Movement', with particular focus on the period 1973–1996. [34]

Because of the issues raised as part of the goals of the event, it seemed right to draw on the resources at Fuller's SWM. A number of their faculty were asked to present on various subjects. Both McGavran and Winter gave major plenary presentations. All the SWM faculty were present, as well as Fuller President Alan Hubbard and a number of alumni. According to the Bulletin of FTS, SWM Dean Arthur Glasser 'has prepared an extensive 'Unreached People Survey'. This data, gathered from missionaries and national church leaders, will be the basis for much of the discussion at Lausanne.' [35] McGavran and Winter's presentations emphasized

> … the startling figure that 2,700 million people remained unevangelized, but that nevertheless they could be reached if we were to break down the world's population into 'people groups', distinguish between E1, E2 and E3 evangelism, and remember the 'great new resources for world evangelization' constituted by the younger churches. [36]

In addition, 'Dr. Winter finally spoke to the confusion of 'mission' and 'evangelism'' He explained that mission involved cross-cultural, cross-linguistic, and cross-racial evangelizing while evangelism refers to taking the gospel to one's own people whether inside or outside the homeland'. [37]

While most people remember Winter's presentation at Lausanne as focusing attention on billions of unreached peoples in major religious blocs culturally separated from those who know Christ, SWM student Bruce Graham noted that central to Winter idea was there was a need for a different or new kind of evangelism. Perhaps we haven't made progress in these areas because we can't communicate well. 'We developed core ideas, pie charts, etc. that ended up pushing people to go to these groups, … but the vast majority go taking the same kind of evangelism as if they were reaching their own people.'[38]

In reporting on the 1974 event in the World Vision magazine, Dayton quoted Winter as saying, 'Most of us are people-blind! Because we have lived most of our lives with people very much like ourselves, we tend to ignore

---

Lifestyle; a large consultation in Pattaya Thailand following up the Lausanne '74 theme of 'Let the Earth Hear His Voice' with, 'How Shall They Hear?'

[34] Klas I. Lundström, 'Gospel and Culture in the World Council of Churches and the Lausanne Movement with Particular Focus on the Period 1973–1996' (PhD dissertation, Uppsala University, 2006).

[35] From undated and unnumbered pages in a FTS promotional newsletter. This was the first publication in MARC's Unreached Peoples book series.

[36] Stott, *Making Christ Known*, xv.

[37] Chaeok Chun, 'The All-Asia Mission Consultation', (MTh thesis, Fuller Theological Seminary, 1975), 80.

[38] Comments made during a USCWM staff discussion after Ralph Winter's death; July 28, 2009.

people quite different than ourselves or to think them 'strange'. All over the world, differences of race, language and culture are generally considered a nuisance rather than a blessing. But the Bible is not people-blind.' [39]

As Winter reflected on the issues of hidden or unreached people groups and the need to mobilize workers to go to these people, in discussions with faculty Winter tried to talk Fuller into starting their own center focused on world missions. It would be more than the SWM. It would seek a closer connection with the sending agencies and would seek to collaborate with them and others involved in mission. It would not be more academics, but would be modeled after the coordinating offices in New York City at 475 Riverside Drive that housed the mission arm of a number of denominations. Winter had hoped that Fuller would open such an office building or 'implementation annex' nearby.

There were many reasons for such a building or quasi-independent organization, as Charles Kraft noted:

> We talked often of setting up another organization that would not be hampered by academic rules and regulations. It would be lean, mobile, flexible and adaptable to carry out the 'activist' ideas we generated that didn't fit into our academic programs.
>
> We even had more or less formal discussions over a two-year period involving both outsiders and Fuller insiders. In these meetings our ideas began to converge into the concept of a major 'annex' to SWM that would implement new strategies and functions essential to the things we were talking about in class. [40]

In the process of presenting the paper at Lausanne, and bouncing these ideas off of mentors like McGavran and younger leaders and students, Ralph and Roberta felt that God was calling them to start such an 'annex' or center. In 1976, Winter finally left Fuller to implement this vision and start the US Center for World Mission (USCWM). McGavran said to Winter that Ralph 'had bigger fish to fry' and encouraged him in founding the USCWM which has focused on 'frontier missions' since 1976.

Researching and cataloging unreached people groups, strategies for reaching them, mobilizing the body of Christ for prayer and service among the unreached, training programs, such as Perspectives on the World Christian Movement, publishing books through William Carey Library, producing generic missions publications such as Mission Frontiers Magazine as well as journals focused on those areas of missions most neglected, have been the hallmarks of Winter's US Center for World Mission. This mission institution, started to serve the mission agencies with workers on the ground, grew out of many of his experiences and reflections, especially from his exposure to students and other faculty at the Fuller School of World Mission. It represents

---

[39] Edward R. Dayton, 'A New Way to See the World', *World Vision* 18:9 (October, 1974), 9.

[40] Charles H. Kraft, *SWM/SIS at 40: A Participant/Observer's View of Our History* (Pasadena: William Carey Library, 2005), 132-33.

one significant way in which the SWM has had a lasting impact on evangelical missions worldwide that will continue for years to come.

Bibliography

Chen, Stephen Lei. 'Church Growth: Textbook for Theological Education by Extension'. MA thesis, Fuller Theological Seminary, 1977.

Chun, Chaeok. 'The All-Asia Mission Consultation'. MTh thesis, Fuller Theological Seminary, 1975.

Conn, Harive M. *Theological Perspectives on Church Growth*. Seoul: Sung Kwang Publishers, 1981.

Dayton, Edward R. 'A New Way to See the World'. *World Vision* 18:9 (October, 1974), 7-9.

Fong, Bruce W. *Racial Equality in the Church: A Critique of the Homogeneous Unit Principle in Light of a Practical Theology Perspective*. Lanham, MD: University Press of America, 1996.

Glasser, Arthur F. 'Church Growth at Fuller'. *Missiology* 14:4 (1987), 401-20.

Kraft, Charles H. *SWM/SIS at 40: A Participant/Observer's View of Our History*. Pasadena: William Carey Library, 2005.

McGavran, Donald A. *The Bridges of God: A Study in the Strategy of Missions*. New York: Friendship Press, 1955.

– *Church Growth and Christian Mission*. New York: Harper & Row, 1965.

– *Crucial Issues in Missions Tomorrow*. Chicago: Moody Press, 1972.

– *Effective Evangelism: A Theological Mandate*. Phillipsburg, NJ: Presbyterian and Reformed Publishing Co., 1988.

– *Understanding Church Growth*. Grand Rapids: Eerdmans, 1980.

McGavran, Donald A., ed. *Church Growth Bulletin, Volume 1*. South Pasadena: William Carey Library, 1969.

– *Church Growth Bulletin Volume 2*. South Pasadena: William Carey Library, 1977.

McGavran, Donald A., Donald Anderson and George G. Hunter. *Church Growth: Strategies That Work*. Nashville: Abingdon, 1980.

McIntosh, Gary (ed.). *Evaluating the Church Growth Movement: 5 Views*. Grand Rapids: Zondervan, 2004.

McPhee, Arthur G. 'Pickett's Fire: The Life, Contribution, Thought, and Legacy of J. Waskom Pickett, Methodist Missionary to India'. MA thesis, Asbury Theological Seminary, 2001.

Middleton, Vernon J. 'The Development of a Missiologist: The Life and Thought of Donald Anderson McGavran, 1897–1965'. PhD dissertation, Fuller Theological Seminary, 1990.

Mulholland, Kenneth B. 'Donald Mcgavran's Legacy to Evangelical Missions'. *Evangelical Missions Quarterly* 27:1 (January, 1991), 64-70.

Pickett, Jarrell W. *Christian Mass Movements in India: A Study with Recommendations*. New York: Abingdon, 1933.

Shenk, Wilbert R. 'Church Growth Studies: A Bibliography Review', In Wilbert Shenk (ed.). *The Challenge of Church Growth: A Symposium*. Elkhart, IN: Institute of Mennonite Studies, 1973.

Shenk, Wilbert R. and George R. Hunsberger (eds.). *American Society of Missiology:*

The First Quarter Century. Decatur, GA: The American Society of Missiology, 1998.

Stott, John R. W. *Pasadena Consultation on the Homogeneous Unit Principle*. Wheaton: Lausanne Committee for World Evangelization, 1978.

– *Making Christ Known: Historic Mission Documents from the Lausanne Movement, 1974–1989*, Grand Rapids: Eerdmans, 1997.

Winter, Ralph D. *Theological Education by Extension*. South Pasadena: William Carey Library, 1969.

– 'Church Growth Calculations: Facts and Fallacies, No. 1'. *Church Growth Bulletin*, 6:4 (March, 1970).

Wodarz, Donald M. 'Church Growth: The Missiology of Donald Anderson McGavran'. PhD dissertation, Pontificia Universitas Gregoriana, 1979.

PERSONAL REFLECTIONS

Ezra Sargunam and Andrew Swamidoss

***Editors' Note**: A major impact of the Fuller School of Intercultural Studies has been its role in training church and mission leaders from the Majority World. Two of these leaders, from India, reflect on the influence of Donald A. McGavran and Ralph D. Winter, two of the original faculty members of the School of World Mission, now the School of Intercultural Studies.*

On Donald A. McGavran

Ezra Sargunam
Bishop of the Evangelical Church in India
and an Indian *challaji* (disciple) of Donald McGavran

While teaching in the Madras Theoogical Seminary and College in 1972, I was asked to present a paper on 'Urban Church Planting' in Chennai, India. At the time I was also pastoring a church on Mandapam Road in Kilpauk, and we had set a goal for planting 100 churches. Donald McGavran knocked on my door the next day, saying, 'You are the kind of man I am looking for – you already speak my language. I want to invite you for a doctoral programme at the School of World Missions in Fuller Seminary'. He offered me full scholarship. Since it was very difficult for me to leave my family and ministry for two or three years, I agreed to take up a one-year Master's programme.

McGavran's Famous Slogans and Pertinent Church Growth Principles

It was during my sojourn in the US between 1972 and 1973 that I was exposed to the church growth principle comprising the 'people-groups' concept – reaching the unreached and the least-reached people groups, beginning with the most responsive ones. It was there that I came across the famous slogans of Donald A McGavran: 'win the winnable', 'harvest the harvestable', 'reach the reachable', 'go where the fish are found and biting', 'make conversions with minimum social dislocation', and the phenomenal India-specific approach – plant caste churches, have an urban strategy; begin with cities and then move on to the home villages of the urban migrants.

On Ralph D. Winter and Donald A. McGavran

Andrew Swamidoss
Dean of the India Graduate School of Missiology

A Memorial Tribute to Ralph D. Winter

With the passing of Ralph Winter [May, 2009] an era has passed away in front of our eyes. Dr. Ralph Winter was a missiologist par excellence, a think tank towering over all other think tanks energizing them with new vision. I knew him since the 1970's when he was teaching at Fuller and I was a student in the School of Theology under Professor Ralph Martin. I was fascinated and blessed by Dr. Winter's writings always. What a depth and what an analysis! Amazing! I pray that US Center for World Mission he founded will bring out many more Winters in the days to come.

Influence of McGavran and Winter upon Andrew W. Swamidoss

I was a graduate student in Fuller School of Theology in the seventies – 1974–79. McGavran used to say, 'Andrew, you are in the wrong School. Acts of the Apostles must be practiced, not just studied in theory.' I was doing my research in Acts of the Apostles under Martin getting trained to be a professor of New Testament, which I was for 10 years. But due to the influence of McGavran and Winter and the Fuller School of World Mission, in 1989 I switched over to developing a school of missions at Yavatmal along with Samuel Devadason, who had the Doctor of Missiology degree from the Fuller School of World Mission.

We were following the example of Dr. McGavran and Dr. Winter who were committed missiologists who not only could give strategic advice concerning field situations, but were committed to training others to be part of a think tank. Ralph Winter's vision for the US Center for World Mission in the seventies and his walk over the campus to claim it and the faith that he had in raising money to purchase the campus were for me a wakeup call. I took his example as a challenge when we developed the School of Mission at Yavatmal and raised one million US dollars.

McGavran's Homogenous Unit Principle and the Caste System

McGavran was born in India, where he also served as a third generation missionary. With such a background and experience, he was able to make observations that led to formulating general principles that have influenced many people for church growth. As an illustration of McGavran's Homogenous Unit Principle at work in India, Devadason tells the story of a village where he baptized four young men and told them they should proclaim the gospel. The result of their preaching and a power encounter was the whole village turning to Christ and 196 people were baptized. This has happened in village after village.

Some leaders have complained that the Homogeneous Unit Principle promotes the caste system in India. I do not agree. Just as water flows in the line of least resistance, the progress of the gospel happens along the lines of the castes better than otherwise. I believe the caste system could be abolished if Christian ministers encouraged inter-caste marriages. Since they do not do this, the problem perpetuates. The caste system is not promoted by the Homogenous Unit Principle, which is simply an observation of social realities.

I met with McGavran just six weeks before he died. He told me, 'Andrew, if Europe could be evangelized tribe after tribe, India can be evangelized tribe after tribe and caste after caste'.

LAUNCHING A MOVEMENT: A HISTORY OF THE PERSPECTIVES COURSE

Yvonne Wood Huneycutt

Editors' Note: *In the United States more people have taken the Perspectives on the World Christian Movement course than any other single missions course. Taught at local churches and schools around the country, this course has shaped the average evangelical church-goer's thinking on mission more than any other event, and continues to generate energy for frontier missions among evangelicals today.*

Background

I sat transfixed. Bewildered. Amazed. What is this speaker saying? How could I just now be hearing such significant information? After all, I was raised in church, in a strong mission-minded denomination. I served in church staff positions. I had a seminary degree, for goodness sake. How did I miss this? This is revolutionary. My perception of missions was shattered in the space of two hours. My insight into scripture was enlarged in the space of two weeks. My understanding of God, myself, the world and my role in it was transformed over the course of a semester.

My experience may be radical, but it is not unusual. Thousands have testified to similar shifts in perspective as a result of participating in the *Perspectives on the World Christian Movement* course. From college students to college professors; from business executives to stay-at-home moms; from pastors to Sunday School teachers; from missionary candidates to seasoned missionaries, the wide variety of participants in the Perspectives course have entered a movement has been reshaping mission endeavours from the last quarter of the twentieth century up until the present.

Launched in 1974, the Perspectives course has influenced tens of thousands of believers across the globe over the past three-and-a-half decades. In addition to those who have taken the Perspectives course, or derivatives of the Perspectives course, thousands more have used the *Perspectives Reader* as a textbook in college and seminary classes. There is no way to calculate the additional hundreds of thousands of lives that have been directly influenced by those who have studied the Perspectives material and embraced the call and promise of God for world evangelization through praying, giving, going, and living for God's eternal purpose: that 'a great multitude ... from every nation, tribe, people and language [will some day be] standing before the throne and in front of the Lamb' (Rev. 7:9, NIV).

Ralph Winter, the originator of the Perspectives course, used to say that Perspectives joined a movement of God that was already in progress in history. The first part of this chapter, therefore, will present an historical overview of the major trends in American culture and in missions leading up to the mid-seventies. The next section will document the early development of the Perspectives course, up through 1981 with the publication of the first *Perspectives Reader* and *Study Guide*. The Perspectives course not only joined a movement of God, but itself became a movement, contributing to and accelerating major mission trends. Therefore the final section will briefly consider the future of the expansion and development of the Perspectives course into the twenty-first century, including escalating world-wide reach.

Historical Context

'The day of the missionary is over. We have completed the missionary task; all that remains is local evangelism by the national church.' This was the thinking of much of the Christian church as the 1960's came to a close. The celebrated fact of the time was the recognition of the 'younger churches' – those planted by earlier mission efforts – on every continent and in almost every country. This led many to believe that Christ's Great Commission was fulfilled and all that remained was a clean-up job by the national churches within each country.[1] Furthering this popular belief was a call by some in the 'younger churches of the Third World', as they were then called, for a moratorium on missions.[2]

Global Realignments

What precipitated this sentiment in both the national and western churches that the missionary vocation was no longer welcome or appropriate? A principal answer lies in one of the most massive global political realignments in history. In his book, *The Twenty-Five Unbelievable Years, 1945-1969*, missiologist Ralph Winter recounts how rapidly the world shifted from a colonial-dominated landscape to a vast array of newly-independent nations. At the end of World War II in 1945, Europeans had virtual control over 99.5% of the world outside of the West. In a brief twenty-five year period, western nations lost control over all but five percent of the non-western population of the world. Missionary presence was often equated with colonial rule; therefore, in the

[1] Donald A. McGavran, 'Introducing Crucial Issues in Missions', in Arthur F. Glasser, Paul G. Hiebert, C. Peter Wagner and Ralph D. Winter (eds), *Crucial Dimensions in World Evangelization* (Pasadena: William Carey Library, 1976), 169-70.

[2] David M. Howard, 'Editorial: A Moratorium on Missions?' *Evangelical Missions Quarterly* (January 1975), http://www.emqoline.com/emq_article_read.php?ArticleID=2655.

minds of many in both the Majority World and the West, as one form of western dominance was shed, so should be the other.

Such rapid change brought with it unrest, resulting in regional conflicts. Many newly-independent nations turned to authoritarian governments, often embracing Marxism and coming under the shadow of the Soviet Union. Not only did communism seem to be gaining ground, but in the West, Christianity seemed to be losing ground. In American society, the Vietnam War fed the youth revolt of the sixties, fostering anger and disillusionment with 'the establishment'. David Howard, InterVarsity director of the Urbana student mission conventions in the early seventies, commented that 'the anti-government, anti-establishment, anti-family, anti-church attitudes were also expressed in anti-mission reactions. Seldom have missions been looked upon with less favor by students than during that decade.'[3]

Societal Trends

Secularism replaced the Judeo-Christian worldview in American media, government and educational systems. Salvation takes on a whole new meaning when the immortal soul is dismissed. Indeed, the very meaning of salvation was the theme of the World Council of Churches' Bangkok assembly in 1973. They defined salvation exclusively in this-worldly terms as a struggle for economic justice and human dignity against exploitation and oppression, solidarity with the marginalized poor and hope against despair.[4] The purpose and goal of mission accordingly turns upon the definition of salvation.

Simultaneously in Catholic circles salvation began to be equated with socio-political liberation. Arising out of Latin America and emerging from the reforms of Vatican II (1962–1965), liberation theology focused the mission efforts of the church on working for political and economic liberation for the oppressed and marginalized masses, even if it meant revolution. Many liberal denominations embraced it while most evangelical denominations condemned it, especially for its Marxist-leanings.[5]

Alongside secularism, another societal trend in the early seventies was the rising tide of pluralism. The world was shrinking due to astounding advances in technology. International travel, international trade, global telecommunications and massive immigration into burgeoning cosmopolitan cities all combined to heighten international awareness and intercultural contacts. Beginning in the 1950's, secularization and massive immigration started to erode the Christian percentage of America.[6] Familiarity with those of other religions made it harder

---

[3] David M. Howard, 'The Road to Urbana and Beyond', *Evangelical Missions Quarterly* (January 1985), http://www.emqonline.com/emq_article_read.php?ArticleID=2855.

[4] David J. Bosch, *Transforming Mission: Paradigm Shifts in Theology of Mission* (Maryknoll: Orbis Books, 1991), 396-97.

[5] Bosch, *Transforming Mission*, 432-42.

[6] David B. Barrett and Todd M. Johnson, *World Christian Trends, AD 30 – AD 2200: Interpreting the Annual Christian Megacensus* (Pasadena: William Carey Library, 2001), 330.

to conceive of an acquaintance going to hell for holding a non-Christian belief system. The plurality of religions and the outworking of secularism produced a relativism of truth. Writing in 1976, renowned missiologist Donald McGavran summarized the current environment, 'It is unpopular today to think in terms of one true religion and the others all false '.[7]

Negative View of Missions

The amalgamation of all of these and other factors – a collective guilty conscience over colonialism, rapid moral degeneration, alluring materialism, the struggle for racial equality, shocking political assassinations – permeated the American church at the turn of the decade with a spirit of negativism and despair. With the nightly news showing horrible footage from Vietnam, popular books making dire predictions about global overpopulation, reports on the seriousness of the drug problem in the public schools, the ubiquitous fear of communism and the cataclysmic threat of the arms race, the entire country was in a funk.

Ralph Winter reflects on those days.

> I wrote a book in 1969 called the *Twenty-Five Unbelievable Years*. The title of every chapter was negative on the grounds that I did not think it would arouse interest if it took an optimistic approach. That is how bad the negativism was in popular Christian culture at the time. That's why McGavran's famous lecture, 'The Sunrise (not the sunset) of Missions' was so shocking to so many people.[8]

The prevailing controversy of the day revolved around the question of what the primary purpose and mission of the church should be: evangelism or social action? This issue was seen at the time in terms of a dichotomy and not holistically. Liberal theology and religious pluralism had shifted much of the church away from the conviction of the Christian responsibility to evangelize.

At the close of the sixties the view of missions among evangelical students was similarly grim. To get a clear picture, I will quote at length from a 1970 article in *Evangelical Missions Quarterly (EMQ)*. The authors of this article catalogue the contemporary student impressions of missions.

> *Missions as 'out of it'*. Many students consider missions not much more than a dead cause because missions seem so irrelevant to the issues and problems of the day. ... Students still accuse *missionaries of being drab*. In emphasizing devotion to God and sacrifice for His work, many evangelical missionaries seem to deny certain essential aspects of personality and beauty. ... *Missions as traditional and inflexible*. Students fear that missions strategy and policies have not changed in the last twenty years. Frequently the terminology they hear from the missionary on the campus is very much the same that they heard as children; this gives rise to the suspicion that perhaps the whole enterprise is static and unimaginative. ...

[7] McGavran, 'Crucial Issues', 166.
[8] Ralph D. Winter, interview by author, June 20, 2005, audio recording.

> Missions as non-personal. Youth are desperately scared that they might get involved in an organization where they are just another cog, going around in circles like the next one! ... Missions as unsuccessful. ... Because students question the validity of the institutional church here at home, they also question the validity of exporting institutional churches overseas. They also question the need for North American missionaries abroad when there is a national church in existence among all ethnic groups. They have nagging suspicions that missionaries have exported more Americanism than Christianity. And here's another honest doubt: If missions are 'out of it' at home, they're probably not doing such a hot job overseas. ... *The whole concept of the missionary has become 'foreign' to the students.* They see the missionary as having a totally different life orientation and style. *They can hardly imagine themselves in a similar role; far be it from them!* (italics mine) [9]

This, then, is the negative environment preceding the 1974 launch of the *Perspectives on the World Christian Movement* course. However, to borrow a phrase from a popular song of the decade, a change was 'blowing in the wind'.

A New Spiritual Vitality: Urbana '73

Emerging from the turbulent 60's, the 'Jesus Movement' erupted on the national youth scene. Beginning on the west coast, hippies turned from drugs to Jesus and found in Him the love, freedom and purpose they were looking for. Christianity began to take on a radically different appearance as they melded their music and youth culture with their new-found faith. The radical activism that ignited protests in the sixties now found expression in bold and passionate witness to their faith. This change was noticed at the Urbana '70 missions convention, which recorded an upsurge in attendance. Although still not enamored with the institutional church, 'this generation of students is looking for and finding spiritual vitality centered around the person of Jesus Christ'.[10]

The Urbana student mission congress is held every three years (previously at the University of Illinois at Urbana) in order to mobilize each new student generation for missions. The planners of Urbana '73 decided they had had enough of negativism.

> Students have heard much about colonialism, paternalism, western imperialism (religious as well as political), failures of mission policies, racism in missions, superiority attitudes of missionaries, ad infinitum. ... There comes a time when negativism can no longer produce positive results. In my opinion, we have reached that point in missions. ... Therefore, the planners for Urbana '73 ... have decided to take a positive approach. ... We want to sound a forward-looking note

---

[9] Phil Schwas and Rick Melick, 'How to Close the Gap Between Students and Missionaries', *Evangelical Missions Quarterly* (October, 1970), http://www.emqonline.com/emq_article_read.php?ArticleID=2451.

[10] James W. Reapsome, 'Urbana '70: One Man's Impression', *Evangelical Missions Quarterly* (April 1971), http://www.emqonline.com/emq_article_read.php?ArticleID=2462.

of hope based on the sovereignty of God as the Lord of history who will fulfill all of his purposes.[11]

The call for a positive outlook hit a chord. The following year an entire issue of the *Evangelical Missions Quarterly* was devoted to the 'remarkable expansion' of the 'evangelical missionary enterprise'. Editor Jim Reapsome proclaimed, 'There is no sign we can detect that missions are going out of business'.[12] It was noted that although mission interest had woefully declined within liberal Christian institutions, among conservative evangelicals mission interest and commitment was on the rise. Several Bible schools had added a year of missions to their programs. Many seminaries, including Fuller, Concordia and Trinity, had established a school of world mission within the past decade.

Missiology, a fairly new discipline, was maturing. The American Society for Missiology was founded in 1973, with its new publication, *Missiology: An International Review*. Other journals and publications were founded to feed and inform the growing evangelical interest in missions. William Carey Library publishing house was established to enable mission titles to be printed and distributed economically (because mission books do not sell in large quantities, most publishers will not print them). Missiologist Herbert Kane comments, 'Thirty years ago a new book on missions was an event. Not so today. Mission books are coming off the press so rapidly that one hardly has the time to read them, much less the money to buy them.'[13]

But it is what happened at Urbana '73 that sounded a trumpet call and proclaimed a new day in missions had indeed arrived.

The Urbana student mission conventions had begun back in 1946, held in December of every third year.[14] Billy Graham usually gave a keynote address in which he would challenge students to sign a commitment card to pursue God's call on their life regarding missions. Attendance at the conventions gradually rose over the years but the number of students signing commitment cards experienced a sharp decline during the 1960's. At Urbana '70, only fourteen percent of the 12,304 students in attendance signed the commitment cards. Then suddenly, and quite unexpectedly, there was a sharp turnaround. At Urbana '73 when the challenge was issued for students to commit themselves

[11] David M. Howard, 'Urbana '73 Theme Emphasizes Positive View of Missions', *Evangelical Missions Quarterly* (January 1973), http://www.emqonline.com/emq_article_read.php?ArticleID=2521.

[12] James W. Reapsome, 'Editorial: A Positive Outlook', *Evangelical Missions Quarterly* (January 1974), http://www.emqonline.com/emq_article_read.php?ArticleID=2585.

[13] J. Herbert Kane, 'Changes Observed in Missiological Studies', *Evangelical Missions Quarterly* (January 1974), http://www.emqonline.com/emq_article_read.php?ArticleID=2590.

[14] The first 'Urbana' convention in 1946 was actually held in Toronto, Canada. It moved to the campus of the University of Illinois at Urbana-Champaign two years later, where it adopted its name. The convention continued to be held at Urbana until it moved to St. Louis, Missouri in 2006.

to whatever course God had for them in world missions, Urbana leaders were surprised at how many stood up and responded. Thinking that they did not understand the challenge, students were told to sit down and the challenge was repeated, this time making it harder. Even more students stood up in response! It was the largest response in Urbana history. That weekend twenty-eight percent of the 14,158 students signed a commitment card. More cards came into InterVarsity Christian Fellowship's headquarters over the next weeks, raising the total to thirty-eight percent. At the next convention in 1976, the percentage of students signing commitment cards grew to *fifty percent*![15] Students had left the negativism of the 1960's behind; God was stirring a new generation of students for His global purpose.

It is at this point, with the large and unexpected student response at Urbana '73 that the story of the *Perspectives on the World Christian Movement* course begins.

Urbana '73 Follow-up: Development of the Perspectives Course through 1981

Ralph Winter, professor at the relatively new School of World Mission at Fuller Theological Seminary in Pasadena, California, heard the report of the unexpected student response at Urbana '73. Could this be the beginnings of another Student Volunteer Movement, he wondered.

Fuller School of World Mission Background

Working alongside Donald McGavran at Fuller Seminar was formative for Winter. His wife, Roberta elaborates,

> Although in Guatemala we had seen the wonderful changes that the gospel brought into a community, we were surprised at Fuller by Dr. McGavran's exuberant conviction that we were in the sunrise, not the sunset of missions. Like others, we had heard plenty of the bad news of the world, as reported in the newspapers. At the School of World Mission we were privileged like few others to have access to the good news, the wonderful news that God was no liar: that as He promised, His gospel was spreading and growing, often out of control, all around the world.[16]

McGavran's thinking about church planting movements among people groups also deeply influenced the Winters. Through his own study of how the gospel flowed throughout history from one cultural basin into another, Winter became convinced that a separate church planting movement was needed for

[15] David M. Howard, 'What Happened at Urbana – its Meaning for Missions', *Evangelical Missions Quarterly* (July 1977), http://www.emqonline.com/emq_article_read.php?ArticleID=2572.

[16] Roberta H. Winter, *I Will Do a New Thing* (Pasadena: William Carey Library, 1987), 18.

every people group on earth in order for the church to complete the Great Commission. This would require a massive change in strategy among mission agencies. It would also require multitudes of new missionaries.

Back at the beginning of the twentieth century the Holy Spirit had moved upon a whole generation of students calling them into the mission fields of the world. They were motivated by the motto 'the evangelization of the world in this generation' and began what is referred to as 'The Student Volunteer Movement'. By 1945 around 100,000 students had signed a pledge committing themselves to 'foreign missions' and 20,000 of those actually ended up overseas. The ones who did not go faithfully prayed for and supported their fellow student missionaries. The Student Volunteer Movement (SVM) made possible great progress in world evangelization during the twentieth century. Yet now in the last quarter of the twentieth century, most of those SVM missionaries were retiring. A new wave of recruits was needed to replace them.

Responding to the Move of the Holy Spirit at Urbana '73

Suddenly, in 1973 a new surge of mission interest appeared among Urbana students. Could the Holy Spirit be moving again among another student generation? Ralph Winter explored the possibility of another SVM in a 1974 article in *Christianity Today*, 'Is a Big New Student Mission Movement in the Offing?'[17]

With the newly expressed interest in missions, Winter was concerned that those students would have no idea how to follow up on their Urbana decision and that their flame of passion, if not fueled, would gradually be extinguished. Winter immediately contacted his long-time friend David Howard, InterVarsity's Urbana director. He challenged InterVarsity to offer a follow-up course for the students who had indicated missions interest. Considering his overwhelmed staff, Howard's response was, 'Ralph, we've had more crying women in this office than we've ever had in one month. We can't do anything more!' Winter then offered to conduct a follow-up course himself if InterVarsity would release the students' contact information, something InterVarsity had never done. Howard responded to Winter with his own challenge. 'You need to answer five questions before we will consider giving out our address list: (1) Who will teach? (2) What will you teach? (3) Where will you hold the class? (4) Who will sponsor it? and (5) Who will hold the bag financially?' If the questions were intended to dissuade Winter, they did not. Over the course of the next two weeks, Winter made about 200 phone calls, attaining answers to all five questions, much to Howard's surprise.[18]

Amid an already busy schedule, Winter set about organizing and promoting a summer follow-up mission course for the Urbana students. He wanted the

---

[17] Ralph D. Winter, 'Is a Big New Student Mission Movement in the Offing?' *Christianity Today*, (May 10, 1974).
[18] Winter, interview.

course to be credit-bearing so that it would not be an extra financial or time burden on the students. He also wanted to challenge students, not simply to a missionary career, but to lay hold of the total task of world evangelization. If they would embrace the total task of fulfilling the Great Commission, then they could work out under God's leading what their individual role in that task is to be. An early oft-repeated motto in the Perspectives course was, 'Every major decision you make will be faulty unless you see it from God's perspective'.[19]

Winter also had four daughters and was looking at the college generation through their eyes. He recalls, 'My own kids didn't have a knowledge of missions. My oldest, who is very sharp, asked me one day, 'Dad, who is William Carey?' I was shocked. I could see through their eyes that something foundational was needed.'[20]

Winter first addressed the task of establishing a board of directors. He gathered together about twelve mission executives living in the Wheaton area to discuss the project. Out of that group he formed a small five-man board and incorporated. The original board consisted of Winter, Ted Ward, Charlie Mellis, Jack Frizen and Warren Webster.

The course was planned for the summer of 1974 and named the *Summer Institute of International Studies* (SIIS). The name and nature of the course was patterned after Wycliffe Bible Institute's *Summer Institute of Linguistics* (SIL) which Winter had taken for credit when he was a student. SIIS became the forerunner of the Perspectives course.

InterVarsity unfortunately did very little to promote the course, merely sending out a letter to the Urbana card-signers. As they did not alert their campus staff, very little interest was generated. Out of the 5000 Urbana card-signers, only two students registered for SIIS as a result of InterVarsity's efforts.

When Winter saw that InterVarsity was not going to do very much to promote the course, he was able to get Billy Graham to mention it twice on his 'Hour of Decision' radio program. He also succeeded in convincing Harold Lindsell, editor of *Christianity Today* and one of Winter's former professors, to allow Winter to write a full-page ad/article in *Christianity Today*. The article questioned if another Student Volunteer Movement might be emerging and also announced the upcoming SIIS course. For a more direct approach, Winter enlisted his college-age daughters to get on the phone before 8:00 a.m. west coast time every morning for weeks, calling Urbana students inviting them to the class. Through all these means they were able to enroll twenty-nine students for the first *Summer Institute of International Studies (SIIS)*.[21]

---

[19] Steven C. Hawthorne, 'History of the Perspectives Course', speech delivered to consultation of Perspectives coordinators, July 14, 2004, Pasadena.
[20] Winter, interview.
[21] Ralph D. Winter, personal recollections at a celebration gathering on the thirtieth anniversary of the Perspectives course, July 13, 2004, Pasadena, audio recording.

Precursor to the Perspectives Course: The Summer Institute of International Studies

Winter asked an old friend, Herbert Kane, to be the dean of the Institute. As he contacted other mission professors, he realized that most of them already had their summer schedules in place and could, at best, give only one week to the program. As a last resort they decided to have a different professor come in each week to teach. Kane fretted that such a structure would be way too confusing and messy to function and dropped out from serving as dean. It turned out to be a popular feature of the course and Perspectives has continued this practice to this day. The only downside, Winter recalls, was that that first summer each visiting professor wanted to assign a term paper for their week of teaching, thereby overloading the students.[22]

Winter developed a ten-week curriculum, divided into two sessions. Each professor taught for a week on the subject that he was assigned. The four-section structure of the course, Biblical, historical, cultural and strategic, came from the structure of the Fuller School of World Mission curriculum. Halfway through the first session the students became very excited about what they were learning. Winter shut the school down for an entire day and had them write their friends encouraging them to come to the second session, especially since many of them were only able to attend the first session. As a result, they were able to enroll about the same number of students in the second session.[23]

SIIS was held at Wheaton College where the students lived and studied for the entire summer session. The visiting professors also lived in the dorms and ate with the students during their week of teaching. They held class in the morning, ate lunch together, had free time in the afternoon, ate dinner together and had wonderful prayer times in the evenings. One of the students, Bruce Graham, remembers running around the track for exercise in the afternoons with famed missiologist Dr. Arthur Glasser. Almost every evening either the visiting professor or one of the many missionaries in the Wheaton area would come and sit on the floor and share their life story. It was a rich time for the students having so much access to the professors, most of whom were also former missionaries. Students were not only picking up knowledge, they were being mentored by some of the most experienced mission leaders of the day.[24]

The roster of the original SIIS professors read like a Who's Who in missions: Dr. Ralph Winter, Dr. Arthur Glasser, Dr. Paul Hiebert, Dr. C. Peter Wagner, Dr. Harvey Conn, Dr. Herbert Kane, Dr. Ted Ward, David Howard, and Elizabeth Elliott. The class was coordinated by Alvin Martin, the extension director at Fuller at the time and a former missionary to Israel. Credit was extended through Whitworth College in Washington State.[25]

---

[22] Winter, interview.
[23] Winter, personal recollections.
[24] Bruce Graham, interview by author, July 13, 2005, email.
[25] Graham, interview.

On the first day of the first SIIS course, Dr. Arthur Glasser stood up and read to that small group of twenty-nine students a passage from Zechariah 4:10: 'Do not despise the day of small beginnings'. Looking back at that beginning, Bruce Graham, who became very influential in the development of SIIS into what is today known as the Perspectives course, emphasizes that SIIS was more than a just a course to those first SIIS students:

> The alumni out of these earlier classes felt like we were becoming part of a student movement for missions after earlier student mission movements. This was not a course or a program for us, but a cause to live for. Many alumni stayed connected and recruited others into the movement. We just wanted to be together and work together toward a world-size cause that had eternal significance.[26]

The sense that another Student Volunteer Movement might be igniting and that they were part of it powerfully captured and motivated the SIIS students.

Lausanne '74

In the middle of the first SIIS session, Ralph Winter dropped in on his way to Lausanne, Switzerland for the International Congress on World Evangelization sponsored by the Billy Graham Evangelistic Association. This congress drew more than 2,300 evangelical leaders from 150 countries (see http://www.lausanne.org/lausanne-1974/lausanne-1974.html) for study and discussion of the church's evangelistic and missionary mandate. Winter was on the program to deliver a plenary address on the final day of the congress. Still working on his presentation, he shared with the SIIS students the groundbreaking challenge he was going to deliver at Lausanne. Bruce Graham, an engineer from Massachusetts Institute of Technology, recalls Winter, a fellow engineer from California Institute of Technology, asking him to help draw up pie charts to illustrate the present state of the world in terms of evangelization.[27]

It is not an overstatement to say that Winter's address at Lausanne '74 so radically altered the focus and strategy of global mission efforts that a line of demarcation can be drawn between pre-Lausanne '74 understanding and efforts and post-Lausanne '74 efforts. In a day when so much contemporary thought asserted that the day of the missionary was over, the church is planted in every country of the world, and the remaining non-Christians in the world can be reached by the ongoing evangelism of the national church, Winter's address came as a bombshell.[28]

---

[26] Graham, interview.

[27] Bruce Graham, personal recollections at a celebration gathering on the thirtieth anniversary of the Perspectives course, July 13, 2004, Pasadena, audio recording.

[28] The text of this address, 'The New Macedonia: A Revolutionary New Era in Mission Begins', can be found in Ralph D. Winter and Steven C. Hawthorne (eds), *Perspectives on the World Christian Movement – A Reader*, 4th ed, (Pasadena: William Carey Library, 2009), 347-60.

Building on McGavran's missiology, Winter introduced the whole concept of unreached people groups, referring to them as 'hidden people groups'. The terminology 'unreached people groups' came a few years later. Using examples from India and Indonesia, Winter demonstrated how the existing church within each of those countries, are not and could not evangelize all of their fellow countrymen without crossing significant barriers of both language and culture – a truly *missionary* task. India and Indonesia were given as potent examples of how most every geographical country consists of hundreds or thousands of separate cultural-linguistic ethnic groups. He supported his research biblically, noting that when the scripture spoke of 'nations' it was usually referring to cultural-linguistic ethnic groups, not geo-political countries.

Introducing the labels 'E-1', 'E-2' and 'E-3' to define increasingly difficult levels of the evangelistic task, Winter established how the national churches' evangelistic outreaches will only reach those from their own culture (E-1); it will take a different kind of cross-cultural outreach (E-2 and E-3) to reach those around them of different languages and cultures. Winter concludes: 'We are thus forced to believe that until every tribe and tongue has a strong, powerfully evangelizing church in it, and thus an E-1 witness within it, E-2 and E-3 efforts coming from outside are still essential and highly urgent.'[29] He then drove the point home, asserting 'cross-cultural evangelism must still be the highest priority. Far from being a task that is now out-of-date, the shattering truth is that at least four out of five non-Christians in the world today are beyond the reach of any Christian's E-1 evangelism.'[30] In other words, if every local church in the world were to effectively evangelize everyone within their range – those speaking the same language and inhabiting the same culture – four out of every five non-Christians in the world would still be completely untouched, beyond the range of any existing church or the present efforts of any mission. Winter called attention to the huge Muslim and Hindu spheres as examples of millions of non-Christians lacking any gospel witness within their language and culture. 'Why is this fact not more widely known?' Winter asked. 'I'm afraid that all our exultation about the fact that every *country* of the world has been penetrated has allowed many to suppose that every *culture* has by now been penetrated.'[31] Winter called this 'people blindness'.

A New Way of Viewing the Unfinished Task

Winter's address at Lausanne '74 was controversial and caused quite a stir. Yet Donald McGavran commented, 'Nothing said at Lausanne had more meaning for the expansion of Christianity between now and the year 2000'.[32] As the implications of his challenge sunk in, over the next few years it prompted widespread discussion and eventual changes in mission goals and strategies.

[29] Winter, 'The New Macedonia', 353.
[30] Winter, 'The New Macedonia', 353.
[31] Winter, 'The New Macedonia', 353.
[32] Donald A. McGavran, introductory comment to Winter, 'The New Macedonia', 347.

Ten years later in an interview with *Evangelical Missions Quarterly*, the heads of the two largest evangelical missions associations – Wade Coggins of the EFMA[33] and Edwin (Jack) Frizen, Jr. of the IFMA[34] – pointed back to the significance of this historic crossroads. When an interviewer asked, 'If you could pick out only one thing, what would be the most significant thing that has happened in world missions since 1964?' Coggins replied, 'The rise of [indigenous] mission agencies and missionaries in Africa, Asia, and Latin America'. But then added,

> A second development, if you permit, is the new way of viewing the unfinished task. The unreached people group movement has caught the imagination of a lot of people and convinced them that there is indeed a remaining task. ... This concept also challenges missions as they seek to find unreached peoples and prepare strategies to reach them.[35]

Jack Frizen responded,

> My choice is the renewed focus on unreached people groups and penetrating the frontiers still remaining. This has influenced missions agencies at home and in the field to evaluate the work of their missionary staff, to see if they are in fact reaching out to unreached peoples. It has helped new mission agencies of churches in developing countries to make their own mission goals without working toward an institutional approach to their work. In North America, the movement has given a renewed vision to many supporting churches, prospective candidates, and missionary training schools.[36]

Through his writing and speaking over the next months and years Winter continued to call attention to the unfinished task of world evangelization – namely, the unreached people groups. Through statistics, charts and graphs he also visually portrayed the grossly disparate distribution of the world's missionary force.

For example, in September 1976 Winter delivered the opening address, entitled 'The Grounds for a New Thrust in World Mission', to the joint conference of the Interdenominational Foreign Mission Association (IFMA), the Evangelical Fellowship of Mission Agencies (EFMA) and the Association of Evangelical Professors of Missions. Using carefully drafted graphical charts drawn precisely to scale of population figures relative to each other (his engineering degree was not wasted), Winter helped mission agency executives

[33] The Evangelical Fellowship of Mission Agencies (EFMA) was renamed The Mission Exchange in 2007.

[34] The Interdenominational Foreign Mission Association (IFMA) was renamed CrossGlobal Link in 2007.

[35] Dean Merrill, 'It's Our 20th Birthday: Interviews with Wade Coggins and Edwin L. Jack Frizen, Jr', *Evangelical Missions Quarterly* (April, 1984), http://www.emqonline.com/emq_article_read_pv.php?ArticleID=2819.

[36] Merrill, *EMQ*, http://www.emqonline.com/emq_article_read_pv.php?ArticleID=2819.

visualize the extent of the remaining task. His comments on the Hindu world reveal the research and reasoning he presented for each of the major blocks of unreached people groups – Chinese, Muslim and Hindu:

> Once more, if we are sensitive at all to the heart of God, we must be stunned and crushed by the vastness of the unreached populations within this major block of mankind. But the second message is still more shocking: it is the stubborn fact not often recognized that a relatively small number of people in India are reachable by normal evangelistic efforts on the part of even the Christians in India. ... A reliable – but staggering – report indicates that 98% of all current evangelistic efforts in India, whether missionary or national, are not even focused on non-Christians, but (as is true in the USA) are attempts of believing Christians to reach nominal Christians and bring them back into the vital fellowship of the church. (emphasis his)[37]

The size of believing communities within Muslim peoples, whether in Asia or Africa, was so small that it could not even be shown graphically on the chart. And the size of the missionary force working among the vast Muslim sphere was graphically illustrated as barely more than a dot on the page.

At this same mission executive meeting, Winter proposed the establishment of a major mission center that would focus attention on the Chinese, Hindu and Muslim blocks of unreached peoples. The US Center for World Mission would later be birthed out of this thinking.

Alumni Catch the Vision to Continue SIIS

The students of the first *Summer Institute of International Studies* in 1974 returned home to share their new insights with their churches and friends, seeking to mobilize them to mission among unreached peoples. Two of those students, Bruce and Christy Graham, were to play a large role in the future development of SIIS. They returned from the first SIIS to Park Street Church in Boston and started a missions fellowship where they shared many of the things they had learned in SIIS. The following summer they returned to attend the second *Summer Institute of International Studies*, mobilizing twenty-two students to join them. They piled in a car caravan to travel from Boston to Wheaton, stopping by the famous 'Haystack Prayer Meeting' monument on the way. The 'Haystack Prayer Meeting' was where in 1806 the first American students consecrated themselves to foreign missions, leading to an active recruitment of students into mission service and the establishment of the first ever American mission society.[38]

---

[37] Ralph D. Winter, 'The Grounds for a New Thrust in World Mission', in Arthur F. Glasser, Paul G. Hiebert, C. Peter Wagner and Ralph D. Winter (eds), *Crucial Dimensions in World Evangelization*, (Pasadena: William Carey Library, 1976), 472.

[38] Timothy C. Wallstrom, *The Creation of a Student Movement to Evangelize the World* (Pasadena: William Carey International University Press, 1980), 24-29.

The 1975 SIIS, held again at Wheaton College, was similar to the first, however a few extra weeks were added at the end so that returning alumni could obtain further scholastic credit. Charlie Mellis, former president of Mission Aviation Fellowship and on the SIIS board of directors, coordinated the class. It is unclear how many students actually were in the class; estimates given from thirty-five-year-old memories range from 45 to over 100. The second SIIS course concluded with a field trip to Guatemala. Winter, along with two of his daughters, Linda and Beth, joined the students returning back to the country they had served as missionaries. They travelled in a caravan of seven cars driving day and night from Chicago, down through Mexico into Guatemala. Winter recalls that twice they were lost and the caravan separated in the huge metropolis of Mexico City. In Guatemala they visited several mission stations in the day and gathered in the evening to learn from and critique both the good and the bad of the mission station strategies. It was very illuminating to the students, as what often looked good on the surface, might not be so healthy in terms of long-term strategy.[39] They also began to dream together on this trip about forming a missions community focused on unreached peoples. They were highly motivated by Charlie Mellis' new book, *Committed Communities: Fresh Streams for World Mission.*

A challenge for the students was how to maintain this student mission movement between summer courses. They decided to start an SIIS newsletter and set up Student Conferences on World Evangelization (SCOWE), planned and conducted by the alumni. At home alumni also began small Bible study and prayer groups, called the Fellowship of World Christians, to mobilize others and to nurture their own mission commitment. All of this was stimulated by and modelled after the historic Student Volunteer Movement.

One of the participants in the 1975 SIIS class was David Bryant, now known internationally for promoting Concerts of Prayer, serving as chairman of America's National Prayer Committee and through the many books he has authored. In 1974 Bryant had noticed Winter's article in *Christianity Today* questioning whether another Student Volunteer Movement might be in the making. Bryant also noticed that the author was a professor at the Fuller School of World Mission (SWM). By the fall of that year he had moved to Pasadena and was enrolled in Fuller. As he stood knocking on the door of Winter's office one day, he was confronted by a sign on the door: 'God cannot lead you on the basis of facts you do not know'. That sign and Winter's influence led to his long-term involvement with SIIS and as an author and instructor in the Perspectives course.[40]

Bryant completed his master's degree in missiology at Fuller SWM, raised support and joined the staff of SIIS in 1975 as National Coordinator of the

[39] Ralph D. Winter, interview.

[40] David Bryant, personal recollections at a celebration gathering on the thirtieth anniversary of the Perspectives course, July 13, 2004, Pasadena, audio tape recording.

program. In this capacity he developed curriculum, shaped the day-to-day structure of the classes, designed field trip experiences and gave oversight to the course. SIIS opened an official office in Pasadena in the fall of 1975. In January of 1976, Bryant conducted a one-month intensive course on the campus of Erskine College, a Christian college in Due West, South Carolina. Around forty enrolled in that class, coming from all over the nation. The summer of 1976 saw SIIS back on the Wheaton College campus, with Bryant coordinating a class of around eighty, all students in-residence as previously.

World Christian Terminology

In preparation for his classes, Bryant developed a 'World Christian Psalter' – a songbook comprised of popular hymns and choruses, rewritten with a world missions focus and application. He also developed a daily inductive Bible study series with 'World Christian' themes for students to use in their personal devotionals and small group meetings. Bryant taught the students about 'World Christian discipleship'. He later popularized the term 'World Christian' through his highly influential book, *In the Gap: What It Means to Be a World Christian*, published in 1979. Bryant had been introduced to the term 'World Christian' in a lecture by Winter at Fuller School of World Mission (it was first used in the title of a 1927 YMCA publication). 'I reconstituted it', Bryant explains, 'to refer to what it means to live a life that is fully wrapped around Christ and His global cause on every level of practical daily discipleship'.[41] *In the Gap* was promoted at Urbana '79 and became a well-read book among young people for the next twenty years.

For the 1976 SIIS class, Bryant spent much time negotiating with the leaders of the major student organizations to secure their support and recruit from among their ranks. He developed a thirty-page catalog for the course that was mailed out to nearly 3000 who wrote in for more information. The well-attended 1976 course provided specialized modules for those from organizations such as InterVarsity, Navigators and Campus Crusade for Christ to be able to study and share together.

But then a division arose. During the summer of 1976, the SIIS board came to a disagreement over the nature of the course. Some wanted to see it continue to expand in order to mobilize a new wave of World Christians, while others wanted to focus on the academic nature of the class, keeping it small to refine the pedagogy. It was at this point that David Bryant resigned from SIIS, taking a position as Missions Specialist for InterVarsity Christian Fellowship, where he served for the next twelve years continuing to mobilize students into World Christian discipleship. Bryant credits Fuller's School of World Mission (SWM) and SIIS for having had a profound influence on him and his ministry. The 'World Christian Discipleship' department of InterVarsity in the 1980's flowed out of *In the Gap*, which flowed out of the School of World Mission and the

---

[41] David Bryant, interview by author, August 15, 2005, email.

Summer Institute of International Studies. 'Above everything else, SWM, SIIS and Perspectives have each provided the same fundamental overhaul of my whole world view, and it has done so in two major directions: (1) a massively enlarged Christology and (2) an abounding, unrelenting hope about the task before us and its ultimate outcome.'[42]

Development of a Standard Curriculum

Up until this time the SIIS courses did not have a codified curriculum. The four-section structure was in place from the beginning, adopted from the structure of the Fuller School of World Mission. The curriculum consisted of various readings – often photocopied – from multiple sources. The Lausanne Occasional Papers coming out after the 1974 Congress provided a wealth of resources on current mission issues.

With rising student interest in missions, Moody Bible Institute asked Peter Wagner to develop a curriculum for an introductory missions course in their extension program. Wagner in turn asked Arthur Glasser to write the theological dimension of the curriculum, Ralph Winter to write the historical dimension, while he set about writing on the strategic dimension of missions. Paul Hiebert was chosen to write the cultural and anthropological dimension.[43] These four missiologists worked together to produce a highly relevant, cutting-edge, insightful text for the day: *Crucial Dimensions in World Evangelization*, published in 1976. Contributing authors to the text were well-known mission professionals McGavran, Alan R. Tippett, Roger Greenway, Edward Murphy, Warren Webster, J. Robertson McQuilkin and Ralph R. Covell. Besides the sections mentioned above, additional topics covered were church/mission tensions, Third World missions and an introduction to Theological Education by Extension. For some reason Moody Bible Institute never used the curriculum. However, it became a foundational text for the next several years for the *Institute of International Studies* (the name was changed from SIIS to IIS when the course was no longer held only in the summer). It was, in fact, in structure and format, a forerunner to *Perspectives on the World Christian Movement: A Reader*.

Founding of the US Center for World Mission: A Home for the Persepctives Course

Another critical foundation stone was laid in 1976. Ralph Winter was increasingly burdened that there needed to be a world missions center focused on unreached people groups. Winter proposed the concept to mission leaders, Fuller faculty and students whenever he could, and although interest was generated, no one accepted the challenge of establishing such a center. For months Winter struggled over a decision of whether to resign from Fuller and

---

[42] Bryant, interview.
[43] Ralph D. Winter, personal recollections.

focus on starting such a center. ''I must admit,' he told the other professors, 'that this project may very well fail. But I am overwhelmingly convinced that God wants someone to try it. No one else seems willing, so I guess I'll have to.''[44] Such a sentiment is characteristic of Winter. He has been known over the years for saying, 'Don't do things others can do; do things others can not or will not do'.

Letting go of financial security and a prestigious career, Ralph and Roberta Winter launched out on the riskiest venture of their lifetime, confident in faith that God was calling them to found the US Center for World Mission. With no financial provision in sight, they negotiated to buy the nearby campus of Point Loma College in Pasadena, California. The college was relocating and needed desperately to sell the property. The Winters, with no money, were competing with a religious cult with plenty of money, to purchase the property. For a period of months, both the cult and the newly formed US Center for World Mission occupied the property at the same time. Roberta Winter recounts the fascinating story of intense spiritual warfare and divine miracle after miracle which paved the way for full purchase and occupation of the campus in her book, *I Will Do a New Thing*. The US Center for World Mission (USCWM) was formally founded in November of 1976. Most of the original staff were SIIS alumni whose worldview and lives had been dramatically changed; they felt strongly that they were part of a new movement of God stirring up the church to finish the task of world evangelization. Winter had taught them to work for a cause, rather than a career. They had lived and studied in community, many keeping in contact with each other throughout the year. It was a natural next step to follow their passion to Pasadena to staff this exciting new world mission center.

Understanding World Evangelization (UWE): Follow-up Curriculum for Urbana '76

In a year of laying critical foundations, 1976 yielded yet another advance in the development of the Perspectives course. Once again it came about through the Urbana student missionary convention.

Student interest in missions was continuing to swell, evidenced by the increased attendance and response at Urbana '76. When on the fourth night of the convention, Billy Graham once again issued his customary call for students to commit themselves to God and His global purposes, several thousand stood. Fifty percent of the students signed mission commitment cards! In an offering taken to advance student ministry around the world, $300,000 was given or pledged – possibly the largest student offering ever given to date in history.[45]

---

[44] Roberta H. Winter, 32.
[45] Howard, 'What Happened at Urbana'.

> Billy Graham was asked in his press conference, 'What do you sense about these students here?' He said, 'They are not asking the hard questions they used to ask. They are asking the practical questions, 'What can I do? I am ready to move. I want to do something for the Lord. I want to be in on what God is doing.''[46]

Once again Ralph and Roberta Winter designed a follow-up curriculum for Urbana students wanting to pursue a mission interest. They came to Urbana to introduce the new curriculum, *Understanding World Evangelization* (UWE). Developed by the same four missiologists who produced the *Crucial Dimensions* text, it consisted of a study guide tied to four books, along with a cassette-taped introduction. The four study texts were: *Crucial Dimensions in World Evangelization*; *The Twenty-Five Unbelievable Years: 1945-1969* by Ralph D. Winter; *Frontiers in Missionary Strategy* by C. Peter Wagner; and *Stop the World, I Want to Get On*, also by Wagner. UWE was developed for SIIS. The added benefit, however, of the UWE curriculum was that it was designed to make possible totally independent study; indeed, the expectation was that most students would take the course this way. Both college and graduate credit were available through Westmont College for the course.

John R.W. Stott, the famous British evangelical Bible expositor, was scheduled to deliver the opening Bible lecture at Urbana '76. Sitting in the large assembly hall was a student with only a mild interest in missions but a profound eagerness to hear Dr. Stott – a student by the name of Steve Hawthorne. He recalls that morning vividly:

> It was about 10:15 on the morning of December 28, 1976 when Stott took the stage. With his grand British accent, Stott announced the title of his address: 'The Living God is a Missionary God.' I expected good exposition but I did not expect an integrated focal point. Stott presented the entire Bible as a single escalating story of God accomplishing His purpose among all the peoples of the earth. The first chapter of the *Perspectives Reader* is the transcript of that very address by Stott.[47]

Hawthorne completed the follow-up UWE correspondence course in the spring of 1977 while concurrently taking graduate courses at Point Loma Nazarene University in San Diego, California. At the end of 1978, Hawthorne and his wife Barbara moved onto the campus of the US Center for World Mission. They joined the Haggai Community founded by Bruce and Christy Graham. Inspired by Charlie Mellis' book, *Committed Communities*, members lived in community preparing, like the Moravians of old, to go off together as committed teams into the mission field. The Haggai Community was the first member organization of the US Center for World Mission. The vision of the USCWM was to attract many mission agencies and organizations to locate on

---

[46] Howard, 'What Happened at Urbana'.
[47] Steven C. Hawthorne, interview by author, June 11, 2005, audio recording.

its campus in order to collaborate together. Soon many other organizations established themselves at the Center, staffed by SIIS alumni, such as the Zwemer Institute for Muslim Studies, the Institute of Chinese Studies, the Institute of Hindu Studies, and the Fellowship of Arts and Cultural Evangelization (FACE). Keeping the *Institute of International Studies* [48] in operation was a major endeavor of the USCWM, one in which Hawthorne would eventually play a major role as co-editor of the Perspectives course with Ralph Winter.

Decline, Reorganization and Expansion

Even though many of the SIIS alumni, the key to new student recruitment, were now living and working in Pasadena at the USCWM, the SIIS board wanted to continue to hold the *Summer Institute of International Studies* at Wheaton College. An additional class for the summer of 1977 was planned for Boulder, Colorado at the ministry headquarters of The Navigator's. Due to disagreement on the board over the direction SIIS should take, enrollment plummeted. The Wheaton class had to be cancelled due to lack of students. The Boulder class enrolled only fifteen. Charlie Mellis, the administrator of SIIS at the time, wanted to dissolve the course. Winter intervened, convincing the board to transfer it to the Center staff at Pasadena. The USCWM would take all the financial responsibility for the course. Bruce and Christy Graham assumed administrative oversight for the *Institute of International Studies* (IIS) dropping the term, 'Summer'. Looking back, Winter reflects that the failure of the 1977 classes was actually a good thing, for it allowed them to relieve a divided board of responsibility and bring the IIS under the auspices of the USCWM.[49]

The Graham's coordinated an intense one-month in-residence course in January 1978, held on the campus of the USCWM. A major change came when in 1979 the course was expanded to a full semester, conducted in the fall, spring and summer, granting sixteen credit hours (four for each of the four sections of the course – Biblical, Historical, Cultural and Strategic). The frontier mission vision had matured to such a level that now four fully developed courses could be offered. Many of the IIS students both lived and worked at the USCWM. Additionally the Graham's led IIS alumni on short term outreaches to India in 1978–1980, solidifying commitment to world mission. Today many of those students are still active in career missions in various parts of the world.[50]

With the semester-long expansion of the course, it was recognized that the Biblical section of the UWE curriculum was shorter than the others; consequently there were not enough readings to fill up a four week, four credit-hour section. As the overseer of curriculum development, Bruce Graham asked

---

[48] Hawthorne, interview.
[49] Ralph D. Winter, interview.
[50] Graham, interview.

Steve Hawthorne to collect more readings for the Biblical section. As a volunteer for IIS, Hawthorne's assignment was to sit in on all of the classes in the Biblical section, take notes on the lectures, and then devise a test to be given on Friday morning after the speaker left. He graded the tests over the weekend, beginning the process all over again the following Monday. In the process he gathered more Biblical articles – photocopied from existing works – and designed the curricula for the Biblical section.

The format for the semester-long IIS course was the same as it had been for the SIIS course at Wheaton. The students lived in residence as a learning community and the speakers would spend an entire week with the students. Hawthorne fondly recalls how they did not simply teach the material; they also poured out their hearts along with their fascinating life stories. Some of the speakers during that time (1979–1980) were Donald McGavran, J. Christy Wilson, Jr., Elizabeth Elliot, Harvey Conn, David Hesselgrave, Don McCurry, Sam Wilson of the Zwemer Institute, and many other stellar figures of the mission world.[51]

The Penn State Class: The First IIS Extension Course

Realizing that only a handful of students would ever be able to come to Pasadena to study, the USCWM staff began to dream of taking IIS to students via extension classes. Enrolled in a 1978 summer intensive IIS class were Jay and Olgy Gary, preparing to join USCWM staff. While raising ministry support in Pennsylvania, the Gary's visited with a former colleague on staff with Campus Crusade for Christ at Pennsylvania State University. That encounter led to the first official IIS extension course. Jay Gary recounts the progression of events.

> We shared with Phil how reaching hidden peoples was key to fulfilling the Great Commission, and how students needed to be awakened to this challenge. He was open to this vision and invited us to bring a SCOWE, a Student Conference on World Evangelization, to his beach project the following summer of 1979.... That band of Campus Crusade for Christ students attending the SCOWE in Lake Tahoe was blown away by what they learned. Phil then invited me to come back that coming winter to do a SCOWE for Penn State students. At that time, Penn State had the largest concentration of Christian students active in campus ministries out of all the universities in the US. I remember telling Phil, 'We will come, but only if you let us run an IIS Extension course following the conference....' Phil agreed. During that fall leading up to the conference, I spent time at Penn State, sharing the story of the Student Volunteer Movement, how it began with 100 students banding together to fulfill the Great Commission. It too had started at a conference. I began to ask others, 'Could God be raising up a Penn State 100?' The SCOWE conference at Penn State drew some 450 students. Greg Livingstone, Ralph Winter and I shared the platform. By the end of the first

---

[51] Hawthorne, interview.

> evening, two students had registered for the course. I remember telling Fran Patt, the conference coordinator, 'Those two are Caleb and Joshua'. By the end of the conference, 65 students had signed up. Sensing that God was still at work, I delayed my trip back to Los Angeles. I set up camp and by week's end we reached our prayer goal of 100 students registered for that Spring term, starting in less than 4 weeks. I returned to Pasadena, took a leave from my job as director of Personnel at the Center, and Olgy and I drove back to Penn State – to lead the first 'Perspectives' extension class.[52]

Once again Winter and IIS intersected with a movement of God already in progress among American students. Hundreds were coming to Christ each year on the Penn State campus through the active witness of students in the university Christian organizations such as Navigators, InterVarsity and Campus Crusade for Christ.

Fran Patt, who later opened the first USCWM Regional Office, was a recent graduate when approached by Phil Hardin about coordinating the Student Conference of World Evangelization (SCOWE) on the Penn State campus. Patt had met Winter and Gary when they conducted the SCOWE at the Lake Tahoe Campus Crusade summer project in 1979. Patt recalls that is when he became interested in the ministry of the USCWM. 'I had been working with international students; but I hit a wall every time I ran into a Muslim, Hindu or Buddhist student. Jay gave me a copy of Crucial Dimensions in World Evangelization which opened my eyes.'[53]

Patt worked with Jay Gary to set up the SCOWE on Penn State's campus the first week of February 1980. They went to each university organization to arouse interest and recruit. Gary, however, failed to mention to Patt that the SCOWE was intended to be a forerunner to a follow-up semester-long course.

Speaking at the SCOWE, Ralph Winter laid out the challenge of unreached people groups. Greg Livingstone, then director of North Africa Mission, laid out the challenge of North Africa – once the heartland of Christianity, now almost completely devoid of Christians. Livingstone really captured the imagination of the students, stirring their passions. North Africa Mission had a goal of planting twenty-five churches in North Africa by the year 2000. Livingstone told the students, 'There's nothing stopping us from getting into these countries, but I can't promise I can get you out'.[54]

One of the students called out to Livingstone, 'What's happening in Libya?' At the time, Libya was considered one of the most difficult countries to get into in the world. Livingstone replied, 'We don't have anybody in Libya. The last missionaries that were there were arrested and sentenced to eight years in

---

[52] Jay Gary, 'Perspectives Marks 30th Anniversary', *Helping Faith Communities Cultivate Foresight*, July 13, 2004, http://www.jaygary.com/Perspectives_30thanniversary.shtml/ [accessed July 21, 2004].
[53] Fran Patt, interview by author, August 7, 2005, transcript.
[54] Patt, interview.

prison. We are, however, looking for four men to go to Libya to see if they can get in and stay in.'[55]

Such a challenge would not slip by unnoticed. Four Penn State students subsequently volunteered to go to Libya: Al Stahl, Harry Gray, Greg Fritz and Bob Sjogren. Fran Patt recollects, 'I remember sitting down specifically with Stahl, Sjogren and Fritz to challenge them to attend the SCOWE, telling them that it will change their lives'.[56]

Within a week after the SCOWE, Jay Gary convinced Fran Patt to help him run the IIS course, even though Patt had never heard of it before. Unfortunately, he was able to attend only the first couple of sessions before having to leave to help with the family business.

The first IIS class meeting began unusually, Patt recalls. A blizzard arose that morning. Ralph Winter was flying in to speak, but became stuck in Pittsburgh due to the snow. The airlines told Winter that there was no way he was going to get to Penn State that night. Back at Penn State they began to pray. They called all the student ministry leaders and asked them to get their students praying. The blizzard stopped for about one hour – just enough time to get Winter's plane airborne. As he landed at Penn State, the snow began in earnest again, shutting down the airport. When Winter arrived to teach, he shared his adventure with the students, who had been praying all day. 'You could have heard a pin drop,' Patt remembers, 'as the students realized God's intervention in answer to their prayers. Dr. Winter was powerful that night. He spoke for two hours and the students stayed around another hour-and-a-half asking him questions.'[57]

The IIS class met twice a week, on Tuesday and Thursday for ninety minutes. On one of those days an outside speaker taught the lesson. On the other day Gary reviewed the lesson and the students met in small discussion groups. They used the curriculum, *Understanding World Evangelization*, and added David Bryant's new book, *In the Gap*. By this time the course consisted of twenty lessons. Westmont College issued independent study academic credit. Seventy-seven excited students were enrolled in this first-ever IIS extension class. Some of the visiting professors for the Penn State class were Winter, Greg Livingstone, Roberta Winter, Walter Hannum, George Patterson, and William Miller.[58]

One of many significant outcome of the Penn State IIS class is the story of Bob Sjogren, who was also one of the four who had volunteered to go to Libya. He eventually went on to develop his own mission mobilization and teaching ministry. For years he taught a seminar entitled 'Destination 2000', which distilled many of the Perspectives concepts. Sjogren states, 'the principles taught in Perspectives of 'blessed to be a blessing' and the understanding that

[55] Bob Sjogren, interview by author, August 5, 2005, transcript.
[56] Patt, interview.
[57] Patt, interview.
[58] Gary, interview.

the Abrahamic Covenant is the Great Commission in the Old Testament were foundational to me.'[59]

Fran Patt later wrapped up his commitment to his family business and joined the staff of the USCWM. He returned to Pennsylvania and opened the first regional office of the USCWM – the Eastern Regional Office – which he continues to direct. His first staff members were a couple from the Penn State class. Another student, Sue Richard, from the Penn State class also went on to join USCWM staff, later becoming his wife.[60]

These and other students from the Penn State 1980 IIS class went on to influence and mobilize other individuals who in turn became key church and mission leaders with significant ministries focused on the unfinished task of world evangelization. This mobilization dynamic has been a hallmark of the IIS/Perspectives course from the beginning.

A Published Text

In preparing for the 1980 Penn State class, the USCWM staff realized that the IIS curriculum needed to be revised into a format more suitable for an extension class. Bruce Graham, director of IIS in Pasadena, began the process through organizing curriculum ideas and researching material then he recruited Steve Hawthorne to develop the curriculum so that it could be presented as one course in other regions. At this time *Understanding World Evangelism* was the base curriculum, but the staff had been adding photocopied articles and sections from other resources and books. As the frontier mission movement grew, IIS had grown with it, expanding into four complete courses (Biblical, Historical, Cultural and Strategic) studying the burgeoning amount of material being written on the subjects. Now it was deemed more strategic to condense the course back down to a single semester course, still covering all four aspects but in a less extensive way, in order for more students to have access to the course.

As a volunteer assigned to condense and codify the IIS curriculum, Hawthorne relates, 'I was just amazed and thrilled to be part of it all'. Yet he began to sense a calling to the task as well. He remembers telling a group of friends, 'I'm going to help put together this curriculum'. 'It just occurred to me that God was giving that project to me as my assignment. It was a holy moment for me.'[61]

With the Graham's leaving for India, Darrell and Linda Dorr (Winter's daughter) took over the administration of the IIS courses in Pasadena. Jay Gary assumed directorship of the total IIS program. The number of courses jumped to seven per year in 1980 and 1981. A handful of others took the course via independent study. After the successful Penn State course, Jay Gary attempted two other extension courses, one at Wheaton and one California State

[59] Sjogren, interview.
[60] Patt, interview.
[61] Hawthorne, interview.

University at San Luis Obispo. Even though the classes were credit-bearing and initiated with a well-attended SCOWE, they did not emulate the success of the 1980 Penn State class. Gary realized that the key for successful extension classes was well-trained coordinators to run them. One successful program was run during that time, however, at a church near Goleta, California by Rick Love, who later became the international director of Frontiers mission agency.

Jay and Olgy Gary pursued a passion to train IIS alumni to coordinate extension classes all over the country. As a couple they went back to school to earn a Master's degree in curriculum development. Their focus was to develop a coordinator training curriculum. During the day they ran the current IIS program, while at night they attended school for the purpose of enhancing the future of the program.[62] In retrospect, the development of trained coordinators was as important to the success of the Perspectives course as the development of curriculum.

Under Gary's leadership, Hawthorne began to design learning objectives and gather articles for the codified text that would become the Perspectives Reader and Study Guide. The development process progressed from educational objective design, to crafting a study guide, to production of the text. Most of the articles gathered were already in print somewhere, but per the educational objectives, they realized that some articles needed to be commissioned. The primary focus at that time was still on expanding IIS courses into universities throughout the country. The 'screaming omission', Hawthorne admits, is that they did not include the Lausanne Covenant in that first edition of the Perspectives Reader.[63]

By the spring of 1981 Hawthorne was working full-time on curriculum development. Winter sent him out to meet with numerous mission leaders in order to learn and obtain articles from them. Back at the Center, Hawthorne and Gary would present articles they selected to Winter for his review and approval. The title of the text, *Perspectives on the World Christian Movement*, originated with Gary.

As the curriculum neared completion, Winter sent Hawthorne out to enlist certain well-known mission leaders to be published with Ralph Winter as co-editors (David Hesselgrave, Herbert Kane, Lloyd Kwast and Donald McGavran). Hawthorne contacted each one of them and each one responded in like manner. They felt that the text was already well-edited and therefore it would not be appropriate for them to be identified as co-editor. They each proposed, however, that they could be listed as a contributing editor. When the curriculum team reported this back to Winter, he asked the team which one of them did the most work on the text. Everyone sat silent. Finally someone said,

---

[62] Gary, interview.
[63] Hawthorne, interview.

'Steve did the vast majority of the work'. Much to Hawthorne's surprise, Winter replied, 'You are the co-editor, then'.[64]

At that time Ralph and Roberta Winter were preoccupied with securing the finances to establish the USCWM; neither was able to be as deeply involved in the curriculum development as they wished. When asked about his role as co-editor of the Perspectives text, Winter replied,

> It would be more accurate to say Bruce Graham, Jay Gary and Steve Hawthorne – and to some extent me – were the editors of the *Perspectives Reader*. I laid the groundwork from which they drew the documents, but I didn't select the documents. I objected to some and insisted upon others, but most of the work was not done by me. My name is just on the book because Steve said we need your name on the book.[65]

In the summer of 1981 a group of esteemed mission professors met with Winter and the curriculum team on the USCWM campus. They had assembled the basic structure and articles and for several hours the team presented their work. To their delight the professors profusely praised the text. Hawthorne recollects, 'I remember David Hesselgrave leaning back and saying, 'This is a book we have all been waiting for! Everyone will use it!''[66]

To ascertain how very much the Perspectives text was forward-thinking, Winter relates this revealing episode:

> When we were readying the 1981 curriculum to be published, Steve Hawthorne and Jay Gary came to my house seeking my approval on the complete curriculum. I said, 'We've got to put in there that the Great Commission is found in the Abrahamic Covenant'. They responded, 'Nobody else believes this; we can't put that in there'. We were at an impasse. Then I was asked to speak at the dedication of the Billy Graham Center at Wheaton College. Walter Kaiser was there also. I had recently seen his book on the Old Testament. In it he regularly mentioned 'the Promise' referring to the Abrahamic Covenant. I approached him and said, 'You know, the Abrahamic Covenant is not only a promise; it is a mandate, a commission'. He said, 'Well, you can call it a Great Commission if you want'. I was really quite surprised. I told him, 'I can't go around saying that. I need someone like you to say that. Do you have that in print?' He replied, 'You quote me, and I'll put it in print'. A few days later I received a cassette tape of a chapel talk that he had given at Trinity Seminary called 'Israel's Missionary Call'. We put that address by Kaiser in the *Perspectives Reader*. That was the single most provocative thing in the book in those days. That's what shocked a lot of seminary students and is what gives people a totally new view of the Bible. We later found

[64] Hawthorne, interview.
[65] Winter, interview.
[66] Hawthorne, interview.

> out that lots of other people down through history believed this, but at that time we were really on shaky ground.[67]

Finally the *Perspectives Reader* was introduced at Urbana '81. With the introduction of the new textbook, the course ceased to be called *Institute of International Studies* and became *Perspectives on the World Christian Movement.* The stage was now set for the Perspectives course and textbook to expand in its reach, mobilizing and educating increasing numbers of students for world evangelization. It had been a challenging eight years (1974–1981) laying the foundations of the course, pursing vision in the face of obstacles, mobilizing students to recognize and do something about the overlooked and unreached people groups of the world. Perspectives (in its original form of SIIS) came on the scene in the midst of a weary, pessimistic church and a very negative student generation. Yet, as Winter remarks, 'We were not simply going upstream. The Holy Spirit produced a change, which affected us. We didn't affect the change; we were affected by that change and we simply responded to it.'[68]

As the Perspectives course responded to the move of the Holy Spirit among the student generation in the latter half of the 1970's, so the US Center for World Mission and Perspectives would continue to both respond to and catalyze change in mission thinking and involvement throughout the remainder of the century.

A World-Wide Reach

What is it about the Perspectives course that makes it so life-changing? What is the unique contribution of this course?

David Bryant affirms that it is the course's Christology. 'Seeing King Jesus and what He is doing. He is leading this victory celebration in one generation after another … and seeing the eschatological dimension to all of this … that it will all be summed up. That is what this course is all about.'[69] Ultimately, Bryant adds, the course is about hope. Hope is not something wistfully wished for, but rather a firm and secure confidence that God's promises and purposes will surely be fulfilled, thereby granting purpose, certainty and destiny to the life that is grounded upon such a hope.[70]

Arthur Glasser, the founding father of the Biblical section of Perspectives who first developed its Christology, states, 'The inductive method of Bible study informs Perspectives. It drives you back to scripture. It is one of the most

---

[67] Winter, interview.
[68] Winter, interview.
[69] Bryant, personal recollections.
[70] Bryant, recollections

valuable contributions of the Perspectives program.'[71] Indeed seeing scripture and history afresh through the eyes of God's purposes being fulfilled is what student after student comments upon as being so revolutionary.

Yet maybe Ralph Winter said it best,

> What is it about the course that changes people's lives? Not any one thing. It is the Holy Spirit working through the people that run the course and speak in the course and write the course that changes people's lives. The very idea that God is still around and at work creates a sense of awe in the average student. They may believe in God, but they've grown accustomed to the idea of God and have no more awe of God. The Perspectives course is not what we are really promoting. We are promoting the awe of God. The course is an earthen vessel in which something very much more important is being carried.[72]

The first thirty-five years of Perspectives have laid a strong foundation. In the days ahead the movement is on course, through a well-developed administrative office operating out of the Northwest Arkansas office of the USCWM, to continue to expand in North America. In addition, a Perspectives Global Office is actively coordinating the translation and adaptation of the course by leaders around the world into new languages, formats and cultures.

Alumni of the Perspectives course affirm that this movement, to quote a phrase from Henry Blackaby in his popular study, *Experiencing God*, 'saw what God was doing and joined him'. Probably the most critical next step is how the course is to take shape in other cultures. Considering how God has used this course in North America over the past thirty-five years, what can be envisioned for its future among Chinese, Africans, Latinos, Arabs, South Asians and others?

If Ralph Winter were still living he might ask as he did in 1973, 'is another Student Volunteer Movement in the offing?' If a new Volunteer Movement does explode on the scene, this time it will reflect not merely the North American segment of the world's peoples, but will flow from the active global Church that has emerged with its own leadership during this past century, declaring God's glory so that His salvation may reach to the ends of the earth (Isa. 49:1-6).

Bibliography

Barrett, David B. and Todd M. Johnson (eds.). *World Christian Trends, AD 30–AD 2200: Interpreting the Annual Christian Megacensus*. Pasadena, CA: William Carey Library, 2001.

[71] Arthur F. Glasser, personal recollections at a celebration gathering on the thirtieth anniversary of the Perspectives course, July 13, 2004, Pasadena, audio recording.

[72] Ralph D. Winter, personal recollections.

Bosch, David J. *Transforming Mission: Paradigm Shifts in Theology of Mission.* Maryknoll: Orbis, 1991.

Bryant, David. Interview by author, August 15, 2005. Email.

– *In the Gap: What It Means to Be a World Christian.* Ventura, CA: Regal Books, 1979.

– Personal recollections at a celebration gathering on the thirtieth anniversary of the Perspectives course, July 13, 2004. Pasadena, CA. Audio recording.

Crawley, Winston. *World Christianity: 1970–2000.* Pasadena, CA: William Carey Library, 2001.

Gary, Jay. Interview by author, June 26, 2005. Email.

– 'Perspectives Marks 30th Anniversary'. In *Helping Faith Communities Cultivate Foresight,* July 13, 2004. http://www.jaygary.com/Perspectives_30thanniversary.shtml/ (accessed July 21, 2004).

Glasser, Arthur F. Personal recollections at a celebration gathering on the thirtieth anniversary of the Perspectives course, July 13, 2004. Pasadena, CA. Audio recording.

Glasser, Arthur F., Paul G. Hiebert, C. Peter Wagner and Ralph D. Winter (eds.). *Crucial Dimensions in World Evangelization.* Pasadena, CA: William Carey Library, 1976.

– *Understanding World Evangelization: Cultural Dimensions in International Development*. Pasadena, CA: William Carey Library, 1977.

Graham, Bruce. Interview by author, July 13, 2005. Email.

– Personal recollections at a celebration gathering on the thirtieth anniversary of the Perspectives course, July 13, 2004. Pasadena, CA. Audio recording.

Hawthorne, Steven C. Interview by author, June 11, 2005. Audio recording.

– 'History of the Perspectives Course'. Speech delivered to consultation of Perspectives coordinators, July 14, 2004. Pasadena, CA.

Howard, David M. 'Editorial: A Moratorium on Missions?' *Evangelical Missions Quarterly* (January 1975). http://www.emqoline.com/emq_article_read.php?ArticleID=2655.

– 'The Road to Urbana and Beyond'. *Evangelical Missions Quarterly* (January 1985). http://www.emqonline.com/emq_article_read.php?ArticleID=2855.

– 'Urbana '73 Theme Emphasizes Positive View of Missions'. *Evangelical Missions Quarterly* (January 1973). http://www.emqonline.com/emq_article_read.php?ArticleID=2521.

– 'What Happened at Urbana – its Meaning for Missions'. *Evangelical Missions Quarterly* (July 1977). http://www.emqonline.com/emq_article_read.php?ArticleID=2572.

Kane, J. Herbert. 'Changes Observed in Missiological Studies'. *Evangelical Missions Quarterly* (January 1974). http://www.emqonline.com/emq_article_read.php?ArticleID=2590.

McGavran, Donald A. *The Bridges of God.* rev ed. New York: Friendship Press, 1981. Original edition published in 1955 by World Dominion Press in London.

– 'Introducing Crucial Issues in Missions'. In Arthur F. Glasser, Paul G. Hiebert, C. Peter Wagner and Ralph D. Winter (eds). *Crucial Dimensions in World Evangelization*. Pasadena, CA: William Carey Library, 1976, 165-89.

Mellis, Charles J. *Committed Communities: Fresh Streams for World Mission.* Pasadena, CA: William Carey Library, 1976.

Merrill, Dean. 'It's Our 20th Birthday: Interviews with Wade Coggins and Edwin L. Jack Frizen, Jr'. *Evangelical Missions Quarterly* (April 1984). http://www.emqonline.com/emq_article_read_pv.php?ArticleID=281.

Patt, Fran. Interview by author, August 7, 2005. Transcript.

Reapsome, James W. 'Editorial: A Positive Outlook'. *Evangelical Missions Quarterly* (January 1974). http://www.emqonline.com/emq_article_read.php?ArticleID=2585.

– 'Editorial: the Unexpected Turnaround'. *Evangelical Missions Quarterly* (April 1975). http://www.emqonline.com/emq_article_read.php?ArticleID=2656.

– 'Urbana '70: One Man's Impression'. *Evangelical Missions Quarterly* (April 1971). http://www.emqonline.com/emq_article_read.php?ArticleID=2462.

Schwas, Phil and Rick Melick. 'How to Close the Gap Between Students and Missionaries'. *Evangelical Missions Quarterly* (October, 1970). http://www.emqonline.com/emq_article_read.php?ArticleID=2451.

Sjogren, Bob. Interview by author, August 5, 2005. Transcript.

Wallstrom, Timothy C. *The Creation of a Student Movement to Evangelize the World.* Pasadena, CA: William Carey International University Press, 1980.

Winter, Ralph D. Interview by author, June 20, 2005. Audio recording.

– 'The Grounds for a New Thrust in World Mission'. In Arthur F. Glasser, Paul G. Hiebert, C. Peter Wagner and Ralph D. Winter (eds). *Crucial Dimensions in World Evangelization*. Pasadena, CA: William Carey Library, 1976, Appendix.

– 'The New Macedonia: A Revolutionary New Era in Mission Begins'. In Ralph D. Winter and Steven C. Hawthorne (eds). *Perspectives on the World Christian Movement – A Reader*, 4th ed. Pasadena, CA: William Carey Library, 2009, 347-60.

– *The Twenty-Five Unbelievable Years, 1945–1969*. Pasadena, CA: William Carey Library, 1970.

– 'Is a Big New Student Mission Movement in the Offing?' *Christianity Today* (May 10, 1974), 12-15.

– Personal recollections at a celebration gathering on the thirtieth anniversary of the Perspectives course, July 13, 2004. Pasadena, CA. Audio recording.

Winter, Roberta H. *I Will Do a New Thing*. Pasadena, CA: William Carey Library, 1987.

PENTECOSTAL MISSIONS AND THE INFLUENCE OF FRONTIER MISSION MISSIOLOGY

Alan R. Johnson

Editors' Note: *Pentecostals are typically considered separately from evangelicals, even though the theological and missional stance of millions of Pentecostals largely draws from evangelical convictions. Anyone who would understand evangelical engagement in frontier mission must understand the many ways Pentecostals fit into that picture.*

At the celebration of the centennial of Edinburgh 1910 we find that the composition and character of global Christianity changed greatly over the past 100 years. The Southern shift in the locus of the Christian faith is now a well documented phenomena and the subject of scholarly interest.[1] The past century has also seen the rise of a new stream of Christianity represented in Pentecostal and Charismatic forms of the faith. These two phenomena are related since the shift of the center of gravity of the Christian faith to the south has been statistically a Pentecostal/Charismatic one.[2] The essays in this volume document another megashift that has happened in the past 100 years in the arena of missiology. Corwin observes that the shift was not so much a new vision as it was a new way to look at the old vision: 'that for the first time in the modern period the [mission] task was now couched primarily in terms of *ethne* or peoples and religious blocks, rather than in geographic or geo-political terms'.[3] Known as frontier mission missiology, the special plea of this stream of mission thinking is to take the gospel to people groups that lack Christians, churches, and church movements adequate to evangelize their people on their own.

My interest here is to explore the relationship between these two megashifts. One is a missiology that has generated an evangelistic focus on people groups that do not have existing church movements, while the other began as an evangelistic church movement that has generated a phenomenal amount of

---

[1] Philip Jenkins, *The Next Christendom: The Coming of Global Christianity* (Oxford: Oxford University Press, 2002), 2, 3.
[2] Allan Anderson, 'Towards a Pentecostal Missiology for the Majority World', in Grant McClung (ed.), *Azusa Street & Beyond* (Gainesville FL: Bridge-Logos, 2006), 169-70).
[3] Gary Corwin, 'Sociology and Missiology: Reflection on Mission Research', in Edward Rommen and Gary Corwin (eds), *Missiology and the Social Sciences: Contributions, Cautions and Conclusions* (Pasadena: William Carey Library, 1996), 20-21).

cross-cultural mission with great success in raising up younger churches all over the globe. On the face of things it would seem that these two shifts were made for each other, with the one calling for evangelistic activity where the gospel has not been preached or believed, and the other born in the fires of revival with the compulsion of the Spirit to evangelize the world. However, as it played out in the last quarter of the 20th century, classical Pentecostal mission agencies in general did not bend their efforts or structure themselves to mobilize their vast resources for the challenges articulated by frontier mission missiology. What caused the mission arms that developed out of classical Pentecostal denominations to have a relatively slow response to the notion of unreached people groups? I endeavor to build an account to answer this question and then move to a discussion of ways that Pentecostals can draw from their own theological and historical roots to turn their massive numbers and spiritual vitality towards the remaining unreached peoples.

Classical Pentecostals and Their Presence among Unreached Ethnolinguistic Groups

Trying to define Pentecostal/Charismatic Christianity is notoriously difficult. Wonsuk Ma reminds us that these movements are not homogeneous and the terminology used to describe them is not standardized.[4] He offers a classification system with three major streams: Classical Pentecostals (roots in the Azusa revival in 1906, believe in a unique experience of baptism in the Holy Spirit as evidenced by speaking in other tongues); Charismatic (or Neo) Pentecostals (who may not subscribe to the doctrinal position of a separate baptism in the Holy Spirit, but are open to the supernatural work of the Spirit); and Indigenous (or Neo-Charismatic) Pentecostals (highly diverse and often with doctrinal emphases orthodox Christians reject or are uncomfortable).[5] Coming chronologically in the first wave of renewal at the turn of the last century, classical Pentecostal denominational mission structures are older, more established, and have large networks of national churches outside their home borders. Thus it is possible to track their response to the rise of frontier mission missiology from the mid-1970s to the present.

In critically examining the interface between classical Pentecostal mission agencies and the challenge of frontier missions to plant the church among the unreached, some qualifications are necessary. First, to make the assertion that these agencies were slow to respond does not mean that there was no response. Pentecostals place great value on personal calling and the leading of the Spirit. There have always been people called and led to work among groups of people that have had little or no Christian presence. Second, the achievements of the classical Pentecostal denominational mission agencies have been stunning. As

[4] Wonsuk Ma, 'When the Poor Are Fired Up: The Role of Pneumatology in Pentecostal-Charismatic Mission', *Transformation* 24:1 (2007), 28.
[5] Ma, 'When the Poor', 28.

an example, the Christians associated with churches planted or associated with the mission arms of only six of these denominations number nearly 82 million.[6] Third, although full documentation on this does not yet exist, we know that some of the cross-cultural workers generated from these newer church movements are ending up among the unreached. Finally, in the last decade there is evidence of increasing numbers of workers, structures, and initiatives within many of these agencies and their national churches that are devoted to aspects of frontier mission, often focusing on a particular religious block or the unreached in a geographic region.

It is in point of fact the phenomenal success of classical Pentecostal missions that brings into deeper contrast the realities of their massive growth in some places, and little fruit in others. This is matched by the fact of large numbers of personnel in highly successful places and a corresponding dearth of workers among places and peoples with arguably the least Christian witness. What is at issue here is not the sending of discrete individuals with a call to an unreached people group, but rather the agency level choices that did not utilize their structures and energies to encourage and facilitate new ministry thrusts from their cross-cultural workers and national churches to the ethnolinguistic groups with the least witness of the gospel.

A full documentation of my assertion of a slow response to the challenge of unreached people groups is beyond the scope of this paper. Additionally, there are inherent limitations in trying to gather data related to work that engages unreached groups. Classical Pentecostal missions keep statistics at the level of the nation-state and not by people group, thus it is impossible to know precisely how many actual members of their teams are working directly with such groups. The various missions define their regions in different ways as well, and the countries that make up regions change, making it hard to compare data. The work done by Majority World churches connected to classical Pentecostal movements is still in its early stages and has not been documented for the most part.

However, it is possible to delimit a geographical area that is unreached people group dense, and compare over time the number of personnel located in this area. Taking 1970 as a baseline, before the dissemination of frontier mission missiology post-Lausanne in 1974, we can then see how missionary placement changed or did not change over the decades up to the present. A significant increase in field staff would be a solid indicator that something happened in response to the challenge of unreached peoples. Similarly if

---

[6] The information here is taken from the denominational websites or from articles in Wikipedia that reference denominational documents and refers to their worldwide constituents/adherents. Assemblies of God 2009 estimated constituents, 63,089,711; Church of God of Prophecy, one million; Church of God (Cleveland), six million; International Foursquare, eight million; International Pentecostal Holiness Church 2000, 3,410,890 including members and affiliates; Pentecostal Church of God (Joplin), 500,000.

percentages stay relatively the same, and percentages in other areas where the church exists stay the same or grow, it is an indicator that response was limited. The number generated by this exercise is not the actual total of people working among the unreached (due to the fact that many workers are connected to the national church and its needs in these countries) but only the potential maximum number of workers.

The area that I have chosen for comparison among five classical Pentecostal agencies is the region that includes North Africa, the Middle East, Turkey and the Central Asia republics, and the South Asian countries including India and those surrounding it. For convenience I am using the Assemblies of God World Missions designation for this area, Eurasia. By Joshua Project database figures this area contains arguably the highest density of discrete unreached ethnolinguistic groups in the world.

	1970	1990	2000	2009
Assemblies of God World Missions				
Total Career Staff	889	1663	2401	2719
Total In Eurasia	78	86	261	308
Percent of Total Staff in Eurasia	8.8	5.2	10.9	14.6
International Pentecostal Holiness Church				
Total Career Staff				97
Total In Eurasia				7
Percent of Total Staff in Eurasia				7.2
Foursquare				
Total Career Staff	71	40	65	88
Total In Eurasia	1	2	4	8
Percent of Total Staff in Eurasia	1.4	5	6.1	9.09

Table 1 Percent of Workers In An Unreached People Group Dense Part of the World (Eurasia)

What this information shows is that even with the ability to enter the newly accessible countries of Central Asia after the 1989 dissolving of the Soviet Union, the relative percentage of these missions' total field staff in this area has not changed drastically. Two missions have statistical information on their websites measuring their personnel placement in terms of well known measures relating to the unreached and least-reached. The Assemblies of God 2010 current facts and highlights sheet shows 34.2 percent of their staff working in places that are less then 2 percent evangelical, which are the Joshua Project categories 1 and 2. The Pentecostal Assemblies of Canada website says of their 254 workers that 'Nineteen per cent ... serve in Restricted Access nations or in places closed to the open preaching of the gospel. Another 18 per cent work in the 10/40 window'. While these numbers are very commendable, the fact that 60 plus percent of their mission teams are working where the global church is largest and growing fastest, indicates a less than aggressive response to the challenge of unreached ethnolinguistic groups.

Missiological Factors Shaping Response

I now want to examine some missiological factors that may have shaped the response of one classical Pentecostal mission agency towards peoples and places in the world with the least Christians. The context for my observations is my own agency, Assemblies of God World Missions, USA. While there are numerous external factors involved in missionary placement, my focus here will be explicitly on internal missiological issues. Although other organizations will have different issues, I believe that much of the discussion that follows will be relevant not only to classical Pentecostal agencies, but to any agency that finds the bulk of their teams working outside of unreached groups.

Conceptions of National Church and the Unintended Loss of the Pioneering Dimension

Founded in 1914, with one of its stated priority purposes being the evangelization of the world, the Assemblies of God noted in their 1915 General Council that missionaries were to evangelize using New Testament methods. At their 1921 Council in St. Louis they formally adopted the goal of establishing three-self 'native churches',[7] and delineated to the Foreign Missions Department the nature of the New Testament practices they were to follow in six key principles.[8] The second stated, 'The Pauline example will be followed so far as possible, by seeking out neglected regions where the gospel has not yet been preached, lest we build upon another's foundation (Rom. 15:20)'.[9]

It was not until the 1930s that indigenous self-governing church organizations at the nation-state level began to appear with El Salvador being one of the first.[10] Some twenty years later, veteran missionary Melvin Hodges who worked in Central America, was asked to put the practical steps of indigenous church development into book form. This short and clearly written book became a seminal piece in Assemblies of God missiology and as testimony to its enduring value, it is still in print nearly 60 years later and remains a popular missions text in the evangelical world.

The power of the indigenous national church concept cannot be underestimated in the exponential growth of the Assemblies of God worldwide

---

[7] Gary B. McGee, *This Gospel Shall Be Preached: A History and Theology of Assemblies of God Foreign Missions to 1959* (Springfield MO: Gospel Publishing House, 1986), 95-96.
[8] McGee, *This Gospel*, 95.
[9] McGee, *This Gospel*, 96.
[10] McGee, *This Gospel*, 148.

fellowship of churches. While recognizing its fruitfulness as a mission concept, I want to look at some of the unexpressed assumptions that grew out of the specific historical context of its development that may have impacted our response to unreached people groups. In current usage national church almost always is equated to mean the church movement within the boundaries of a nation-state. In rereading Hodges, I am not necessarily sure that such jump was in his mind as he wrote.

The book, following its title, is primarily about planting an indigenous three-self church or churches. Only six pages of the text are dedicated to the formation of a national church organization.[11] Indigeneity was much more the focus than development of a national organization. Although the unifying factor of the Spanish language among the various peoples in his experience in Central America meant that the fledgling national church would encompass the boundaries of the nation state, his words leave open the possibility for other scenarios. He allows for the needs of geographical features, political boundaries, differences of language, and transportation facilities to be accommodated. 'When distance, language or political barriers make it impractical to unite the churches into one district, it is advisable to divide the district into smaller units with a sectional conference or council in each area.'[12] Hodges used terms like conference, district and section, taken from AG organizational structure in the USA, to illustrate the form of organization he is suggesting.[13] Only later does he introduce the term, 'national church'.[14] My sense is that in Hodges' mind the notion of national church and its structure along the lines of AG USA polity was quite clear to his audience thus he felt no need to define or defend it. But his own comments do not demand, and leave the door open for organizing around language or other factors that would separate groups, and not simply geography. Thus it appears that the notion of one national church along nation-state lines came to be assumed, and was not required by the missiological concept.

Another assumption entered the mix as a result of the rapid growth of these national church organizations. There was a natural movement from the idea of the missionary planting the first individual churches and facilitating the development of an indigenous national church movement to partnering with that movement.[15] There is a logical shift in role from the pioneering work that established the church to working with the young organization to strengthen it and pursue its agendas. It is interesting to note that when Hodges did talk about the need for redistribution of missionaries because there were too many in one

[11] Melvin L. Hodges, *The Indigenous Church* (Springfield MO: Gospel Publishing House, 1976), 92-97.

[12] Hodges, *Indigenous Church*, 94.

[13] Hodges, *Indigenous Church*, 93-94.

[14] Hodges, *Indigenous Church*, 95.

[15] Melvin L. Hodges, *The Indigenous Church and the Missionary* (South Pasadena: William Carey Library, 1978), 5. Also see Morris Williams, *Partnership in Mission* (Springfield, MO: Empire Printing Company 1979).

locale, it was not for the purposes of pioneer church planting among the unreached, but for the good of the indigenous church.[16]

The principle of partnership is also an extremely powerful concept because it forms the basis for an ongoing relationship to help emerging indigenous national church movements grow and prosper. Without such a notion, it is too easy to get something started and then back away, thus truncating the movement and not allowing it to truly become capable of evangelizing its own people without outside resources. For us in the Assemblies of God, the definition of national church, like Winter's notion of Pauline missiological breakthrough, is a very robust concept.[17] What is problematic however is the unwarranted jump that makes partnership with the national church such a dominant theme that it suppresses the ability of the mission to act as an apostolic band to take the gospel where it has not been preached. While that conclusion is never formally stated, in practice, partnership becomes a primary value that shapes placement and ministry trajectory. This is true not only on the side of the mission agency, but can come from national churches as well. Majority World church movements, jealous to husband resources for their needs, are capable of citing chapter and missiological verse back to missionaries when they propose working outside of their boundaries to reach out to an unreached people group.

When we stand back for a moment and look at these two concepts, linking the ideas of 'indigenous national church' and 'partnership' enabled a level of fruitfulness that could only have been dreamed for in the early years. However, surfacing some of the assumptions that are currently connected with each reveals ideas that hinder rather than facilitate a move towards unreached people groups. I see the shift in primary emphasis from proclamational pioneer church planting to partnership with existing church movements as something that was never planned. It was a natural change of attention to what was happening as new movements blossomed. However, the unintended consequence of the partnership concept was the erosion of the pioneering dimension of Pentecostal mission that was so salient in their early days. My guess is that this development may have been aided by an assumption that the Pentecostal experience would always lend towards urgency in proclamation and thus it was not something that needed to be worried about. What the passage of time has now revealed is that it is quite possible to remain doctrinally and stylistically Pentecostal, yet lose one's evangelistic fervor.

At the same time, the gradual cementing of the meaning of 'national church' along nation-state lines unwittingly marginalized unreached ethnolinguistic groups outside of the primary ethnicity of the existing national church. Missionaries find that national churches want them to work in their orbit and

---

[16] Hodges, *Indigenous Church*, 96.

[17] See Alan R. Johnson, *Apostolic Function in 21st Century Missions*, J. Philip Hogan World Missions Series (Pasadena: William Carey Library, 2009), 113-14.

not with those who they may have a history of problems or animosity. Another problem set has to do with how the new converts in an unreached group will relate to the existing church. Do they start their own 'national church'? Do they come under the existing one? Rather than legitimating and validating pioneer work among the unreached, the hardening of these concepts and their associated assumptions slowed the process down by raising concerns were not taken from our reading of Scripture, but rather grew from limitations in our use of these concepts.

The Impact of Missions Success on the Ability to Engage Least-Reached, Resistant, and Unresponsive Peoples

In hindsight, it appears that the incredible success of our mission endeavors actually caught us all by surprise. The doctrine of indigeneity valued and predicted strong, robust, Pentecostal, zealous, evangelistic, national church movements. But when it happened so suddenly, it was natural that some missiological points were neglected or lost in the scramble to stay at the front of the wave. The impact of mission success was a key factor in creating a particular ethos and self-understanding in mission; contributed to a lack of reflection on and missions praxis for the unreached, resistant, and unresponsive; and its suddenness hindered the development of missions policy for responding to it. All of these factors combined to work against a systemic response to the challenge of unreached peoples.

THE SELF UNDERSTANDING AND ETHOS OF CLASSICAL PENTECOSTAL MISSIONS

The advent of frontier mission missiology in the mid-1970s came at a time when the national churches founded by classical Pentecostal agencies were beginning to explode exponentially.[18] To put it simply, to be a Pentecostal missionary, meant that it works. The era of painstaking sowing, rejection, and persecution in many fields became memories as big crusades, big churches, big institutions, and big buildings sprung up all over the globe. New missionary candidates raised on stories of powerful Pentecostal mission success came to the agency interested in going to such places and reduplicating such methods. The opposite side of the coin is that this success ethos creates an environment where people working in circumstances with slower response feel a great deal of pressure to 'produce' the results that are expected from Pentecostal mission. Both at the denominational level in the local churches and at the agency level successes were cheered and given high profile, and it was natural that numerically unfruitful fields among the unreached world received correspondingly less attention. The overall effect of such a self-understanding is to constrain those who will respond to the challenges represented by the unreached.

---

[18] Randy Hurst, 'The Secret of Accelerating and Lasting Growth', *Today's Pentecostal Evangel* January 26, 2006, 24-25.

SUCCESS AND THE DULLING OF CONTEXT-SENSITIVITY

Another impact of the success ethos is that the way Pentecostals 'did church' became a part of their style, or mode of faith expression. Pentecostal/Charismatic worship forms jumped beyond the boundaries of their own churches and became the trademark of cutting edge churches in a globalized world. The difficulty in terms of mission is the fact that while this style fits well in a globalized segment of the world, it does not touch the heart of millions of people in the unreached world who are either turned off, offended, or confused by globalized music, worship styles, and the equation of Christianity with western culture. This stylistic identity that starts at the grassroots level of the constituent churches of classical Pentecostal organizations combined with the success ethos at the agency level means that the cross-cultural workers sent out in the time frame examined here were not well prepared to deal with the context issues that they faced among unreached populations. Their ministry toolkits were limited to reproducing globalized style Pentecostal/Charismatic forms.

A LACK OF THEOLOGICAL REFLECTION ON HOW TO HANDLE THE RESISTANT AND UNRESPONSIVE

One of the strengths of Pentecostal mission is the emphasis on the leading of the Holy Spirit, and getting involved in what the Spirit is manifestly doing in the world. Wilson, in his biography of J. Philip Hogan, who served for 30 years as the executive director of the Assemblies of God missionary program, provides a number of illustrations from Hogan's thinking that show the sense of dependence on the guidance of the Spirit.[19] It is the Spirit who leads laborers to strategic harvest opportunities [20] and prepares peoples, communities, cities, and nations for sudden harvest.[21] Being strategic in this sense is going where God is pouring out his Spirit.[22] Success in part flowed also from an intentional focus on where the Spirit was working.

Again, it seems natural that in an era of explosive growth all over the globe, there was little time to think about the resistant, unresponsive, and those separated from the gospel by barriers of language, religion, and social standing. The result was that there has not been serious Pentecostal missiological reflection on working among those who do not respond quickly. There is no theology of sowing and preparation and creating a value system that honors such work. The practical on-field result of this theological gap is that cross-cultural workers find it hard to persevere in the face of no results and gravitate towards work with existing churches that is more capable of quantification and amenable to being reported to constituents.

---

[19] Everett A. Wilson, *Strategy of the Spirit: J. Philip Hogan and the Growth of the Assemblies of God Worldwide 1960–1990* (Carlisle, Cumbria: Regnum Books International), 1997.

[20] Wilson, *Strategy*, 64, 136.

[21] Wilson, *Strategy*, 67, 136.

[22] Wilson, *Strategy*, 72.

LACK OF REFLECTION ON MISSIOLOGICAL PRINCIPLES FOR EXIT FROM FULLY INDIGENOUS NATIONAL CHURCHES

If there is a lack of theological reflection on how to deal with the unresponsive, the other side of the coin is that we never developed a missiology of success that gave us an explicit exit strategy. By this I mean how we respond as a mission to the successful formation of strong indigenous national churches which is our stated goal. Indigenous national churches are inherently needy; it never feels as if there are enough workers. Without a theology of success we have no decision-making tools to help us decide what needs to be done and how to respond to the demands of national churches long after they are fully indigenous or as they are in last stages of the transition time moving towards it. The result is that over time the New Testament dimension of crossing cultural boundaries to present that gospel and the Pauline theme of going where the gospel is not yet present becomes obscured.

Classical Pentecostals and Frontier Missions: Towards a Greater Engagement

If in the past classical Pentecostal agencies have been slow to respond to the challenges of the final unreached peoples, the good news is that the present is showing signs of significant shifts towards a greater engagement. These signs are hopeful that the future will see the turning of the energy of these movements towards the frontier task that remains. I now want to look at some missiological issues that may help facilitate a greater engagement with unreached ethnolinguistic groups by classical Pentecostals all over the world. Each of these points could be expanded upon; my purpose here is not to be exhaustive or comprehensive, but rather is to set forth a tentative outline of a potential agenda that both established and emerging missions can begin to discuss and seek to implement in their work.

I envision this as a reflective process, taking the powerful concepts that have already been developed and proven to bear fruit, and not discard them or move past them, but rather revisit them in light of the challenges of the unreached and bring to them fresh insights that will sharpen our focus and practice. I see the goal of this exercise as synthesizing a conception of mission that:

- Integrates the guidance of the Spirit, the power of the indigenous national church/partnership notions, and a lens to see 'peoples' without the gospel.
- Legitimates the role of the apostolic band that goes where Christ is not known.
- Brings a unified identity to all cross-cultural workers and affirms the value of the multiplicity of gifts in the missionary team.

The series of reflections here provide an outline and some examples of the issues that are potential content for this process.

Reflecting on Pentecostal History: Restoring Evangelistic Zeal

The early Pentecostals saw the coming of the Holy Spirit as a restoration of the church and harbinger of the return of the Lord. The mission impulse was grounded in a sense of urgency that Christ be proclaimed to reap a final harvest. In Assemblies of God history, they pledged themselves to the greatest evangelization the world had ever seen. Now, 100 years distant from the Azusa revival the Lord has not returned, the fires of evangelism have waned among the western based denominations, and the perception of missions on the part of many constituent churches is that missionaries train local people to do ministry. While doctrinally affirming that the coming of the Spirit is empowerment for mission, practically we have developed systems that concentrate on supportive activities among emerging churches. There needs to be an intentional linkage on the part of denominational and missions leaders that the coming the Spirit is still a relationship that pushes people to go to those who have not heard the gospel. The fact of the documented existence of unreached ethnolinguistic groups needs to be held up to our movements as a primary place of labor for Spirit empowered workers.

To argue that western originating cross-cultural workers are relegated to only a training role so that Majority World people can finish the task is faulty at two points. First, it assumes that people who themselves are not burning with a zeal to proclaim the good news among the unreached are able to communicate that burden to others. Second, it introduces a limitation that is not warranted by Scripture, restricting the apostolic task to others while ignoring it ourselves, to our spiritual peril. The reality is that the best way to revive evangelistic zeal among the western churches is to trumpet the need of all the tribes and tongues to hear the gospel. For every worker envisioned by the Spirit who moves out of their own cultural setting there will be dozens that take up the task among their own.

Reflecting on Key Missions Concepts: Revisiting the Indigenous National Church and Partnership

The problems with some of the unwritten assumptions connected to the concepts of the indigenous national church and partnership I discussed above invite revisiting these notions in order to clarify and strengthen them. Expanding the concepts to make room to enable mission structures to relate to an existing national church while at the same time pioneering in another people group is a first step. This means loosening the connection between national church and the nation-state and opening the doors to creatively structuring varying forms of relationship between church movements with two or more distinct ethnic groups within the boundaries of a single nation-state. Similarly, the notion of partnership needs to be updated so that it allows for an incoming mission team to have the blessing and freedom to work apostolically in planting the church among an unreached group. The bottom line is that we cannot allow the concepts of national church and partnership to harden in such a fashion that they prohibit or inhibit the ability of the mission team to work outside the boundaries of the existing national church and its people group among an unreached group.

Reflecting on the Work of the Holy Spirit

For Pentecostals, the role of the Spirit in calling the workers is central to placement. However, research shows that there are a number of elements that coalesce in the calling to mission. Information via a variety of sources such a missionary narratives, missions conventions, missionary experience, and counsel play an important role in this. This means that it is an act of missionary statesmanship to make the needs of the unreached world known. Constituent churches of the home base as well as missionary candidates coming to the agency need to know that there is a world that has not yet heard, understood, or responded to the gospel.

If a candidate comes to a mission organization evincing a call to missions but has never heard of the unreached world, it is incumbent upon the mission leadership to make those facts known and ask that such a candidate spend time in prayer over this information asking God for guidance. I am not suggesting in any way that we squelch the work of the Spirit, nor is this an exercise in suppressing individual guidance in favor of corporate guidance. My point is very simple and is grounded in a big assumption: that it is impossible for the Holy Spirit not to be calling workers to the unreached, given what we know from Scripture about God's concern for all the peoples. The databases of the world's unreached peoples are public documents. At the very least prayer for these groups needs to be engaged at the highest levels of our mission leadership, in our local churches, in our mission teams, and among the emerging national churches we relate to. To pray seriously about such groups will be to place ourselves in the line of fire to hear the voice of the Spirit who calls workers into the harvest fields.

Reflecting on Our Current Placement: The Need for Spiritual Genetic Modification

If we generate prayer for new workers to the least reached, what do we do with the 60-70 percent working among the existing church? Some have mistakenly taken the call to the unreached as also being a call to redeploy existing cross-cultural workers to work among them, and as an implicit negative judgment upon those working with the church. This is not the case. It was a great misfortune that Ralph Winter's views on this were underplayed and ignored as people group thinking gained more prominence in mission circles.[23] He consistently maintained that to take language and culture competent workers out of their setting and put them into new learning curves among the unreached

[23] Ralph D. Winter, 'Are 90% of Our Missionaries Serving in the Wrong Places?' *Mission Frontiers* November–December (1991), 34-35.

is not a policy of wisdom. There is much strategic work that can be done for the frontiers of mission from their current place of service.

I like to compare the awakening of having a 'lens' to see 'peoples' as a spiritual genetic modification. This DNA level change in the worker produces changes at the level of why they do things, reorients the ultimate goals of their work, and may even change their whole focus. If our mission staff living among the existing church movements in the Majority World began to turn the energies of those churches towards prayer for the unreached, and to help develop mission sending structures and train workers to go to the unreached, what would the impact be? To infect all of the ministerial training apparatuses among these churches with the biblical theology of mission and a burden for the unreached would be an incredibly strategic work. In my own corner of the world as I have had opportunities to train Asian leaders, I have discovered that our Majority World churches often do not share our missiology. In addition to this, their views of mission are shaped by the experience of receiving the gospel in a flow of transmission from the West. Too often mission is defined by their perceptions of what western cross-cultural workers have done and are doing. When they have never seen anyone go to the unreached, they do not see it as part of the mission agenda. If our existing mission staff can get the vision for the unreached, they can become key players in passing that burden on to the church movements to which they relate.

Reflecting on the Biblical Text: A Theology of the Hard Work

The Holy Spirit's work in bringing response to the message and guiding the worker, combined with the ethos of Pentecostal mission success has created a blank spot for what to do with the places that are *not* currently receptive/responsive. In addition to this, the western passion for tangibility and quantification has shaped a view of mission that makes results the primary evaluative tool for determining success. This results in avoiding work that does not produce immediate and measurable results; thus many important activities that are preparatory to harvest are neglected. This value system is often transmitted from the West into the newer emerging missions, making the criterion of successful mission numerical results alone and discouraging any activity that does not meet that standard. All of this highlights the need for what I call a theology of the hard work. Such a theology is grounded in reflection on the biblical text that will strengthen workers for the foundational tasks of clearing the fields, preparing the ground, and planting the seed needed for harvest.

In John 4:35-38 as Jesus is talking to his disciples about the present harvest, he makes the statement that others have done the hard work (John 4:38), and they are now reaping the fruits of those labors. When I went back and worked through commentaries on this passage, I discovered that scholars are not really sure of the antecedents that Jesus is using here. Who are the 'others'?, what harvest Jesus is talking about?, where did he send them to reap?, who are the reapers drawing their wages?, and so on. What is quite clear however, is that Jesus is acknowledging here the well known agricultural fact that in order to get a harvest you must do hard preparatory work first. It encouraged me greatly that Jesus recognizes and honors the hard work. He notes that both the sower and the reaper rejoice together (John 4:36).

A theology of the hard work is founded on Jesus' acknowledgement of the role of hard work in preparing for a harvest. He lets his disciples know that they are standing on the shoulders of others; that those who have gone before have done the really difficult labor and now they will reap. Today, in the excitement of the worldwide expansion of the church there is a diminished tolerance for the often backbreaking labor of preparation for a harvest. I look forward to seeing classical Pentecostal missions new and old fill out their theologies of victory and success with perspectives on hard work in preparation for harvest that includes the role of suffering, and living among the nations to declare the glory of God. This kind of theological reflection will provide future workers among the hardest places to serve joyfully for God's glory even when they are not seeing tangible results yet.

Reflecting on the Future: Mobilizing Classical Pentecostal Movements to Go to the Unreached

I have saved what is the most important issue and what I consider to be the most exciting possibility for this final point. One thing that makes the Pentecostal/Charismatic stream of faith so dynamic is the continual, unplanned, often unexpected wind of the Holy Spirit that blows and raises up new vision and visits and transforms bodies of believers and their communities. As classical Pentecostals we need to believe God for a mighty visitation that will bring the vision and spiritual power to turn the movements that are associated with us all over the world towards the unreached ethnolinguistic groups.

Imagine what could happen if tens of millions of believers suddenly could 'see' peoples and begin to order their lives, churches, and movements around making Christ known among such neglected groups. Beyond the obvious benefits of large numbers of people being aware and praying for the unreached, there are two particular ways in which a mobilization of classical Pentecostals would have a huge impact for frontier mission. The first is the vast pool of workers that could be released into unreached harvest fields. Majority World missions among classical Pentecostal movements are taking off, and it needs to be steered in the direction of places that do not have existing church movements. It would be a great tragedy for the Majority World churches to develop cross-cultural sending structures only to have people sent to work with the existing church somewhere else. It is entirely understandable how emerging Majority World missions structures want to emulate the work of the missionaries who were sent to them. This highlights the critical need for missions education and information so that these younger agencies can be aware of the needs of the unreached. It is ironic that many younger missions structures have come into existence with a vision to send people not to cross cultural boundaries, but geographic ones, often in pursuit of reaching the diasporas of their own people, while neglecting cross-cultural opportunities right within the borders of their own nation state to work among an unreached people.

The second impact of an awakening to see unreached peoples has to do with the informal ministry of millions of lay people in classical Pentecostal movements around the world that literally rub elbows with unreached peoples every day. If we could bring training down to our local churches and pastors to enable them to bear witness to the Muslims, Hindus, and Buddhists that live around them, these believers would have access to the lives of millions of people that are much more culturally near to them than any expatriate worker.

Conclusion

At the time of Edinburgh 1910, no one could have predicted the megashifts brought to the mission world by the concepts of frontier missions and the vitality and success of Pentecostal churches. Although organizations and missions growing out of classical Pentecostal roots have been slow to respond to the challenges of the unreached world in the past, there are reasons to be very hopeful about the coming together of these streams. The first signs of hope are the explicit structures that are emerging within classical Pentecostal missions in the West that focus on the unreached, and the mobilization for mission happening in the younger churches. The second is that the reasons for slow response are amenable to being addressed, and there is every reason to believe that revisiting key concepts and Pentecostal experiences can lead to a massive turning of the weight and spiritual energy of these movements towards the needs of the unreached.

Bibliography

Allen, Roland. *Missionary Methods: St. Paul's or Ours*? Grand Rapids: Eerdmans, 1962.

Anderson, Allan. 'Towards a Pentecostal Missiology for the Majority World. In Grant McClung (ed.). *Azusa Street & Beyond*. Gainesville, FL: Bridge-Logos, 2006, 169-89.

Barrett, David B. and Todd M. Johnson. 'Annual Statistical Table on Global Mission: 2004'. *International Bulletin of Missionary Research* 28:1 (2004), 24-25.

Barrett, David B., Todd M. Johnson, Christopher R. Guidry, and Peter F. Crossing (eds.). *World Christian Trends, AD 30–AD 2200: Interpreting the Annual Christian Megacensus*. Pasadena: William Carey Library, 2001.

Barrett, David and Todd Johnson (eds.). *World Christian Encyclopedia: A Comparative Study of Churches and Religions in the Modern World, AD 1900–2000*. Oxford: Oxford University Press, 1982.

Corwin, Gary. 'Sociology and Missiology: Reflection on Mission Research'. In Edward

Rommen and Gary Corwin (eds). *Missiology and the Social Sciences: Contributions, Cautions and Conclusions*. Pasadena: William Carey Library, 1996, 19-29.

Hodges, Melvin L. *The Indigenous Church*. Springfield, MO: Gospel Publishing House, 1976.

– *The Indigenous Church and the Missionary*. South Pasadena: William Carey Library, 1978.

Hurst, Randy. 'The Secret of Accelerating and Lasting Growth. *Today's Pentecostal Evangel* (January 26, 2006), 24-25.

Jenkins, Philip. *The Next Christendom: The Coming of Global Christianity*. Oxford: Oxford University Press, 2002.

Johnson, Alan R. 'Analyzing the Frontier Mission Movement and Unreached People Group Thinking Part 3: Critical Analysis of the Missiology of the Frontier Mission Movement'. *International Journal of Frontier Missions* 18:3 (2001), 121-28.

– *Apostolic Function in 21st Century Missions*. J. Philip Hogan World Missions Series. Pasadena: William Carey Library, 2009.

Johnstone, Patrick and Jason Mandryk. *Operation World: 21st Century Edition*. Carlisle, United Kingdom: Paternoster, 2001.

Klaus, Byron and Douglas Petersen (eds.). *The Essential J. Philip Hogan*. The J. Philip Hogan World Missions Series. Springfield, MO: Assemblies of God Theological Seminary, 2006.

Kraft, Charles H. 'Why Isn't Contextualization Implemented?' In Charles H. Kraft. *Appropriate Christianity*. Pasadena: William Carey Library, 2005, 67-79.

Luce, Alice E. 'Paul's Missionary Methods'. *The Pentecostal Evangel* (Jan. 8, 1921_, 6-7.

– 'Paul's Missionary Methods'. *The Pentecostal Evangel* (Jan. 22, 1921), 6, 11.

– 'Paul's Missisonary Methods'. *The Pentecostal Evangel* (Feb. 6), 6-7.

Ma, Wonsuk. 'When the Poor Are Fired Up: The Role of Pneumatology in Pentecostal-Charismatic Mission'. *Transformation* 24:1 (2007), 28-34.

McGavran, Donald A. *Understanding Church Growth*. Grand Rapid: Eerdmans, 1987.

McGee, Gary B. *This Gospel Shall Be Preached: A History and Theology of Assemblies of God Foreign Missions to 1959*. Springfield, MO: Gospel Publishing House, 1986.

Miller, Donald E. and Tetsunao Yamamori. *Global Pentecostalism: The New Face of Christian Social Engagement*. Berkeley: University of California Press, 2007.

Rance, DeLonn L. 'The Empowered Call: The Activity of the Holy Spirit in Salvadoran Assemblies of God Missionaries'. PhD dissertation, Fuller Theological Seminary, 2004.

Synan, Vinson. *The Spirit Said 'Grow': The Astounding Worldwide Expansion of Pentecostal & Charismatic Churches*. Monrovia, CA: MARC, 1992.

Walls, Andrew F. *The Missionary Movement in Christian History: Studies in the Transmission of Faith*. Maryknoll: Orbis, 1996.

Williams, Morris. *Partnership in Mission*. Springfield, MO: Empire Printing Company, 1979.

Wilson, Everett A. *Strategy of the Spirit: J. Philip Hogan and the Growth of the Assemblies of God Worldwide 1960–1990*. Carlisle, Cumbria: Regnum Books International, 1997.

Winter, Ralph D. 'Are 90% of Our Missionaries Serving in the Wrong Places?' *Mission Frontiers* (November–December 1991), 34-35.

International Initiatives

THE INFLUENCE OF UNREACHED PEOPLES THINKING ON FRANCOPHONE AFRICAN THEOLOGICAL EDUCATION AND MISSION

Moussa Bongoyok

Editors' Note: *Global South Christians have been characterized as deeply conservative theologically, and thus are engaged as evangelicals in their thinking and praxis. The impact of unreached peoples thinking and frontier missions among Christians in Francophone Africa makes a helpful case study.*

A thousand students went through Ralph Winter's classes at Fuller's School of World Mission and one can hardly imagine the wealth of experience that they shared with him. As a good professor should, he listened to them. He collected, organized, analyzed the data and drew the necessary conclusions. Here is Winter's own testimony about what he discovered:

> For me this was a glorious introduction into the global phenomenon of Christianity and it led to some disturbing conclusions. I began to write and promote insight into the idea that thousands of minority groups in every country were still walled off from missions by the tendency of many missions to assume that the churches they established could easily bridge the many ethnic differences which make most countries into a linguistic mosaic. Realizing that this perspective was an overlooked dimension that affected the strategies in virtually all fields, it became serious enough so that, it seemed to me someone would have to stop teaching and begin actively promoting outreach to these additional totally pioneer fields that were invisible to anyone with American melting pot assumptions.[1]

The result of this new learning experience, and the hard work of analysis that accompanied it, is known today: he came out with a unique thinking on unreached people groups that go beyond theoretical consideration and that has shaped global missions since his address at the Lausanne '74 conference.

Fuller School of World Mission was instrumental in the genesis and early developments of Winter's thinking on unreached people groups. He was still at Fuller when he presented his ground breaking paper entitled 'The Task of Highest Priority: Cross-Cultural Missions', at Lausanne in 1974. The ethnic groups that were hidden in the eyes of church leaders and missionaries came to

---

[1] Ralph D. Winter, *Frontiers in Mission* (Pasadena: WCIU Press, 2008), 2.

a new light. The task ahead was clearly identified and the arguments were very convincing.

Influence of Winter and the Fuller School of World Mission on Education and Mission in Francophone Africa

It must be said that Bangui Evangelical Graduate School of Theology relies heavily on visiting professors due to the limited number of resident African professors. Professor Nzash U. Lumeya, a missiologist and Old Testament specialist, was one of those visiting while I was a student at Bangui. Professor Lumeya had been exposed to the ideas of Winter and to the teachings of the School of World Mission as a student there, and he played a key role in transferring the flame he received from California to the heart of Africa. He not only spoke about mission, but his whole life was (and is still) missions. No matter what he taught, he ended up referring to mission and unreached peoples. The amazing thing about him I noticed when I was a student is that he did not only teach but was actively involved in missions as well. During the week-end and holidays, while other faculty members were enjoying rest after an intense week of teaching, he was usually on his way to the forest among the Bamenga who were then an unreached pygmy people group. He brought some students and local pastors with him because he did not want to be involved alone. He wanted (and he still wants) other people to be involved.

Professor Lumeya encouraged one of the leading denominations, *Eglise de la Cooperation Evangélique en Centrafrique* (Cooperation Evangelical Church in Central African Republic), to start a Missiology Institute in order to train African missionaries. That institution is still active today. He himself taught in that school in addition to his teaching load at Bangui Evangelical Graduate School of Theology. Later, his former students took over the leadership and teaching at that institution when he relocated to Kinshasa, in the Democratic Republic of Congo, his home country. Even there, his heart for the unreached people groups did not stop. In October 1990, he went ahead and created an even more important Mission School, known in French under the name of *Centre Universitaire de Missiologie* (The University Center for Missiology). This school trains up to the Master's level. Although he is still actively involved with that school, he did not stop there; he also founded the Fresno School of Mission that he currently leads.

Why is Lumeya's teaching ministry and impact on Bangui Evangelical School of Theology so important for the whole Francophone Africa? To understand this, it is important to underline the fact that the seminary in Bangui is the premier evangelical theological institution for Francophone Africa. It was founded in 1977 by the Association of Evangelicals in Africa. It trains students from all French Speaking Nations and the graduates of this institution are now in key leadership positions in most of the denominations, Christian organizations and theological schools of Francophone Africa. Because of this impact on the ground, it succeeded in creating the Council of Theological Institutions in French-Speaking Africa known in French under the name of *Conseil des Institutions Théologiques d'Afrique Francophone* (CITAF).[2] The council created a curriculum for all levels. That curriculum is in use in almost all the evangelical institutions in Francophone Africa, with mission studies occupying a good place within this theological education. The current leader of CITAF is Abel Ndjerareou, the former President of Bangui Evangelical Graduate School of Theology and current Coordinator of Transafrican Education Network.

Francophone African Missionaries

This short historical background explains why the training and passion for the unreached people groups received from Bangui Evangelical School of theology have permeated French speaking nations. Many graduates, including myself, ended up teaching missiology, founding and leading mission schools, speaking in various gatherings on unreached people groups or launching church planting movements. They faithfully ran with the flame received from Professor Lumeya and ultimately from Winter and the School of World Mission by God's permission.

But Lumeya was not the only person who spread the passion for the unreached people groups in Francophone Africa. The participants from the Lausanne gathering of 1974 and the following gatherings were deeply touched by Winter's presentations. When they returned to their home countries, they shared the information with their colleagues and they ran with the idea. Inside the Association of Evangelicals in Africa, Rene Daidanso did an extraordinary job not only in his home country, Chad, but throughout the continent. He not only taught about the importance for evangelizing and reaching the unreached people groups but he successfully mobilized the evangelical denominations of his country. He organized systematic evangelism in his whole country starting in 1993. Today, the entire population has had opportunity to hear the gospel and many hundreds of new churches have been planted, including some among the unreached people groups. Many countries, like Cameroon, caught the vision and have started to follow his example.

Dave Richards, a missionary from New Zealand who was based in Burkina Faso, pulled together a team and began missionary training based on a short French language course that is part of the family of courses in the Perspectives movement.[3] He organized many seminars on unreached people groups during

---

[2] CITAF's website is http://www.citaf.org.

[3] This course is called in French '*Cours abrégés de mission mondiale*' (Abridged Courses of World Mission), based on the three volume work edited by Jonathan Lewis. *Mission modiale* is published in Abidjan, Ivory Coast by *Centre de Publications Evangéliques* [CPE]). The same publishing company translated and published many

the second half of 1990s and early 2000s. Through his ministry, mission agencies and church leaders and individual Christians in Francophone Africa got key training on unreached people groups and how to reach them with the gospel.

One of the lasting results of these courses is the creation of an excellent international missionary training center, *Institut Missiologique du Sahel* (Missionary Institute of the Sahel) that started training French speaking missionaries in 2003 in Ouagadougou Burkina Faso. Pastors and Evangelists came from various French speaking nations in West and Central Africa. Because they have already been trained in Bible Institutes and Theological Schools, they receive a supplemental nine months of residential and intensive training on missions. Professors come from various backgrounds and countries and who have a solid academic training in missiology and/or outstanding experience in the mission field. During their training, students spend several weeks on the field in order to practice what they have learned in the classrooms. Graduates of that school are actively engaged in work among the unreached people groups and some graduates have even founded similar schools in their home countries.

Countries like Benin, Burkina Faso, Cameroon, Chad, Central African Republic, Congo Democratic Republic, Ivory Coast, Madagascar, Mali, Niger, Senegal, Togo, are showing promising signs as far as mission and education are concerned. Increasing numbers of workers are participating in church planting among the unreached people groups. Even economically challenged countries like Burkina Faso have sent African missionaries to Europe and Asia. Since the 1990s there is a growing number of missionaries from Cameroon, Central African Republic, Congo Democratic Republic, Ivory Coast and Mali to other countries throughout Africa. Some of them are currently active in Europe, North America and Asia. These developments hold good promise for the future.

Possible Future Impact

As of 2010, many French speaking countries have schools where people can get training in missiology although most of them are at diploma level or lower. However, none is offering a Ph.D. in missiology yet and the need is becoming more and more crucial for several reasons. Qualified professors of missiology and Islamic studies are needed; African mission agencies and local mission executives lack proper training; mission strategists need research centers and updated data on unreached people groups; current mission professors and leaders of Mission Institutes need places where they can continue their education and earn the necessary academic credentials.

TEE (Theological Education by Extension) materials in French. These documents are successfully used throughout French speaking nations.

Institutions like Fuller Theological Seminary and William Carey International University can bring a unique contribution by training scholars at doctoral level (Doctor of Missiology and Ph.D.). Both schools have started cohort-based distance education programs at that level with the potential to train thousands of leaders in the next ten to fifteen years. Graduates from these programs have the potential for a major impact not only on the French Speaking nations but on the entire world, given the fact that most African French speakers are able to function in several languages. I envision a large missionary sending-base in Francophone Africa that will bear much fruit in the kingdom of God and create a revolution in Christian mission endeavor. The question is: are we ready to invest time and energy in order to train this giant that is still half asleep?

One cannot speak about training in missiology without at least mentioning the diversity of training model. William Taylor's observation is true: 'New models are emerging, local churches are increasingly designing their own programs, and training options are readily available on the internet and in different languages'.[4] The model provided by Theological Education by Extension (TEE) has not said its last word yet. Winter brought to Fuller the first teaching on TEE. That teaching, coupled with his prior accomplishments in that area, together with his colleagues James Emery and Ross Kinsler, changed the paradigm of numerous church leaders, missionaries and mission agencies around the world whose approach to theological education was basically restricted to residential seminary training. He helped Fuller and many other institutions pave the way and provide solid foundation to TEE that has become today a worldwide movement.

There are many good testimonies to the benefits of TEE, such as the following one by Helena Hooper, which is just one testimony among hundreds.[5]

> The introduction of TEE has been of immense help, especially for the AIC's [African Independent Churches], as they have had to remain in their contexts and yet acquire theological education and serve their churches faithfully. TEE has been called 'the Bible going to the people' and the text as 'the book is the teacher', which is more than an adequate description of what it does. It has trained and empowered more people at a given time than the average theological seminary can.[6]

An advantage of TEE is that it succeeded in drawing interest even from Africa Independent Churches that are still hesitant to send their leaders to exiting Bible schools and seminaries. These churches cannot be neglected when

[4] William Taylor, 'Training', in Jonathan Bonk (ed.), *Encyclopedia of Missions and Missionaries* (New York: Routledge, 2007), 444.
[5] Cf. Kinsler and Snook.
[6] Helena Hooper, 'TEE among African Instituted Churches', in Ross Kinsler (ed.), *Diversified Theological Education* (Pasadena: WCIU Press, 2008), 89.

we know that in the Kimbanguist church alone there were seven million members in 1996 according to the World Council of Churches sources quoted by Allan H. Anderson.[7] When it comes to TEE, they do not feel threatened and yet they still get access to doctrinal teaching that draws them closer to other Christian denominations and even produces changes in their way of handling church administration, evangelism, mission and social involvement.

There is a genuine need to continue to develop a missiological education by extension based on the TEE model that is accessible both online and through traditional venues of education.[8] With the advent of new communication tools, there is a growing number of cyber-cafes even in remote regions of Africa where internet connection was unknown only ten years ago. Many countries are aggressively developing networks and facilitating the import of computers for the benefit of their populations. Online education has a brilliant future in Francophone Africa and worldwide provided Christian Schools and Churches will develop and implement proper strategies for greater results.

Effective strategies for distance (including online) education must take African philosophies of education into consideration. The important thing is to train people who are or will be fully involved in evangelism, mission, discipleship, leadership training, church and mission administration or similar activities and also lay men and women. If seminaries and Christian universities are to successfully meet the challenge of unreached people groups in Africa and worldwide, they must give a solid, holistic, and accessible training in missiology to all the mature members and let them contribute to the spread of the gospel wherever the Lord places them. Christianity cannot afford to rely primarily on specialists and clergy members who, by the way, are becoming fewer each year.

Conclusion

Winter's insights into the importance of theological and missiological education by extension and his robust advocacy on behalf of unreached people groups have impacted the world. Even distant villages of Francophone Africa have felt the transforming influence of Winter's thinking on unreached people groups and they have responded well. The impact is observable in training institutions and mission activities inside these countries, from these countries to neighboring countries, and beyond the African continent. The most exciting part of this development is that this is only the beginning of a movement that will result in more French Speaking Africans on the front lines of global missions. There is also a price to pay in prayer, research, training and strategic

---

[7] Allan H. Anderson, *African Reformation* (Trenton NJ: Africa World Press, 2001), 125.

[8] Compare Winter's World Christian Foundations study program, www.worldchristianfoundations.org, which packages a missiological view of God's purposes in history in a distance-based format, adaptable for online, individual or group mentoring sessions at the graduate, undergraduate or certificate level.

actions. I pray that God may give our generation many people who will have the same vision, wisdom, passion, and determination as Winter, for the glory of God and the advance of His kingdom!

Bibliography

Anderson, Allan H. *African Reformation*. Trenton, NJ: Africa World Press, 2001.

Hooper, Helena. 'TEE among African Instituted Churches'. In Ross Kinsler (ed.). *Diversified Theological Education*. Pasadena: William Carey International University Press, 2008.

Mulholland, Kenneth. 'Winter, Ralph D.' In A. Scott Moreau, Harold Netland and Charles Van Engen, (eds.). *Evangelical Dictionary of World Missions*. Grand Rapids: Baker, 2000.

Snook, Stewart G. *Developing Leaders through Theological Education by Extension*. Wheaton: The Billy Graham Center, 1992.

Taylor, William. 'Training'. In Jonathan Bonk (ed.). *Encyclopedia of Missions and Missionaries*. New York: Routledge, 2007.

Kinsler, Ross, ed. *Diversified Theological Education*. Pasadena: WCIU Press, 2008.

Winter, Ralph D. *Frontiers in Mission*. Pasadena: William Carey International University Press, 2008.

Winter, H. Roberta. *I Will Do A New Thing*. Pasadena: William Carey Library, 2002.

History and Growth of the Korean Missions Movement

Timothy K. Park

Editors' Note: *Among Evangelicals, no Global South country is better known for its recent church growth and for its engagement in sending out missionaries than Korea. In this chapter the author explains significant components of the story behind that reality.*

The Korean Church has been a missionary church almost from the beginning. Now the Korean Church has become the second largest missionary-sending church in the world,[1] and is leading the missionary movement of the Asian churches.

Brief History of the Korean Church Mission

Mission history of the Korean church can be divided into three periods: (1) mission during the Japanese colonial rule (1907–1957); (2) mission after the independence of Korea (1955–1991); and (3) the current mission (1980–present). Each period is unique in terms of its characteristics.

Mission During Japanese Colonial Period (1907–1957)

The Korean Church's missionary work outside of the Korean peninsula began as early as 1907, when the self-supporting, self-governing Presbytery of the Presbyterian Church in Korea was formed. As the first native Presbytery was constituted, seven men, the first graduates of the Theological Seminary of Korea, were ordained as ministers. Yi Ki-Poong, one of the seven, was commissioned to Jeju Island [2] as the first Korean Protestant missionary. A missionary committee was appointed to administer the missionary effort, and the presbytery ordered the whole Church to make a special offering for this work of propagating the Christian faith.[3]

---

[1] Norimitsu Onishe, 'Korean Missionaries Carrying Word to Hard-to-Sway Places', New York Times, November 1, 2004.

[2] Jeju is an island about sixty miles off the southern coast of the mainland of Korea. It was known to foreigners as the Island of Quelpart.

[3] George Lak-Geoon Paik, *The History of Protestant Missions in Korean 1832–1910* (Seoul, Korea: Yunsei University Press, 1929).

The missionary movement of the Korean Church gradually won the support of the believers, and the Church sent missionaries to other parts of the world. In 1909, the church ordained a second group of nine ministers. The Church sent one of them, Choi Kwan-Heul, as a missionary to Vladivostock, Siberia. In the same year, the Presbytery also sent Han Suk-Jin to minister to the Korean students in Tokyo, and Pang Hwa-Chung to minister to the Korean emigrants in California and Mexico.[4]

In 1912, the Presbyterian Church in Korea made a resolution to send three ministers to Shantung, China – the birthplace of Confucius and Mencius – to mark the organization of the General Assembly. In the following year in 1913, the three ministers went into the mission field. 'Again, as an expression of the joy of the Church in the great event, a 'thank offering' was taken throughout Korea and the three pastors and their families were sent to open a real foreign mission work in the Chinese language for the Chinese in Shantung, China.'[5]

The Korean Church sent about eighty missionaries outside the Korean peninsula during the Japanese colonial regime. The missionaries were sent to Jeju Island, Siberia, Japan, California, Mexico, Manchuria, Shantung, Shanghai, Nanking, Peking, and Mongolia, among others. Most of the missionaries were sent to minister to the Korean immigrants in other countries. Some of them also engaged in evangelizing the natives and the second-generation Koreans, whose languages and cultures were vastly different from the people in Korea.

The most significant of the Korean Church's missions was its mission to Shantung, China, because it was the first to be solely focused on the natives. In fact, it was the first mission carried out by Asian people to other Asian people, since the days of the apostles. Though Korea was a destitute, powerless nation, the Korean Church sent a message across the globe that even a young, poor, and powerless Majority World church could carry on a hefty load of missionary responsibilities.

Unlike the western churches and today's Korean Church, the Presbyterian Church in Korea dispatched her missionaries to Shantung, China in consultation with the American Presbyterian Mission that began work there already and with the approval of the Chinese Church. They worked in the areas where both the Chinese Church and the American Presbyterian Mission assigned them. They, unlike many of today's Korean missionaries, did not transplant their home church in the field. They transferred their membership to the Chinese Church, and served as members of the Chinese Church.

They worked in harmony with the fellow Korean missionaries and in partnership with the Chinese Church and the foreign missions in the field. After their country's loss of sovereignty to Japan, the Korean missionaries carried on

---

[4] Paik *History*, 390.

[5] C. A. Clark, 'The Missionary Work of the Korean Presbyterian Church', *Korean Mission Field* 30:8 (August, 1934).

their missionary responsibilities from the position of weakness. Denominations played a major role in the missionary movement of the church during the Japanese colonial rule.

Mission After Independence of Korea (1955–1991)

After World War II, the missionary movement of the Korean Church was greatly hindered due to political strife in the Far East. The Communist Revolution in the Mainland China and the Korean War compelled the Church to temporarily suspend its missionary work. Although Korea was restored to sovereignty in 1945, the country still suffered from the consequences of war. Nevertheless, the Korean Church soon resumed its missionary work.

Thus, the missionaries during the three decades after Korean Independence carried out their responsibilities without any strong political, ecclesiastical, or financial support. They also carried on their missionary responsibilities from a position of weakness. During this period, most worked under or in partnership with the western missions, as well as with the churches within their mission fields.

Current Korean Mission (1980–Present)

This period can be characterized as 'mission in affluence'. Multiple factors contributed to the phenomenon, including explosive church growth, economic growth, increase in immigration, improved diplomacy, higher education, and accumulated missionary experience. These factors, among others, have enhanced the missionary movement of the Korean Church in recent years. Abundant resources of Korea, however, were not always beneficial. A rise in wealth also brought negative consequences, such as an increased dependence on material resources than on the Holy Spirit and the Word. In doing so, receiving peoples were inadvertently taught to depend on the missionaries and their material resources.

Current Situation of the Korean Mission

The Korean Church has emerged as a new missionary force in the 20th century and has aggressively launched its missionary enterprise into the world. There is a strong sense among church leaders that the Lord is using the Korean Church to usher in his kingdom.

1. Number of Korean Missionaries: According to a survey recently conducted by the Korea World Missions Association, 20,840 Korean missionaries are working in 169 other countries as of January 30, 2010.[6]

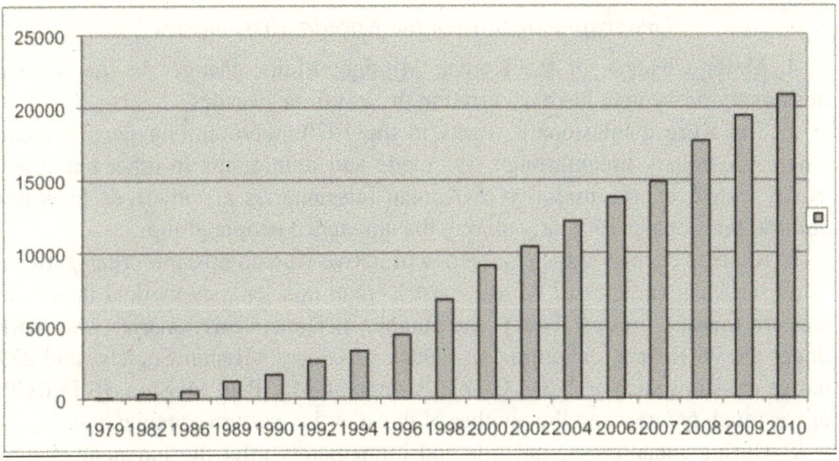

Figure 1. Increase of Korean Missionaries

2. Kinds of Missionaries: In terms of years of service, the number of career missionaries who have served more than three years is 20,819 (94% of total missionaries), and the number of short-term missionaries[7] is 1,311 (6%). While the number of short-term missionaries is increasing gradually, the number of career missionaries increases at a greater rate. In terms of vocation, the number of ordained ministers, including spouses, is 14,697 (66% of total number of missionaries), while the number of lay missionaries is 7,433 (or 34% of the total). The proportion of ordained to non-ordained missionaries is significant.

3. Countries in Which the Korean Missionaries Are Working: Geographical data of Korean missionaries shows that 5,760 (26% of total number of missionaries) are working in Northeast Asia (7 countries) including AX and Japan. 3,810 (17.2%) are in Southeast Asia (11 countries), 1,724 (7.8%) are in Central Asia (10 countries), 1,191 (5.4%) are in South Asia (6 countries), 1,030 (4.7%) are in Eastern Europe and Eurasia (22 countries), 1,038 (4.7%) are in Western Europe (18 countries), 2,325 (10.5%) are in North America and Caribbean Countries (6 countries), 842 (3.8%) are in Latin America (19 countries), 897 (4.1%) are in South-East Africa (20 countries), 349 (1.6%) are in Central and West Africa (20 countries), 809 (3.7%) are in North Africa and Middle East (18 countries), 760 (3.4%) are in the Pacific/Oceania (11

[6] They are sent by 96 Korean denominations and 229 Korean missions at home and abroad. *Korea Missions Quarterly* 9:3 (Spring, 2010), 79.

[7] Short Term Missionaries in this statistics are those who serve in the fields less than three years. Those who visit fields for a couple of weeks are not counted.

countries), 240 (1.1%) are classified as missionaries-at-large and non-residential missionaries, 1,355 (6.1%) are missionaries in home-assignment, apprenticeship, and furlough.[8]

Geographical Data of the Korean Missionaries

4. Major Changes of the Korean Mission: Major changes in the Korean missionary movement have occurred in the last three decades.

a. The Korean missionary works in the 1970s were among people group where missionary breakthrough was made and immigrants in other countries. Today, however, the majority of Korean missionaries are involved in cross-cultural missions, particularly among the unreached people groups.

b. Another change is the emergence of native Korean mission organizations. After the independence of Korea, most Korean missionaries worked under the western mission groups. Today, the number of Korean missionaries who work under the 96 Korean denominations, such as Global Mission Society, and 229 native missions such as UBF, Global Partners, GMF, Paul Mission, INTERCP, etc. is much greater than the number of those in the western organizations.

c. During Japan's colonial rule and immediately after the independence of Korea, the missionary movement was carried on mainly through denominations and local churches, with the exception of a few mission organizations. Today, however, the movement has been carried on both by denominational missions and mission organizations. The number of Korean missionaries sent by mission organizations is slightly greater today than that sent by denominations.

d. Another change in Korean mission after 1980s is in the Korean church's mission from 'mission from a position of weakness' to 'mission from a position of strength'. During Japan's colonial rule and after the Korean War, the missionaries carried out their responsibilities from a position of weakness. During the last three decades, however, they have carried out their responsibilities from a position of strength. Instead of relying on the life-changing power of the Holy Spirit and the Word of God, Korean missionaries today tend to rely on the material resources of the Korean Church.

Contributing Factors to the Growth of the Korean Mission

Various factors have contributed to the missionary movement of the Korean Church. These include divine, human, organizational and contextual factors.

1. Divine Factors: Manifestations of the power of God, including revival movements, kept missions growing.

a. Revival movements, particularly the Great Revival Movement in Pyongyang in 1907, contributed to the growth of mission. Because of the fire of spiritual movements, the Korean Church experienced a dynamic vigor in

---

[8] *KMQ* (Spring 2010), 80-81.

sending missionaries out to surrounding nations. It was customary for the Korean Church to have two revival meetings every year, in the spring and the fall. This tradition helped keep the Korean Church spiritually strong.

b. Manifestations of the power of God and of the Holy Spirit also contributed to the widespread missionary movement. Healings of the sick were often seen in the missionary works on the Island of Jeju.

2. Human Factors: Human factors, such as a spirit of gratitude and capable leaders are notable contributions to the growth of mission of the Korean Church.

a. Koreans by nature are a people who pay a debt of gratitude when they are shown grace. When the Presbyterian Church in Korea dedicated one out of seven of its first ordained ministers as missionary to the Island of Jeju, they were expressing their joy and gratitude to God for founding the Presbytery in 1907. The sending of three missionary families to Shantung, China was also an expression of gratitude to God for establishment of the General Assembly of the Presbyterian Church of Korea, and to China, where they learned the ethical standards of Confucius and Mencius. On both occasions, the Church collected a 'thank offering' throughout the nation to support these missionaries.

b. There were many capable leaders in the Korean Church who made a great impact on the Korean missionary movement. Rev. Kil Sun-Choo, one of the Presbyterian Church in Korea's first ordained pastors, Dr. Helen Kim of Ewha Woman's University, Dr. David J. Cho of Korea International Mission, Dr. John E. Kim of Chongshin University, Joon Gon Kim of the Korea Campus Crusade for Christ, and Tai-Woong Lee of Global Missionary Fellowship are among those who made significant contributions to the growth of Korean mission.

3. Organizational Factors: From the outset, the Korean Church created a mission committee to organize and coordinate missionary works. The Church also collaborated with the western mission groups. The Korean student groups also played a significant role in contributing to the movement.

a. Much of the success of today's growth of mission in the Korean Church is due to the organization of missions committees. By creating structures, the missionary works were simultaneously conducted according to the church's structure (modality) and mission's structure (sodality). When one group was in need of support, the other undertook those responsibilities. In recent years, hundreds of native missions have emerged. Some examples are the Korea World Mission Council (KWMC), Korea World Mission Association (KWMA), World Korean Missionary Fellowship (WKMF), and Mission Korea (MK). These groups have facilitated much of the missionary movement in the past three decades.

b. The typical missions committee of the early Korean Church was comprised of both Korean and western missionaries. The western missionaries mentored the Korean missionaries and helped them to enter into the new mission fields. Unlike today's missionaries, the early missionaries often worked in partnership with the western mission organizations and the national churches, especially in China.

c. Students have played a crucial role in the widespread growth of the Korean mission. During the Japanese colonial rule, students organized missionary societies and sent or supported missionaries. After Korea's independence from Japan, students at Ewha Woman's university, Chongshin University, and Daejon University among others started their own student missionary movement. Since 1990, Mission Korea (led by Chul Ho Han) has held bi-annual mission conferences for students and young Koreans. About 45,000 students have attended the conferences held by Mission Korea and among them, 29,000 have made commitments to serve as missionaries in 2008 alone.

4. Contextual Factors: The contextual factors that have contributed to the spread of the Korean mission movement are: increased Korean immigration, growing influence of the international missionary movements, spread of information, Korea's burgeoning economy, and improved diplomatic ties with foreign nations.

a. Immigration Growth: Political, social and economic conditions in Korea have led to a rise in immigration to countries all over the world. Through immigration, Korean emigrants have become a great missionary force. Wherever Korean Christians have gone, their churches have accompanied or followed them for the quickening of the peoples among whom they have come to live. This is true to the North in Manchuria and Siberia, to the South on the Island of Jeju, to the west in Shantung, China, and to the East in Hawaii, Mexico, on the west coast of America, and among the Korean students in the city of Tokyo.[9] Korean emigrants and residents have served as missionary forces for the evangelization of the world.

b. International Conferences: The success of Korea's missionary movement is connected to international conferences. For example, the first mission to China was strengthened by the International Missionary Council held in Edinburgh in 1910 and the mission to Thailand was related to the work of the World Council of Churches.

c. Information Distribution: The spread of information through newspapers and magazines has stimulated Christians to be aware of their missionary responsibility and has served as a call to action. *The Korea Mission Field*, a monthly publication by the Evangelical Missions in Korea, was distributed to foreign missionaries in Korea and to their sending and supporting bodies. The Christian Messenger, a weekly joint-publication by Methodists and Presbyterians in Korea, was also used as a great informational source. These newspapers shared news about missionaries and their works with the public. The Christian Messenger stirred up the missionary spirit within the Korean Church by printing an article about the missionary David Livingstone in forty-

---

[9] C. A. Clark, 'Korean Student Work in Tokyo', *Korea Mission Field* 11:7 (July 1915).

four consecutive issues. This newspaper also published news about Korean missionaries in other countries. Today, many Christian newspapers and mission journals distribute information about Korean missionary works in many nations.

d. Burgeoning Economic Growth: With the dynamic growth of the Church, Korea's economy has also achieved an incredible growth during the last decade. Abundant material resources of Korea have had both positive and negative effects on Korean mission.

e. Diplomatic Ties with Foreign Nations: Korea's economic growth and successful hosting of the Seoul Olympic Games in 1988 created opportunities for Korea to establish diplomatic ties with almost all nations in the world. Doors were opened wide and today Koreans can travel almost anywhere with a Korean passport.

Strengths and Weaknesses of the Korean Mission

Like any organization, the Korean missionary movement has its strengths and weaknesses.

1. Strengths include: (a) dynamic church growth; (b) ample financial resources; (c) widespread Korean diaspora; (d) strong diplomatic ties with foreign nations; (e) high levels of education; (f) long mission history; and (g) deep passion, courage and commitment for the cause of the Great Commission.

2. Weaknesses include: (a) an unbalanced mission theology; (b) mono-cultural perspective; (c) lack of field research; (d) inappropriate missionary deployment; (e) improper selection and training of missionaries; (f) competitive individualism; (g) weak administration of mission organizations; and (h) lack of cooperation among the sending, receiving, and supporting bodies.

While remaining faithful to the preaching and teaching of God's Word, the Korean Church has in some aspects neglected its social responsibilities. Many leaders have become church-oriented instead of kingdom-oriented. It is imperative that the leaders preach the gospel in both word and deed. Theology produces methodology. The Korean Church must practice a mission theology that incorporates all spheres of society, including politics, business, media, culture, and education.

The Korean culture is in essence mono-cultural. This creates a tendency for missionaries to impart their culture to the people and the churches they serve. It is important to respect the host cultures and communicate the gospel in a way the people of the host culture can accept. Unfortunately, some Korean missions and missionaries work without accurate information or a workable strategy for their fields.

Many missionaries have also been inappropriately selected, trained, and deployed. This results in a lack of cooperation, creating problems of competition among missionaries in the field. Local church pastors who may not have proper knowledge and experience are often in a position of control over their missionaries and their ministries.

Summary

The Korean Church has been a missionary church almost from the beginning of the church. The Korean missionaries are willing to go to any place of the world risking their lives for Christ even to the hardest-to-evangelize corners of the world. The Korean Church's bold faith projection to send one million tent-making missionaries by 2020 and 100,000 career missionaries by 2030 continues to challenge Korean believers around the world. The Korean Church is expected to play an important and unique role in the missionary movement in the 21st century.

Although the Korean Church only received the gospel at the end of the 19th century, it started its cross-cultural mission in the early 20th century – showing churches around world that even a young church can get involved in the missionary work. The Korean Church reconfirmed the biblical principles that even a destitute church suffering under persecution can carry missionary responsibility, and that the work of the lay people is important in the world evangelization. The Church showed that spontaneous ministry of the gospel by lay people, translation of the Bible into native languages, practice of indigenous church planting, thorough teaching of the Bible, right selection and on-the-job training of workers, revival and spiritual renewal, and mission from a position of weakness are essential.

In light of this overview of the missionary movement of the Korean, here are several suggestions for the Korean Church and other Asian churches to consider for more effective mission in the 21st century:

Establish a mission theology that is biblically sound and culturally relevant. The focus must be on the kingdom of God, not on transplanting denominational teaching. Missions should include both bringing people to Christ and enhancing God's rule on earth. Expanding the missionary's own denominational church and imposing his theological tradition should not be considered as legitimate mission work.

Pray for revivals and renewals of the church that the church may continue to become a dynamic and missional church.

Promote dependence on the Holy Spirit and the Word of God, instead of material resources or funding. Careless mission subsidizing will result in dependency problem and will discourage the spontaneous missionary movement.

Build effective partnerships with local churches and other mission organizations at home and abroad. One-way missionary work without consulting national churches and other mission organizations should be avoided. Partnership, particularly in the area of missions research and development is needed. Korean missionaries should not only try to help evangelize the nations, but also help train national churches become missionary churches by showing them examples, educating them on mission, and connecting them for their missionary works in other nations.

Avoid paternalism of the people among whom the missionary works. This only hinders the indigenization of the gospel and the independent spirit of local churches. Instead, missionaries should develop methods that promote self-sustenance in local churches, as the early foreign missionaries did to Korea, according to the Nevius[10] principles.

Continue to hold mission conferences for students and other believers.

Develop viable methods through in-depth field studies, discerning each missionary's unique gifts to ensure strategic deployment and effective ministry.

Learn from past success and failures to better adapt to changing trends as we move into the 21st century.

Develop mission leaders who will lead the missionary movement of the church.

---

[10] Also known as the three-self formula – a self-supporting, self-propagating and self-governing church.

DEBORAH XU: THE STORY OF A CATALYTIC LEADER IN THE CHINESE HOUSE CHURCH MOVEMENT

Yalin Xin

Editors' Note: *Evangelicals around the globe have rejoiced over the burgeoning of the Chinese House Church movement over the past several decades. This case study gives us a better perspective on some of the significant issues in China from an evangelical perspective.*

History has witnessed the phenomenal church growth in China for the past three decades from almost ground zero at the end of the Cultural Revolution in 1976 to the estimated 70-80 million Christians now. Prominent in the midst of this growth are the house church networks in central China, which have grown to be significantly large in membership. The Word of Life (WOL) church is one of the largest house church networks that originated in Henan Province three decades ago.[1] It is also among the most dynamic Christian movements in the history of the Chinese church, with its network of house churches extending to all 23 provinces in China, its ministry covering significant portion of China's rural population, and its membership in tens of millions.[2]

One of the key elements in historical Christian renewal movements is the role played by key leaders.[3] Women leaders at all levels in the WOL have been the backbone of the movement since the beginning three decades ago. Transformed by the Spirit of God, these women dedicated themselves as ready vessels to God and played important roles in this dynamic Christian movement among the rural population. Among these female leaders, Deborah Xu stands out as the recognized 'aunt' of the network, who has had significant influence on the direction, operation, and result of the movement.

Deborah Xu served in the WOL movement as an evangelist, teacher, counselor, leader, theologian and a model. She started to engage herself in

---

[1] The Word of Life movement is also known as Born Again movement, Born Again Family and, sometimes, the Full Scope Church.

[2] For statistic reference of the number of Christians in the Word of Life Church, see Patrick Johnstone, et al, *Operation World* (Cumbria, UK: Paternoster, 2001), 160; Paul Hattaway, *Back to Jerusalem* (Carlisle, UK: Piquant, 2003), 63; David Aikman, *Jesus in Beijing* (Washington, DC: Regnery Publishing, 2003), 86.

[3] See Howard A. Snyder, 'Church Growth Must Be Based on a Biblical Vision of the Church as Vital Community of the Kingdom of God', in Gary L. McIntosh (ed.), *Evaluating the Church Growth Movement – Five Views* (Grand Rapids, MI: Zondervan, 2004), 209-36.

Christian ministry in her teenage years and has served in the house churches for five decades. She made herself available for Christian ministry as she felt called of God and became catalytic in the WOL movement. She is looked to as the top female leader of the movement, an inspiration to those in ministry, and a model for many female Christians in the network.

Early Years and Family Influence

Deborah was born in 1946 in a well-to-do family in Nanyang, Henan Province in central China. Her grandparents became the first Christians in the family during the time when Marie Monsen, a Norwegian missionary, was ministering in Henan. One of Deborah's great aunts was discipled through Marie's ministry and became a strong believer who in turn influenced the rest of the family. Deborah's grandmother and mother were both strong holders of faith and set examples for the younger generations such as Peter and Deborah Xu.[4] In her early childhood, then, Deborah was fully imbued in the teaching, preaching and hymn-singing of the natural house church in her house as well as the Christian witnesses of the adults in the family.

Historically, the development of Chinese Christianity has been intimately interwoven with the theological cross-fires of the time. Denominationalism became a more relevant reality for the Chinese Church from the second half of the nineteenth century when over sixty different mission societies from the West sent their missionaries to various parts of China. At the turn of the twentieth century, however, the theological division between the modernists and the fundamentalists also drew lines within the Chinese Church. This was going to have great implications later on as history witnessed that the gap was only getting wider by the decade, especially after the creation of the Three-Self Patriotic Movement (TSPM) in the early 1950s, whose leaders were chosen primarily from the Modernist camp. TSPM, then, became the officially sanctioned organism to supervise the affairs of the Christian churches in China.[5] The house church network of which Deborah became a leader would be in direct contrast as non-TSPM sanctioned and therefore often subject to suppression from the authorities.

While the modernist-fundamentalist controversy was going on in China in the early 20th century, Marie Monsen's ministry seemed to have left more distinctive marks on the parts of China she served for the majority of her missionary career – Henan Province, where Deborah was born and grew up.

---

[4] Peter Xu is Deborah's elder brother who is recognized as the founding leader of the Word of Life Movement. He is presently residing in the US and serves as the president of the Back to Jerusalem Gospel Mission.

[5] The Three-Self Patriotic Movement (TSPM) is a mechanism created by the Chinese government in 1954 through which the church could be monitored and regulated in accordance with the goals of the new Communist regime that came to power in 1949. It is a government-recognized institution that governs the affairs of the Christian Church in China.

Though Deborah was never able to meet with Marie Monsen in person, Marie's influence as a powerful revivalist and teacher in Henan and northern China greatly inspired Deborah even at the beginning of her faith journey. Characteristics of Marie's theology and ministry were evident in Deborah – a tradition, or ripples of renewal, that was passed on to her through family members of faith who were fruits of Marie Monsen's ministry.

Marie Monsen – Norwegian Evangelical Lutheran Missionary to Henan

In conversation with believers among the WOL movement about the history and stories of the church, the name of Marie Monsen is often and commonly mentioned with appreciation, as someone who dedicated herself to mission in central China as well as a model in ministry that has had significant impact on the WOL movement.

Who was Marie Monsen? The Norwegian Journal of Gender Research has this to say about Monsen,

> One prominent Scandinavian woman missionary who became a successful religious authority in her own right was Marie Monsen (1872–1962) in the Norwegian Lutheran Mission. Her Christian calling and personal religious experience legitimized her own roles as a preacher for men as well as for women and children in China, and as spiritual counselor for male Christian leaders.[6]

Marie Monsen was born and grew up in Bergen, Norway. Her mother was among the advocates in the popular movement led by Hans Nielsen Hauge (1771–1824), which inspired women in ministry and an evangelical missionary movement.[7] Marie responded to the missionary call and joined Norwegian Lutheran Mission (Det norske lutherske Kinamisjonsforbund, later called Norsk Luthersk Misjonssamband).[8] She went to China in 1901 and was stationed in Nanyang, Henan Province. She engaged in educational ministry there, running a girl's school and training Chinese Bible women. In the later part of her time in China, because of evacuation of the Norwegian Lutheran Mission (NLM) from Henan due to social and political instability, Marie Monsen travelled extensively in Northern China, preaching in churches and organizations, instrumental in 'instigating a religious awakening among missionaries and Chinese church leaders'.[9]

Marie Monsen was regarded as the catalyst for the famous Shantung Revival that swept multiple cities and counties in Shantung Province and sent its ripples

---

[6] Inger Marie Okkenhaug, 'Women in Christian Mission: Protestant Encounters From the 19th and 20th Century', *Kilden* (Web Magazine), special edition of *Kvinneforskning* (*Journal of Gender Research in Norway*). Article published January 30, 2004.

[7] See Susanne Soltvedt, 'Hans Nielson Hauge: The Influence of the Hauge Movement on Women of Norway', *UW-la Crosse JUR*, Vol. II (1999), 1-4.

[8] See Lisbeth Mikaelsson, 'Marie Monsen: Charismatic Revivalist – Feminist Fighter', *Scandinavian Journal of History* 28 (2003), 121.

[9] Mikaelsson, 'Marie', 125.

back to Henan Province where she had served in the previous years. Marie Monsen was known for her stress on repentance and born-again spirituality, which left a long-lasting mark on the spirituality of Christians to whom she ministered. Leslie Lyall comments on the role of Marie Monsen,

> The pioneer of the spiritual 'new life movement', the handmaiden upon whom the Spirit was first poured out was Marie Monsen of Norway. Her surgical skill in exposing the sins hidden within the Church and lurking behind the smiling exterior of many trusted Christian – even many a trusted Christian leader – and her quiet insistence on a clear-cut experience of the new birth set the pattern for others to follow.[10]

One of Deborah Xu's great aunts, who came to faith through Maria's ministry, often shared with Deborah about how Maria Monsen was empowered by the Spirit of God leading revival meetings and ministering among women in Nanyang, Henan. In her ministry, Maria always stressed the confession of sins. After each revival meeting she would talk with members of the congregation one by one, checking to make sure that one was saved and finding out those who only pretended to be saved by imitating others in their confessions. Marie stressed what she called the experience of 'suffering from the disease of sin' – that after one, on hearing the message of the gospel, felt it spoke to the heart and became troubled by it. And from this 'disease' one started to regret ever having had previous misconduct and bad behavior. 'Maria always made sure that a believer was filled with the Spirit, and born again, receiving the baptism of the Spirit, just as what happened in Acts. The foundational work in a person's coming to faith is to be, first of all, filled with the Spirit.'[11]

Marie Monsen was one of the most important female figures among the missionaries in Norway. Her ministry embodied 'an unusual blend of feminist commitment, religious fervor and educational zeal ... Marie Monsen's career is a demonstration that spirituality is a sphere open to be negotiated by women, provided they have the charisma or the type of religious experience that is acknowledged as valid and reliable also by the powerful men in their organization.'[12]

Family and Extended Family

In rural China, family, and sometimes extended family, live under one roof or in close vicinity. Children imitate and learn from adults from an early age in participation of their share of responsibility of farm and housework within the family. They also, in the meantime, pick up religious beliefs and ethics from the teaching and modeling of the adult members of the family. By the time

[10] LeslieT. Lyall, 'Historical Prelude', in Marie Monsen (ed.), *The Awakening* (London: Lutterworth Press, 1961), 21.

[11] Personal interview with Deborah Xu in Los Angeles, California in 2009.

[12] Lisbeth Mikaelsson, 'Marie Monsen: Charismatic Revivalist – Feminist Fighter', *Scandinavian Journal of History* 28 (2003), 123.

Deborah was born, her family had been Christians for three generations. Those family traditions and examples of faith would help ground Deborah solidly as a follower of Jesus Christ as she grew up and became one of the most dynamic female leaders of the house church network.

Great Aunt, Mrs. Lin

Deborah's great aunt, Mrs. Lin, was an eager student of Marie's teaching and often attended the chapel where Marie was ministering in Nanyang. Mrs. Lin would often share with Deborah her conversion experience through the ministry of Marie Monsen, which naturally shaped Deborah as she grew in knowledge and faith. Deborah today vividly recounts her great aunt's born-again experience:

> One day she felt 'caught' by the Spirit, feeling urged to confess all the sins in her life. She was not able to open her mouth, however, and her face was pale, obviously under attack from the devil. She struggled so much, recognizing herself as a pool of filthy water, shining on the surface, and yet rotten and stinky under. The Spirit had just made a stir of that dirty water, and she was feeling sick. After this experience, she felt completely released from the bondage of sin and was born again, laughing and rejoicing.[13]

Mrs. Lin became a transformed person through Marie's ministry. In the midst of the Cultural Revolution (1966–1976), Mrs Lin bore witness to her fellow villagers how Jesus could bring peace and joy even in the difficulties and hardship of life. China was experiencing great national turmoil and people were on the brink of despair, losing confidence in the government for providing solutions to natural and human disasters in the Chinese society. The rural population took the harshest blow when natural disasters, mixed with the consequences of government policy errors, left people with hunger and poverty.

Deborah recalls, 'even in the 1960s, my aunt would always sing hymns wherever she was, working in the fields, doing housework at home, visiting neighbors, and made she every opportunity to share the gospel with people. She started to hold meetings in her house, and people would gather around her listening to her telling the Bible story. Often times at the house church meeting, she would heal people of sickness and command the evil spirits to leave the demon-possessed.'[14] As Deborah often followed her aunt to the meetings, she would serve alongside her aunt, reading from the Bible, teaching, praying and healing. Sometimes when needed, Deborah would go to the neighbors herself to teach and conduct healing on behalf of the sick, an important experience of internship for young Deborah.

[13] Personal interview with Deborah Xu in Los Angeles, California in 2009.
[14] Personal interview with Deborah Xu in Los Angeles, California in 2009.

GRANDMOTHER

Another figure in the family who had had great influence in Deborah's faith is her grandmother. Grandma came from a big family with some of its members working as local officials. She was good in Chinese literature, well versed in ancient Chinese poems, and was able to quote freely from Chinese classics. Grandma became a Christian during the time when Marie Monsen was serving in the region, and was inspired by Marie's championship in both education and feminism. Grandma was known as an advocator of feet-unbinding and education for women, and was respected in the area as an educated, righteous, and good Christian. As an educated and influential woman in the neighborhood, Deborah's grandma always drew attentive ears to her sharing from the Bible. Deborah was among the best audience of her grandma's preaching. 'She often emphasized words and phrases such as 'life', 'born again', 'repentance', and 'sin'. She would also often sing and teach people to sing from a Lutheran hymn book.'[15] All of these were identifiable characteristics of Marie Monsen's ministry.

Rural people were sensitive to the evil spirits which, they believed, were often involved in disturbance, sickness, and misfortunes. Local remedies for these problems generally included appeasing the evil spirits by burning incense in the local shrines or temples. Grandma, however, bore witness to power of God over evil spirits in her reaction to such incidence. Deborah recalls,

> When my grandma heard the village bells ring during the night – an indication, which was generally believed by the locals, that the evil spirits was making a stir, she would sit up the whole night long singing Jesus' acts as recorded in the Bible. When the evil spirits disturbed, she would command them to leave with authority. At night when crossing the fields grandma would sing 'Jesus' Soldiers' at the disturbing evil spirits so that people would not fear, recognizing Jesus had power over the evil spirits.[16]

As a woman of strong faith, Grandma was a great influence on Deborah as well as on the rest of the family. Deborah's brother, Peter Xu, was full of gratitude when he remembered his grandma and called her the Abraham of the family and a witness for God.

> Every night Grandma would lead the whole family to kneel down and pray to God, she would always end the family prayers with a hymn: 'I now lie down to sleep peacefully. Pray that our heavenly Father will sustain me until morning. If I am called to leave this world tonight, please save me to return to your paradise.' Every morning when she woke up, she would begin the day with prayer. And prayer accompanied her throughout the day: when she was walking, she prayed that 'my feet will walk in the truth of your word'; when she washed her face, 'water cleanses the face, and blood cleanses the heart. Worshiping the true God, I

[15] Personal interview with Deborah Xu in Los Angeles, California in 2009.
[16] Personal interview with Deborah Xu in Los Angeles, California in 2009.

> am cleansed inside out'; when she swept the floor, 'cleanse my heart of all filth'; when cooking, 'fuel my spiritual fire'. All day long I heard her call on the name of the Lord. And she did so all her life.[17]

Mother

Deborah's mother was also active in evangelistic work in the neighborhood. She was very good at teaching hymns in the house church meetings and instrumental in spreading the gospel in the neighborhood. When Grandma was old and could no longer walk on her own, Deborah's mother would carry her on her back to worship in the local chapel that was four miles away. People were touched by their faith and testimony and even years later they still talk about how the mother carried the grandmother on her back and walked for miles in order to attend Christian meetings.

Growing up in such a family of faith, Deborah was presented with good examples to follow even from a very young age. Her own faith grew even as she naturally imitated the adults in the family in what they exemplified in life and ministry. She received much support in her faith journey because of the opportunity she had to be born in such a family of faith.

Beginning of Ministry

'I grew up in a Christian family, and it was only natural for me to follow the models of the women in the family and to dedicate my life for Christian ministry. As a teenager I did not think of anything else in terms of my future vocation apart from being a preacher or an evangelist.'[18]

Deborah stood out in the family and in the village as bright and gifted. Coming to Christian faith at a very young age, Deborah was known for her kindness toward others and seriousness about her faith. Siblings would often find her on her knees in the dirt of the fields or behind the hay, committing herself to long prayers, totally oblivious of the things that were going on around her. Her older sister recalls, 'she would always unreservedly point out the sins in us and urge us to repent before the Lord in prayer. She would also encourage us to have faith. She was an encourager, sometimes like a big sister instead of a younger sister'.[19]

Deborah would also give up her own things to her siblings or whoever she saw as in need without ever seeming to be concerned for her own need. She would sleep on the hotel floor so that others in company could sleep on the beds. Once Deborah saw Sister M appearing cold on a winter day. She went

---

[17] Yalin Xin, *Inside China's House Church Network* (Lexington, KY: Emeth Press, 2009), 78.
[18] Personal interview with Deborah Xu in Los Angeles, California in 2009.
[19] Personal interview with Deborah's elder sister in Shanxi, China in 2010.

quietly inside the room, took off her own sweater and offered to Sister M, who, when putting it on, still felt the warmth in the sweater.[20]

In 1963, at the age of seventeen, Deborah prayed a prayer of dedication to the Lord as she later wrote down on one of the calendar pages: 'Lord, you love me so much. How can I repay the love you have shown to me. I promise you this day that I will remain celibate all my life to serve you'. Her brother, Peter Xu, found the note folded in a Bible by accident. Tears ran down Peter's face when he read this prayer note.[21] Peter was appreciative of his sister for her dedication and the blessing she brought to ministry: 'I'm extremely thankful that the Lord made my sister as my spiritual partner. She was called by the Lord when she was 17 years old and dedicated her whole life to the Lord. She serves as a beautiful example in the front lines. Brothers and sisters [designate] her as a mother of the church'.[22]

As a teenager, Deborah took over the responsibility of teaching the children after school. Every afternoon, children in the neighborhood would gather around in the yard waiting for Deborah, who would tell Bible stories, teach songs of praise, and share from the Word of God. Many of these children were to become future evangelists and co-workers among house churches. These early exercises in teaching and leadership were important experiences for Deborah as she devoted herself to more pervasive involvement in the house church ministry once churches started to grow significantly in number and size in a wave of revivals during the 80s.

Like everybody else in rural China, as a young adult Deborah would go to work in the fields daily with the rest of the villagers. Her maturity and kind-heartedness won her the trust and support of the young girls and their parents in the village. They respected her as an older sister with wisdom and character. So young girls would come to visit Deborah with questions and open hearts, which provided an opportunity for Deborah to teach these young girls from the Bible and lead them to faith in Jesus Christ. Soon, some twenty girls became regulars in the house church meetings with Deborah being the leader, where they would engage in prayer, singing, and listening to what Deborah would share from the Bible.

Hymn singing was a lot of fun for the young girls in the village. Deborah taught them note by note, often accompanied by body movement as well, providing an opportunity for the girls to be expressive in a context where such activity was not always encouraged. They soon learned enough hymns to sing along whenever possible, so that one would often hear hymn singing in the village. The teenagers were so enthusiastic and joyful about learning hymns and the Bible that they would keep copying the hymns and Bible verses during

---

[20] Personal interview with Deborah's elder sister in Shanxi, China in 2010.
[21] Personal interview with Peter Xu in Los Angeles, California in 2010.
[22] From *Christianity Today* (Web-only), 48 (February 2004) 2.

and after the gathering. 'It was like a scene in the Millennium', Deborah recalls.[23]

God allowed trials to come across Deborah's path, preparing Deborah for the challenges in ministry later on. After she had made the promise to the Lord to remain single in order to serve him wholeheartedly, she would often encounter temptation that would stir some inner struggle – 'spiritual conflict' as she would call it. In order to win over the conflicts, Deborah would create ways to deal with the situation. She once even cut off all her hair so that she would look like a boy and even asked her niece to call her 'uncle'.[24] Her determination influenced a lot of girls who would later learn from Deborah's example to remain celibate in ministry. Deborah's dedication was later to be a model that was encouraged and promoted among the WOL leaders and evangelists.

Later on, young people from other villages also came for the meeting at Deborah's place, and it became necessary that meetings be organized in multiple places to meet the growing need. Deborah then took some helpers with her to the neighboring villages to organize house church meetings. These meetings were always filled with people.

As more house churches were established in the nearby villages, Deborah started to make itinerant visits to each of these house churches within the county boundary. The teaching in the house churches revolved around the theme of the cross. She always identified God as the source of revivals as the house churches started to grow. 'The Spirit of God worked mightily in these meetings, drawing people to the house church meeting from every home.' Very often the house was filled with people, in the sitting-room, bedrooms, walkways, and courtyard. People would use loose bricks as stools in the yard. As the crowd grew when there was no longer any room inside the yard, loud speakers were used so that people sitting outside the house could hear.

The presence of the Spirit was evident. Some sick were healed as they were still on their way to the meeting place. The weeping of those in repentance was loud and touching as the Holy Spirit 'made a stir in the hearts of the people. Open confessions were commonplace in the revivals and people came out of the meetings completely changed. This was how the Spirit worked in the house church gatherings in the 1970s.'[25]

This was the period of time that was also referred to as the period when 'revival furnaces' multiplied in the early 1970s. Revivals started through Deborah's (and her mother's) ministry were like a 'revival furnace', producing heat to its surroundings and drawing people to it. Soon 'the whole neighborhood became Christian and became a spiritual center. Without notice, the 'revival furnace' spread outward and more 'furnaces' were created.'[26]

---

[23] Personal interview with Deborah Xu in Los Angeles, California in 2010.
[24] Personal interview with Peter Xu in Los Angeles, California in 2010.
[25] Personal interview with Deborah Xu in Los Angeles, California in 2010.
[26] See Yalin Xin, *Inside China's House Church Network* (Lexington, KY: Emeth Press, 2009), 83-84.

When the local authorities started to come to disturb the meetings and make arrests, Deborah and her co-workers would move from place to place to avoid being targeted. Wherever they went, they would continue leading the revival meetings. Thus more house churches were established as they ministered in new areas.

Leader of the House Church's First Trans-provincial Mission Team

The basic and foundational structure of the Word of Life (WOL) movement is the house church, established through the evangelistic ministry of itinerant evangelists sent by the Gospel Band, which is closely related to and supported by Theological Education (underground seminaries or training schools). Thus the Established Churches, Theological Education, and the Gospel Band form a solid support for the whole WOL movement, often intimately illustrated by Christians as an ancient Chinese cooking vessel supported by three solid legs. The three constituent parts of the WOL work closely together to keep the ministry wheel spinning outward, thus enlarging the WOL network.[27] This movement dynamic gradually took shape in the early 1980s after the first WOL trans-provincial mission.

In the early 1980s, the churches in Henan experienced great revivals and the house churches expanded outwards. Nanyang district in Henan where Marie Monsen was based during the first quarter of the 20th century became the center of the revived house churches and the base where future ministry was directed. Leaders of the WOL received requests from various parts of China for evangelistic teams to be sent to the regions. In prayer and fellowship the WOL leaders decided to send out their first trans-provincial evangelistic team to Sichuan Province, the hometown of Xiaoping Deng, then paramount leader of China.

In the early 1980s, seventeen young evangelists were chosen to form the first trans-provincial evangelistic team to enter Sichuan province. Deborah was the leader of the team of evangelists who were then designated as 'Messengers of the Gospel' (hereafter, MGs). This may have been the first trans-provincial mission team sent from the house churches in China.

They got on the train with one-way tickets to Sichuan. The team had one contact in Sichuan. Their aim was to share the gospel with the people in Sichuan. They did not have a guaranteed financial provision for the duration of their mission; neither did they have money for the return tickets. What they had was prayer and trust in the Spirit of God. It may have looked like a doomed mission humanly speaking, with only a goal and direction, leaving the rest to the leading of the Holy Spirit. But the result was a big boost for the faith of believers and encouragement for further mission efforts in the years to come.

---

[27] For a more detailed description of the WOL structure, see Yalin Xin, *Inside China's House Church Network* (Lexington, KY: Emeth Press, 2009), 137.

As soon as the team arrived at Sichuan, they started to busy themselves in preparation for the work. Through arrangements the team was received into a hospitality family where they started to host evangelistic meetings as well as sending out evangelistic pairs to the neighboring villages.[28] Deborah went with local Christians to the homes of new believers and seekers to get rid of the idols such as paintings and clay idolatry figures. This was an integral part of the house church ministry at that time because it was common for rural homes to have idolatry images and altars even after the households had begun coming to faith. The WOL leaders ruled that it was unacceptable to have images and altars which hindered work of the Holy Spirit in the lives of new believers and seekers. The team also evangelized people on the streets and entered every home where they were invited to share the gospel message. All of these MGs carried portions of the Bible, hymn booklets, and gospel tracks on their backs as they went from place to place, distributing them as they saw needs.

Deborah and her teammates were in prayer most of the time as they walked to a new village. They took every opportunity to share the gospel message with anyone they met, on the streets, outside peoples' houses, and even in the fields. Sometimes, after interacting with people for a while, they were invited into the house. Often the host family would go out and invite extended families and neighbors to the meeting, who were eager to hear the Christian message. 'This was where we bore most of our evangelistic fruit. People would come to a house church meeting, being taught the truth from the Bible, opening their hearts to the Lord Jesus and being saved, being given the portions of the Bible and other materials. We then laid hands on some who already had the calling and gifts for leadership roles. Thus a house church was established.'[29]

In less than a month, sixteen house churches were established through the ministry of the evangelists.[30] Even the village's Party Secretary's house became a house church. Hospitality families were established so that future evangelists could be received and discipleship trainings could be housed there. Deborah attributed the result of the evangelistic effort totally to God, 'The hearts of the people were wide open to the gospel at that period of time. This was of course the work of the Spirit who heard our prayers and already went ahead of the team and prepared the hearts of the people.' Seekers and new believers were all eager to receive the Christian materials and request contact information from the team members for future guidance.[31]

Then one day all seventeen MGs were arrested in Sichuan after they were rounded by the local police. One female team member claimed responsibility

---

[28] Hospitality Family (*jie dai jia ting*) is a term commonly used among the house churches in central China referring to devoted Christian families that open their houses or other properties for the purpose of holding various house church meetings, trainings, and receiving co-workers, etc.

[29] Personal interview with Deborah Xu in Los Angeles, California in 2009.

[30] See Yalin Xin, *Inside China's House Church Network* (Lexington, KY: Emeth Press, 2009), 87.

[31] Personal interview with Deborah Xu in Los Angeles, California in 2009.

for the Christian literature in the team's possession. As they were detained in the local police station, all seventeen MGs fasted for seven days and nights appealing to God in prayer for each other and for the situation. They were then sent back to the detention center in Henan where they served terms of differing lengths. All of them were released before the Chinese New Year in 1983. This was the beginning of the Gospel Band in the WOL church as it started to explore strategic evangelization into the surrounding regions and provinces. The stories and examples of the church's first trans-provincial mission have become part of the training and reference for future MGs.

Upon release, the MGs came together for fellowship and reflection, and felt God was teaching them the spiritual value and significance of service and ministry in the Lord by means of chains and imprisonment. 'Our faith increased because the mark of the cross, which we saw as a reward, was added onto our physical bodies. And the Macedonian call became louder to our ears.'[32] After that evangelistic teams were dispatched back to Sichuan on many occasions. Deborah was able to reflect on this mission experience and use it in her teaching and training of evangelists in the years to come as she found herself speaking at leadership training sessions, co-workers' retreats, and providing counsel to female evangelists.

WOL Training Manuals

The WOL house church network is known for systems of training and organizational structure that were developed to meet the need of the growing house churches under its umbrella. It is sometimes referred to as the 'Full Scope Church' by the authorities because of extensive regions in China that it covers. The training system started from evangelistic meetings, after which it moved on to Life Meetings, Truth Meetings, and underground seminary trainings of different levels. There was also training for pastoral and administrative elders of local house churches that were called Pillars' Theological Education.

This training system was supported primarily through Theological Education (TE), one of the three constituent parts of the WOL movement. As the network started to grow significantly, there was great need for training manuals that could be used in training and teaching. Commissioned by the church, a committee was formed, with Peter Xu as the leader and Deborah as the primary contributor, to reflect biblically and theologically, write and edit the first training manual for the house church. The work came out in handwritten form in 1984, titled, 'Seven Principles'. It basically addressed seven areas of theology and ministry that the WOL Christians judged as important and relevant: (1) salvation through the cross, (2) the way of the cross, (3) discerning

---

32 Personal interview with Deborah Xu in Los Angeles, California in 2009.

the adulteress, (4) building the church, (5) providing for life, (6) interlink and fellowship, and (7) frontier evangelism.

When the manual came out, it was immediately hand-copied into multiple copies and used in leadership trainings and retreats, and received very positive responses. Soon the manual was revised for print, so that, from 1985 on, thousands of copies were available at network conferences for leaders from various regions to take back to their home areas for teaching and training purposes. The manual was designed to be used in all levels of ministry within the WOL network, from Life Meetings, Truth Meetings, short-term training, to all levels of TE training. From time to time special committees were organized for revisions and additions to the manual as Christians in the network constantly reflected on the Word of God in ministry.

As a recognized leader and mentor in the network, Deborah was always sought out by younger co-workers in the network for sessions of consultation on both spiritual and physical concerns. Almost on top of the list of common questions and doubts that many young evangelists had was about marriage. As a simple matter of fact, the backbone of the WOL house church network was the young adult evangelists, and the majority of these young adult evangelists were female. It was only natural that these young evangelists became interested in fellow co-workers of the opposite sex and started dating. And issues would then emerge.

The WOL church encouraged those serving in different levels of ministry to remain celibate while in service. Leaders of the WOL network, such as Deborah and many other female leaders, including regional, district, and even area leaders primarily consisted of those who were committed to remain celibate for the sake of ministry. The rationale for this appeal was based on practicality and not on theology. 'When remaining single in Christian service, one would devote himself/herself more wholeheartedly to the work without being distracted by issues that families tended to have.'[33] Of course, the theological stress on imminent eschatological expectation at least played its role here as well in a community whose theology leaned toward a pre-millennium, dispensationalist view.

The WOL church had passed a 'Co-workers' Code of Behavior' that clearly discouraged casual dating and marriage proposals without first seeking God's will and the approval of the church.[34] Sometimes young evangelists were disciplined and stopped from their ministry for dating without consultation with leaders of the church. This caused a lot of frustration among the young co-workers. In the face of these issues and concerns, Deborah went on her knees praying to God for wisdom and instruction. She studied the biblical teaching on the topic and reflected on the reality of the WOL church of the time, before she

[33] Personal interview with Deborah Xu in Los Angeles, California in 2009.

[34] See '*Ye di shen xue yuan gen zong bao dao zhi er*' (Report of the Seminaries of the Fields, Part Two). *Zhong guo yu jiao hui* (China and the Church) 57 (Jan.–Feb., 1987).

committed herself to writing a training manual, *Marriage and Celibacy,* that was later pervasively used in the house churches. Issues were dealt with and agreement was achieved in the community.

In *Marriage and Celibacy* Deborah recognized that marriage was instituted by God as a blessing for humans and should not be treated lightly. She referenced biblical teachings in God's blessing on marriage to humans as they were found in Matthew 19:4-6, Genesis 2:18, 24-25, 1 Cor. 7:1-3, 9-28, Proverbs 18:22, and Proverbs 19:14. She warned against casual pursuit of the opposite sex as it was modeled in Genesis 6:1-3. The booklet paid attention to culture and cultural traditions as it addressed various aspects in marriage including the significance of marriage, the objective of marriage, proposal in marriage, engagement, and wedding from a biblical perspective.

On the emerging reality of disproportional ratio of male and female Christians, thus posing a problem for marriage within the Christian community, Deborah examined the reality of the situation and asked God to raise more brothers in the church. In conjunction with the church's call for more devoted ministry through celibacy among its leaders, she made a practical appeal: 'May there be no marriage in the church that is outside the biblical principle and God's will. If God does not change the reality of the shortage of brothers, sisters need to accept this blessing and dedicate themselves to Christ as virgins, so that Deborah's wish be fulfilled a hundred fold.'[35]

Teacher, Revivalist, Leader and Model

In 1983 the Chinese authorities launched a nation-wide counter-crime campaign in which the house church leaders became targets of opposition. Deborah was the team leader in the mission trip to Sichuan and was the natural target. So she left home and stayed with hospitality families wherever she went. Because of her strong faith, knowledge of the Bible, and experience in walking with the Lord, she and several other co-workers took the responsibility of leading the first training classes of the underground seminaries that were to be established in the next few years, first in Henan, and later into other provinces.

Unique in the WOL network, leaders stressed biblical and theological training in ministry. The initial organized training started in the beginning of 1980s when five- to seven-day intensive training sessions were often organized to equip committed believers for effective evangelism and church ministry. The trainees would then return to their home churches to involve themselves in evangelism as well as discipling new converts. This went on until the time was ripe for establishing more formal theological training schools. Toward the end of 1985, the first house church seminary, locally termed Theological Education, was established in S County, Henan Province. It was a three-month intensive

[35] Deborah Xu, *Marriage and Celibacy*, unpublished booklet.

training program and was known as 'the Seminary of the Field' through published literature on the underground church.[36]

Seminary and Theological Education

Deborah was actively involved in taking charge of the ministry of establishing the seminary. This included meeting with potential trainers for fellowship and interviews (and often times this involved a time of training), finalizing location, organizing prayer support chains, and supervising the recruiting of student trainees, etc. She both gave leadership to Theological Education and taught at the training sessions. Often these trainings took place in hospitality families in more remote villages. Students were in the closed-up location for the entirety of their training, totally immersed in the learning, devotion, prayer, worship, and community. As the teacher of the seminaries, Deborah would also take on the responsibility of counselling the student trainees. God had given her the gift of counselling even when she was still a teenager in the village, and now the experience had helped her to be more effective in mentoring these devoted young Christians who would soon go out as MGs into frontier evangelism.

Revival

The mid-1980s was a time when Christianity experienced a phenomenal revival in various parts of China. There was the gradual freedom in the air when the Cultural Revolution (1966–1976) ended. 'The church in many areas of China is growing at a staggering rate, as we have seen…the spectacular growth of the church in many parts of China is evidence of a remarkable work of the Holy Spirit.'[37]

The WOL church was able to make use of the freedom of the time to engage more broadly in evangelistic ministries in Henan and surrounding areas. As the church sent out evangelistic teams to various regions, with some ground work done, they would organize evangelistic meetings, followed by Life Meetings, Truth Meetings, and short-term training. In the process house churches were established, local leaders were chosen, and dedicated believers were selected for more training to be future MGs. Thus, a cycle of ministry was gradually taking shape that was to become the norm of WOL ministry in the years to come.

Revival was taking place in multiple regions among the WOL house churches and the ripples of revival naturally expanded outwards. Typically in the ministry pattern of the WOL system, MGs were instrumental in the revivals as they travelled from place to place ministering among the people. 'The hearts of the people were ready for the gospel before it was preached to them. In revival meetings, co-workers needed to pick out those from the family who

---

[36] See '*Ye di shen xue yuan gen zong bao dao zhi yi*' (Report on the Seminary of the Fields) *Zhong guo yu jiao hui* (China and the Church) 6 (Sept.–Oct., 1986).

[37] Tony Lambert, *The Resurrection of the Chinese Church* (Wheaton, Ill.: OMF IHQ Ltd., 1994), 156.

were ready for the message to participate in the meetings. Sometimes people in the family fought to be included in the meetings. All wanted to participate and yet it was up to the decision of the responsible co-workers.'[38]

Deborah provided support for the MGs who were responsible for leading the revival meetings, typically through prayer and encouragement as she identified prayer for God's Spirit to work in these meetings as basic to yielding of fruits. So she was on her knees multiple hours a day on her own and with fellow co-workers petitioning and interceding. Fasting was a common practice for the WOL co-workers in ministry like this. Very often those who were involved in leading the revival meetings would fast 2-3 days before the events ever took place. 'Without prayer, there is no power', as Deborah often stressed.

Deborah recalled one of the series of revival meetings in the mid 80s in Henan,

> Every night baptism in hundreds for 2 months. Sometimes when the Holy Spirit had already prepared the hearts people were saved even before the preaching. Hospitality family would cook all day long with smoke coming out of the chimney all the time. Police noticed and came to disturb. When they entered the courtyard, they were overwhelmed with headache. One police head was sickened with cancer. A believer went to evangelize him, asking him to cry out to God for healing and help, and he came to faith.[39]

Deborah was a model for many women leaders of the WOL network and other house church groups. She was often looked up as gifted, devoted, and empowered for ministry. She was also a big sister, aunt, and someone who was always ready to others. Many of those who came to faith through Deborah's ministry eventually became co-workers in the house churches. 'She was a trumpet of God, calling people to service. She was an encourager of believers for ministry', as one of the former MGs said. The MGs who came back for retreats would always gather around Deborah with stories and questions to share with her. And Deborah would always deal with the questions in Bible studies she led in retreats.[40]

Persecution

After Peter Xu was arrested in 1988 due to plans to meet with Billy Graham, the task of leading the movement naturally revolved around Deborah, who sought every decision from God in prayer and fellowship. Deborah, together with Sister J, took on the leadership role in the network, organizing national and regional co-workers' meetings, directing training affairs, visiting with leaders of various levels, etc., when Xu was not around.

---

[38] Personal interview with Deborah Xu in Los Angeles, California in 2009.
[39] Personal interview with Deborah Xu in Los Angeles, California in 2009.
[40] Personal interview with Sister M in Henan, China in 2010.

When opposition became fierce, revivals took place all the more as house church gatherings were intensified and underground training strengthened. Deborah travelled from place to place, holding leadership meetings, teaching at training centers, and preaching in revival meetings. The news of Peter Xu's arrest in 1988 actually became an encouragement for Deborah, as well as for others serving in the network, to persist in what she felt called to do, ready to bear marks of persecution. She had already put fear behind her facing the fact that, as a top leader of the WOL network, she was in constant danger of being targeted by the authorities. And she had indeed been arrested on multiple occasions and put in detention or under house arrest.

Leadership

In trials like severe external opposition against the church and internal difficulties, Deborah demonstrated herself as a leader of great wisdom and strong faith in the Lord. She encouraged fellow Christians with examples of the early church in Acts, how, in prayer, fellowship, encouragement and support, Christians stood in solidarity with one another. In one of the interviews Deborah shared the story of one female MG, Sister L, who was planning to return to her hometown for a visit with elderly parents and siblings after years of ministry away from home. On hearing of the news that Peter Xu was arrested, Sister L immediately gave up the furlough opportunity and continued her ministry where she was. To WOL Christians, harsh times as such were the moments when they especially needed to stay with 'family'. Deborah explained, 'I was in the leadership of organizing training/meeting/fellowship during the time when Peter was not around. Sister J was another leader of the church, organizing the fellowship meetings and training. Whenever unexpected difficult situations arose among members of the house churches, people would come to me for advice and counselling. This just came naturally over the years.'[41]

On one occasion, in the mid-1990s, Deborah had to leave J City, where she had been teaching, to N City to organize a month-long annual conference that involved representatives of WOL pastors from across the country. Deborah was responsible for coordinating the speakers for the conference, making sure of the hospitality family and supplies for the event, security precautions, making necessary communication, etc. During conference, Debora led prayer meetings as well as participating in fellowship and consultation with pastors from different regions who came with reports as well as questions. This was typically a time when the network examined the work in different parts of the country and reflected on the ministerial experience. Visions and directions of the movement were also shared in the meetings as participants engaged in reflecting on the Word of God together. Deborah's room was always full of

[41] Personal interview with Deborah Xu in Los Angeles, California in 2009.

people day and night, sharing, consulting, studying the Bible, praying, and singing.

When Peter Xu was released in 1991, he went to P City for a leadership meeting. After hearing reports from regional leaders, Peter realized that the WOL network was growing even while he was locked away in the three years between 1988–91. Persecution is often identified as a factor for church growth. Christian solidarity, however, in times of opposition, and persistence in ministry empowered by the Holy Spirit, preaching, evangelizing, teaching, serving and loving spoke volume to believers.

Deborah's teaching and preaching often stressed the repentance of sins and importance of possessing new life in Christ through rebirth. One of verses she often quoted in her sharing was from Acts 2:37, 'When the people heard this, they were cut to the heart and said to Peter and the other apostles, 'Brothers, what shall we do?' Peter replied, 'Repent and be baptized, everyone of you, in the name of Jesus Christ for the forgiveness of your sins. And you will receive the gift of the Holy Spirit.'' She would train those serving in the house churches to prepare sermons that allowed the Spirit of God to cut right to the hearts of the congregation, to convict and revive. In time this stress naturally became a measure by which believers evaluated preachers – whether or not the message cut to the hearts. Deborah recalls, 'everyone wanted to hear more when the message cut right to the hearts, and felt disappointed when it did not.'[42]

Deborah shared from her experience of identifying those who did not possess new life through the rebirth experience. 'You find such in all levels of the church ministry who seem to be able to teach and speak, and yet without life, sooner or later they will fall into temptation and bring damage to ministry. So it is important to identify those who need to be born again before they can be trusted with any forms of ministry of the church.'[43] As a frequent speaker in leadership training sessions and retreats, Deborah made sure that those serving in the ministries of the church got the message so that not only leaders themselves reexamine themselves constantly of their relationship with God as they serve, but also they would, in their ministry, partner with God in producing born-agains rather than the merely 'saved' Christians.

This emphasis seems natural when we take into consideration of the legacy left by Marie Monsen in her ministry in Henan and her role in Shangtung Revival in the early 20th century, when she was known for her radical insistence on a thorough repentance of one's sins and being born again of all true Christians. It was then quite common a phenomenon that in revival meetings she conducted, 'The people were struck to the bone with God's conviction, were sickened by their sin, and revival broke out', while Christians

---

[42] Personal interview with Deborah Xu in Los Angeles, California in 2009.

[43] Personal interview with Deborah Xu in Los Angeles, California in 2009.

were renewed through a thorough repentance and rededication of their lives to God.[44]

Prayer

Deborah is known as a woman of prayer among fellow house church believers. For almost all her life she has been on her knees for extended long prayers and intercession everyday. Even as a young teenager, Deborah was already exercising intimate communion with God in her unique style, spending time wherever and whenever she could on her knees. This was often witnessed by her siblings and peers. She cultivated a habit of communicating with God multiple times a day, praising God, letting God know her inner thoughts and struggles and questions, asking God to show His will in decisions she needed to make, blessings on the things she intended to do, and interceding for the needs of others, spiritually and physically.

Later on as she started to take on more responsibilities of the network as it grew significantly in size and influence, her prayer life became more evidently witnessed and appreciated by co-workers around her. 'She would seek God's will in prayer for everything before she makes any move or decision, which is also an emphasis of the WOL teaching, that in everything seek the will of God in prayer until the Spirit brings unity in community so that everyone is on the same page as to what measures should be taken', said Sister S.

In almost every kind of meeting of the house churches, i.e. prayer meetings, Bible studies, co-workers' meetings, retreats, leadership meetings, fellowship meetings and underground seminary training, people would often find Deborah already on her knees in prayer well before the meeting started. And fellow Christians respected Deborah as a powerful prayer warrior because in her prayers she was able to engage God's promises in Scripture. 'She prays with the Bible', as one of her fellow co-workers said. Years of prayer on her knees left clear marks on Deborah as well as many other believers of the WOL: thick callous on the knees. To Deborah, and others in the house churches, praying on her knees is a natural expression of humbleness when approaching a holy God in honor and respect.

Confession of Faith of House Churches in China

In 1998, Deborah, representing the WOL house church network, participated in the drafting of the 'Confession of Faith of House Churches in China'. Representatives from four large house church networks came together in Beijing studying, praying, and reflecting on the Word of God for the sake of drafting a united declaration of faith. The rational behind this effort was, first of all, a practical step in the unity process. After separating from one another for

---

[44] Paul Hattaway and Joy Hattaway, 'From the Front Lines', *Asia Harvest* (March, 2002), 4.

more than a decade, leaders of house church networks came back together for fellowship and unity. 'A spirit of unity prevailed among them, believing that it pleases the Lord for them to come together as members of the same body of Christ and to promote spiritual unity among them for more effective evangelism in the next century.'[45] Since then, there had been some collaboration in ministry across the different house church networks such as joint training sessions and mutual fellowship meetings. Secondly, this Statement served as clarification over controversies, primarily fabricated accusation from the authorities against these large house church groups.

> In order to arrive at a common standard of faith among house churches in China, in order to establish a common basis for developing unity among fellow churches in China and overseas, in order to let the government and the Chinese public understand the positions of our faith, and in order to distinguish ourselves from heresies and cults, top leaders of a few major house church groups have come together in a certain village in North China in November, 1998, to pray together, to search the Scriptures, and to draft the confession of faith as shown below.[46]

The Confession dealt with seven doctrinal categories that reflect the basics of orthodox historical Christianity: The Bible, Triune God, Christ, Redemption, the Holy Spirit, the Church, and the Last Days. Jonathan Chao, the late president of China Ministries International, helped organize and facilitate the important work. The committee of representatives convened for three days, reflecting on the important biblical and theological themes, each from a slightly different perspective, and yet reaching unity in the process of fellowship with one another. The Statement of Faith came out in published form in CMI's journal, *China Prayer Letter and Ministry Report* in February, 1999 as an expression of unity movement among the house churches as well as a defence of their orthodoxy in theology in the midst of controversies on heresies and cults, as well as accusations against the house churches. The backlash of the publication, though, was the arrest of several of the participants.

Back to Jerusalem Ministries

Spreading the Gospel back to Jerusalem (BTJ) has been considered to be a call from God to the Chinese Christians to carry on the task of evangelization to all the remaining unreached areas in the world west of China, which includes Asia, the Middle East, and North Africa. Although the original vision was not clearly defined and promoted, in comparison to the BTJ vision as it is understood presently, in the first attempts by Christians from several different institutions

---

[45] David Aikman, *Jesus in Beijing* (Washington, DC: Regnery Publishing, 2003), 295.
[46] Jonathan Chao (trans.), 'Chinese House Church Confession of Faith', *China Prayer Letter and Ministry Report* 149 (November, 1998–February, 1999), 2-4. See also David Aikman, *Jesus in Beijing* (Washington, DC: Regnery Publishing, 2003), 297.

and churches in the 1930s and 1940s, testimonies of their convictions, success and failure, suffering, and perseverance continue to impact believers. Simon Zhao was one such example, whose calling and experience had inspired many people. He had continued to minister after his release from prison where he spent many years of his life for the sake of spreading the gospel to the western part of China and beyond. He was among the few first-generation BTJ evangelists who was still living in the 1990s.

In the renewal of the BTJ vision, however, Deborah played an integral role in that she was instrumental in reconnecting the key figure in the early BTJ movement in the 1940s with the house church community in central China in the 1990s. Here is the story:

Bringing back Simon Zhao

When MGs from Xinjiang came back to report about believers who shared the BTJ vision, and stories about Simon Zhao experience and testimony in the early BTJ mission, leaders of house church networks assigned Deborah and Sister L the task of going into Xinjiang to bring back Simon Zhao to the house churches in central China. This was an important task because house church networks had just started to explore ways for unity after having been separated from each other since the mid-1980s. Bringing back Simon Zhao to rekindle the evangelistic vision given to the Chinese to take the gospel back to Jerusalem was the common desire shared among the leaders of different house church networks. And therefore, Deborah and Sister L went as representatives of united house church networks in China.

Without the knowledge of Zhao's exact location, Deborah and Sister L went through county after county looking for Simon Zhao. Due to the poor transportation system in that part of the country and also lacking supply for themselves, they frequently had to ask for rides on construction transportation trucks to take them wherever possible and covered the rest of the journey on foot. It was weeks before they eventually found Zhao in a meeting one night where he was preaching. They waited until the end of the gathering before confronting him with their intent. Deborah assured Zhao the confidence and conviction of Christians in China's Midland (Henan Province and its surrounding areas) that it was God's appointed time for the BTJ vision to be renewed among the house churches. Zhao listened carefully without a response, as he always waited upon what he received from the Lord before making any decision. The group prayed together, and in prayer they sought God's blessing as well as spiritual unity among them in this effort.

Early the next morning, Deborah saw Zhao on his knees in the grass on the nearby hill. He came back and kept quiet before God and wept in prayer. Everyone present knelt with him in prayer realizing that God was dealing with him. Scriptural verses poured out from Zhao's prayer, from which Deborah joyfully sensed that God had sanctioned her mission to bring Zhao to the house churches. Rising from his prayer Simon Zhao informed Deborah of his decision to go to Henan to meet with the house church saints there.

Because Zhao needed time to make proper arrangements for his ministry before he could travel to Henan, and Deborah had to leave without him for her responsibilities in TE-3 training at the house churches. She left money for Zhao, who was in his 80s then, to take a sleeper train to Henan, and made arrangements for him to stay with hospitality families in L City when he arrived. Deborah later understood that Simon Zhao never took a sleeper, nor even a seat. He just found some space on the floor of the train all the way from Xinjiang to Henan and donated the rest of the money to someone in need! Christians in the house churches were greatly touched by the testimony of Simon Zhao even before he spoke about the Back to Jerusalem vision.

Zhao was taken into different house church gatherings to share about his experience and the BTJ vision. He was in high demand from revival meetings, leadership meetings and underground seminaries. In one of the underground seminaries where Ruth Xu (Deborah's sister-in-law) was in charge of training, Simon went in and wrote 'Antioch' on the board as he started immediately to narrate the acts of the apostles. Eloquently as he spoke, students and teachers were much encouraged by his knowledge of the Bible, richness in his teaching, and confidence in the fulfilment of the BTJ vision.

Deborah made arrangements for Simon Zhao's itinerary while he was in Henan. Zhao spoke primarily on the BTJ vision as he also shared and taught many of the poems and hymns he had written in prison. He became a key advisor for the WOL and other networks and was mightily used by God at the time when he was able to provide much-needed insight to the leadership of the WOL from his experience and faith. Christians looked up to him as a model of what God's workers should be, and loved him dearly. Leaders constantly went to him for fellowship and advice. As Simon Zhao frequented revival meetings, leadership meetings and other forms of fellowships among the house churches, his presence brought great encouragement and affirmation to the house church Christians. Zhao went to be with the Lord on December 7, 2001, in Pingdingshan, Henan Province, among the Christians he loved and who loved him. He left behind him stories, testimonies, songs and poems that Christians continue to tell and share and find encouragement from.

'Prayer Warrior' of BTJ – Mission Continued

Deborah has always been a woman of prayer. Since the early years of her Christian journey she developed a life of dependent prayer. Since coming to the US she has been actively involved in prayer support, among other speaking and teaching responsibilities, for the Back to Jerusalem ministries. She typically spends many hours of her day in prayer, and sometimes the entire day. She is convinced that God will fulfill his promise through agents he has called in mission with him. And above everything else, she sees prayer as the prerequisite for any ministry attempt.

Her prayer almost always starts with a sense of humility before God, and thanksgiving for his salvation. She always grasps God's words in the Bible and claims the promise there. In humility she acknowledges herself as an unworthy vessel God graciously chooses to work with; in faith she dares to claim victory based on the promises in the Bible. To Deborah, spreading the gospel all the way back to Jerusalem is already assured and will be fulfilled in God's timing.

Deborah is also actively involved in establishing and participating in prayer groups in North America where she has been since 2005, frequently speaking in churches and fellowship gatherings, testifying to the miracles of God in the China, advocating the BTJ vision, and encouraging young Christians for dedication to Christian service. Whenever she prays, fellow Christians take note of the charisma and authority that accompany her prayer. In one of the prayer groups specifically for BTJ ministries, fellow Christians who are encouraged by the presence of the Spirit within Deborah call her 'Prayer warrior'. Deborah hopes to establish a prayer base in Jerusalem in the near future, where she could pray, and invite others to join her in prayer, for God's provision and empowerment of BTJ ministries through which the gospel may be preached to unreached nations all the way back to Jerusalem. As a leader and member of the renewed community of house churches in China, Deborah continues to make herself available to God in channeling the ripples of renewal to the global church.

Bibliography

Bays, Daniel. 'Christian Revivals in China, 1900–1937'. In Edith Blumhofer and Randall H. Balmer (eds). *Modern Christian Revivals.* Urbana: University of Illinois Press, 1993, 161-79.

Carlberg, Gustav. *China in Revival*. Rock Island, Ill.: Augustana Book Concern, 1936.

Chao Jonathan (trans.). 'Chinese House Church Confession of Faith'. *China Prayer Letter and Ministry Report* 149 (Nov. 1998–Feb. 1999).

Culpepper, C. L. *The Shantung Revival.* Dallas, Tex.: Baptist General Convention of Texas, 1968.

Hattaway, Paul. *Back to Jerusalem.* Carlisle, UK: Piquant, 2003.

Hattaway, Paul, and Joy Hattaway. 'From the Front Lines'. *Asia Harvest* (March, 2002), 2-11.

Johnstone, Patrick, et al. *Operation World.* Cumbria, UK: Paternoster Lifestyle, 2001.

Lambert, Tony. *The Resurrection of the Chinese Church.* Wheaton, Ill.: OMF IHQ, Ltd., 1994.

Lyall, Leslie T. 'Historical Prelude'. In Marie Monsen (ed.). *The Awakening: Revival in China, a Work of the Holy Spirit.* London: Lutterworth Press, 1961, 17-21.

Mikaelsson, Lisbeth. 'Marie Monsen: Charismatic Revivalist – Feminist Fighter'. *Scandinavian Journal of History* 28 (2003), 121-34.

Monsen, Marie. *The Awakening: Revival in China, a Work of the Holy Spirit.* Trans Joy Guinness. London: Lutterworth Press, 1961.

Okkenhaug, Inger Marie. 'Women in Christian Mission: Protestant Encounters from the 19th and 20th Century.' *Kilden* (Web Magazine). Special edition of *Kvinneforskning* (*Journal of Gender Research in Norway*). Article published January 30, 2004.

Snyder, Howard A. 'Church Growth Must Be Based on a Biblical Vision of the Church as Vital Community of the Kingdom of God'. In Gary L. McIntosh (ed.). *Evaluating the Church Growth Movement – Five Views*. Grand Rapids: Zondervan, 2004, 209-36.

Xin, Yalin. *Inside China's House Church Network: The Word of Life Movement and Its Renewing Dynamic*. Lexington, KY: Emeth Press, 2009.

'Ye di shen xue yuan gen zhong bao dao zhi yi' (Report on the Seminary of the Fields, One). *Zhong guo yu jiao hui* (*China and the Church*) 6 (Sept.–Oct. 1986), 13-16.

The Use of 'Means' to Fulfill the Great Commission

Relating Church Hierarchies to Mission Agencies: Healing a Breach in the Protestant Church

Robert A. Blincoe

Editors' Note: *Over the course of the 20th century, every new decade saw more new evangelical mission agencies founded in the United States than the prior decade. Agencies have played a central role in evangelical missions over the past century, and this chapter helps us see this development in the historical and theological contexts of evangelical missions.*

Introduction

The Protestant mission paradigm, as conceived by Luther and Calvin and taking classic shape in the generation of Reformers that followed them, assumed that ecclesiastical hierarchies should retain for themselves the authority to initiate God's mission to all the world. However, in Bishop Stephen Neill's words, this paradigm achieved 'exceedingly little'.[1] Not even in the Dutch Golden Age of the late 16th and 17th centuries, when Protestant ships sailed the oceans, did this paradigm produce results comparable to those achieved by Catholic orders sailing those same seas. Some early Protestant mission advocates, such as Justinian Welz and Adrian Saravia, opposed the hierarchical mission paradigm, but the church came down hard on them. Only with the publication of William Carey's *Enquiry* in 1792 did a more effective and biblical paradigm gain considerable acceptance among Protestants, despite ecclesiastical suspicion that continues today.

Ecclesiastical suspicion that mission agencies, however successful, are a threat to church unity or have no biblical basis has, unfortunately opened a breach in the Protestant Church, but it is one that can be healed. It is important to address these suspicions and, if possible, normalize the relationship between ecclesiastical hierarchies and mission agencies.

It is my thesis that in order for Protestant church governments to achieve the greatest good, by which I mean creating durable and effective solutions to many of humanity's greatest social problems, it will be necessary for them to

---

[1] Stephen Neill, *A History of Christian Missions*, rev. ed. (New York: Penguin Books, 1986), 222.

negotiate new social contracts with the voluntary associations that their members are starting or joining.

Ralph Winter's Formulation of the Concepts of Modality and Sodality

William Carey's innovative mission organization is an effective 'operating system' that dozens, even hundreds of activists have copied. 'The Protestant missionary movement that arose', Andrew Walls wrote, 'became possible only by means of these new structures'.[2] However, when Ralph Winter published 'The Two Structures of God's Redemptive Mission' in 1974, he challenged readers to consider that the existence of such structures was not something new. Winter pointed out that Paul's missionary band – a second structure unlike the congregation in that the missionary band was mobile, voluntary, task-oriented and comprised only of adults – also had roots in the New Testament Jewish mission experience. Winter wrote:

> The structure we call the New Testament church is a prototype of all subsequent Christian fellowships where old and young, male and female are gathered together as normal biological families in aggregate. On the other hand, Paul's missionary band can be considered a prototype of all subsequent missionary endeavors organized out of committed, experienced workers who affiliated themselves by making a second decision beyond membership in the first structure.[3]

An Objection to Winter's Theory Considered and Refuted

Bruce Camp raised an objection to Winter's 'two structure' theory when Camp stated, 'The idea that an expression of the universal church may limit its constituency based on sex, age, talent, gifts, or other criteria is completely foreign to Christianity. It violates both scripture teaching (1 Corinthians 12:21) and early church practice (Acts 1–2)'.[4] Thus, Camp, like the early Reformers and many today, stated that in the New Testament there is only one church structure, the congregation and its superstructure, the denomination. But historical research reveals that the two structures to which Winter refers evolved from two first century Jewish structures, the synagogue and the *khevra*. The synagogue evolved into what we think of as the congregation, and the *khevra*, or Jewish missionary band, evolved into the missionary bands of the book of Acts.

---

[2] Andrew F. Walls, *The Cross-Cultural Process in Christian History: Studies in the Transmission and Appropriation of Faith* (Maryknoll: Orbis, 2002), 17.
[3] Ralph D. Winter, 'The Two Structures of God's Redemptive Mission', *Missiology* 2:1 (1974), 122.
[4] Bruce Camp, 'A Theological Examination of the Two-Structure Theory', *Missiology* 21:2 (1995).

Khevra is the Hebrew word for 'membership society', 'association', 'fraternity', 'guild'. It is related is *khaver* (kha-*VER*) meaning 'friend'.[5] There were several *khevrot* (plural of *khevra*) in New Testament times: Pharisees, Essenes, Sadducees, and others, some quite informal, comprised of a rabbi and his chosen disciples.[6] *Khevrot* still exist today.[7] The Pharisees were a *khevra*, organized to perform tasks and achieve certain goals. F. F. Bruce says the Pharisees 'banded themselves together in local fellowships or brotherhoods'.[8] Alfred Edersheim writes that 'the Pharisees were a regular 'order', and that there were many such 'fraternities''.[9] If we do not see them explained as such in the New Testament, it is because 'the New Testament simply transports us among contemporary scenes and actors, taking the then existent things, so to speak, for granted'.[10]

Membership had its requirements, including 'mutual scrutiny and encouragement, regularly scheduled meetings for worship, usually the evening of Shabbat. Study of the Torah and a communal meal were also part of these gatherings'.[11] We don't know much about the wandering band of exorcists in Acts 19, but we do know that they were on a mission to cast out demons. It is reasonable to say that John the Baptist invited 'disciples' to join his *khevra*. Jesus called twelve to go on a preaching mission that he organized; the disciples would have recognized themselves as members of a *khevra*, as would the Jews who met them.

While all Jews could belong to a synagogue, only some Jews met the requirements (or had the inclination) of joining a *khevra*. These two kinds of organizations – synagogue and *khevra* – are the structures with which Jews like Peter and Paul would have been familiar. According to Daniel J. Elazar, these two structures have a normal relationship in Jewish society today. In his article, 'Jewish Organization Patterns in the United States', Daniel J. Elazar observes that Jews in the United States belong to all manner of membership organizations that are voluntary and task-oriented. Jews do not demean these voluntary structures as 'para-synagogue' organizations, as though the synagogue were the center of the Jewish activities. Membership in Jewish

[5] Robert Ezra Park and Herbert Adolphus Miller, Old World Traits Transplanted (New York: Harper and Brothers Publishers, 1921), 127.
[6] The Qumranic community describe the Pharisees, Sadducees and 'Essenes'. 'The monastery at Qumran was probably the extreme expression of Sadduceeism' and were probably 'partisans of Judas Maccabee', differing from the 'normative Sadduceeism of the Herodian period', according to Robert Eisenman (*The Dead Sea Scrolls and the First Christians* [Rockport, MA: Element Books, 1996], 51).
[7] For examples of modern day *khevrot*, google *khevra* or *chabura, chevra* or *havurah*.
[8] F. F. Bruce, *New Testament History* (London: Nelson, 1969), 78. Also Ralph P. Martin, *New Testament Foundations: A Guide for Christian Students* (Grand Rapids: Eerdmans, 1975), 86. Also Alfred Edersheim, *Sketches of Jewish Social Life in the Days of Christ* (London: The Religious Tract Society, 1876), 169ff.
[9] Edersheim, *Sketches*, 169.
[10] Edersheim, *Sketches*, 169.
[11] Clarence H. Wagner, Jr. www.bridgesforpeace.com

special-purpose associations is often more important than membership in the synagogue, with the result that 'the essential community of interest and purpose is reflected in a well-nigh complete panoply of organizations'.[12]

In sum, Winter said that in the New Testament we observe 'the pre-existence of a commonly understood pattern of relationship, whether in the case of the church [patterned after the Jewish synagogue] or the missionary band [patterned after the Jewish Pharisees] which Paul [had] employed earlier as Saul the Pharisee'.[13] 'We will consider the missionary band', Winter writes, 'the second of the two redemptive structures in New Testament times'.[14] For Winter, Pellowe says, 'neither structure is more central than the other, although the church structure regulates the specialized structure, on the principle that the specialized reports to the more general'.[15]

Thus, Paul and the apostles adapted two Jewish structures when they formed the structures of the New Testament church. There was never a time when the congregation was 'the single divine instrument' of God's work in the world. Nor are mission agencies an afterthought, or to be casually treated as 'parachurch'.

In the next section we will explain William Carey's most important analogy – the resemblance of mission agencies to private trading companies – that we might understand the relationship between church hierarchies and mission agencies in terms of their resemblance to the relationship between free-world governments and private corporations.

Voluntary Societies, Like Trading Companies, Are 'Little Republics'

Free world governments everywhere have legalized the right of their citizens to form corporations. The private trading company is, Peter Drucker said, 'the first autonomous institution in hundreds of years, the first to create a power center that was within society yet independent of the central government of the national state'.[16]17 And what a change corporations have made! 'The company', write Micklethwait and Wooldridge, editors at the Economist, 'is the basis of the prosperity of the West and the best hope for the future of the world'.[18] 'By contrast', they continue, 'civilizations that once outstripped the West [but] failed to develop private-sector companies' – the authors mention

---

[12] Daniel J. Elazar, 'Patterns of Jewish Organization in the United States', in Ross P. Scherer (ed.), *American Denominational Organizations* (Pasadena: William Carey Library, 1980), 132.
[13] Winter, 'Two Structures'. 122.
[14] Winter, 'Two Structures', 124.
[15] John Pellowe, 'Leading Ministries into Christian Community: A Practical Theology for Relations between Churches and Self-Governing Agencies' (PhD dissertation, Gordon-Conwell Theological Seminary, 2007), 88.
[16] Quoted in John Micklethwait and Adrian Wooldridge, *The Company: A Short History of a Revolutionary Idea* (New York: Modern Library, 2003), 54.
[17] Quoted in Micklethwait and Wooldridge, *The Company*, 54.
[18] Micklethwait and Wooldridge, *The Company*, xiv-xv.

the Islamic world – 'fell farther and farther behind'.[19] The US had 5 ½ million corporations in 2001; North Korea apparently has none. 'Today the number of private-sector companies that a country boasts is a better guide to its status than the number of battleships it can muster. It is also not a bad guide to its political freedom.'[20] In their description of a totalitarian regime, Carl Friedrich and Zbigniew Brzezinski include as one of six distinguishing traits the prohibition of private, non-government organizations.[21] By contrast, in a democratic system 'a multitude of independent, voluntary, non-government associations' transfers some power from the state to the individual'.[22] The enduring relevance of economist F. A. Hayek's warning against centralized control, sounded in his 1944 classic *Road to Serfdom*, demonstrates the need for citizens to guard their freedom to form special-purpose associations. Hayek's main point is that 'coordination of activities through central direction and through voluntary cooperation are roads going in very different directions: the first to serfdom, the second to freedom'.[23]

'The limited liability corporation is the greatest single discovery of modern times',[24] proclaimed Nicholas Murray Butler (d. 1947), president of Columbia University and recipient of the 1931 Nobel Peace Prize. Butler added, 'Even steam and electricity would be reduced to comparative impotence without it'.[25] This praise is warranted because, as Micklethwait and Wooldridge wrote, 'the company itself was an enabling technology'.[26] Peter Drucker agreed: 'This new 'corporation' could not be explained away as a reform. ... It clearly was an innovation'.[27] It was a paradigm shift.

Carey said that the corporation that he proposed was like a private trading company. In his *Enquiry*, Carey uses the word 'company' twice in reference to the Dutch East-India Company and once referring to private trading companies in general.[28] Such a company is clearly what Carey had in mind when he made his famous proposal:

> Suppose a company of serious Christians, ministers and private persons, were to form themselves into a society, and make a number of rules respecting the regulation of the plan, and the persons who are to be employed as missionaries, the means of defraying the expense, etc., etc. This society must consist of persons

---

[19] Micklethwait and Wooldridge, *The Company*, xxi.
[20] Micklethwait and Wooldridge, *The Company*, xx.
[21] Constance E. Smith and Anne E. Freedman, *Voluntary Associations: Perspectives on the Literature* (Cambridge: Harvard University Press, 1972), 33.
[22] Smith and Freedman, *Voluntary Associations*), 34.
[23] Friedrich A. von Hayek, *The Road to Serfdom* (Chicago: University of Chicago Press, 1994), xiii-xiv.
[24] Micklethwait and Wooldridge, *The Company*, xx-xxi.
[25] Micklethwait and Wooldridge, *The Company*, xx-xxi.
[26] Micklethwait and Wooldridge, *The Company*, xx-xxi.
[27] Micklethwait and Wooldridge, *The Company*, 54.
[28] William Carey, *An Enquiry into the Obligations of Christians to Use Means for the Conversion of the Heathens* (Leicester: Baptist Missionary Society London, reprinted by Ann Ireland, 1792), 36, 37, 81, 82.

> whose hearts are in the work, men of serious religion, and possessing a spirit of perseverance; there must be a determination not to admit any person who is not of this description, or to retain him longer than he answers to it.[29]

Carey was fortunate to make his proposal after the year 1779. In that year Parliament passed an Enabling Act that authorized English citizens to organize public or private schools and associations apart from the authority of the Anglican Church. Robert Raikes took advantage of this law in 1780 to organize a Sunday School of which the Anglican Church disapproved. Thus 'it is unlikely that anything like the Sunday School could have arisen without the legal sanction of the Enabling Act'.[30] With Raikes we see 'the clear connection between a free society and the growth of independent religious organizations. Prior to 1779, the philanthropy of Robert Raikes (or anyone else) would have been stifled by the laws of the country and the prejudice of those in ecclesiastical power'.[31] Today, more than four centuries after the establishment of the Virginia Company one may forget that the government had to act before citizens could form themselves into private companies:

> No matter how much modern businessmen may presume to the contrary, the company was a political creation. ... Businessmen might see the joint company as a convenient form; from many politicians' viewpoint, it existed because it had been given a license to do so, and granted the privilege of limited liability. In the Anglo-Saxon world, the state might decide that it wanted relatively little in return: 'these little republics', as Robert Lowe called [the corporations], were to be left alone.[32]

Thus, mission agencies resemble private trading companies not only by the fact that a board of directors holds an executive accountable for a desired outcome, but by the fact that a church hierarchy must act to recognize and regulate mission agencies, just as a free world government recognizes and regulates corporations.

Suspicion at High Levels

But many church leaders are suspicious of special-purpose associations. Church and denominational officers are alert to every threat to their control, asking,

---

[29] Carey, *Enquiry*, 81-82. Note that a member could be ousted from the society for failing to qualify, even after he had joined. In other words Carey foresees a screening process to get in, and if a member fails to keep his pledge, he or she can be removed from the group. All mission societies organize themselves in this way.

[30] Wesley Kenneth Willmer, J. David Schmidt, and Martyn Smith, *The Prospering Parachurch: Enlarging the Boundaries of God's Work* (San Francisco: Jossey-Bass, 1998), 37.

[31] Willmer, *Prospering Parachurch*, 37. Today, of course, a pastor is expected to manage a Sunday School, the New Testament basis for which has become somehow obvious to most members of the church.

[32] Micklethwait and Wooldridge, *The Company*, 54.

'Aren't mission agencies doing what we local churches are supposed to do? Is money that should be going to the church being siphoned off by mission groups?'[33] 'The simple fact', Walls states of William Carey's era, 'was that the Church as then organized, whether episcopal, or presbyterian, or congregational, could not effectively operate mission overseas. Christians had accordingly to 'use means' to do so'.[34] The voluntary society 'subverted all the classical forms of Church government, while fitting comfortably into none of them'.[35]36

Hence the suspicion of church leaders that William Carey and all who follow his pattern have subverted the authority of the local church. So there is tension between the governing ecclesiastical structures, which value order, and the founders and members of mission agencies, which value autonomy. Max Warren says we must accept 'the inevitability of tension', but adds that 'too much tension makes administration impossible'.[37] Bauer adds helpfully:

> If mission structure leaders could understand and accept the fact that the congregational structure is an organ of coordination that is primarily concerned with organization, unity, worship, nurture and service for existing members, and if congregational leaders could understand that the mission structures largely consists of action and mobility in order to fulfill their specific tasks, then perhaps each structure could be more accepting of the other. With acceptance and understanding would also come a favorable reduction in tension between the two.[38]

The Term 'Parachurch' in Light of the 'Two Structures' Paradigm

As mentioned, ecclesiastical hierarchies sometimes use the term 'parachurch' as a pejorative because, as Stephen Board wrote, 'It is widely held that 'if the churches were really doing their job the parachurch groups wouldn't be necessary''.[39] 'Unlike the relative acceptance such structures have in the case of the orders in the Roman Catholic tradition', writes Winter, 'the same thing within Protestantism is ignored, despised or denigrated by such phrases as parachurch structures'.[40] Winter continues, 'In truth, modern American congregations are so far removed from the ecclesias of the New Testament that

---

[33] Walls, *Missionary Movement*, 246.
[34] *Walls, Missionary Movement*, 246. Italics are in Walls' essay.
[35] *Walls, Missionary Movement*, 247.
[36] *Walls, Missionary Movement*, 247.
[37] Max Warren, *Crowded Canvas: Some Experiences of a Life-Time* (London: Hodder & Stoughton, 1974), 157.
[38] Bruce L. Bauer, 'Congregational and Mission Structures', (PhD dissertation, Fuller Theological Seminary, 1982), 11.
[39] Stephen Board, 'The Great Evangelical Power Shift', *Eternity* 30:6 (1979), 19.
[40] Ralph D. Winter, 'Global Cross-Cultural Mission Collaboration: 1910 to 2010' (Unpublished paper, William Carey International University, 2008), 2. Italics are in original.

it would be just as reasonable to refer to our contemporary congregations as 'paramission' structures'.[41] Parachurch, when used as a pejorative, is a distortion of the now arguably demonstrated 'two structures' New Testament paradigm. We err, Winter says, when we refer to the congregation and its denominational superstructure 'as the church *as if there were no other structure making up the church*' [emphasis is in original].[42] Eugene TeSelle agrees, pointing out that 'before there was a 'local' ministry in the churches, there was an 'itinerant' ministry by which churches were founded and by which they were edified in an ongoing way... Mission has an original authority in the Christian church'.[43]

In the essay 'Para-Parochial Movements: The Religious Order Revisited', Darrell L. Guder corrects a perception which 'parachurch' implies, that perception being 'almost a church, resembling a church'.[44] He asks that we start, again, with a missiological approach to understanding the purpose of the church:

> The view of the church which emerges from this missiological approach is, then, *highly instrumental*. The church is God's instrument for the accomplishment of God's purposes. The way in which the church is to be structured to do that is defined by the mission, nature and purposes of God. Such a missiological approach obviously places in question any attempt to restrict the forms of Christian mission to a particular tradition, or structure, or hierarchy. The church is emphatically for the sake of mission. The organizational implication of this missiological position is to relativize the question of forms and structures. It makes a term like 'para-church' with its 'first class church' and 'second class church' implications ultimately impossible [emphasis added].[45]

'The fundamental question, then', Guder emphasizes, 'is not one of structure as much as it is a question of mission: What is the mission of the church and how does that mission define its forms?'[46]

---

[41] Winter, 'Global Collaboration', 2. 'We do wonder about the assumption', Winter writes, 'that the denomination was a divinely instituted structure, while the societies were merely human creations' (Ralph D. Winter, 'Protestant Mission Societies and the 'Other Protestant Schism'' in Ross P. Scherer, ed., *American Denominational Organization* [Pasadena: William Carey Library, 1980), 200-201.

[42] Winter, 'Two Structures'.

[43] Eugene TeSelle, 'Church and Parachurch: Christian Freedom, Ecclesiastical Order, and the Problem of Voluntary Organizations', (Nashville: Vanderbilt University, 1994). This essay was originally prepared for a funded research project on 'the church and the groups', initiated and conducted by Eugene TeSelle, Professor of Systematic Theology in the Divinity School, Vanderbilt University.

[44] Darrell L. Guder, 'Para-Parochial Movements: The Religious Order Revisited' (Nashville: Vanderbilt University, 1994).

[45] Guder, 'Para-Parochial Movements', 7.

[46] Guder, 'Para-Parochial Movements', 5.

Darrell Guder on Karl Barth's 'Special Working Fellowship'

Guder then introduces Karl Barth's theology of 'special working fellowships of the Church' (*besondere Arbeitsgemeinschaften der Kirche*), which Barth locates in section 72 of his *Dogmatics*, 'The Holy Spirit and the Sending of the Christian Community'.[47] Barth sees the role of sodalities, Waldron Scott has pointed out, as 'proper and even indispensable to Christian ministry'.[48] Barth's theology of special working fellowships is 'thoroughly missional',[49] Guder writes. Barth 'understands that the one unifying mission of the church can express itself in a number of organizational ways'.[50] 'Not all Christians will belong in the same way to the same kind of community. There will be a vast variety of special working fellowships, all going about the activity demanded of all Christians'.[51] But, under the empowerment of the Holy Spirit, they will do so 'in a particular form of thought, speech and action, Christian witness being given in a particular way'.[52] For Barth a 'multiplicity of the ministry of witness' is 'normal and legitimate':[53]

> The Holy Spirit does not enforce a flat uniformity. Hence the Christian community, quite apart from the natural individuality of its members and the consequent dangers, cannot be a barracks, nor can its members be the uniformed inhabitants, nor can their activity be the execution of a well-drilled maneuver. Their divine calling and endowment are as such manifold. They are always new and different.[54]

Guder states that our challenge today 'is to move from church with mission to missional church'.[55] I believe this crisis has developed in part because of the breach that has opened between church and voluntary society in the Protestant experience. The future effectiveness of the church to bring the ideals of Jesus to bear on our world depends on making a paradigm shift. Members of voluntary structures that have confidence in their organizations are adapted from patterns practiced by Jesus Christ and Paul the apostle. Sodalities apparently exist

---

47 Karl Barth, *Church Dogmatics*, IV/3 (Edinburgh: T. & T. Clark, 1957), 830. This is Section 72, No. 4. Guder writes, 'No. 4, is translated 'The Ministry of the Community', but should be translated 'The Service of the Community'. This translation in the English edition is unnecessarily clericalizing and out of touch with Barth's whole argument!' (private correspondence, July 31, 2010).

48 Waldron Scott, 'Karl Barth's Theology of Mission', *Missiology* 3:2 (1975), 221.

49 Guder, *Continuing Conversion*, 184.

50 Guder, *Continuing Conversion*, 184.

51 Barth, *Dogmatics*, 856.

52 Barth, *Dogmatics*, 856.

53 Barth, *Dogmatics*, 856. There is also an abnormal multiplicity of ministries which is abnormal, and 'from below', Barth writes. This derivation 'jeopardizes and perhaps to a large degree actually hampers this ministry' that is, the ministry of the Holy Spirit in granting to the church different services of calling (Barth, *Dogmatics*, 855).

54 Barth, *Dogmatics*, 855.

55 Darrell L. Guder and Lois Barrett, *Missional Church: A Vision for the Sending of the Church in North America* (Grand Rapids: Eerdmans, 1998), 6.

among all peoples and all cultures. Their members are eradicating root problems everywhere. As Carey said, there is a 'glorious prize' that 'stretches our every nerve' and we should never imagine 'that it was to be obtained in any other way'56 than forming special-purpose associations.

A Self-Governing Missional Model

The authors of *The Prospering Parachurch* show that 'the [governmental] freedom that allowed Robert Raikes to begin his first Sunday school in a rented kitchen is still with us. This freedom is the necessary environment for the parachurch'.[57] Today's ecclesiastical leaders need to give 'a license' to their church citizens to organize themselves for mission. Richard Hutcheson suggests that Protestants look to the Catholics for a self-governing missional model:

> The Roman Catholic Church developed admirable structures for carrying out these missional activities in the various lay and priestly religious orders. These have been permitted to be self-governing internally. Teaching orders, missionary orders, charitable and serving orders could focus on their own particular missional interests, and they have had free access to church members to develop support and collect funds. ... The Protestant equivalent of the Roman Catholic order has been the voluntary association.[58]

Hutcheson attempts to persuade denominational leaders that a centrally planned and administered missional structure prevents citizens with special interests from allocating any of the funds they contribute. A denominational program which sets out to affirm rather than resist the pluralism of the constituents would probably include, Hutcheson suggests, most of the following elements: [59]

1. Acceptance of the existence, within the denomination, of special-interest mission associations.
2. Integrated planning of a full range of mission activities, substantively as well as nominally responsive to the intentions of various groups of donors.
3. Integrated promotion by the denomination of a full range of mission activities, together with acceptance of promotion by consensus groups of their own mission goals.
4. Full utilization of the widespread Christian commitment to the church itself, which leads to generalized giving to the whole mission of the church by many, but with full acceptance also of designated giving to particular causes.
5. A guarantee that all designated contributions go to the cause designated.

---

[56] Carey, 'Enquiry', 80.
[57] Willmer, et al, *Prospering Parachurch,* 37-38.
[58] Richard G. Hutcheson, 'Pluralism and Consensus: Why Mainline Church Mission Budgets Are in Trouble', *Christian Century* 17 (July, 1977), 618.
[59] Hutcheson, 'Pluralism and Consensus', 624.

6. A willingness for the constituency to affect the missional priorities through its designated giving, without the kind of ecclesiastical shell game which compensates for increased giving in one area by shifting an equivalent amount of no designated money away from that area.
7. An intention to serve the needs and reflect the concerns of all groups within the constituency.

In a new social contract denominational leaders would recognize the right of mission agency boards of directors to set budgets and raise funds and direct funding, thus validating the independent nature of voluntary societies. This would repair the breach after the manner of the Roman Catholic pattern. As Ralph Winter wrote,

> A single, highly centralized denominational board cannot by itself fully express the vision and energy of the whole constituency of the denomination, especially as the tradition becomes older and more diverse internally. It is likely that the most creative structural changes for US denominations in the near future will be in this area.[60]

A Denominational Structural Change: How Lutherans Today Recognize and Regulate Voluntary Societies

Until 1996 leaders in the Lutheran Church Missouri Synod (LCMS) were proponents of centralized mission planning and budgeting. No pastor or church member could initiate a mission effort. But this has changed; since 1996 LCMS pastors and church members have formed a galaxy of mission agencies; ecclesiastical leaders, for their part, recognize and promote these mission agencies. The LCMS has even assigned a staff person to coach LCMS members through the legal process of forming corporations and opening bank accounts. The number of new mission initiatives began to increase:

The number of mission agencies grew to 52 agencies in 1999, to 65 in 2003 and 75 by 2008. These voluntary societies are doing specialized work with the official consent and promotion of the Missouri Synod headquarters, but without its control. Some of the seventy-five mission agencies on the ALMA web site include:[61]

Alaska Mission for Christ: sharing Christ in the last frontier through the use of well trained laity, especially in areas too remote or sparsely populated to allow service by ordained clergy.

---

[60] Ralph D. Winter, 'Churches Need Missions because Modalities Need Sodalities', *Evangelical Missions Quarterly* 7 (July, 1971) 195.

[61] http://www.alma-online.org. ALMA lists only those agencies that pay the annual $85 membership fee and agree to work in cooperation with the member agencies and with the LCMS . There are 35 additional LCMS mission agencies that have not joined ALMA.

Apple of His Eye Ministries: Planting messianic congregations among Jewish people

Friends of Indonesia: Helping Indonesian believers grow in body, mind and spirit, as well as partnering with them to share Jesus' love with those around them.

Hmong Mission Society: Proclaiming of the Gospel to the Hmong people of North America and throughout the world.

Missio Dei Network: providing theological materials to foster learning communities that encourage, form and equip mission leaders for missiological bridge-building in the 21st century.

Sudanese Lutheran Mission Society: telling the Good News to the Sudanese who do not know about Jesus

Tien Shan Mission Society: Spreading the Gospel of Jesus Christ among the Dungan people of the Tien Shan Mountain region of Central Asia (Kyrgyzstan).

Each Lutheran mission agency has its own board and its own by-laws. Each one obtains from the IRS its own Tax Identity Number in order to open up its own bank account. Once a new mission initiative obtains its 501(c)(3) status, the society can apply to the LCMS headquarters in St. Louis to become a Recognized Service Organization (RSO). RSO status allows an agency to solicit funding and provides a number of privileges, such as the opportunity to include its staff in the denomination's pension and health-care plan. Organizations with RSO status agree to submit an annual audit and promise to work in ways that support the aims of the denomination. Mission groups that seek a partnership status with the denomination's mission arm enter into a five to seven year agreement to work together in mutually beneficial ways. Some ALMA agencies choose not to participate in RSO.

Through its partnership office a LCMS staff member advises pastors and lay members on the process of incorporation, and provides a starter kit for setting up a mission agency. ALMA also helps new mission agencies to effectively raise funds and communicate to Lutheran churches.

ALMA hosts an annual gathering of its member agencies to help them network with one another and to interface with the mission staff of LCMS World Mission. It's a win-win for denomination and the mission agencies. 'In a time of financial limitations and in response to the initiative of many different mission groups in the LCMS it makes sense to work closely with the independent Lutheran mission agencies' said Steve Hughey, Director for Mission Partnership and Involvement at the Lutheran church headquarters.[62]

[62] Telephone interview with Steve Hughey, March, 2002.

The LCMS Mission Structure: An Example for Other Denominations

Lutheran Church Missouri Synod has validated the right of its members to form 'little republics'. 'Our concern', Hughey said 'is to get the task of missions done' by partnering with small voluntary associations.[63] In a pluralistic church such as the LCMS, members with ideas that interest only a minority of the entire church membership can work in harmony with church officials. This pattern should encourage other denominations to do likewise. Paul Pierson concurs: 'Ecclesiastical structures (Presbyterian and Anglican) are suited for stability and stationary organization – not conducive to the frontier situation which requires more freedom'.[64] The historical data supports these statements, as we have seen. The data does not corroborate the statement by Paul A. Beals that 'normally the local church initiates the sending of missionaries'.[65] I think Beals pulled this thought out of the air; all empirical evidence is to the contrary. An individual or a group may approach the church board and persuade it to act; but in that case the board is responding to the initiatives begun elsewhere. As long as there are new missions to undertake, men and women must organize themselves into voluntary societies.

Four Types of Denomination-Mission Agency Relationships

At the May 22-24 1975 'Consultation on Voluntary Societies', Ralph Winter described four kinds of relationships between denominations and mission agencies. He published this in *Evangelical Missions Quarterly* in 1974 and subsequently developed it in a major article in *Missiology* in 1979.[66] Winter explains the four kinds of relationships:

Type A Missions are (1) related to a specific church body; (2) administrated by that church through a board appointed by ecclesiastical processes; (3) funded by that church through a unified budget which discourages (or prevents) local churches from affecting the percentage going to the mission structure.[67]

---

[63] Hughey, March, 2002.

[64] Paul E. Pierson, 'Historical Development of the Christian Movement', (Classroom lectures, Fuller Theological Seminary, 1985), 204.

[65] Paul A. Beals, *A People for His Name: A Church Based Missions Strategy*, Rev. ed. (Pasadena: William Carey Library, 1985), 115.

[66] Ralph D. Winter, 'Seeing the Task Graphically', *Evangelical Missions Quarterly* 10:1 (1974), 11 ff. Also, Ralph D. Winter, 'Four Kinds of Church-Agency Relationships in 'Protestant Mission Societies: The American Experience'', *Missiology* 7:2 (1979), 203.

[67] The following denominations have a 'Type A' mission society: Presbyterian Church (USA), Episcopalian, Methodist, and Reformed Church. At the May 1974 Consultation on Voluntary Societies the Episcopalian representative, Sam van Culin said, 'We have a Type A organization in our church. It is funded directly through an organized method in the church, and it is directly related administratively to the Church through a thing called the Executive Council. Within our charter, every baptized member of the Episcopal Church is described as a member of this Domestic and Foreign Missionary Society (DFMS)' (Sam van Culin, 'Remarks', in Robert A. Blincoe (ed.), *Consultation on Voluntary Societies* [Evanston, IL, May 22-24, 1974]).

Type B Missions differ from Type A missions only in the elimination of the third characteristic mentioned. This type of mission raises its own support. It does not depend on a certain percentage of a church budget. Most Type A missions used to be of this kind.[68]

Type C Missions, such as the Conservative Baptist Foreign Mission Society [today WorldVenture], sustain a close relation to a church body (the Conservative Baptist Association) but neither its administration nor its budget are determined by the official processes of that church.[69]

Type D Missions acknowledge no special relation to any specific church (although churches may choose to regard a certain Type D mission as their official expression in overseas work). All mission agencies belonging to the Cross Global Link (formerly IFMA) are of this type. By comparison, the former EFMA (now Mission Exchange) includes all four types.[70]

The first three types, A, B, and C, are similar in that they are all denominationally-related mission agencies. William Carey's 'Baptist Missionary Society' was of Type C, barely escaping from Type D because Carey 'secured the limp backing of a local Baptist conference of churches'.[71] Winter favors Types B and C, but especially Type C.

All Catholic orders are Type C. American Protestant mission agencies mostly fall into Type A or Type D, extremes that Winter refers to as 'the Bear Hug or Abandonment Syndrome'.[72] In Type A, the church hierarchy understands itself to be a missionary society, the only missionary organization to which its members should join or fund. In Type B the church hierarchy has negotiated an agreement with certain mission associations to accept designated giving in exchange for certain administrative controls. In Type C the church hierarchy recognizes and names many mission associations that members who are in good standing are initiating or joining, in exchange for an annual report. I am advocating for Type C denomination-missions relations. When Robert Weingartner describes the 19th century Presbyterian women's societies as 'a

[68] The Presbyterian Church (USA) has three Type B mission societies: Presbyterian Frontier Fellowship, The Outreach Foundation, and the Medical Benevolence Foundation. The Assemblies of God has a Type B mission structure.

[69] The Presbyterian Church (USA) has three Type B mission societies: Presbyterian Frontier Fellowship, The Outreach Foundation, and the Medical Benevolence Foundation. The Assemblies of God has a Type B mission structure.

[70] At its founding in 1984 the Methodist Mission Society was a Type C mission society but in 2008 its board decided to become a Type D mission society.

[71] Winter, 'Protestant Mission Societies', 204. In his *Enquiry* Carey suggested that members of each denomination organize a mission agency particular to their own church. William Carey suggested that each denomination begin its own mission society (the Baptist Missionary Society sent Carey to India) He writes that 'each denomination should engage separately in the work. There is room enough for us all without interfering with each other' (Carey, *Enquiry*, 83).

[72] Winter, 'Protestant Mission Societies', 204.

loose confederation of quasi-independent groups and agencies'[73] he is referring to a Type C denomination-mission relationship.

Conclusion

Good governments, both political and church, negotiate social contracts with special-purpose associations that their restless members organize in order to create durable and effective solutions for many of humanity's great problems. William Carey said he proposed that Christians organize special-purpose associations because he was ambitious to 'do something' to eradicate the root evils in the world, evils which he called the 'ignorance and barbarism' that are subjugating 'our fellow creatures, whose souls are as immortal as ours'.[74] Sociological data indicate that it is the nature of societies everywhere for its members to join other likeminded members to achieve particular outcomes. In addition, historical data indicates that the 1792 publication of William Carey's small pamphlet, An *Enquiry into the Use of Means*, did bring to a sudden end the 270-year period of Protestant mission doldrums, inaugurating the Protestant mission era. Ralph D. Winter's 'Two Structures' paradigm is closer to what is in the Bible, and to what is in nature, and closer to what history teaches, than the paradigm which posits the congregation and its ecclesiastical hierarchy to be the single divine instrument of God's redemptive mission.

But there has been resistance. Thomas Kuhn's theory of 'paradigm shift and resistance' helps us to understand why ecclesiastical structures, past and present, have reacted against Carey's paradigm. Kuhn wrote that 'people are persuaded to change paradigms if they believe that the new model is closer to nature, closer to what is 'really there''.[75] I believe the data I have persuaded shows that the 'Two Structures' model is closer to what is really there.

One denomination has repaired the breach. Other ecclesiastical structures can follow the lead of the LCMS. At LCMS headquarters, the church validates the corporations that its citizens initiate. Voluntary associations, like corporations, become centers of power, 'little republics' that responsible governments are bound to regulate but not manage. But 'it is imperative', Robert Worley wrote, 'that there be a political style that encourages the development of openness and visibility of these differences and enables minority groups to form coalitions and be active politically without being

[73] Robert Weingartner, 'Missions within the Mission', in Scott W. Sunquist and Caroline N. Becker (eds), *A History of Presbyterian Missions*, 1944–2007 (Louisville: Geneva Press, 2008), 111.

[74] Carey, *Enquiry*, 68. The particular works to which Carey put his hand on behalf of the people of India are well known and beyond the subject of this dissertation. For an essay on Carey's good works see Vishal Mangalwadi and Ruth Mangalwadi, *The Legacy of William Carey: A Model for the Transformation of a Culture* (Wheaton: Crossway Books, 1999).

[75] Thomas S. Kuhn, *The Structure of Scientific Revolutions* (Chicago: University of Chicago Press, 1962), 206.

labeled 'enemies''.[76] Bonaventure, St. Francis' immediate successor, offers an apt illustration, comparing the friars of his day to the unnamed fishermen in 'the second boat', the one that aided Peter in hauling in the extraordinary catch of fish (Luke 5:4-11). 'Without the help of the second boat', Bonaventure said, 'the catch of fishes would surely be lost'.[77] For the sake bringing in the extraordinary catch William Carey launched a second ship. Those who desire to overcome evil might be wise to initiate special-purpose associations in order to address and eradicate the great problems of our day. As Andrew Walls has written,

> From age to age it becomes necessary to use new means for the proclamation of the Gospel beyond the structures which unduly localize it. Some have taken the word 'sodality' beyond its special usage in Catholic practice to stand for all such 'use of means' by which groups voluntarily constituted labor together for specific Gospel purposes. The voluntary societies have been as revolutionary in their effect as ever the monasteries were in their sphere. The sodalities we now need may prove equally disturbing.[78]

Bibliography

Anderson, Gerald H. *Biographical Dictionary of Christian Missions.* New York: Macmillan Reference USA, 1998.

Bailey, Kenneth E. *A Tale of Three Cities: An Analysis of Presbyterian Mission Policies.* Pasadena: Presbyterian Center for Mission Studies, 1989.

Barth, Karl. *Church Dogmatics.* Vol. IV/3. Edinburgh: T. & T. Clark, 1957.

Bauer, Bruce L. 'Congregational and Mission Structures'. PhD Dissertation. Fuller Theological Seminary, 1982.

Beals, Paul A. *A People for His Name: A Church Based Missions Strategy.* Rev. ed. Pasadena: William Carey Library, 1985.

Board, Stephen. 'The Great Evangelical Power Shift'. *Eternity* 30:6 (1979).

Bosch, David J. *Transforming Mission: Paradigm Shifts in Theology of Mission.* Maryknoll, N.Y.: Orbis Books, 1991.

Camp, Bruce. 'A Theological Examination of the Two-Structure Theory'. *Missiology* 21:3 (1995).

Carey, William. *An Enquiry into the Obligations of Christians to Use Means for the Conversion of the Heathens.* Baptist Missionary Society London, 1792.

Ecclesiastical History Society. Summer Meeting (1985: Oxford University), W. J. Sheils, Diana Wood, and Ecclesiastical History Society. Winter Meeting. *Voluntary Religion: Papers Read at the 1985 Summer Meeting and the 1986 Winter Meeting of*

---

[76] Robert C. Worley, *Change in the Church: A Source of Hope* (Philadelphia: Westminster, 1976, 46.

[77] John R. H. Moorman, *A History of the Franciscan Order: From Its Origins to the Year 1517* (Chicago: Franciscan Herald Press, 1988), 141.

[78] Andrew F. Walls, 'The Fortunate Subversion of the Church', in *The Missionary Movement in Christian History: Studies in the Transmission of Faith* (Maryknoll: Orbis, 1996), 253-254.

the Ecclesiastical History Society. [Oxford, Oxfordshire ; New York, NY, USA]: Published for the Ecclesiastical History Society by B. Blackwell, 1986.

Guder, Darrell L. *The Continuing Conversion of the Church.* The Gospel and Our Culture Series. Grand Rapids: Eerdmans, 2000.

– 'Para-Parochial Movements: The Religious Order Revisited'. Nashville: Vanderbilt University, 1994.

Guder, Darrell L., and Lois Barrett. *Missional Church: A Vision for the Sending of the Church in North America.* Grand Rapids: Eerdmans, 1998.

Hayek, Friedrich A. von. *The Road to Serfdom*. Chicago: University of Chicago Press, 1994.

Hutcheson, Richard G. 'Pluralism and Consensus: Why Mainline Church Mission Budgets Are in Trouble'. *Christian Century*, 17 (July, 1977).

Kuhn, Thomas S. *The Structure of Scientific Revolutions*. Chicago: University of Chicago Press, 1962.

Micklethwait, John and Adrian Wooldridge. *The Company: A Short History of a Revolutionary Idea*. New York: Modern Library, 2003.

Moorman, John R. H. *A History of the Franciscan Order: From Its Origins to the Year 1517*. Chicago: Franciscan Herald Press, 1988.

Moreau, A. Scott, ed. *Evangelical Dictionary of World Missions*. Grand Rapids: Baker, 2000.

Pellowe, John. 'Leading Ministries into Christian Community: A Practical Theology for Relations between Churches and Self-Governing Agencies.' PhD Dissertation. Gordon-Conwell Theological Seminary, 2007.

Pierson, Paul E. Pierson, Paul E. 'Historical Development of the Christian Movement'. Unpublished Classroom Lectures, Fuller Theological Seminary, Pasadena, 1985.

– *The Dynamics of Christian Mission: History through a Missiological Perspective*. Pasadena: William Carey International University Press, 2009.

Schnabel, Eckhard J. *Early Christian Mission*. Downers Grove: InterVarsity Press, 2004.

Scott, Waldron. 'Karl Barth's Theology of Mission'. *Missiology* 3:2 (1975).

Skreslet, Stanley H. 'Impending Transformation: Mission Structures for a New Century'. *International Bulletin of Missionary Research* 23:1 (1999).

Smith, Constance E. and Anne E. Freedman. *Voluntary Associations: Perspectives on the Literature*. Cambridge, Mass.: Harvard University Press, 1972.

TeSelle, Eugene. 'Church and Parachurch: Christian Freedom, Ecclesiastical Order, and the Problem of Voluntary Organizations'. Unpublished Paper, Vanderbilt University, Nashville, 1994.

Van Culin, Sam. 'Remarks.' In Robert A. Blincoe (ed.). *Consultation on Voluntary Societies*. Evanston, IL, May 22-24, 1974.

Walls, Andrew F. *The Cross-Cultural Process in Christian History: Studies in the Transmission and Appropriation of Faith.* Maryknoll, N.Y.: Orbis Books, 2002.

– *The Missionary Movement in Christian History: Studies in the Transmission of Faith*. Maryknoll: Orbis, 1996.

Warren, Max. *Crowded Canvas: Some Experiences of a Life-Time*. London: Hodder & Stoughton, 1974.

Weingartner, Robert. 'Missions within the Mission'. In Scott W. Sunquist and Caroline N. Becker (eds). *A History of Presbyterian Missions, 1944–2007*. Louisville: Geneva Press, 2008.

Willmer, Wesley Kenneth, J. David Schmidt, and Martyn Smith. *The Prospering Parachurch: Enlarging the Boundaries of God's Work*. San Francisco: Jossey-Bass, 1998.

Winter, Ralph D. 'Churches Need Missions Because Modalities Need Sodalities'. *Evangelical Missions Quarterly* 7:3 (July, 1971), 195, ff.

– 'Global Cross-Cultural Mission Collaboration: 1910 to 2010'. Unpublished Paper, William Carey International University, Pasadena, 2008.

– 'A Plea for Mission Orders'. Unpublished Paper, COEMAR Conference, Chicago, August, 1970.

– 'Seeing the Task Graphically'. *Evangelical Missions Quarterly* 10: 1 (1974).

– 'The Two Structures of God's Redemptive Mission'. *Missiology* 2:1 (1974), 121-139.

Worley, Robert C. *Change in the Church: A Source of Hope*. Philadelphia: Westminster, 1976.

Gathering, Collating and Meshing Information on the Frontiers: Identifying Unreached Peoples

Jim Haney

Editors' Note: *For much of the last quarter of the 20th century, evangelicals focused on understanding the concept of 'people groups' as a foundation for frontier mission. This chapter helps us see both the historical framing and the not yet fully resolved issues that remain.*

An Opening Biblical Perspective

After the flood, Noah's descendants became the 'nations' listed in Genesis 10. At first all spoke the same language, but when they began seeking to make a name for themselves, God confused their language and caused them to separate and spread out over the earth. After this, God looked for a faithful man, one who was not bent on making a name for himself but who submitted to God. The call of Abram is recorded in Genesis 12:1-3 (NIV):

> The Lord had said to Abram, 'Leave your country, your people and your father's household and go to the land I will show you.
> I will make you into a great nation
> And I will bless you;
> I will make your name great,
> And you will be a blessing.
> I will bless those who bless you,
> And whoever curses you I will curse;
> And all peoples on earth
> Will be blessed through you.'

We have a better understanding of the peoples of the world today than ever before. We are blessed with computers, transportation, communication and many breakthroughs that have resulted in globalization with new markets, strategic alliances and vast networks – the world is flat indeed.

While it is flat, it is not yet full – full of the glory of God. There are competing forces for God's glory among the nations, and these forces race to the edges of our world along with us. As we look at our world, it's trends and drivers; it is easy to be swept away by over-optimism or to be paralyzed by signs of impending doom. We look to research, to fruitful practices and an increasing knowledge base that enlightens our partnerships and networks. But we need to be cautious in our stewardship of what we know and what we say, or, as Samuel Zwemer cautioned in 1911, an over-reliance on ourselves may lead analysts to over-estimate trends and under-estimate God.[1]

In *L'envoi* to the Readers of 'Edinburgh 1910', the official message from the conference delegates to the members of the church in Christian lands, those delegates, now long gone, remind us of their hopes, later to be greatly affected by the outbreak of World War I and followed by the Great Depression. Their words inform us today:

> Dear Brethren of the Christian Church,
>
> We members of the World Mission Conference assembled in Edinburgh desire to send you a message which lies very near to our hearts. During the past ten days we have been engaged in a close and continuous study of the position of Christianity in non-Christian lands. In this study we have surveyed the field of missionary operation and the forces that are available for its occupation. For two years we have been gathering expert testimony about every department of Christian Missions, and this testimony has brought home to our entire Conference certain conclusions which we desire to set forth.
>
> Our survey has impressed upon us the momentous character of the present hour. We have heard from many, of the awakening of great nations, of the opening of long-closed doors, and of movements which are placing all at once before the Church a new world to be won to Christ. The next ten years will in all probability constitute a turning-point in human history. ... If those years are wasted, havoc may be wrought that centuries are not able to repair. On the other hand, if they are rightly used they may be among the most glorious in Christian history. ...
>
> But, it has become increasingly clear to us that we need something far greater than can be reached by any economy or reorganization of the existing forces. We need supremely a deeper sense of responsibility to Almighty God for the great trust which He has committed to us in the evangelization of the world. ... Assuredly, then, we are called to make new discoveries of the grace and power of God, for ourselves, for the Church, and for the world; and, in the strength of that firmer and bolder faith in Him, to face the new age and the new task with a new consecration.[2]

---

[1] Samuel M. Zwemer, *The Unoccupied Mission Fields of Africa and Asia* (New York: Student Volunteer Movement for Foreign Missions, 1911), n.p.

[2] Gairdner and Mott, *Echoes*, 277-79.

The Languages and Dialects of the World

We have reminded ourselves of God's call to Abram and his faithfulness to that call. We have listened once again to the echoing voices of the delegates of Edinburgh from near-recent history. Now, we find ourselves in a task that is both sobering in its scope and celebratory in its advance. In research, we realize that our understanding of the nations is partial; in our walk with God, we need a deeper sense of responsibility to almighty God for the great trust which He has committed to us of identifying the nations He loves.

When we consider the peoples of the world today, we must acknowledge the vision of Wycliffe Bible Translators who for many years have taken up the task of bringing God's Word to the peoples of the world in the aftermath of Babel. With Pentecost came the compelling vision of the nations hearing God's Word in distinct languages, and many have gone before us to learn languages and dialects while living among people groups to engage them with Scripture. Today, we are grateful for the listing of languages that is available to us in SIL's Sixteenth edition of the *Ethnologue*, which started humbly in the form of 10 mimeographed pages in 1951 and included 45 languages. With this, the Church takes up the challenge of communicating the gospel to the people groups of the world who speak 6,909 living languages and are referenced by three-letter ISO 639-3 codes.[3]

When it comes to dialects, there is even more room for divergence and dialects are just that: divergent speech varieties [4] that may have considerable overlap with each other within a language. For this reason and others, it seemed wise to drop the dialect extension formerly associated with languages that were coded with a three-letter, two-number code known as the ROPAL (Registry of People and Languages) code. Today, Global Recordings International maintains the ROD (Registry of Dialects)[5] while working to assure that whenever a people group cannot understand a previously recorded gospel presentation, they will provide one in the new dialect.

The Peoples of the World

People groups are not the same as language groups, although many people group names and language names are identical or similar. Because some people groups speak multiple languages and because some languages are spoken my multiple people groups, they must remain distinct categories.

Today, there are three primary global lists that account for the peoples of the world – the CPPI (Church Planting Progress Indicators, IMB), the JP (Joshua

[3] Paul M. Lewis, *Ethnologue: Languages of the World* (Dallas: SIL International, 2009), 7, http://www.ethnologue.com/web.asp.

[4] Lewis, *Ethnologue*, 9.

[5] Harvest Information System Website, http://www.harvestinformationsystem.info/, https://extranet.imb.org/sites/HIS/registries/Registry%20of%20Dialects/Forms/AllItems.aspx [accessed March 30, 2010].

Project), and the WCD (World Christian Database). All three lists are available online and are updated as their editors discover new information.

In addition, the WCD (which requires a membership fee to view the data) is published hardbound as the *World Christian Encyclopedia*, second edition. The three lists trace their beginnings to David B. Barrett, formerly of the Southern Baptist Foreign Mission Board (today, IMB).

According to Patrick Johnstone, WEC International, each of the three lists has their 'specific assumptions, emphases, ministry foci and informant networks, and each aiming to develop and maintain a high degree of information-sharing and correlation'.[6] Since each is edited differently and contains different factual material, the lists are somewhat different in their coverage or segmentation of the world's peoples. The following table shows how each of the list accounts for the peoples of the world.[7]

Count of People Groups by Affinity Blocs for CPPI, JP and WCD

	CPPI	JP	WCD
Arab World	508	573	581
East Asian Peoples	330	454	471
Eurasian Peoples	956	1,970	1,901
Horn of Africa-Cushitic Peoples	164	160	189
Iranian-Median	237	273	261
Jews	81	181	226
Latin-Caribbean Americans	1,096	1,127	1,110
Malay Peoples	847	1,018	999
North American Peoples	334	369	457
Pacific Islanders	1,477	1,563	1,605
South Asian Peoples	1,401	3,718	966
Southeast Asian Peoples	471	615	546
Sub-Saharan African	2,742	2,994	3,182
Tibetan / Himalayan Peoples	548	770	658
Turkic Peoples	217	311	291
Unclassified	174	254	232
Grand Total	11,583	16,350	13,675

Although each of the lists accounts for the peoples of the world differently, it is interesting to note that each list shows nearly identical populations for the world and the countries of the world. Segmentation preferences account for

[6] Patrick Johnstone, 'Affinity Blocs and People Clusters: An Approach Toward Strategic Insight and Mission Partnership', *Mission Frontiers* (March–April 2007), 9.

[7] People groups website: www.peoplegroups.org [accessed March 15, 2010]; Joshua Project website: www.joshuaproject.net [accessed March 15, 2010]; World Christian Database, query by Peter Crossing [received March 31, 2010]. From a confluence of the three lists by Jim Haney.

these differences in the list, and simplistically speaking, this is somewhat like three people who each buy a loaf of bread in the market, and each cuts the loaf of bread in a different number of pieces. Each list may be used separately, but list holders who edit the CPPI, JP and WCD urge users to compare similar information from each list for greater depth of understanding and to use the unique facts that each list provides to the user.

Because each of the lists is segmented differently, list holders code their people group lists with three levels of ROP (Registry of Peoples) codes so that they may be joined and compared.[8] On the highest level, the peoples of the world are coded to show their affinity bloc (ROP1). Affinity blocs are further subdivided into people clusters (ROP2). Finally, people clusters are divided into people groups (ROP3). People group population segments, like dialects, are divergent and overlapping, so the lists do not attempt to provide (ROP4) coding. But this is not to say that the segmentation of any people group is not important – it is very important at the level of ministry teams as they look at unengaged or unreached portions of their people group, such as those living in particular cities, classes, castes, and clans.

For further information about the three lists, see 'Which Peoples Need Priority Attention',[9] a back issue available from *Mission Frontiers* online. Also see 'A Comparison of Global People Group Lists'[10] on the Joshua Project website.

Additionally, we call on our partners to continue to sharpen what we know of people groups through diligent regional and local research initiatives so that our knowledge of our world will grow. If partners choose to maintain their own databases, we urge that they key their data to the language, dialect, people, geography, religion and resource registries found at the Harvest Information System website.[11] Our goal is not to create a single global super-database, but to connect what each organization tracks and is important to them.

People Group Priorities

Joshua Project

The Joshua Project Progress Scale provides an estimate of the progress of church planting among a people group or country. The scale is derived from a comparison and integration that looks at the following sources as they relate to each people group:[12]

Percent Evangelical

---

[8] Harvest Information System Website, http://www.harvestinformationsystem.info [accessed March 15, 2010].

[9] Justin Long. 'Which Peoples Need Priority Attention? Seeking Agreement on the 'Core of the Core'', *Mission Frontiers* (March–April, 2007), 18-23.

[10] http://www.joshuaproject.net/people-list-comparison.php [accessed March 15, 2010].

[11] http://www.harvestinformationsystem.info/ [accessed March 15, 2010].

[12] Joshua Project website, http://www.joshuaproject.net/definitions.php?term=12 [accessed March 15, 2010[.

Percent Adherent
Church Planting Indicator (CPI)
Global Status of Evangelical Christianity (GSEC)
Other Progress Indicators.

The resulting integration of the data from these sources results in three distinct stages, each of which is subdivided.

Stage	Level	Level Description
Unreached / Least-Reached Less than 2% Evangelicals and Less than 5% Christian Adherents	1.1	Very few, if any, known Evangelicals. Professing Christians less than or equal to 5%
	1.2	Evangelicals greater than 0.01%, but less than or equal to 2% Professing Christians less than or equal to 5%
Formative / Nominal Church Less than 2% Evangelicals and Greater than 5% Christian Adherents	2.1	Very few, if any, known Evangelicals. Professing Christians greater than 5%.
	2.2	Evangelicals greater than 0.01%, but less than or equal to 2% Professing Christians greater than 5%.
Significant / Established Church Greater than 2% Evangelicals	3.1	Evangelicals greater than 2%, but less than or equal to 5%.
	3.2	Evangelicals greater than 5%.

Out of 16,350 people groups on the Joshua Project list, 6,648 are classified as 'Least Reached'. For more information on how the Joshua Project determines priority people groups, see 'A Model for Determining the Most Needy Unreached or Least-Reached Peoples', by Dan Scribner, Joshua Project.[13]

World Christian Database

In the January–February 2002 edition of *Mission Frontiers*, Todd Johnson and Peter Crossing offered a methodology for determining priority by the presence or absence of 24 basic Christian ministries within each people group of the world.[14] They defined an 'untargeted people' as one with fewer than 15 basic ministries, and they gave these a code beginning with 1 and a decimal number for the number of basic ministries each people group had. So, a people group that had five of the 24 basic ministries achieved a T rating of 1.05. At that time, there were 815 people groups with a T rating of T 1.0 to T 1.15.

Some of the 24 basic ministries are as follows:

---

[13] Dan Scribner, 'A Model for Determining the Most Needy Unreached or Least-Reached Peoples', *Mission Frontiers* (November–December, 2004), 6-13.

[14] Todd M. Johnson and Peter F. Crossing, 'Which Peoples Need Priority Attention? Those with the Least Christian Resources', *Mission Frontiers* (January–February, 2002), 16-23.

Local affiliated Christians or church members
'Jesus' Film in mother tongue or related language
Audio
New Reader Portions (NRP) or Scriptures
New Testament published in mother tongue
Personal evangelism

In the January–February 2005 edition of *Mission Frontiers*, the number of untargeted peoples had grown to 926 because of the addition of new people groups to the database. While still affirming the validity of this approach to determine priority, Johnson and Crossing recommended a wider use of their data, especially in light of the advent of the online version of the WCD. In this article they suggested a customized approach for using the WCD.[15] They suggested that users come to the vast amount of data with their own priorities and determine for themselves how WCD data informs their mission. For example, someone with a heart for the providing Braille Bibles for people groups could go to the online database and use the query tool to get a list of those people groups who are still without Braille Bibles.

Today, out of 13,675 people groups in the WCD, 1,197 are classified as 'untargeted peoples.'

Global Status of Evangelical Christianity

The Global Status of Evangelical Christianity, IMB, is a model that describes the progress of the gospel among the peoples of the world by considering three main conditions:

- Percent Evangelical
- Accessibility to the Gospel
- Church Planting Activity within the Past Two Years (none, localized and widespread)

Based upon these criteria, each people group receives a GSEC Status. Unreached people groups or people groups who are less than 2% Evangelical have a GSEC Status of 0-3. Unlike the Joshua Project, IMB does not consider % adherents in determining unreached status. Unreached people groups who have not had at least one new Evangelical church started among them in the past two years are considered Last Frontier People Groups. These have a GSEC status of 0-1. People groups equal to or greater than 2% Evangelical are no longer considered as unreached.[16]

---

[15] Todd M. Johnson and Peter F. Crossing, 'Priority Peoples: A Customized Approach', *Mission Frontiers* (January–February, 2005), 8-14.

[16] People Groups website, www.peoplegroups.org [accessed March 21, 2010]. For a full explanation of these and other terms see FAQs on this site.

Last Frontier

Unreached

Status	Description
0	No evangelical Christians or churches. No access to major evangelical print, audio, visual, or human resources.
1	Less than 2% Evangelical. Some evangelical resources available, but no active church planting within past 2 years.
2	Less than 2% Evangelical. Initial (localized) church planting within past 2 years.
3	Less than 2% Evangelical. Widespread church planting within past 2 years.
4	Greater than or equal to 2% Evangelical
5	Greater than or equal to 5% Evangelical
6	Greater than or equal to 10% Evangelical
7	Unknown

Today, out of 11,583 people groups on the CPPI list, 6,661 are classified as unreached. For more information on how IMB determines priority people groups, see 'The Global Status of Evangelical Christianity – A Model for Assessing Priority People Groups'.[17]

Engaging the Peoples of the World with an Initial Church Planting Team

We have shown that from Edinburgh 1910 to Tokyo 2010, the call to make disciples of all nations has continued as strong and compelling as ever. Still, with all that has been done to work among people groups throughout the world, there are many unreached people groups left. Why is this?

There is no easy answer to this question.

In many cases, faithful people have labored long giving their entire lives to seeing just a handful of new believers emerge. Other Christian workers seem to

[17] Scott Holste and Jim Haney, 'The Global Status of Evangelical Christianity: A Model for Assessing Priority People Groups', *Mission Frontiers* (January–February, 2006), 8-13.

have been at the right place at the right time and seen a mighty outpouring of God's Spirit. Looking across time, generations have come and gone in some areas of the world causing the Church to weaken, struggle and die. In other areas of the world, those who dwelt apart from Christ have experienced an awakening, and today they are part of a mighty movement of God.

Today, we need strategies for reminding the Church of its mission. Without mobilization, new partners will not understand or sense the compulsion of the unfinished task and their part in it. Once mobilized and committed to the harvest force, new teams must have a sense for the priority of unreached peoples, particularly those that are unengaged, having no church planting methodology underway among them.

Engagement is a serious step. When a man and a woman share the news of their engagement to be married, they are telling family, friends and others that they are making a life-long commitment to each other. When missionaries engage people groups, a similar commitment is warranted.

Jeff Liverman, of Frontiers, says that engagement is characterized by four criteria:[18]

- An apostolic effort in residence
- A commitment to work in the local language and culture
- A commitment to long-term ministry
- Sowing in a manner consistent with the goal of seeing a Church Planting Movement emerge

Paul Eshleman of the Finishing the Task initiative has reminded the Church for many years that it is unfair that some people groups have never had an opportunity to hear the gospel and believe. Jerry Rankin of the International Missionary Board (IMB) often asks: 'What reason can any of us give for depriving any people group of their first opportunity to hear the gospel?'

Still, with 2000 years of Christian history behind us, there are 3,706 people groups (CPPI) today that are not engaged with a single church planting team on the ground, implementing a church planting strategy; 495 of these have a population of at least 100,000.[19]

Establishing the Engaged Peoples of the World in Christ

Mobilizing the Church to go, partner and initially engage the unengaged people groups of the world is a compelling starting point, but there is much to be done after engagement teams arrive. The task of the engaging team is to sustain their effort and see their witness spread through multiplying teams of disciples and churches so that the Church is established within that people group.

---

[18] Jeff Liverman, 'Unplowed Ground: Engaging the Unreached', in J. Dudley Woodberry (ed.), *From Seed to Fruit: Global Trends, Fruitful Practices, and Emerging Issues among Muslims* (Pasadena: William Carey Library, 2008), 23.

[19] People Groups website, www.peoplegroups.org [accessed March 15, 2010].

So beyond the list of unengaged people groups, what can we say about under-engaged peoples – those that are perhaps newly engaged or barely engaged? We have already provided some hints about this in the 'People Group Priorities' section where the JP, T, and GSEC scales were discussed. These scales are based on data found in the spreadsheets offered by the list holders. In addition, each list affords additional facts that can help us understand both the provisions and the needs of the under-engaged.

For example, let's say that you want to use the JP list to compare the conditions of various under-engaged people groups. First, download the JP list from their website, open it and find the CPTeam column. Choose Y, and the list will show you only those people groups that have church planting teams. Next, look at the JPScale column, this will tell you the status of these people groups. Even though they all have church planting teams, they have different JP Scale values. Let's say that your focus is on the Arab Bloc; filter the Affinity Bloc column for the Arabs. You will find 84 least reached people groups (Levels 1.1 and 1.2), which have at least one church planting team but are still considered to be least reached.

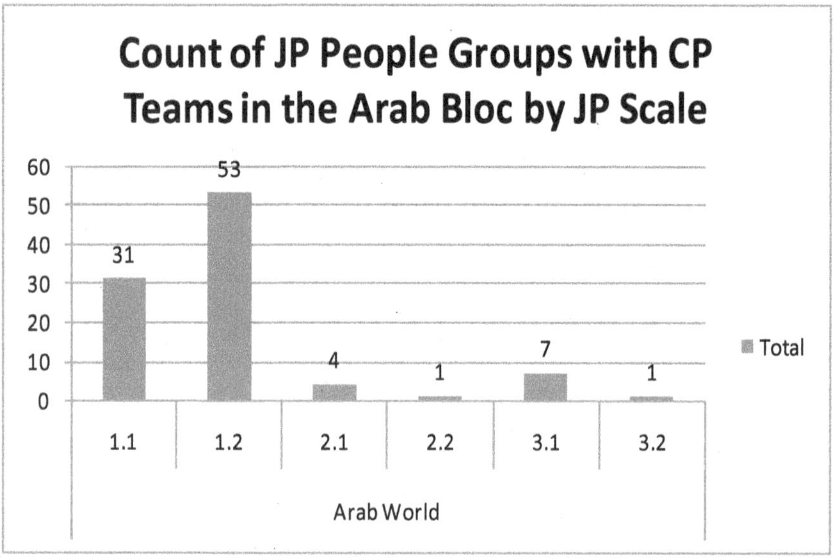

Beyond this, the Joshua Project list provides additional information under the following column headings: AudioRecordings, BibleYear, Church100, CPI, GospelRadio, GSEC, JF, LeastReached, NTYear, PCChristian, PCEvangelical, Population, PortionsYear, PrimaryReligion, RankMinistryTools, RankOverall, RankProgress, Language.

Using the CPPI, the picture is similar. Using a listing of engaged people groups in the CPPI, we filter it for the Arab Bloc people groups only and then show these by GSEC scale. You will find 91 unreached people groups that have some Evangelical resources, but have not had a new church planted in the previous two years (Level 1).

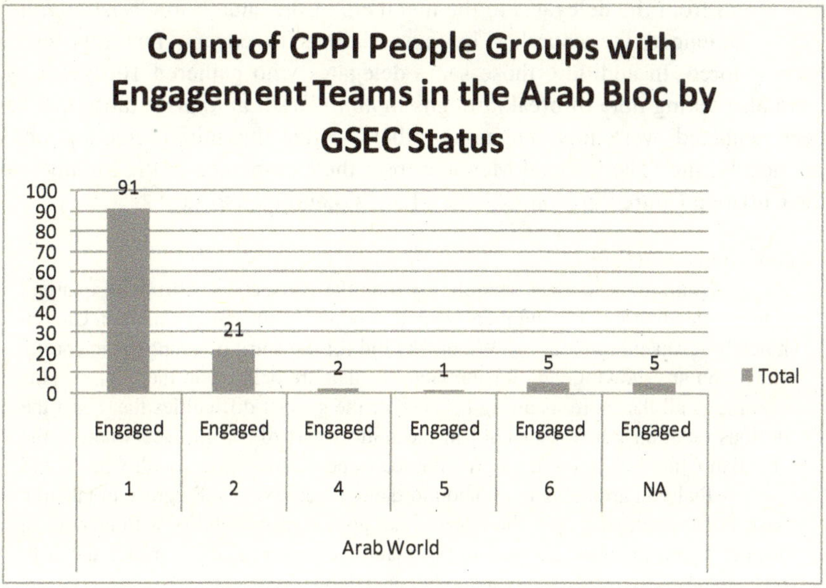

Beyond this, the CPPI list provides additional information under the following column headings: Population, Language, Religion, Congregations, Evangelicals, Percent Christian, Engagement Status, Evangelical Presence, Written Scripture, Audio Scripture, Jesus Film, Radio Broadcast, Gospel Recordings, Bible Stories, Physical Exertion, Freedom Index, Threat Level. (Some of this information is restricted or modified for sharing with partners for research and strategic purposes.)

Using the WCD, we can look further to find the status of each of the 24 basic ministries or entry points. Using information collected by FTT (Finishing the Task), which seeks to see at least one missionary placed for every population segment of 50,000, we can discover how many missionaries are in place and how many more are needed. In addition to all of this, we have the knowledge base of frontline engagers [20] who can tell us even more about the extent to which a people group is engaged.

As a team continues to engage a single people group, their goal is to multiply disciples and see the church established according to the harvest that God brings. Statistics are useful to help us know the extent to which each people group is progressing.

---

[20] Frontliners: 'boots-on-the-ground', those who live among the people for which they provide information.

Enlisting the Established in Christ in the Harvest Force

But unless those we engage and establish emerge as harvest force partners to join us, we have not gone far enough. This message started with an echo from Edinburgh from the delegates to the members of the church in *Christian lands.* They challenged the churches in those nations to engage fervently in the harvest force. In addition, those same delegates who gathered 100 years ago were also taking note of breakthroughs in *non-Christian lands* – those that had been engaged were now engaging others. After the initial greeting noted previously, the 'The Official Message from the Conference to the Members of the Christian Church in Non-Christian Lands' continued to say :[21]

> Dear Brethren in Christ,
>
> [N]othing has caused us more joy than the witness borne from all quarters as to the steady growth in numbers, zeal, and power of the rising Christian Church in newly -awakening lands. ... We thank God for the spirit of evangelistic energy which you are showing, and for the victories that are being won thereby. ... This example is all the more inspiring because of the special difficulties that beset the glorious position which you hold in the hottest part of the furnace wherein the Christian Church is being tried. We rejoice to be fellow-helpers with you ... and to know that you are being more and more empowered by God's grace to take the burden of it upon your own shoulders. Take up that responsibility with increasing eagerness, dear brethren and secure from God the power to carry through the task; then we may see great marvels wrought beneath our own eyes.

And with this sentiment, we must ask of the new harvest force, 'Who are your harvest fields, and who has God prepared you to reach?' Unless the established Church emerges and becomes part of the harvest force in engaging others, they remain unfinished themselves. As we track the number of home missionaries and foreign missionaries these new partners send out, we need to also record who these missionaries are engaging in their own countries and beyond.

Confirming the State of the Unfinished Task

In the early 1990s I was a church planter in Northern Ghana. I planted churches and conducted lay pastoral training among the Frafra, Tampulma, Kusasi, Bimoba, Mamprusi, Fulbe, and Konkomba people groups. Along the way, I worked with the Assemblies of God, Evangelical Presbyterians and Evangelical Lutherans to survey Northern Ghana and look for unreached people groups in unchurched places.

As we conducted our work, I remember discussing together the possibility of bypassing an area of the North that we knew to have Christian missionaries in three separate stations. Ultimately, we decided to make the trip, and it was good

[21] Gairdner and Mott, *Echoes*, 280-81.

that we went, even though the area was hard to reach and we had to dig our four-by-four out of the mud more than once. After some time, we arrived at the first of the three missionaries.

The first missionary we found to be a brilliant but rather reserved translator who was working on a mother-tongue literacy project. He told us all about how he had learned the language, developed orthography and was teaching the locals how to read their own language. We were quite excited to hear of the progress, and asked him how he was using this ministry to share the gospel with this unreached people group. The translator gave us an odd look and added that it was not his intention to share the gospel through this means or any other because his assignment did not include that, and if he were to do that, the Muslims would make him leave.

As we continued our survey, we reached another missionary late the next morning. We met up with a very zealous young man who had taken up shovel and dynamite to provide hand-dug wells for his adopted people group. As much as he was able to show his progress and skills in well drilling, he told us that he had not yet brought himself to share the gospel, and he was soon to leave for another station.

As we continued our survey wtih the last of the three missionaries, we met a Catholic missionary and his wife. They offered us some hand-squeezed lemonade, and it was wonderful, as were they. However, there was uneasiness to our dialogue, and he ultimately expressed his deep concern that we would try to come to his area to plant new churches, especially since the locals could ask him to leave before he would have the opportunity to finish his Ph.D. on traditional healing practices.

What does this illustration have to do with confirming the state of the unfinished task? It shows us that whether we are talking about the accuracy of a people group list or the state of the gospel among the listed people groups, someone has to go to the field to get ground truth. For those who are unable to go to the field themselves, they must rely on the information that comes to them, evaluate the quality of that information, and decide whether they feel it is the best possible source of truth for their needs.

Concerning the three lists – CPPI, JP and WCD – various sources are used and various experts have been consulted, even within a single column of data. Some information on each of the lists changes slowly; other information changes relatively quickly. There is not space here to discuss the data sources for each piece of information for the three lists, but there is space to talk about ways to sharpen our research and improve the state of the data.

Confirming through Field Assessments

No researcher is able to personally check out everything that she or he gathers and reports; this is why researchers weigh various sources of information in their analysis before settling on what they are going to use. However, there are times when fieldwork is necessary, and this usually comes when a researcher receives a report that is difficult to believe. In these cases, assessment teams are formed, trained and sent out.[22]

We have learned a great deal by doing field work in cooperation with other mission agencies and field workers. There have been Church Growth Strategy Studies, base counts and surveys, and in recent years, Church Planting Movement assessments. We learn a great deal about people groups in research projects such as these, and sometimes we learn a lot about ourselves. This kind of research helps to identify problems that exist as well as exciting breakthroughs that have occurred.

Field Assessments help us to see whether engagement reports are accurate; they help us to identify and understand fruitful practices; they help us to test our hypotheses before reaching conclusions, and they help us get to know great people that God is using in many hard places.

Confirming through Reporting

For the most part, research improves as it is published and used. Another way of saying this is that data accuracy is often proportional to data usage. Someone who conducts a research project and sticks it in a drawer may be personally satisfied, but if the research never sees the light of day and remains untested, it is unlikely to improve. On the other hand, someone who conducts a research project and makes it public for everyone to see will likely receive feedback generated by the posting. If this feedback is ignored, the data is unlikely to improve.

Researchers not only post results to inform others; they post results to gather new and better information, often through direct feedback. Those who provide feedback expect researchers to listen to them, take their feedback seriously, respond in a timely way, and provide an explanation as to the usefulness of their feedback. If the feedback results in a change to the data, the list holder should let the person providing the feedback know when the change will be reported. If the feedback does not result in a change to the data, the list holder should let the person providing the feedback know why the feedback will not result in a change to his research report.

IMB welcomes feedback from those who use CPPI data. Observations and suggestions are needed to improve the CPPI. When feedback is received, it is acknowledged and referred to an IMB Global Research staff liaison who discusses the feedback with one or more IMB strategy research associates on the field. IMB prefers firsthand, well-documented information whenever possible. Since changes to CPPI data are not made at the level of the global office, all feedback is referred to field workers, and it is they who must make the change to the data using the web-based CPPI reporting tool. When feedback

[22] Team composition, training that agrees upon research methodology, methodological pitfalls, logistics, and on-site conduct must be discussed thoroughly before any fieldwork is conducted so that the best information may be found without harm to the work.

results in changes to the CPPI, changes are reflected on the peoplegroups.org website within one to eight weeks.

The Joshua Project makes every effort to respond to questions, comments and feedback within two working days. If changes to Joshua Project data are suggested, the suggestions are evaluated against other sources, most notably the Ethnologue, the World Christian Database, Operation China and other books from Asia Harvest, research materials published in Southeast Asia, refined census data for South Asia, other census data, CPPI data, field input and other web searches. In addition, they will often consult their main data editors, Patrick Johnstone and Omid. If requested changes can be justified, they change their in-house master files promptly. These changes are then reflected on the Joshua Project website within approximately two weeks depending on their web update cycle.

The World Christian Database generally relies more heavily on published sources of data and information than on field sources, and hence the major revision cycles are geared towards publications such as the UN's population revisions (every two years), the Ethnologue (printed every few years), Bible Society annual reports for new translations, and censuses as they become available. While the ISO for example is continually updating language codes online, WCD will generally wait until a new revision of the *Ethnologue* is printed before incorporating these new languages and codes. Similarly, until a new scripture translation has reached the UBS library and is published in their annual report it will generally not appear in WCD. That said, the sheer volume of new specialist books and other publications appearing daily on all topics of relevance to world evangelization means that the database is being continually edited, and these edits are incorporated in WCD quarterly updates. Feedback from users is welcomed, particularly where it points to published material, and will be added in the context of this research cycle.

Confirming through Virtual Conferencing

With the advent of Skype, it is now convenient to conference with people all over the world almost effortlessly. One Global Network is utilizing this new tool to confirm the CPPI list and engagement information for people groups on the list, particularly those people groups upon which the Global Network is focusing – unengaged, unreached Muslim people groups that are 100,000 in population and larger. This list is called the 247 list since there were 247 on the list when the goal to engage these people groups was initiated.

One task force that is part of the Global Network works through a feedback facilitator who follows a process for list and engagement review. The basis of the review is the quarterly 247 list report that is securely posted on a portal for the Global Network research contacts and others. When the report is viewed, feedback is generated and directed to the feedback facilitator. This feedback does not result in immediate changes to either the list or the engagement report; instead, the feedback facilitator arranges a Skype meeting so that the feedback offered can receive first-hand review from frontline engagers; usually two or more the Global Network partners take part in a review.

The frontline engagers are the main voices solicited for these meetings. As Global Network partners provide names to the feedback facilitator of those who live in the country and/or among the people cluster to be reviewed, they are provided a spreadsheet for their review at least one month in advance of the Skype meeting. This gives them time to work through the list and edit what they see.

When the day of the meeting comes, the feedback facilitator begins the meeting and confirms that the people needed are in the 'room'. This includes the person responsible for CPPI edits (IMB), Global Research (IMB) and the feedback initiator and frontline engagers.

As the first pass is made through the part of the list under review, anyone can suggest the addition or deletion of people groups on the list. As this discussion takes place, the feedback facilitator notes consensus for changes to the list in the Skype chat window, which serves as a whiteboard that can be saved and distributed later. It is in this kind of environment that changes are made to the CPPI list or deferred until more research can be conducted.

The second pass through the list asks for confirmation of engagement teams on the ground. Sometimes, the frontline engagers will say that one of the people groups on the list is no longer engaged – a team was there last year, but they are no longer there. Sometimes they will confirm that a people group is engaged, and they will share more about what that team is doing. If a change to engagement status is to be recorded, consensus is needed within this group. When consensus is reached, it is noted on the virtual whiteboard.

When the second pass is finished, closing remarks are made and a follow-up meeting is scheduled for matters that have been deferred. After the meeting, the IMB field representative changes the CPPI for those items that have received consensus. Meeting notes, participant identities and locations, and identity of engagement teams remain confidential throughout the process.

Final Remarks: Research for the Greater Glory of God

We stand on the shoulders of many researchers who have gone before us and given their lives to understanding the unfinished task. Research, in its many forms, provides mission critical information to inform decision making so that our activity moves toward fulfilling the mandate of the Great Commission. Our research must be focused and cooperative so that we can stay the course making sure that every nation is engaged, established in the Church, and part of the global harvest force, to the greater glory of God.

Bibliography

Baird, Annie L. Daybreak in Korea: *A Tale of Transformation in the Far East*. New York: Revell, 1909.

Barrett, David B., George T. Kurian, and Todd M. Johnson (eds.). *World Christian Encyclopedia: a Comparative Survey of Churches and Religions in the Modern World*. Oxford: Oxford University Press, 2001.

Cary, Otis. *A History of Christianity in Japan*. New York: Revell, 1909.

Clark, Francis E. *The Continent of Opportunity; the South American Republics – Their History, Their Resources, Their Outlook. Together with a Traveler's Impressions of Present Day Conditions*. New York: Revell, 1907.

Gairdner, W. H. T., and John R. Mott. *Echoes from Edinburgh, 1910*. New York: Revell, 1910.

Harvest Information System Website, http://www.harvestinformationsystem.info.

Holste, Scott and Jim Haney. 'The Global Status of Evangelical Christianity: A Model for Assessing Priority People Groups'. *Mission Frontiers* (January–February, 2006), 8-13.

Johnson, Todd M., Kenneth R. Ross, and Sandra S. Lee (eds.). *Atlas of Global Christianity 1910–2010*. Edinburgh: Edinburgh University Press, 2009.

Johnson, Todd M. and Peter F. Crossing. 'Which Peoples Need Priority Attention? Those with the Least Christian Resources'. *Mission Frontiers* (January–February, 2002), 16-23.

– 'Priority Peoples: A Customized Approach'. *Mission Frontiers* (January–February, 2005), 8-14.

Johnstone, Patrick. 'Affinity Blocs and People Clusters: An Approach toward Strategic Insight and Mission Partnership', *Mission Frontiers* (March–April, 2007), 9.

Joshua Project Website, www.joshuaproject.net.

Latimer, Robert Sloan. *Under Three Tsars: Liberty of Conscience in Russia, 1856–1909*. London: Morgan & Scott, 1909.

Lewis, M. Paul. *Ethnologue: Languages of the World*. Dallas: SIL International, 2009. http://www.ethnologue.com/web.asp

Liverman, Jeff. 'Unplowed Ground: Engaging the Unreached'. In J. Dudley Woodberry (ed.). *From Seed to Fruit: Global Trends, Fruitful Practices, and Emerging Issues among Muslims*. Pasadena: William Carey Library, 2008, 23.

Long, Justin. 'Which Peoples Need Priority Attention? Seeking Agreement on the 'Core of the Core''. *Mission Frontiers* (March –April, 2007), 18-23.

People Groups website, www.peoplegroups.org.

Richter, Julius. *A History of Missions in India*. Edinburgh: Oliphant, 1908.

Scribner, Dan. 'A Model for Determining the Most Needy Unreached or Least-Reached Peoples'. *Mission Frontiers* (November–December, 2004), 6-13.

Watson, Charles R. *In the Valley of the Nile: A Survey of the Missionary Movement in Egypt*. New York: Revell, 1908

Woodberry, J. Dudley (ed.). *From Seed to Fruit: Global Trends, Fruitful Practices, and Emerging Issues among Muslims*. Pasadena: William Carey Library, 2008.

World Christian Database, http://worldchristiandatabase.org/wcd.

Zwemer, Samuel M. *Islam, a Challenge to Faith; Studies on the Mohammedan Religion and the Needs and Opportunities of the Mohammedan World from the Standpoint of Christian Missions*. New York: Student Volunteer Movement for Foreign Missions, 1907.

– *The Unoccupied Mission Fields of Africa and Asia*. New York: Student Volunteer Movement for Foreign Missions, 1911.

TOKYO 2010 AND CAPE TOWN 2010 REFLECTIONS

Making Disciples of Every People in Our Generation: The Vision, Purpose and Objectives of Tokyo 2010

Yong Cho and David Taylor

Editors' Note: *One of the four gatherings celebrating the centenary of Edinburgh 1910 took place in Tokyo. For those readers not familiar with the Tokyo 2010 Global Mission Consultation, this helpful overview explains the purpose and framing.*

At the Tokyo 2010 Global Mission Consultation held May 11-14, 2010, over 960 delegates from 73 countries met together. The gathering was sponsored by dozens of national, regional and global mission networks and associations, representing 100,000 cross-cultural missionaries. The purpose of the gathering was to celebrate the progress made in missionary efforts since Edinburgh 1910, assess what remains to be done in making disciples of all peoples, and develop plans for inter-mission cooperation to fully engage the remaining least-reached peoples in our generation.

Following the pattern of Edinburgh 1910, most of the delegates came as representatives of their mission sending structure. Many were the CEOs or top decision makers of both large and small organizations from around the world. Beginning a process that will continue well beyond Tokyo, mission agencies were asked to make specific commitments to send church planting teams to those people groups without any missionary work. A special listing called the Finishing the Task List was distributed at the meeting, detailing the existence of 632 unreached people groups over 50,000 in population without any long-term missionary engagement. Specific commitments were made at Tokyo 2010 to engage 171 of these in the next three years with evangelism and church planting initiatives. Mission organizations also signed up to send out 1,244 oral Bible teams, which will translate and dub Bible video stories for priority language groups where the majority of the population are primarily oral learners. Eighty-five mission agencies also volunteered to help with national surveys in their country to document those areas without access to a culturally relevant local church.

In addition to focusing on the least-reached peoples and places in the world – referred to as the 'breadth' of the Great Commission at Tokyo 2010 – the consultation also brought attention to the 'depth' of the Great Commission mandate, represented by the phrase 'teaching them to obey all that I have commanded' (Matthew 28:20). The Tokyo Declaration issued at the consultation (included in this volume) underscored the importance of this dimension both at the individual level as well as at the social or national level. Under the category of transformation the Declaration made the following affirmations:

> The new believer's worldview must be adjusted to a biblical worldview; his lifestyle changed to increasingly conform to the image of Christ; and his ethical conduct progressively marked by biblical morals. Ideally, this results in individuals applying the gospel of the kingdom to every sphere and pursuit of life – from government to economics, from education to health, and from science to creation care. As a consequence whole communities, cultures and countries benefit from the transforming power of the gospel.

The Tokyo Declaration's emphasis on the transformational dimension of the Great Commission added an element to the Edinburgh 1910 tradition that many mission leaders felt had been a glaring omission in previous gatherings. For this reason the theme and watchword for Tokyo 2010 was established as 'making disciples of every people in our generation'. This watchword built on the earlier watchwords of Edinburgh 1910 and Edinburgh 1980: 'the evangelization of the world in this generation' and 'a church for every people by the year 2000'. The watchword of Tokyo 2010 thus took the 'generation' time frame of Edinburgh 1910, and the people group emphasis of Edinburgh 1980, and added the discipling aspect of Matthew 28:19-20. In doing so, Tokyo 2010 sought to draw attention to an important progression over the last century that has led to greater depth as well as precision in defining how we measure success in fulfilling the Great Commission.

Background and Uniqueness of Tokyo 2010

Tokyo 2010 was the first of four gatherings commemorating the centennial anniversary of the Edinburgh 1910 meeting. Each of these gatherings were designed to have a unique focus and delegation, the combined sum of which should well represent and touch virtually every church and mission tradition in the world – from Pentecostals to Roman Catholics to the Eastern Orthodox community.

The purpose and special contribution of Tokyo 2010 was to reproduce four elements of Edinburgh 1910 which made that gathering historically significant to the global mission community: 1) Delegates came as representatives of all the major evangelical sending agencies and nations of the world, 2) The specific focus was on the final frontiers of the Great Commission, 3) Concerted effort was made to identify and fill in the gaps of inter-mission collaboration, 4) Participating agencies continued to cooperate following the meeting on the national, regional and global level to reach the remaining 'unengaged' non-Christian peoples (today's terminology for what were called the 'unoccupied fields' in 1910).

The Tokyo meeting was first called for by the late Ralph D Winter, convener of Edinburgh 1980. Though two other global meetings were planned in 1980, one sponsored by the Lausanne movement and the other by the World Council of Churches, Winter felt it was necessary to call a meeting that would follow the Edinburgh 1910 pattern, especially with regard to its emphasis on bringing together mission agencies to focus on reaching the final frontiers. Almost the exact same scenario would be repeated thirty years later, though unlike in 1980, the organizers of all the 2010 meetings met together in advance, exhibiting a spirit of cooperation and Christian unity.

The Edinburgh 1980 meeting encouraged mission agencies to focus on the year 2000 as a milestone for seeing a missiological breakthrough – or the birth of an indigenous church with national leadership – in every people group in the world. From out of the momentum of this meeting developed the AD2000 & Beyond Movement, which for ten years became the largest frontier mission network of evangelical agencies and denominations ever assembled. Following the wake of the AD2000 movement, and as the centennial of Edinburgh 1910 approached, Winter convened a meeting of Majority World mission leaders and challenged them to organize a global mission consultation that would follow the blueprint of Edinburgh 1910 and 1980. However, in keeping with the new realities of global mission, this third Edinburgh-type meeting would be held outside of the West, and would be organized primarily by Majority World mission leaders, networks and agencies. At the same time, the meeting was to be a global effort, meaning western participation was welcome and encouraged, but would only represent a minority contribution.

The result of Winter's challenge was that Tokyo 2010 became the first-ever global level meeting following the Edinburgh 1910 pattern that was planned, organized, led and funded primarily by the Majority World mission movement. In contrast, the Edinburgh 1910 meeting had just a handful of participants from outside the West, none of which came as representatives of non-western mission agencies, and none of which were part of the leadership team. Similarly, Edinburgh 1980 had just one person from outside the West on its executive team, although its delegation was made up of one-third Majority World mission leaders – an achievement which was greatly celebrated.

As envisioned, Tokyo 2010 reflected almost the reverse of the Edinburgh 1980 meeting, with around 74% of its delegation coming from the Majority World, and a similar percentage making up its leadership team. These percentages closely resemble the proportions of missionary sending today in the early 21st century. The percentages of delegates coming from various countries and regions also closely reflected their proportional contribution to the global missionary force.

Another unique contribution of Tokyo 2010 to the Edinburgh tradition was its inclusion and elevation of the 'secular peoples of Europe' as a 'frontier mission' priority for the global church. One of the most moving times during the consultation followed the presentation of Stefan Gustavsson, leader of the Swedish Evangelical Alliance, who described the dismal situation of both the society and church in Europe. After his presentation, the entire consultation (most of which represented the fruit of European missionary sending in past centuries) began to intercede for this once Christian continent that is now itself in need of pioneer missionary effort – a phenomenon being referred to as 'reverse mission'. At the same time, many Majority World mission leaders remarked that the very trends which contributed to the decline of the church in Europe are beginning to affect their countries as well. Such a realization brought Tokyo 2010's theme of discipleship into even sharper focus, underscoring the reality that the Christian faith is just a generation away from extinction in every society.

Beyond Tokyo 2010

One of the visions of the Edinburgh 1980 meeting was to see an ongoing global networking structure for mission agencies that would function in a similar capacity to Edinburgh 1910's International Missionary Council (IMC). Although the AD2000 and Beyond Movement helped to facilitate this in part, the central office was disbanded as scheduled in the year 2000. In order to fill in this gap, Ralph Winter convened a small meeting of mission leaders from around the world in the year 2005 to discuss what it would take to bring a global network into reality that would facilitate inter-mission cooperation to finish the task of reaching all the world's remaining unreached peoples. From out of this discussion, the foundations were laid for what has become the Global Network of Mission Structures (GNMS). The first task and priority of this new network was to coordinate efforts for Tokyo 2010, and following this consultation, to help steward whatever visions and plans the Holy Spirit might generate from the gathering.

In the pattern of Edinburgh 1980, coordinating task forces and study groups at Tokyo 2010 were encouraged to think towards a specific milestone, in this case the year 2020, and to ask the question, 'What is it going to take to see a disciple-making movement among all the world's unreached peoples in the next decade?' The media task force, for example, set a goal to form a 20/20 Vision Partnership that would facilitate the development of contextualized media resources for every least-reached people over one million in population by the year 2020. (The significance of prioritizing these larger ethnolinguistic groups is that most of the world's smaller unreached peoples are influenced by or can access media in one or more of the languages of these so called 'mega-peoples').

Altogether, there were 18 coordinating task forces at Tokyo 2010, which focused on areas such as frontier mission training, unreached people intercession, crisis response, missiological research, next generation mobilization, technology and mission, mission associations and networks, field partnerships and cooperation, and unreached people engagement. Each task force was encouraged to develop and discuss strategy papers that would examine the scope of the need in their particular area of focus, identify what is presently being done, and propose specific recommendations to mission agencies for how they might more effectively work together to bridge existing gaps.

From out of this study process, the Global Network of Mission Structures (GNMS) has begun to prioritize specific areas for development that will require central coordination over the next five to ten years. One of those priorities is the formation of national and regional task forces that will assess the progress of missionary deployment among the least-reached peoples and develop specific strategies to engage those population segments without any church planting initiatives. Two large international agencies volunteered at Tokyo 2010's Global Coordination Task Force to help facilitate this process in every country and region that may require it. Another priority is the establishment of special forums to bring together on an annual basis the directors of major international missions, regional and national field leaders of expatriate missions, and coordinators of national mission associations. The latter group, which met together as part of the Mission Associations and Networks Task Force, had already set plans in motion to begin coordinating annual meetings within a few months of the conference.

Finally, the planning of Tokyo 2010 revealed the general lack of global mission intelligence in multiple areas, which the GNMS will begin to address over the next several years. There is still, for example, no existing directory of African or European mission agencies, no global registry for missionary deployment among unreached peoples, and more importantly, no unified listing of the world's priority unengaged peoples and population segments. The latter was addressed at Tokyo 2010 through the creation of the Last Mile Calling (LMC) list, which combines data from the three principle databases of people groups: the World Christian Database, the International Mission Board's database (known as the CPPI, which stands for Church Planting Progress Indicators), and the Joshua Project Database. The LMC list can be viewed online.

In addition to addressing these intelligence gaps, the research department of the GNMS has begun to gather existing mission data into a global directory that will include information on all the world's known mission agencies, mission training centers, mission resources, and unreached peoples. Much of this data will be made accessible to members on the GNMS website. "Membership in the GNMS is open to any evangelical mission agency with a commitment to reaching the final frontiers of the Great Commission" (http://www.gnms.net). A more exclusive directory of mission leaders is also being developed which will be made available only to participating mission agencies. A similar private directory of mission resource people will also be maintained by the Global Network for the purpose of identifying consultants that have expertise in various critical areas, ranging from missionary care to accounting to relief and development.

Towards a Global Strategy to Finish the Task

In keeping with the Edinburgh tradition, the overall purpose of Tokyo 2010 and the GNMS is to build a global alliance of at least 2,000 mission agencies around the world working together to finish the task of reaching all the remaining frontier people groups. Towards this end, the GNMS will act as a forum for developing and stewarding a global strategy to recruit, train, deploy, and empower a new wave of church planting teams among the least-reached such that the goal of 'full engagement' will have been achieved by the year 2020, or at the latest by the year 2025. The value of developing a global strategy with specific objectives and outcomes will be that existing networks, associations, partnerships, sending agencies, training programs, etc., will be able to plug in and take responsibility for a particular component of the strategy. As this is done over the months and years ahead we will be able to more accurately assess what is missing and propose the creation of any new structures needed to fill the gaps.

In the same way that task forces at Tokyo 2010 set decadal goals for the year 2020, participating agencies will also be encouraged to set visionary 2020 goals in relation to reaching the remaining least-reached peoples. As these decadal plans are compiled and analyzed, we will have a clearer picture of what the Holy Spirit is leading us to do together over the next ten years. The critical months following Tokyo 2010 will involve much assessment, reflection, and dialogue with mission leaders about moving forward together to see all peoples fully engaged with church-planting and disciple-making teams in the most efficient and effective way possible.

Tokyo 2010 Declaration: Making Disciples of Every People in Our Generation

Editors' Note: *This Declaration was developed by delegates from a variety of cultures and includes gender specific language which was apparently not a sensitive issue for the writers and signers.*

Preamble

We affirm that mission is the central theme of Scripture, through which God reveals himself to be a God who communicates and works through us by action and word in a world estranged from Him. Furthermore, we recognize that fulfilling and bringing completion to Jesus' Great Commission (Matt. 28:18-20; Mark 16:15; Luke 24:44-49; John 20:21; Acts 1:8) has been the on-going responsibility of the Church for 2000 years.

In this era of missions, we of the Tokyo 2010 Global Mission Consultation value and commemorate the Edinburgh 1910 World Missionary Conference, a hallmark event which stands out as an inspiration and impetus to the modern global mission movement. We celebrate a legacy of 100 years of mission that has transpired since that first world missionary conference.

However, the world has dramatically changed since that conference was convened a century ago. Missions is no longer the predominant domain of western Christianity. Rather, the preponderance of mission activity today is being engaged by Majority World Christians outside of the West. Christ's ambassadors are coming from everywhere around the world and going to anywhere and everywhere in the world. We rejoice that today's mission force is global in composition, bearing a diversity of thought, practice and resources that enriches and energizes Christ's global Cause as never before.

Yet, the corresponding reality is that the present day mission task is so large and complex that no one church, agency, national missions movement, or regional mission block can take it on alone or independently. Also, the understanding of the essence of what is entailed in the remaining task has altered considerably in recent years.

Declaration

We, representatives of evangelical global mission structures, being intent on fulfilling the ultimate objective of the Great Commission, have gathered in Tokyo May 11-14, 2010 at this Global Mission Consultation to make the following declaration. We set forth this declaration in obedience to Christ's final command, as a means of calling Christ-followers everywhere to wholeheartedly embrace and earnestly engage in 'making disciples of every people in our generation'.

Mankind's Need

We affirm that all people are lost apart from faith in Christ. The clear statements of Scripture reveal that every individual, without exception, is a sinner by nature, choice and practice (Rom. 3:9-18, 23). As such, all are under God's wrath and condemnation (John 3:18) because their sin is an affront to the perfect and holy nature of God (Rom. 1:18; 2:2-5). The tragic result of sin is man's alienation from God, leading to everlasting death (Rom. 6:23), and creation's bondage to corruption, subjecting it to futility (Rom. 8:18-21).

God's Remedy

We further affirm that out of love, God sent His only Son, Jesus Christ (John 3:16), to reconcile the world to himself, so that mankind's sin will not be counted against them (2 Cor. 5:19). God's justice for the penalty of sin was satisfied by the atoning death of Christ as a sacrifice on man's behalf. Through Jesus' vicarious death and victorious resurrection, mankind is brought into a restored relationship with God. God offers forgiveness and salvation to all who, through faith, repent of their sin and believe solely in the redemptive work of Christ on the cross on their behalf (Rom. 1:5,16,17; 3:21-26; Eph. 1:7; 2:8-10). Therefore the message of the Great Commission is that 'repentance and forgiveness of sins will be preached in His name to all peoples' (Luke 24:47). Salvation is found in none other (Acts 4:12), nor in any other way (John 14:6).

Our Responsibility

Because of the reality of mankind's dire need and God's gracious remedy, Jesus left with His followers the missional priority of making disciples of every people (Matt. 28:18-20). By this mandate we acknowledge both the breadth of the unfinished task – *all peoples* – and the depth of the task – *making disciples*, as its focus.

We recognize the breadth of our task as geographical, by going 'into all the world' (Mark 16:15); as ethnic, by engaging 'all peoples' (Matt. 28:19; Luke 24:49); and as individual by proclaiming the gospel to 'every creature' (Mark 16:15).

Furthermore, we recognize that the depth of the task contains three essentials that comprise aspects in discipling peoples (Matt. 28:19-20):

> PENETRATION ('GO'): making a priority of going to those who have had little or no exposure to the gospel. Messengers go and encounter non-believers by way of personal encounters, broadcasts, podcasts, printed material, recordings, electronic communications, or any other

innovative means used as a channel of penetrating witness. Thus, the importance of the ministry of evangelizing.

CONSOLIDATION ('BAPTIZING'): gathering new believers into a relationship with Jesus and other believers, which is evidenced by the identifying rite of baptism. To conserve the fruit of evangelism and then be able to systematically disciple believers takes a local body of believers living in corporate harmony. Thus, the importance of the ministry of establishing churches.

TRANSFORMATION ('TEACHING TO OBEY'): teaching Christ-followers to observe His commands with the outcome of transformed lives. The new believer's worldview must be adjusted to a biblical worldview; his lifestyle changed to increasingly conform to the image of Christ; and his ethical conduct progressively marked by biblical morals. Ideally, this results in individuals applying the gospel of the kingdom to every sphere and pursuit of life – from government to economics, from education to health, and from science to creation care. As a consequence whole communities, cultures and countries benefit from the transforming power of the gospel. Thus, the importance of the ministry of teaching.

Finishing the Task

Although none dare predict when the task of making disciples will be brought to completion, we leave Tokyo cognizant of two realities:

1. We are closer now to finishing the task than at any time in modern history.
2. God has entrusted this generation with more opportunities and resources to complete the task than any previous one. We have more mission-minded churches, more sending structures and bases, more missionaries, more material resources, more funding, more and better technology, more information and data, a deeper understanding of the task, and a clearer focus of our responsibility than previous generations. God will require much of our generation.

However, we caution that all these advantages must be matched with a corresponding *will to serve and sacrifice*, coupled with genuine reliance upon the Holy Spirit. We acknowledge that we are engaged in spiritual warfare in which the presence and empowering of the Holy Spirit is essential (Acts 1:8). We give evidence of our reliance on God and His Spirit through frequent and fervent prayer on behalf of the world, the work and the workers (John 17:20-21; Col. 4:3-4; 1 Thess. 5:17).

Our Pledge

Therefore, as representatives of this generation's global mission community, we pledge to obey the Great Commission. We covenant together to use all that God has entrusted to us in this obedience. We will seek to know where people are unreached, overlooked, ignored, or forgotten. We will pray for the Holy Spirit to give strength and guidance as we join with others in changing that neglect, to love and make disciples in the way of the Cross.

We confess that we have not always valued each other or each other's work. We repent of those wrongs and will endeavor to bring an end to competition where it exists, and reconcile where there is hurt, misunderstanding and mistrust. Furthermore, we will endeavor to recognize that each part of the Body has its very own purpose, whether risking their very lives to show God's passion for the salvation of others, or supporting those who lead us forward, or caring for those who quietly support, or fervently pray that His will be done throughout the whole earth. We will respect all mission-engaging individuals and groups as special vessels for God's glory, each endowed with abilities that extend His kingdom in multiple ways.

Finally, we recognize that finishing the task will demand effective cooperative efforts of the entire global body of believers. To facilitate cooperation and on-going coordination between mission structures worldwide, we agree to the necessity of a global network of mission structures. With this in mind, we leave Tokyo pledging cooperation with one another, and all others of like faith, with the singular goal of 'making disciples of every people in our generation'.

Signatories of the Tokyo 2010 Declaration

Global Mission Structures

Ethna to Ethna
Global Network of Mission Structures
Globe Serve
Lausanne Committee For World Evangelization
Muslim Unreached Peoples Network
Nomadic Peoples Network
Third World Mission Association
World Evangelical Alliance – Theological Commission

World Evangelical Alliance – Mission Commission

Regional Mission Structures

Asia Mission Association
COMIBAM International (pending ratification)

Evangelical Association of the Caribbean
Evangelical Missiological Society of US and Canada

CrossGlobal Link of North America

MANI (Movement of African National Initiatives)
SAMA Link
SEA Link
SEA Net

National Mission Structures

AMTB – Associação de MissõesTransculturais Brasileiras (Brazil)
Ghana Evangelical Missions Association
India Missions Association

Japan Evangelical Missionary Association
Japan Overseas Missions Association
Korean World Missions Association

Nigeria Evangelical Missions Association
Philippine Missions Association
Singapore Centre for Global Mission
Swedish Evangelical Alliance
The Mission Exchange, USA
AFCM-OWM (USA)

Missiology and the Measurement of Engagement: Personal Reflections on Tokyo

Kevin S. Higgins

Reprinted by permission,
International Journal of Frontier Missiology, 27:3 (Fall, 2010)

Editors' Note: *This reflection from an agency leader offers a more personal perspective on Tokyo 2010. Over the 20th century, evangelicals integrally linked eschatological concepts with missional work. In this chapter, Higgins integrates thinking on 'engaging' people with the Gospel and 'finishing the task' into a picture of 'closure' for mission, an idea that resonates with many evangelicals.*

Introduction

The Consultation and Celebration held in Tokyo in May, 2010 was one of four events held in 2010 to commemorate in various ways the great Edinburgh 1910 conference. In chronological order the four events included gatherings held in Tokyo, Edinburgh, Cape Town, and Boston. Each was conceived with a unique purpose and audience.

Tokyo will very likely prove to be the gathering most directly connected to the vision of 'finishing the task.' As such, in addition to numerous workshops and plenary addresses devoted to missional and biblical themes and issues across a broad spectrum of concerns, there was a distinctive focus in Tokyo on coordinating as organizations and churches to achieve 'closure' of the missionary task by measuring the extent to which we have reached the unreached and engaged the unengaged. For ease of discussion I will refer generally to this as the closure movement.

In this emphasis on finishing the task, the leadership of Tokyo 2010 was self-consciously standing on the shoulders of prior leaders and movements in the history of the missionary expansion of the church. This great chain was traced again and again in plenary sessions and workshops from Tokyo back through time including (quite selectively): an important gathering in Singapore in 2002 called for by the network of various Centers for World Mission,

InterDev, Joshua Project II and others,[1] the AD 2000 movement; Ralph Winter and hidden peoples (subsequently, unreached peoples); Donald McGavran; Edinburgh 1910 and its emphasis on reaching the world in a generation; the great missionary expansion of the 18th and 19th centuries; movements of monks and migrants; Jesus' final words on reaching all nations; and ultimately back through the Old Testament to Abraham's calling to be a blessing to all nations.[2]

The evangelical missionary effort to complete the Great Commission has successively reworked its terminology and methodology. One major emphasis has been the collection of data about people groups and the status of evangelization and Christian expansion. Depending upon the researcher or the specific database in question, such data may include percentages of exposure to the Gospel, resources or literature available in a people group, the status of church planting, etc. This work of data collection, definition, categorization, communication, and coordination has been immense and has left a lasting legacy for the mission movement to build upon.[3] To describe the data, various attempts at definition have been employed to clarify what constitutes an unreached or unengaged people group. The variety in how such terms are employed results in further variety when attempts are made to list which groups are unreached or unengaged.

Of the major attempts at seeking to bring different perspectives on closure together in a synthesized perspective, Ralph Winter's 2002 article, 'Finishing the Task: The Unreached Peoples Challenge' stands out.[4] Winter discusses four perspectives observed in seeking to define the task of closure relative to understanding which people groups remain unreached. He 'slices' the world into 8 Blocs (cultural and affinity, including Muslim, Hindu, etc.), Ethno-linguistic peoples (of which 3,000 are unevangelized), Socio-peoples

---

[1] See the brief discussion of this event and its focus in Greg Parsons' editorial comments in *IJFM* 19:4 (2002), 5.

[2] See for example, McGavran's seminal article, Donald McGavran, 'A Church in Every People', in Ralph D. Winter and Stephen Hawthorne (eds), *Perspectives on the World Christian Movement* (Pasadena: William Carey Library, 1982), chapter 64. Also, see Samuel Wilson's discussion, 'Peoples, People Groups', in Moreau, *Evangelical Dictionary of World Missions*, 746.

[3] A detailed discussion is beyond the scope of this essay. For a helpful summary, the abridged version of Paul Eshleman's plenary address in Tokyo is a succinct discussion ('The State of the Unfinished Task', *Mission Frontiers* [July-August, 2010], 10-11). Some of the major web-based lists of people groups being consulted in the closure effort include: www.finsihingthetask.com; The Global Status of Evangelical Christianity, a research effort of the International Mission Board, which can be found at http://www.imb.org/globalresearch/sge.asp; and the Joshua Project, at http://www.joshuaproject.net. The statistics in each differ in varying ways since the compilers employ different criteria for measurement.

[4] Ralph D. Winter and Bruce Koch, 'Finishing the Task: The Unreached Peoples Challenge', *IJFM* 19:4 (Fall, 2002), 15-25.

(described as 'peer groups' but clearly larger than the way most might use the term peer, of which 10,000 are unreached), and Unimax peoples.[5]

The last term in the list, 'Unimax', is defined in the way I had come to understand one of the common definitions of a people group: the largest group of people within which the Gospel can spread as a church planting movement without encountering significant barriers.[6] Winter says there is an unknown number of such Unimax peoples, a statement which is important to hold in balance as mission strategists seek to use lists of people groups for the purposes of planning the alignment of personnel and resources for closure. Winter's taxonomy suggests that, in the end, we really don't know the scope of the task remaining.

In Tokyo, there was no attempt to try to come to consensus regarding this variety of definitions and assessments. The reality of the existence of such a variety was acknowledged and maintained. Participants were encouraged to look at and use all of the databases. In one track of the Tokyo gathering mission leaders were encouraged to commit themselves on behalf of their respective organizations to engage specific people groups over the next three years with focused church planting efforts, and to assist in various other strategic tasks such as cooperating in the production/distribution of the *Jesus* Film, etc.

Asking Questions of Myself about Closure

My purpose in this essay is to try to bring to the fore some questions about the approach just described. I do so from two self-conscious perspectives. First, I write as a friend of the 'closure' movement. The organization I direct has crafted its own mission statement largely in keeping with objectives that can be traced to the Great Commission as framed by McGavran, Winter, the AD 2000 movement, and the Finishing the Task effort. The mission of GLOBAL TEAMS is to equip and send teams of missionaries from many nations to multiply disciples of Jesus within cultures least aware of the Gospel. As a friend of the closure movement I have embraced in my thinking, for example, the commitment to the emergence of church planting movements as a key indicator of whether a people group is reached or not.

As such I have encouraged our organization to use the scale developed by the Southern Baptist research effort. (See the scale in Haney's chapter in this volume, "The Global Status of Evangelical Christianity.")

Much of the criteria in this scale is related to the existence and extent of church planting taking place in a given people group. In the case of Global Teams, we have focused strategically on people groups in the 0 to 2 range for

[5] Winter and Koch, 'Finishing the Task'. Winter provides a helpful chart for summary on page 20.
[6] Winter and Koch, 'Finishing the Task', 18.

our pioneer efforts, and see level 3 and above as more appropriately calling for a mobilization effort.

But such criteria for the use of this information presuppose a number of assumptions: what is a church? What is church planting? What constitutes a church planting strategy or plan or even team? What is evangelical Christianity? What is *Christianity* for that matter? I am not suggesting that a scale like this one should provide such definitions, I am merely pointing out that the answers to the questions I just listed would likely be answered in a variety of ways by leaders of organizations who are totally committed to the closure vision. Clarity on this issue is crucial, for the criteria behind our data will directly affect our measurement of closure. The very term 'measurement' implies a clearly articulated standard of reference. On this point Winter's 2002 article offers a helpful perspective, in which he seeks to articulate a difference between measurability and verifiability. He rejects the former and encourages us to think in terms of the latter. He uses the example of AIDS, implying that we are not able to measure, and do not seek to measure, 'how much AIDS' a person has, but we can verify that they have it. Implication: we cannot measure how reached a people group is, but we can verify whether or not they are. [7]

This leads me to my second frame of reference. I also write as one associated closely with the so-called 'insider movement' approach. Many mission strategists, including myself, would like to see the missions community move away from the term 'insider movement', as it does not connote accurately what we are seeking to describe. Instead we are seeking to use language such as 'movements to Jesus within Islam (or Buddhism, etc.)', or 'biblically faithful movements to Jesus within Hinduism (etc.)' I have spent over 20 years in a particular Islamic context and have seen the rise and growth of a movement to Jesus that fosters both an ongoing commitment to remain within the religious community of Islam and to plant and multiply intentional communities of believers in Jesus at the same time. This experience shapes my understanding of how to measure or verify church planting, evangelical Christianity, and thus closure.

These twin convictions have given rise to numerous questions, internally. My questions are birthed from my reflections on certain aspects of the closure movement from the perspective of someone who has witnessed the growth and expansion of a movement to Jesus among Muslims that has not fit the pattern that seems to be assumed by our measurements of whether a people group is engaged or reached.

Tokyo served as the event that for the first time brought both of these sides of my thinking into direct connection in a new and profound way. It was during the time in Tokyo that I first began to ask the questions I raise here. This is just one of the valuable results of the Tokyo event. Because I am shaped by both the closure movement and the so-called insider approach, I have referred to this

[7] See Winter and Koch, 'Finishing the Task', 21.

sub-section as 'asking questions of myself'. These are questions I had not asked prior to Tokyo, which served as the catalyst for seeing these issues as I do now.

A Short Story about Reaching a People Group

First, it might be helpful to say a bit more about my context. For the past twenty years I have been in a position to observe the growth of a movement to Jesus that has intentionally remained within the fabric of Islamic culture and practice. The movement does not describe itself as a Christian movement. However, at the same time, movement leadership intentionally focuses on obedience to biblical teaching and truth and a deepening discipleship as followers of Jesus. Forms of fellowship for believers have emerged, and there has been intentional expansion of the movement both within the original people group in which it was birthed, and beyond that people group to peoples of other languages and in other countries. Regular training for leaders takes place, based upon understanding and applying the Bible in daily life and in addressing theological and cultural questions that arise.

At one point, nearly fifteen years ago, using one of the lists of remaining unreached peoples, we identified a people group in our country that was on the list. I will call them the 'Jedi'. I invited churches to 'adopt' the Jedi and we began to pray for a strategy to reach them with the Gospel. We surveyed the people group with the help of believers from a geographically and culturally-near people.

About two years into that process, and well before we had been able to launch any of the possible plans or strategies conceived from our survey work, I was at a gathering of leaders from the emerging movement. There were new leaders present and I was getting to know them. It turned out that two of these leaders were Jedi, the people for whom we had been praying. These two leaders had become believers and had joined our monthly leader training events, but without any launch of our plans or strategies.

Some Observations about What 'Church' Looks Like in a People Group

This is not to say there was no strategic value to what was happening. As we investigated how this had all come about I realized several important things. First, though we were seeing the Jedi as a distinct people for the purpose of our planning and strategizing, and though they had a distinct language, they saw themselves as part of another, larger, people group, and were seen as such by others around them. Going back to Winter's taxonomy, referenced earlier, the Jedi would be defined by outsiders such as ourselves as an Ethnolinguistic group, within which (according to Winter's model) we would expect to see further distinctions such as Socio-peoples and Unimax groups that would require more segmentation in approach. In fact what we found was that the Jedi identified with a larger Ethnolinguistic group and saw themselves related to that group in terms more akin to what Winter called a Unimax group. The segmentation followed a larger rather than a smaller link.

Second, the decision to 'focus' on this people group, or to 'engage' them, was a distinct decision from my *etic* (outside) perspective, but was not so from an *emic* (inside) point of view. People came to Christ among the Jedi naturally, via lines of relationship. As a result, this people group was, in fact, already 'engaged', and church planting was beginning, before we as missionaries knew it was happening. Those of us in the closure movement would agree that our lists of unreached and unengaged peoples are simply our best understanding of field reality based on available, reported information.

The third observation I would make is that prior conceptions will shape what we find in the field. Since the closure criteria revolve so much around church planting, then our understanding of church will shape how we decide whether church planting is in fact taking place, or not. In our case, as a movement to Christ among Muslims was beginning and growing, I and others sat with key leaders to study the scriptures, seeking to understand and apply biblical teaching about 'church' to the movement: How do we know when a church is planted? What do such churches do when they meet? When and where do churches meet, or when and where does church happen? These are thorny issues for many. Our movement developed a few criteria, based finally in Acts 2:42ff. 'They devoted themselves to the apostles' teaching and to the fellowship, to the breaking of bread and to prayer. … And the Lord added to their number daily those who were being saved.' In our study we concluded that healthy churches are committed to ongoing learning from the Bible, to regular fellowship/being together, to some expression of breaking bread (including meals and some form of the Lord's Supper), and prayer. Based on Acts 14:21ff we also agreed that it was key to assure our movement that, indeed, we had trained leaders.

But during this exercise we did not specify anything like a description of the *form* any of the above functions should take in order to be church. Our focus was on functions we found in scripture, not on specific forms that must be taken as universal carriers of those functions. 'Churches' in our movement might meet at any time, any day, and with any number of people. While such churches generally grew out of already existing social networks, they might be a nuclear or extended family, or a group of families, or a group of non-related individuals with or without a prior friendship or connection already in existence. They might meet weekly, but they might meet less or more frequently.

My sense is that the forms of church and fellowship that are taking shape in this movement would not fit the criteria most would look for in order to determine whether a people group was reached or not. I do not think anyone in the closure movement is suggesting a specific polity (much less denominational form) for 'church'. In fact, I have sensed a genuine flexibility in the viewpoints that are brought to the table. But some of the models presented at Tokyo 2010 in the track devoted to closure were built around measuring the extent of church planting by collecting data for churches such as meeting location, numbers of members, names and addresses of pastors, etc. While I do not see anything wrong with seeking such data, and in some contexts this may well be quite appropriate and helpful, in the context of our movement it would not only be impossible, but also an attempt to measure things we would not see as essential to 'church' and thus not actually informative as to the extent of a church planting effort.

Understanding 'Engagement' and 'Finishing the Task'

This brief window into my background and ministry might help explain the questions I am now posing as I try to understand what 'finishing the task' might look like and how it might be understood when we take such movements into account. But in applying all of this to the closure movement and measurement of engagement and extent to which a people group is reached, I will limit myself to what I see as the two major questions.

How Can We Determine Whether a People Group Is Engaged or Not?

I gave just one example in one country for one people group, but it is a story repeated in other people groups in our region. One nexus of questions this raises for me is how such realities on the ground should shape how we think about measuring and promoting engagement. To rephrase the question, in the example I gave, at which point was the people group I use in the example 'engaged'?

Typically, I have viewed 'engagement' the way I am sure most of my colleagues in the wider evangelical mission movement have done. I have assumed that engaging a people group meant that an organization or church intentionally selected such a people group as a focus for strategy and evangelization. My colleagues and I would include western and Majority World mission and church structures in our understanding. But now I am asking myself, and by extension the wider missions movement, 'If followers of Jesus within Islam, or Buddhism, or Hinduism are reaching a people group by sharing the Gospel and developing appropriate forms of fellowship for believers, is that people now engaged?' Proponents of the so-called insider movement approach have been misunderstood as if we were advocating some sort of individualistic expression of the Gospel. In fact, every such movement I have witnessed personally or have seen described by others has developed very clear forms of *koinonia* among believers.

I am more and more convinced that those of us in the closure movement should find a way to take such movements to Jesus into account as we evaluate what God might be doing to bring the nations to himself. How should we do so? I will suggest a few thoughts at the end of this essay.

How Do We Determine Whether a People Group Is Reached or Not?

I mentioned above that our own organization uses the database and criteria developed by the International Mission Board. As we saw above, the database uses a scale of 0 to 7 to measure the extent to which a people group is reached or unreached. The higher the number the more a people group is considered reached. Among the criteria used in that scale, we mentioned that church planting is key.

But how do we determine, for the sake of measuring the progress of the Gospel, whether a church has been planted, in light of the example I gave above? One organization may set the standard as a gathering of believers that includes at least three family heads. Another says ten families. While both are helpful in making measurement possible, neither can claim to be biblical, strictly speaking.

Some may be tempted to suggest that we should simply claim the words of Jesus as our measure, 'where two are three are gathered together in my name'.... Tempting as that may be, Jesus was not in fact seeking to define church, per se, in that verse but rather the function of discipline within what we call church.

The movements I am most familiar with experience multiplication of believers and they encourage expressions of *koinonia* among disciples. If these movements are growing in number, then would we not want to say that the progress of church planting is also growing in that people group? Of course, the answer to that will depend largely on the perception, and especially ecclesiology, of the person answering.

Elsewhere I have suggested using the description of functions found in Acts 14:21-28 as a grid for understanding the core functions of church: evangelizing, discipleship, ongoing encouragement, appointment of leaders, and remaining relationally connected to a wider network of churches. However, I have also tried to be clear that such functions could take a wide range of formal expression, including forms found in other religious traditions. [8]

Our Posture in Discerning Engagement

I am more and more convinced that those of us concerned about finishing the task of the Great Commission (which could be called a 'closure movement') should find a way to take spontaneous movements to Jesus into account as we evaluate what God might be doing to bring the nations to himself. How should we do so? I would like to suggest a few thoughts about how we in the closure movement might keep 'insider' movements such as I have described on our radar as we seek to assess which people groups are engaged and reached. I turn to that now by way of conclusion.

---

[8] See Kevin Higgins, 'Identity, Integrity, and Insider Movements: A Brief Paper Inspired by Timothy C. Tennent's Critique of C-5 Thinking', *IJFM* 23:3 (Fall, 2006), 117-23.

I have already indicated my dual allegiance to both the closure movement and the paradigm of mission that rejoices in movements to Jesus within non-Christian religious traditions. As such, I personally would be happy to include such movements in any measurement of church planting progress or engagement. However, I know that there is nothing approaching consensus on this point, and that this is likely to remain the case for the foreseeable future. Therefore, addressing others in the closure movement, I would like to suggest the following ways that we might keep such movements in view without requiring that all our colleagues share the same point of view.

Gamaliel-Open

First, I would like to suggest a posture that I will call 'Gamaliel-Open'. A famous passage in Acts portrays Gamaliel who was in apparent opposition to the new Jesus movement taking place among his fellow Jews. Rather than rejecting the new movement, he recommended that his colleagues take a longer view and wait to see what happened, not in compromise of their convictions, but in the awareness that God might be doing something which they would not want to be found opposing should it turn out to be of God. The implications for the closure movement should be clear enough: keeping abreast and aware of the existence and status of such movements as I have described, and doing so with a mindset that allows the possibility of their validity without feeling pressed to express conviction thereof, seems to be a realistic and practical step.

Security-Closed

Second, this would need to be done with another posture, committed with utmost seriousness to remaining 'Security-Closed'. Regardless of what one thinks about the type of movement I have described, there are real human lives at stake. There are those who consider someone who converts to Christianity to be an apostate deserving of death or exclusion from family or society. Therefore, while I do suggest that those who seek to track progress on closure, encourage and foster open discussion about what might be happening in and through such movements among the least reached and unengaged on our various lists, I balance that with a counter call: that the information thus shared and discussed remain within the confines of such meetings, safe and secure. It is an unfortunate fact that the reports of traditional 'church' believers have been the cause of the death and imprisonment of new believers in Jesus within existing religious communities.

Grace-Tongued

Third, I would encourage us all to remain committed to speak the truth, but as 'Grace-Tongued' men and women. This echoes much of what I presented in my own Tokyo address[9] relative to the ongoing dialogue in the mission world about

---

[9] For a summary of my address, see *Mission Frontiers* (July–August, 2010), 12-13

contextualization, Jesus movements, etc. Speaking the truth does not preclude but rather requires speaking in love. There is a need for improvement among evangelicals in the United States in regard to handling missiological and theological disagreements.

Biblically-(re)Formed

Finally, acknowledging that I myself am in constant need of biblical re-tuning and re-adjustment, I would suggest that those of us in the closure movement also embrace fully the hallmarks of the Reformation, including a passion to be continuously 'Biblically-Reformed'. We all come to such issues as our understanding of church with a mixture of vital biblical insight and also inescapable presuppositions due to our differences in denominational heritage. I include in this heritage not only the polities or expressions of church we have embraced, but also those we have rejected. This process of rejection often in turn shapes what we later embrace, and vice versa. None of us believe, become disciples or study the scriptures in a vacuum. We are all shaped by our past and present contexts as we seek to live biblically.

But this much can be said with utmost surety: none of us has a corner on all that the Bible says, and this includes what it says about the church and being the church. As such, if we measure the status of a people group's being reached or not reached based upon the status of church planting, then it seems we would be wise to be humbly open to correction by the Lord of the church as we try to assess and discern what he might be doing, even when it does not coincide with our expectations.

Conclusion

Not every gathering of every closure movement network of leaders and organizations and churches can or will give over large portions of their meeting time to reopen biblical discussions of church. But the values and assumptions outlined above might at least help form our hearts as we engage each other and partner together to complete the task. At the very least, it would seem safe to assume we can join together in praying for the attitude of Gamaliel, the holiness that will enable us to speak with grace-filled tongues, a commitment to giving each other safe and secure places to share what we see God doing, and a desire for his Spirit to continuously reform us in the light of His Word.

CELEBRATION, CONSULTATION AND CONGRESS: FROM EDINBURGH 1910 TO TOKYO 2010 AND CAPE TOWN 2010

Enoch Wan

Editors' Note: *This article provides a comparison of two of the Centennial meetings from the perspective of one who participated in both Tokyo 2010 and Cape Town 2010. Diaspora mission serves as one of the points of comparison, an important development as evangelical mission leaders take note of the realities and implications of global migration which 'liquefies' frontier missions thinking and strategies.*

The dual purpose of this study is to first provide a description of Tokyo 2010 and Cape Town 2010, followed by a comparison of these two conferences with Edinburgh 1910 to glean insights for future reference.

Description of Tokyo 2010 and Cape Town 2010

Tokyo 2010 – A Celebration

The Tokyo 2010 Global Mission: Consultation and Celebration held at Nakano Sun Plaza, May 11 – 14th, 2010 had the theme: 'Making Disciples of Every People in Our Generation' with a focus on 'making of disciples of all nations'. Throughout the 5-day consultation and celebration, 960 delegates from 73 countries were in attendance. It was sponsored by three major networks and sixteen evangelical mission organizations/entities. The three major networks were the Third World Missions Association, the Global Network of Mission Structures, and CrossGlobal Link. The sixteen mission organizations included mission associations from Korea, the Philippines, India, Nigeria, Ghana, Japan, Asia as well as from the United States.

CELEBRATION AND PUBLIC MEETINGS IN THE EVENING

Tokyo 2010 began with Opening Ceremony and Celebration on May 11 when delegates from more than a hundred nations marched in with banners and flags with colorful costumes and impressive performance in music, dance, drama, etc. The Closing Celebration on May 14 included a ceremonial reconciliation of

Japanese aggression toward neighboring countries and US aggression toward Japan.[1]

The celebrations and evening sessions were organized by the host committee of Japanese churches and mission organizations. All evening sessions were open to the public (local participants who registered), thus the attendance increased close to 1,500 in the evenings.

THE MORNING PLENARY PRESENTATIONS

Ten plenary sessions were scheduled in the three mornings beginning with David Cho's 'Kingdom Mission: DNA of the Missionary Task', and ending with Enoch Wan's 'Global Peoples and Diaspora Missiology'. Swedish professor Stefan Gustavsson's presentation on 'Reaching the Secular Peoples of Europe' reported the decline of Christianity in Europe quantitatively and qualitatively to confirm that the center of gravity of world Christianity had indeed shifted to the Global South from the West and the North. It was in Europe that Edinburgh 1910 took place and launched the program of 'the evangelization of the world in this generation'. However, the church in the West has declined due to multiple factors, including secularization, affluence, consumerism, and the confusion of various religio-philosophical frameworks. At the end of the session, delegates rose from their seats and loudly cried out to God in prayers, petitioning for spiritual revival in Europe.

WORKSHOPS AND TASK FORCES IN THE AFTERNOON

Workshops were planned for the three afternoons to encourage active participation by delegates in world mission and post-conference action regionally. Their availability at the website and upcoming published compendium will help us as evangelical mission leaders to expand our horizons and be motivated to take action.

DECLARATION AND CONTINUATION

The 'Tokyo 2010 Declaration', entitled 'Making Disciples of Every People in Our Generation' (included in this volume), was endorsed and signed by representatives of more than two dozen mission organizations/entities at the closing ceremony. It contains a long view for future development and shows a

---

[1] The ceremonial reconciliation was somewhat controversial. One line of thought was that it was inappropriate in the context of Tokyo 2010 – a mission consultation. The opposite view was that the power of the gospel was publicly demonstrated as was reconciliation in Christ. Former traditional enemies can embrace each other with love and forgiveness. After Japanese delegates stood up to confess the sin of aggression and brutalities in colonizing Korea and other nations in South East Asia, in response American delegates also went to the stage to confess their country's sin of dropping atomic bombs on two Japanese cities, killing many innocent Japanese. The scenario was perceived by some as overwhelmingly powerful; yet others felt it was confusing, embarrassing, and unnecessary.

commitment to the Great Commission, calling for strategic and synergetic partnership.

As a follow-through endeavor, the 'Last Mile Calling' (LMC) project was formed to utilize digital means and an internet venue to form many 'Tokyo 2010 communities' for information-sharing, ministry collaboration and strategic partnership. However, the many good ideas and intentions might not be realized in terms of on-going action and activities/ministries due to various factors, such as funding, coordination, and so on.

Cape Town 2010: A Congress

INTRODUCTION

The key text and theme of the third Lausanne Congress on World Evangelization was 'God in Christ, reconciling the world to himself' (2 Corinthians 5:29). In keeping with the spirit and tradition of the previous two Lausanne Congresses on World Evangelism (LCWE – 197e in Lausanne and 1989 in Manila), the third congress, Cape Town 2010, was an international event with historical significance. It was meant not to be just a celebration; but a congress with participation and input from the four corners of the world for evangelism at a global scale. Here is the official report describing the Congress in a summary format:

> The Third Lausanne Congress on World Evangelization was held in Cape Town, South Africa, 16-25 October 2010. The goal of Cape Town 2010 was to re-stimulate the spirit of Lausanne, as represented in The Lausanne Covenant, and so to promote unity, humility in service, and a call to active global evangelization. Some 4,000 leaders from 198 countries attended as participants and observers; thousands more took part in seminaries, universities, churches, and through mission agencies and radio networks globally, as part of the Cape Town GlobaLink. [2]

UNIQUENESS OF CAPE TOWN 2010

There were several unique features of the Congress. One was the 'Table Group at the foot of Table Mountain'. (Table Mountain is one of the most well-known tourist sites of the City of Cape Town.) 'Table Group' was a new format [3] for both the daily Bible study of Ephesians and for group discussions exploring means of more effective evangelism at local and national levels. Participants at the Congress were divided and assigned to tables, six or seven people per table, on the basis of diversity in gender, age, ethnicity, professional interest, etc. Table Group leaders were required to come for pre-congress training and

---

[2] See the report at the official site of Cape Town 2010: http://www.lausanne.org/about.html [accessed December 28, 2010].

[3] This format was experimented at the prior Lausanne gathering for youth leaders first.

provided leadership to nurture friendly relationships among members for fellowship and collective learning.

Another unique feature was the extensive use of technology before, during and after the Congress. A year prior to and leading up to the Congress, the online 'Lausanne Global Conversation' engaged evangelical leaders on every continent. The *Lausanne Website* allows site visitors to 'access current and historical information on global evangelization, learn about national, regional and international gatherings on evangelization and share theological and practical studies and research'.[4]

During the Congress, thousands participated virtually through the 'Cape Town GlobalLink' and 'Lausanne Global Conversation' at multiple sites. 'Organizers extended [the Congress'] reach into over 650 GlobaLink sites in 91 countries and drew 100,000 unique visits to its web site from 185 countries during the week of the Congress.'[5]

Speakers in the plenary sessions, multiplex sessions (similar to workshops/seminars), dialogue sessions (similar to panel discussions), and onstage participants were specifically selected to ensure diversity in gender, age, professional profile, etc. In addition, the many reports, testimonies, and presentations of data all clearly indicated the shift from the traditional Europe-centric pattern of Christian mission to the Global South and East.[6]

Most prominent was the array of leaders on the platform who came from various traditions including African Anglicans, Asian Presbyterians, Latino Protestants and ancient Middle Eastern church traditions. It was reported at the Congress that the last 30 fruitful years in Iran surpassed the past 300 years in terms of people coming to Christ. There was also the visible and artistic parade of clergy attire, worship style, artistic expression from the Global South and East, demonstrating their creativity, variety and cultural/ethnic diversity.

The church in China has grown about 100 fold since the last LCWE in Europe. The 200 delegates selected from China were not allowed by the government of the Peoples Republic of China to attend the Congress. The absence of these delegates and the testimony of a North Korean girl in boarding school uniform sent a strong message to the Church that suffering for the gospel is an ongoing reality. She shared with participants of the Congress that her father had been imprisoned for the gospel and that her mother had died in childbirth in North Korea. Later she had to leave North Korea and was adopted by Christians in South Korea. In spite of her age and small stature, her

---

[4] See the official web site: http://www.lausanne.org/about.html [accessed December 24, 2010].

[5] See the official web site: http://www.lausanne.org/about.html [accessed December 24, 2010].

[6] Leighton Ford said it well, '... Americans will leave Cape Town understanding the importance of listening to and being helped by leaders from other parts of the world.' http://www.christianitytoday.com/ct/2010/september/34.66.html [accessed December 29, 2010].

testimony was impactful as, in tears, she expressed clearly her determination to reach her kinsmen in North Korea.

The explosive growth of Christianity in the Global South and East has come with costly sacrifice as testified by a recently widowed American missionary whose husband was killed by extremists, and an African Anglican bishop who suffered at the hands of a mob led by Islamic clerics. These were just samples of suffering for Christ and the cost of discipleship.

Post-congress Follow-up

There are several aspects to the post-congress follow-up since LCWE is 'a worldwide movement that mobilizes evangelical leaders to collaborate for world evangelization'. LCWE-1 in Lausanne, Switzerland in 1974, was an event but it became an international and inter-continental movement and it was used to mobilize for evangelism. Cape Town 2010 was designed to be more than an event, it was intended to be 'a catalytic event in the life of the church – drawing leaders together in purposeful prayer, humble repentance, strategic dialogue and decisive action'.[7] There are to be many regional post-congress gatherings to continue the momentum generated from Cape Town. For example, Lindsay Brown, international director of the Lausanne Movement, has already reported such meetings held in November 2010 in Ukraine with 153 leaders from across the Eurasian region, and another meeting in December 2010 in Italy with 370 church leaders in attendance. [8]

Post-congress online follow up includes the 'Connect' section on the Lausanne website that offers ways to connect regionally with Lausanne Movement leaders, including subscribing online to the 'Lausanne Connecting Point ENewsletter' and the free monthly online magazine, Lausanne World Pulse (LWP, online at www.lausanneworldpulse.com).

Similar to the well known and widely received 'Lausanne Covenant', 'The Cape Town Commitment', drafted under the leadership of Dr. Chris Wright, will be a legacy of Cape Town 2010 and a contribution to the Church worldwide. 'The Cape Town Commitment' was published in *The Didasko Files* series on 17 March 2011 (English language launch date) and the document in its entirety is accessible at the Lausanne website.

---

[7] 'About Cape Town 2010: The Third Lausanne Congress on World Evangelization', http://www.lausanne.org/cape-town-2010/about.html [accessed February 3, 2011].

[8] Report by Lindsay Brown, http://campaign.r20.constantcontact.com/render?llr=hr96nzn6&v=001L9m-OEIPJ7XZFiomOXGhDNX2JY_Lkl1dGzXG4frAAAllRUjQKAMkasfdNSWWHSkmoHA6dwVoJEgfXx-jv-C8dmOxZZktg9cgPp1DkIjx9QmSlfW6GwDIiw%3D%3D [accessed December 24, 2010].

Comparison of Edinburgh 1910 with Tokyo 2010 and Cape Town 2010

Similarities among the International Gatherings

In this comparative study of the three events, we begin with the similarities between Edinburgh 1910 and Tokyo 2010/Cape Town 2010:

- Major mission agencies gathered together to assess what remained to be done and make plans together to complete it.
- More than 1,000 mission leaders representing many countries came with one objective and question: What is it going to take to complete world evangelization in our generation?
- Approximately 1000 representatives in attendance
- No Eastern Orthodox or Roman Catholic missionary organizations were invited (although there was an invited group of Catholic observers at Cape Town).
- Mission was made front and center in the life of the Church.[9]

Differences in the International Gatherings

There is a centennial gap between Edinburgh 1910 and Tokyo 2010/Cape Town 2010. Table 1 below shows the progress of Christian missions in the 21st century in terms of 'unreached people groups', speed and scale, growth, ratio, mission-sending, resources and approach. The most astounding change is the shifting of the gravity of Christianity from the northern hemisphere to the south and decentralizing from Europe/North America to elsewhere.

ASPECT		EDINBURGH 1910	TOKYO 2010 & CAPE TOWN 2010[10]
UPG		-99% UPG*	-Fewer than 25% UPG
GROWTH	Latin America	-Less than 100,000 evangelicals -of 800 PG*, 750 unreached	-150 million evangelicals -of 800 PG, less than 300 UPG
	Africa	-1.6 million evangelicals -of 2,800 PG, < 100 R*	-175+ million evangelicals -of 2,800 PG, less than 1,000 UPG
	Asia & Pacific	-4 million evangelicals -of 4,500 PG in the region, >200 R	-200+ million evangelicals -of 4,500 PG in the region, 2,200 R
Ratio		-non-evangelicals per evangelical: 20:1	-1970: non-evangelicals per evangelical 13:1; -2010: non-evangelicals per evangelical 7:1

[9] As the Archbishop of Canterbury, Randall Davidson, stated, 'the place of missions in the life of the Church must be the central place, and none other: that is what matters'. See Kenneth R. Ross, 'Edinburgh 1910 – Its Place in History,' http://www.towards2010.org.uk/downloads_int/1910-PlaceHistory.pdf [accessed December 22, 2010].

[10] Adapted from 'Opening Video Script'.

Mission Sending	-EC* sent 25,000 CCM* -99% from the West	-EC sends 220,000 CCM -78% from Majority World
Resources	-Ratio: 20 EC to reach every UPG -transportation: train and steam boat -no digital media nor data base	-EC to UPG:1970-150:1; 2010: 1,000:1 -rich data base, ('Last Mile Calling') for on-going collaboration & partnership
Approach	- Territorial idea, with an activist mentality & a military metaphor of Christian mission[11]	-diaspora mission: non-spatial and from everywhere to everywhere through 'people group' and diaspora approaches.[12]
Center of Christianity	-Concentrated in Europe and North America: Western countries - focus: the West & the Northern hemisphere	-650 million evangelicals globally: 80% in Asia, Africa & Latin America -shifting Southward & decentralizing

Table 1 – Centennial gap between the time of Edinburgh 1910 and Tokyo 2010/ Cape Town 2010[13]

KEY: UPG – Unreached People Groups; EC – evangelical churches; PG – people-group: R -reached; CCM – cross-cultural missionaries

Comparison of Details of the Three Conferences

It is informative to compare the three international conferences in terms of sponsorship and endorsement, venue and time, delegates at meeting, parallel conference and uniqueness. (*See Table 2.*)

Insights Emerging from the Comparison

Of the many insights that can be derived from the comparative analysis of the international conferences, two missiological implications are selectively presented in this study under the titles of 'diaspora missiology' and 'relational paradigm'.

DIASPORA MISSIOLOGY

In the last plenary session at Tokyo 2010, all delegates heard the presentation of two new paradigms, 'diaspora missiology' and 'relational paradigm'. 'Diaspora' is a term referring to 'people on the move from their home land', though biblically and historically it has referred to the Jews of the Old Testament in exile or the Christians of the Early Church in the New Testament.

---

[11] For reference to the 'territorial idea of Christian mission' with an activist mentality and a military metaphor of Christian mission, see Ross, *Edinburgh 2010*, 6-7.
[12] Enoch Wan, 'Global People and Diaspora Missiology', *Tokyo 2010 Hand Book*, 92-100.
[13] Adapted from 'Opening Video Script', *Hand Book of Tokyo 2010*, 8-9, with statistical sources from International Missions Board People Group Database, World Christian Database and USCWM Global Mission Database.

When migrants or immigrants arrive at a new place, they are ready for change in multiple ways, e.g. life style, value system, religious affiliation, etc. People are most receptive to change (including Christian conversion) when they are transient in a new environment (e.g. host society of immigrants, urban centers of migrant workers, refugee camp, etc.). As people move geographically and spiritually, the Church should follow the moving of the Spirit accordingly.[14]

At Cape Town 2010, there were five events focusing on missions related to the 'diaspora' phenomenon: an overview on Wednesday evening; two 'multiplex' presentations, and two 'dialogue sessions' – one each on the last two days of Cape Town 2010. At Tokyo 2010 the last plenary session was devoted, in part, to the topic of diaspora missions.

Migration is a significant demographic phenomenon at a global scale in the 21st century, as more and more people are on the move today than at any other point in human history. At the end of 2008, 214 million people were living outside of their place of birth, which is about 3% of the world's population.[15] (This table does not count those who have moved internally within a country, like the migrant workers of China, who at the end of 2009 numbered 230 million.[16]) Table 3 shows the required changes in paradigmatic conceptualization and pragmatic approach necessitated by the demographic reality of the diaspora in the 21st century.

---

[14] See Wan, 'Global People', 92-100.

[15] United Nations' Trends in Total Migrant Stock: The 2008 Revision, <http://esa.un.org/migration> [accessed July 14, 2010].

[16] National Bureau of Statistics of China: '2009 MW Survey Statistical Report' published March 10, 2010. This report is in Chinese and the translations are by this author; http://www.stats.gov.cn:82/was40/gjtjj_detail.jsp?searchword=-ifbase4-base92-JUMzJUYxJUI5JUE0JnByZXNlYXJjaHdvcmQ9JUMzJUYxJUI5JUE0KzIwMDkmY2hhbm5lbGlkPTY2OTcmcmVjb3JkPTU~> [accessed July 1, 2010].

ASPECT	EDINBURGH 1910	TOKYO 2010	CAPE TOWN 2010[17]
Sponsorship and Endorsement	-Primarily launched by the West -Prior to the formation of WCC -Birthed the ecumenical movement	- Initiated by the US Center for World Mission (USCWM) - Run by US, Korean and Japanese leaders - Evangelical	- Initiated by US-based organizations -Co-sponsored by the LCWE and the World Evangelical Alliance. - Evangelical
Venue	- Edinburgh[18] (Europe)	- Tokyo (Asia)	-Cape Town (Africa)
Delegates at meeting	-Predominantly from the West & male[19]	-Representation from 140 countries of all continents; male & female, young & old.	-Representation from nearly 200 nations, 'most diverse gathering ever'[20] in terms of nationality, denominations and age of delegates.
Parallel conferences	-8 commissions for 2 yrs.(each commission had 20 members) - 1 book[21]	-USCWM sponsored an Edinburgh 1980 meeting (70th anniversary of Edinburg 1910)	-LCWE had a 2nd international conference in Manilla in 1989; multiple conferences and forums
Uniqueness	-The last international mission conference prior to two world wars	-Initiated by one US entity but joined by 3 major networks & 16 evangelical missions	-Hi tech: with most people participating: before, during and post-congress =beyond the event & venue

Table 2 – Summary chart of the three conferences

[17] Adapted from 'Opening Video Script,' Hand Book of Tokyo 2010, pages 8-9, with statistical sources from International Missions Board People Group Database, World Christian Database and USCWM Global Mission Database.

[18] It was held at the 'Assembly Hall' of the 'United Free Church of Scotland' in Edinburgh.

[19] Those in attendance were from US & Britain 500 each, 170 - continental Europe, few from India, China & Japan, none from Africa & Latin America

[20] See John W. Kennedy's 'The Most Diverse Gathering Ever', *Christianity Today* September 2010 54:9

[21] The topics of the 8 commissions covered various topics including evangelism, missionary preparation and cooperation and resulted in the publication of one volume from each commission with total of 9 volumes.

#	CHALLENGE TO CHANGE	OPPORTUNIY [22] (diaspora missiology)	NEW APPROACH (diaspora missions)
1	Old focus: - Polarized/dichotomized - 'great commission' ↔ 'great commandment' - Saving souls↔ social gospel - Church planting ↔ Christian charity - Paternalism ↔ indigenization	New focus: - No longer polarized/ dichotomized - Holistic perspective - No disciplinary compartmentalization	Strong integration: - Evangelism + Christian charity - 'Great Commandment' + 'Great Commission' - Motivate and mobilize diaspora without dichotomy of 'laity' and 'clergy' - Interdisciplinary
2	Old conceptualization: - Territorial: here↔ there - Local ↔ 'global' - Lineal: 'sending' ↔ 'receiving' - Assimilation' ↔ 'amalgamation'	New conceptualization: - Non-spatial; no boundary - Transnational & global - 'Unreached'→ accessible - 'Borderless' → 'ministry without borders'	New approach: - 'Deterritorialization' [23] - 'Glocal' and 'liquid church'[24] - Hyphenated identity and hybridity - 'Mission at our door step' - 'Borderless church,' [25] 'bus church,'[26] - 'Church on the oceans'[27]

Table 3 – Working with Diaspora: Opportunity and Challenge [28]

Diaspora missiology is not simply satisfied with reaching the diaspora groups in terms of pre-evangelistic social service or evangelism (i.e. 'ministering *to* the diaspora.') We want to be engaged in 'ministering *through* the diaspora' (i.e. through their natural network of friendship, kinship abroad and at their homeland). We also want to motivate and mobilize those who are the bridges (through their newly acquired language facility, cultural sensitivity and relational ability) to 'ministering *by/beyond* the diaspora' to engage in cross-cultural missions to those living in their adoptive land. It is therefore missions to the diaspora, through the diaspora and by/beyond the diaspora to

---

[22] 'Diaspora Missions/Missiology' should not be promoted over 'Traditional Missions'. These two strategies are not in competition with each other, but are complementary in light of the global situation of the 21st Century.

[23] 'Deterritorialization' is the 'loss of social and cultural boundaries'.

[24] Peter Ward, *Liquid Church* (Carlisle: Paternoster, 2002).

[25] David Lundy, *Borderless Church* (Authentic Publishing, 2006).

[26] Thomas, Tira and Wan, 'Ministering'.

[27] From Martin Otto's ground-breaking books, *Seafarers: A Strategic Missionary Vision* (Piquant, 2002); and *Church on the Oceans: A Missionary Vision for the 21st Century* (Piquant, 2007).

[28] T.V. Thomas, Sadiri Joy Tira, and Enoch Wan, 'Ministering to the Scattered People', Cape Town 2010 Advance Paper, June 17, 2010, http://conversation.lausanne.org/en/conversations/detail/10540 [accessed July 14, 2010]. (The footnotes found in figure 1 are from this author and not in the original chart).

fulfill the Great Commission. God is moving people geographically and spiritually so the Church should follow the moving of the Spirit accordingly.[29]

In diaspora missions, there is no need to differentiate between the clergy and laity, vocational missionary or expatriate diaspora workers in the fulfillment of the Great Commission in strong partnership. This relational emphasis is the central theme of the LCWE movement: *The Whole Church taking the Whole Gospel to the Whole World.*

RELATIONAL PARADIGM

A relational approach to missions was emphasized at the last plenary session of Tokyo 2010. Participants prayed that they would use not just head knowledge, but heart commitment leading to action. In a relational paradigm, the proper order is heart→head →hand, i.e. 'being' should precede 'doing'. The pragmatic and programmatic strategies of the West are impersonal and non-relational. [30] 'Relational paradigm' is the use of relational framework (e.g. vertical, horizontal, network, etc.) as a coherent conceptual model for understanding and practice. This approach contrasts starkly with the popular practices of western churches that are characteristically programmatic, pragmatic, managerial, impersonal, success-oriented (exclusively quantifiable outcome-based), high-tech but low-touch, etc.

Upon examination of the program and content of Cape Town 2010, one can easily identify a consistent emphasis on 'relationship'. For example, the theme verse of Cape Town 2010 was taken from 2 Corinthians 5:19 – '*God in Christ, reconciling the world to himself*', and the central theme of the Lausanne movement is *The Whole Church taking the Whole Gospel to the Whole World.* 'Reconciliation' is a relational understanding of the doctrine of salvation; instead of the forensic understanding of adoption, atonement and 'justification by faith.' [31]

The plenary sessions in the morning program at Cape Town 2010 were characterized by a 'relational' emphasis. Daily 'plenary session 1' in the morning was a systematic study of the Epistle to the Ephesians: both by speakers and through table fellowship. Ephesians is a book full of doctrinal teaching and practical principles on 'relationships' both vertically and horizontally. The content of all these sessions provided a strong biblical foundation for a 'relation-orientated' theological understanding and practical application in ministry for the 21st century. This is a breath of fresh air to evangelicals who have been obsessed with a quantifiable outcome and success-driven, managerial approach to ministry.

---

[29] See Wan, 'Global', 92-100.

[30] For a critique of the Western way of doing missions, see the 'The Iguassu Affirmation', International Review of Mission 89:353 (2009), 242-48.

[31] For a detailed discussion on a 'relational' reading of Romans from a relational perspective, see Enoch Wan, 'A Missio-Relational Reading of Romans', in *Occasional Bulletin*, EMS 22:1 (Winter 2010), 1-8.

Daily 'plenary session 2' in the morning at Cape Town 2010 had the Christo-centric and relational emphasis in themes such as 'truth of Christ', 'peace of Christ', 'love of Christ', 'will of Christ', 'Church of Christ', and 'Body of Christ'. All of the elements mentioned above form the matrix of a relational framework (vertical and horizontal) for both Christian understanding and ministerial application.

Part one of 'The Cape Town Commitment: A Declaration of Belief and a Call to Action' (liken to 'the Lausanne Covenant')[32] is also highly relational as reflected by its title – 'For the Lord We Love: Our Commitment of Faith'.

All of these 'relational' elements and emphases which were reflected in the program, repeatedly emphasized by speakers, and elaborated upon by ministry reports at Cape Town 2010, are calling the Church back to the essence of Christian faith and practice that should be highly 'relational' in the context of 21st century realities such as broken marriages, dysfunctional homes and a fragmented society. People are starving for 'relationship' and will even run to the 'virtual substitutes' that are flourishing in the form of virtual social networking. Tokyo 2010 and Cape Town 2010 have each emphasized the need for a relational paradigm in the 21st century church.

Conclusion

This study began with a description of Tokyo 2010 and Cape Town 2010, followed by a comparison of these conferences with Edinburgh 1910. Missiological implications from the comparative study selectively focused on two new paradigms for Christian missions in the 21st century: 'diaspora missiology' and 'relational paradigm'.

It is fitting to conclude this study with the following quotation from the opening session of Tokyo 2010 – a centennial celebration with a historical perspective of Edinburgh 1910:

> We are closer than ever to seeing its fulfillment [God's promise to Abraham]: representatives from every nation, tribe, people and language worshipping Jesus in spirit and in truth – from Jerusalem to the ends of the earth.' [33]

---

[32] For details, see http://conversation.lausanne.org/en/conversations/detail/11544.

[33] From 'Opening Video Script', 8, with the words added: (i.e. God's promise to Abraham).

The Third Lausanne Congress: Assessing Cape Town 2010's Contribution to the Cause of Christ

Cody C. Lorance

Editors' Note: *The largest of the four gatherings celebrating the centenary of Edinburgh 1910 took place in Cape Town. It was the third such congress of the Lausanne Movement, with over 4,000 participants and hundreds of additional stewards and invited observers. This personal reflection from a younger evangelical offers perspective on Cape Town that goes far beyond the conference description.*

What Was the Third Lausanne Congress?

Staring at the back of the bus seat in front of me, I sat exhausted and overwhelmed, my jet-lagged mind drowning in a flood of Christocentric significance. It was the end of the second full day of Cape Town 2010, the Third Lausanne Congress on World Evangelization, and I was struggling to get a handle on it. Physically, emotionally, and spiritually I was ready to be back in my hotel room. Preferably, in my bed. So, I tried for a moment to just ignore the man who sat across the aisle from me.

He was Alvaro Fernández Sánchez, but I didn't know that nor would that name have meant anything to me at the time. He is a missionary involved in cross-cultural church planting in Mexico as well as a Bible professor, but I didn't know that either. I only knew him to be another human, a Christian leader no doubt and, I was sure, amazing (like seemingly everyone else at the Congress). I felt my normal introverted nature begin to battle with the gradual realization that God had very likely placed this man next to me on the bus for a purpose. Wisdom eventually won out and I greeted Alvaro.

We began talking about how God was speaking at Cape Town. He reflected a bit on the exposition of Ephesians 2 that theologian Ruth Padilla DeBorst had shared earlier that morning, the theme of reconciliation, and his own context of ministry among indigenous Mexican peoples. And then he directed things back to me, asking what was on my heart.

I said that I wasn't really sure how I could take several more days of this. It wasn't that I felt that too much information had been given to me. It was just so much substance, weightiness. I told Alvaro how I'd often find myself at big

Christian meetings of various kinds and in passing through the crowd I'd overhear snippets of conversations – the latest trends, the cutting-edge ministry gimmicks, the inside denominational gossip, the political stuff, the mind-numbing small talk. But something different was in the air at Cape Town. Earlier that day I had walked down a crowded hall and overheard talk of evangelism and discipleship, global partnership, and testimonies of God's faithfulness. I looked around and saw that very often people from different continents would be gathered together one-on-one or in small groups locked in the most intense conversations, praying, hugging, and laughing.

As I walked that hall, I had in my mind a captivating conversation from earlier in the day with a young leader from Uganda. Gloria Katusiime had spent three years as a missionary in South Asia and, like me, was strongly interested in diaspora missions. We talked intensely for two hours about our common passion for Hindu peoples, we prayed, and we parted with a sense of fullness and divine providence.

'So', I told Alvaro, 'I've just been thinking for the past hour about how weighty and significant and Christ-centered my encounters with other people have been already this week. And then as I walked that hall, I realized that what I've been personally experiencing – which is nothing less than the most profound encounter with God and his Church that I've ever had – is actually multiplied by about 4,000!' I told him, 'The Holy Spirit is here!'

At that, Alvaro sat back in his seat and stroked his thick, grey beard. Then he effortlessly began a discourse that not only took us all the way back to our hotel but through a significant amount of the history of Christian mission. He told stories. He quizzed me. He skillfully placed my Cape Town experience in historic context. But here's what stood out most: 'I was *almost* at the first Lausanne in 1974', he said with a tinge of longing in his voice. 'I had the papers in my hands. I knew Dr. Ralph Winter'. Alvaro proceeded to talk about Winter's historic 'unreached people groups' speech at Lausanne '74 and then declared, 'That speech has shaped and occupied my life for the last *36 years* of ministry! And *that's* Lausanne! *That's* what this is!'

I've been pondering Alvaro's words. I have a strong sense that he was saying something more than simply that the significance of the Lausanne Movement lies in monumental plenary presentations or influential documents. Because, it seemed clear to me, that this too was Lausanne – Alvaro and I riding on a shuttle bus back to our hotel, discussing matters of eternal significance. And before that it was Gloria and me engaged in a similar conversation. And it was those people in the hall from every nation. And long before that it was Alvaro and Dr. Winter. It is in this Christ-centered interaction, the union and communion of God's people with God's people, that we find that mysterious 'spirit of Lausanne'. And if we desire to know what is the contribution of Cape Town 2010 to the body and cause of Christ and what will be the legacy of that third Lausanne Congress, this is where we must look.

I have two primary goals in writing this chapter. My first is to address the question of what will be the most significant and lasting contributions of Cape Town 2010 (CT2010) to the Church of Jesus Christ as it carries out its mandate of making the Triune God and his gospel known among all peoples and nations, tribes, and tongues. Writing just a few months after the close of the Congress makes this a difficult task to say the least. But in his sermon during the closing ceremonies, Lindsay Brown, International Director for the Lausanne Movement, gave me significant help when he said, 'I wonder what the legacy of this Congress will be for the cause of Christ? What will we say when we go home to our families and friends?'[1] By equating the legacy of Cape Town with what the delegates take home with them and share with others, Brown underscored the fact that Lausanne's heart is found in the interaction of the Church with the Church about the things of God. That is, the legacy will be whatever we make it. Or, as Archbishop Henry Orombi, Chair of the Africa Host Committee for CT2010, put it, 'Under God, the legacy of the Third Congress is up to us!' [2]There is a sense in which even this chapter is a participation in the shaping of that legacy. So from the outset I must acknowledge that my perspective is anything but disinterested, universal, or objective – ideals I may strive for, but will nevertheless remain out of reach.

My second yet preeminent goal is directly related to what Doug Birdsall, Executive Chairman of the Lausanne Movement, said in his opening address to the Congress:

> We have come to listen to God and to discern his voice. If God is still speaking to the Church as we enter the third millennium, if he has something to say to us in these opening years of the 21st century, what is it? What is it he wants to communicate afresh? Speak Lord! Your servants are listening.[3]

Seeking to discern what the Spirit of God is saying to the Church through CT2010 must be the primary focus of the following pages because, with all that the Third Lausanne Congress was and will be said to have been, it was chiefly a gathering of Christians who came together to listen to God.

Somewhere between the convention center and my hotel, Alvaro likened CT2010 to the Jerusalem Council of Acts 15. I recalled the words of that council, 'It has seemed good to the Holy Spirit and to us…' (Acts 15:28a). The legacy of the Jerusalem Council, its ultimate contribution to the cause of Christ, was forged in the Christ-centered interaction of the Church with the Church as

---

[1] L. Brown, 'Closing Ceremony – Sermon', online: http://conversation.lausanne.org/en/conversations/detail/11646, 24 October 2010 [accessed 27 December 2010].

[2] The Lausanne Movement, 'The Third Lausanne Congress Opens', online: http://www.lausanne.org/news-releases/the-third-lausanne-congress-opens.html, 16 October 2010 [accessed 31 December 2010].

[3] D. Birdsall, 'Cape Town 2010 Opening Celebration', online: http://conversation.lausanne.org/en/conversations/detail/11322, 17 October 2010 [accessed 27 December 2010].

the Spirit of God spoke into the communion. The same will prove true for CT2010. I will thus proceed to examine the Congress by presenting this communion in terms of its breadth (that is, the Church in its wholeness) and its core (that is, the Lord Jesus Christ). We will see many of the most significant and, I believe, lasting contributions of the Congress flowing out of this communion. And in the end, I believe we will arrive at a clear articulation of what the Spirit of God is saying to his Church today.

The Breadth of the Cape Town Communion

> A most powerfully convincing mark of the truth of the gospel is when Christian believers are united in love across the barriers of the world's inveterate divisions – barriers of race, colour, gender, social class, economic privilege or political alignment. However, few things so destroy our testimony as when Christians mirror and amplify the very same divisions among themselves. – The Cape Town Commitment [4]

Three Impossible Things: The Ephesian Emphasis of the Whole Church

In Paul's letter to the Ephesians, which served as the primary scriptural focus of CT2010, one gets the impression that a follower of Christ who wishes to have anything approaching a meaningful relationship with God must become deeply enmeshed with the life of the Church in its wholeness. In the language of the Apostle, it is the Church who has received 'every spiritual blessing' (1:3) and that has become 'the fullness of him who fills all in all' (1:23). The Church is his 'body' (1:23), his 'workmanship' (2:10), a company of 'fellow citizens' and 'members of the household of God' (2:19), a 'temple' in which the Holy Spirit dwells (2:21-22), and Christ's own bride, the object of his tender care and nourishment (5:25-32).

What is more, it is clear from Ephesians that at least three things of paramount importance are possible only within the context of the whole Church. First, making known the 'manifold wisdom of God' to the invisible realm of evil spiritual 'rulers and authorities' is something that God has purposed to do 'through the church' (3:10-11). This is accomplished as peoples from many different and often mutually hostile nations and cultures become one body through the peace-making cross of Jesus Christ (2:12-3:10). Consequently, the more wholeness is realized among the nations and peoples of the earth through the blood of Christ and the more he himself is manifested as the peace of the Church that truly joins us together as one new humanity, the more awesome the resulting display will be of God's wisdom to the demonic spiritual realm. According to theologian John Piper in his exposition of this

[4] The Lausanne Movement, 'The Cape Town Commitment' (Pre-Publication Version, 2011).

passage at the Congress, 'There isn't anything greater that can be said about the global Church of Jesus but that, through the death of the Messiah, God has created a people in whom he means for his infinite wisdom to be manifest to the cosmic powers of evil'.[5]

Second, it is only together 'with all the saints' that Christ-followers can find the strength to comprehend the multidimensional love of Christ and, through that, be 'filled with all the fullness of God' (3:18-19). Such love, we are told, 'surpasses knowledge' (3:19) and thus lies outside the grasp of a divided and fragmented Church. But when Christians from every family on earth, 'rooted and grounded in love' and indwelt by the Spirit, join together in partnership and communion, the breadth and length and height and depth of divine love is brought into full relief; God is glorified and we are filled (3:14-21).

Finally, we see that outside the context of the whole Church, genuine spiritual maturity is impossible. Paul exhorted us to 'maintain the unity of the Spirit in the bond of peace' for a very practical reason (4:3). There is a single, universal Church and only one Holy Spirit (4:4), but the grace-ministering gifts of Christ are varied and have been distributed to Christians far and wide (4:7). Doug Birdsall's vision of CT2010 being an 'international gift exchange'[6] is exactly what Paul argues is always and at all times required. Paul said that all the saints are to be equipped. All are to attain to the unity of the faith. All are to become spiritually mature. But this is possible for none unless the whole body is 'joined and held together', 'each part working properly' and thus promoting the growth of the Church in the love of Christ (4:16). I dare not presume that all the gifts and manifestations of God's grace exist within the confines of my own local, denominational, or even national church. I need the whole body.

This Ephesian emphasis on the vital importance of the whole Church has always been a core value of the Lausanne Movement which at its inception affirmed that the task of world evangelism required 'the whole Church taking the whole gospel to the whole world'.[7] However, it was a particularly strong theme of CT2010, and flowing out of this emphasis on our need for the full breadth of the Body of Christ came many of the Congress's most significant contributions.

The Will to Represent: Pressing towards the Whole Church

While I was in South Africa for the Congress, a friend and teammate of mine was invited to attend a national consortium focused on church planting and evangelism in the United States. This was a relatively small, invitation-only

---

[5] J Piper, 'Full Session: Bible Exposition: Ephesians 3', online: http://conversation.lausanne.org/en/conversations/detail/10970, 20 October 2010 [accessed 30 December 2010].

[6] Birdsall, 'Cape Town'.

[7] The Lausanne Movement. 'The Lausanne Covenant', online: http://www.lausanne.org/covenant, 1974 [accessed 30 December 2010].

event organized by some leaders in our denomination. My friend is an immigrant to the US from East Africa and was struck by the fact that in a meeting presumably focused on reaching all people groups in the nation, he was the lone African. In fact, besides himself, a small handful of Korean leaders, and one African-American, the other participants at the meeting appeared to be American-born, Caucasian men. It was likely an unconscious and unintentional thing for the organizers. Other immigrant leaders were perhaps invited but unable to attend. My friend may not have noticed a Russian or Polish pastor, a Hispanic church planter, or even a woman amid the crowd. But the point is that in that meeting and countless other Christian meetings like it throughout the history of the family of God, little to no effort was placed in intentionally trying to represent the Church in its wholeness.

Here is where CT2010 has broken the mold, although it was not the first Christian meeting to do so, following in the historic tradition of Lausanne 1974 and Manila 1989, two of the most representative Christian gatherings in history. Beyond that, we may assume that other gatherings of Christians have exercised great intentionality in seeking to be as representative as they could be. However, it is safe to say that nothing on the scale of Lausanne III has ever been either attempted or accomplished. During the opening ceremonies, Doug Birdsall called the Congress 'the most representative and diverse gathering of Christian leaders in the nearly 2000-year history of the Christian movement'.[8] The figures were impressive – more than four thousand carefully selected on-site delegates representing 198 nations, an additional 100,000 people reached through 650 fully interactive GlobaLink sites in 91 countries,[9] and a less formal, social networking system called the Lausanne Global Conversation that allowed countless individual Christians from all over the world to read papers, watch session videos, offer feedback, and even create their own content to share with the global Church. Plenary and multiplex session presenters were likewise carefully chosen so as to pursue both excellence in content and a broad representation of the global Christian community. In addition, a rather complicated selection grid was designed in order to help ensure that more of the Church in its wholeness would be represented than ever before. At minimum, 60% of participants were to be under the age of 50, 10% under age 30, 35% women, and 10% of the delegates were to come from the marketplace.[10]

---

[8] Birdsall, 'Cape Town'. A significant disappointment that must be noted was the shutting out of some 200 Chinese delegates by the government of that country. Though prevented from attending, the delegation nevertheless rejoiced in the face of their persecution and accepted the Chinese government's decision with humble and hopeful submission. See The Lausanne Movement, 'The Third Lausanne Congress Opens', online: http://www.lausanne.org/news-releases/the-third-lausanne-congress-opens.html, 16 October 2010 [accessed 31 December 2010].

[9] The Lausanne Movement, 'The Third Lausanne Congress Opens'.

[10] T. Stafford, 'Teeming Diversity: The Third Lausanne Congress Demonstrated That Global Evangelicalism Has Been Transformed', online: http://www.christianitytoday.

When a friend of mine, a female pastor from Germany, learned about what she referred to as a 'quota system' for selecting participants, she was initially disappointed. 'I want to be here because I deserve to be here, not because of some quota', she told me. However, as she reflected throughout the week, she realized that without such a system she simply wouldn't have been invited to attend. As a young leader under 40, I knew that the same was true for me. Yet all those traditionally marginalized segments of the Church – the young, women, disabled peoples, laity, ethnic minorities, and others – truly belong at the table. In fact, as we have seen from Ephesians, they are needed. That the CT2010 Participation Selection Committee, led by Hwa Yung, understood, prioritized, and actually accomplished bringing them to the table in a historically unprecedented way will stand as a lasting part of the legacy of the Congress. What is more, this intentional effort to represent the breadth of the global Church must also be appreciated as one of the truly significant contributions of Lausanne III to the cause of Christ.

CT2010 modeled for the Body of Christ what it looks like to pursue the biblical ideal and mandate of gathering the Church in its wholeness. This was done in continuity with the two previous Lausanne Congresses, but to a degree of thoroughness which surpassed them. Taken together, the example of the Lausanne Movement's three global Congresses now resounds as an unambiguous call to the global Church to 'go and do likewise'. The mantle of responsibility has now clearly fallen upon the delegates of CT2010, many of whom are key influencers of churches, denominations, and organizations around the world, to pursue the same kind of breadth of representation in the committees, leadership teams, consultations, and conferences that they are and will be a part of. If this is done with faithfulness by a significant number of Christian leaders, it will signal the dawn of a new era in the history of Christ's Church and its partnership in mission.

Before leaving this section, something must be said with regard to the voices of dissension that have openly criticized the Lausanne Movement at this very point for not being representative enough in the planning and implementation of CT2010. Of the more notable critiques on this issue, Latin American missiologist Rene Padilla specifically pointed to the plenary session focused on evangelism strategy as being 'made in the USA' and reflecting 'the obsession with numbers typical of the market mentality that characterizes a sector of evangelicalism in the United States'.[11] Wrote Padilla, 'All too frequently Christian leaders in the North and West, especially in the United States, continue to assume that they are in charge of designing the strategy for the

---

com/ct/2010/december/6.34.html?start=2 , 1 December 2010 [accessed 31 December 2010].

[11] C. R. Padilla, 'Reflections on Cape Town 2010: Lausanne Congress on World Evangelization', online: http://www.micahnetwork.org/en/story/reflections-cape-town-2010-lausanne-congress-world-evangelization, 2010 [accessed 31 December, 2010].

evangelization of the whole world'.[12] Still others lamented the fact that Roman Catholic, Orthodox, or other non-evangelical Christians, while present as official observers, were not invited to serve as delegates to the Congress.

Doug Birdsall, in response to such critiques has offered the following:

> It is a stretch to suggest that the program was planned by Westerners and then sent to the rest of the world. The program chair was Ramez Atallah of Cairo, Egypt. The program director was Grace Mathews from India. The twelve International Deputy Directors from the twelve regions of the world were involved at every stage, including hosting of 20 pre-Congress consultations. The program represented the consensus of hundreds of leaders from around the world. A group of leaders from across Africa met annually in Cape Town for the last three years under the Chairmanship of the Anglican Archbishop of Uganda, Rev. Dr. Henry Orombi to ensure that the program was global in scope and also African in nuance. Two thirds of the speakers were from Africa, Latin America and Asia. They shaped the program. The leaders of the worship team were from South Africa and from Jamaica. It is a slight to these global leaders to overlook their rich contribution and suggest it was planned by the West.[13]

Added Birdsall:

> There were many participants from churches related to the WCC – including Bishop Hwa Yung the Methodist Bishop of Malaysia. There were many Catholics and Orthodox who were there as participants from many places around the world. There was indeed a smaller group of observers who were officially deputized on behalf of the Vatican, the WCC center in Geneva, and the Orthodox Patriarchs. I met with all of them twice during the Congress. They all expressed their desire for more involvement with Lausanne and their desire for ongoing discussions.[14]

The criticisms nevertheless are of tremendous value in that they soberly remind us that CT2010 did not fully arrive at the biblical ideal as presented in Ephesians, a fact that Birdsall himself would readily admit. Nevertheless, we cannot deny that with the third Congress, the Lausanne Movement pressed in more closely to it than anyone ever has.

Christocentric Polycentrism: Equilibrium in the Whole Church

'Over the past century … the center of gravity in the Christian world has shifted inexorably southward, to Africa, Asia, and Latin America'.[15] Philip Jenkins's paradigm-shifting words have been quoted often and the 'southward shift' that he described is a well-documented demographic fact. That CT2010 addressed this issue was a requirement of the times and not particularly unique to Lausanne III. Still it must be acknowledged that the decision to make the pursuit of a new global Christian equilibrium not only a major theme of study but a practical function of the Congress itself was an important one – the result

---

[12] Padilla, 'Reflections'.

[13] Birdsall, D. Email to Cody C. Lorance. 9 January 2011.

[14] Birdsall, Email.

[15] P. Jenkins, *The Next Christendom: The Coming of Global Christianity* (Oxford: Oxford University Press, 2002).

of careful discernment. However, the greater contribution of the Congress on this issue was the distinctly Christocentric treatment of it. The Lord Jesus Christ, obedience and conformity to his word, and the advancement of his gospel to all nations were firmly established as the only legitimate impetuses for the pursuit of global equilibrium in the Body of Christ.

The first and perhaps most profound point of Lausanne III in this arena was to challenge the language of Jenkins and others who have spoken of the 'center of gravity' for the global Christian family as having either a geographic or ethnographic location. Patrick Fung, in his plenary presentation on global partnership, shared the specific example of an idea popular among Chinese Christians 'that the 21st century mission or the next century mission belongs to the Asians or to the Chinese', a harmful concept that he said is sometimes promoted even by western Christians.[16] On this point, the Lausanne Theology Working Group (LTWG) added the following:

> We rejoice in the phenomenal growth of the church in the majority world of the global south, and for that reason we understand the intention of the statement that the 'centre of gravity' of world Christianity has shifted to the south. However we strongly discourage the further use of this term. ... Christianity has no centre but Jesus Christ. We are defined by no geographical centre, but only by our allegiance to the Lordship of Christ and he is Lord of all the earth. The 'centre', therefore, is wherever he is worshipped and obeyed.[17]

Both Fung and the LTWG underscored the importance of this *Christocentrizing* of the global Church by speaking of Christianity's historic polycentric realities. If Christ is the center of gravity for the Christian world, then the reality of his promised presence in his body (Eph. 2:22) necessitates geographic and ethnographic polycentrism. CT2010 did not mark the arrival of this theological reality but rather sounded a clarion call to the body of Jesus Christ to wake up to it in terms of the realities of global mission partnerships. So it was a moment of great historical significance when plenary presenter David Ruiz, self-described as 'a Guatemalan speaking in broken English', announced to the Third Lausanne Congress, 'The era of missions from the West to the earth is finished. Welcome to the era of mission from everywhere to everywhere!'[18] The LTWG heartily agreed:

---

[16] P. Fung, 'Partnership – Equilibrium vs. Diversity in Unity', online: http://conversation.lausanne.org/en/conversations/detail/11611, 24 October 2010 [accessed 4 January 2011].

[17] Lausanne Theology Working Group, 'The Whole Church Taking the Whole Gospel to the Whole World', online: http://www.lausanne.org/documents/twg-three-wholes.html, 2010 [accessed 4 January, 2011].

[18] D. Ruiz, 'Partnership: The Global South', online: http://conversation.lausanne.org/en/conversations/detail/11607, 24 October 2010 [accessed 4 January 2011].

> Christianity, even since the book of Acts, has always been fundamentally polycentric. Anywhere on earth can be a centre, and any centre can rapidly become peripheral. The global nature of the church as 'one throughout the whole wide world' subverts the language of a centre – whether geographic, numerical, or missionary. Mission is from everywhere to everywhere.[19]

The fleshing out of this Christocentric polycentrism in our global mission praxis requires nothing more and nothing less than radical submission to the ancient and timeless principles of the Bible. To begin with, all unworthy motivations for the pursuit global equilibrium must be surrendered before God's supreme agenda of his own self-glorification through the redemption of lost humanity. The exaltation of equilibrium *for its own sake* is not consistent with our mandate to preach Christ to all creation. Said Fung, 'Partnership in the Body of Christ should enhance world evangelization, not global equilibrium'.[20] Secondly, CT2010 reminded us that the kind of equilibrium that promotes faithful, global partnerships in mission requires a level of Christ-imitating humility that most Christians are simply unwilling to embrace. Fung described this as a kind of death [21] and Ruiz as the 'cost of unity'.[22] Ruiz expanded on this by reflecting on Paul's example from 1 Corinthians 4:7-13, saying that, like Paul, we must have humility, 'be ready for humiliation', and 'be willing to be treated without any respect'.[23] A final biblical principle that we must submit to in our pursuit of global equilibrium relates to the concept of giftedness in the Body of Christ.

In the midst of my first full day at CT2010, I was wandering around the convention center looking for a place to eat my dinner. To be completely honest, it felt a bit like high school. I – young, relatively unknown, naturally shy, and easily intimidated – scanned a giant ballroom packed with Lausanne delegates. My eyes landed on a half-full table of Nigerians and one Rwandan, Ruth Ndaruhutse. I timidly took one of the empty seats at the table as Ruth was getting ready to leave. We exchanged a few pleasantries and then, to my delight, she settled back into her chair. Ruth sighed in a kind, motherly sort of way and began to tell me her story.

Ruth Ndaruhutse is Rwanda's national coordinator for the Pan-African Christian Women Alliance. In the capital city of Kigali, she spends her days ministering to women who have been victimized in various ways by the genocidal massacre of 1994. She and her team take care of widows, orphans, rape victims, and others and teach skills that empower them to earn a living.

---

[19] Lausanne Lausanne Theology Working Group, 'The Whole Church'.
[20] Fung, 'Partnership'.
[21] P. Fung, 'Partnering in the Body of Christ toward a New Global Equilibrium', online: http://conversation.lausanne.org/en/conversations/detail/10664, 2010 [accessed 4 January 2011].
[22] Ruiz, 'Partnership'.
[23] Ruiz, 'Partnership'.

She teaches them about forgiveness and reconciliation. She teaches them about Christ. In other words, she incarnates the Savior in a truly remarkable way.

Over dinner, Ruth took her time with me. Imparting to me what I'm certain was only a shred of her spiritual giftedness. She had persevered right on through the unspeakable tragedies of her country. She told me about the losses and the pain – unimaginable stories or cruelty and evil. I had to ask, 'How, sister? How do you do it? How do you forgive?' She replied with profound simplicity, 'You cannot grieve for 15 years. You cannot stay in the past. You have to hope for the future – so, it's like that. It's like that.'

Ruth and so many others have helped me to see that one of the great lessons of Lausanne III is that, as taught in Ephesians, the Spirit of God has distributed the gifts of grace to each Christian in the whole Body of Christ (Eph. 4:7). Consequently, one of the keys to the pursuit of equilibrium in the Church is to recognize this global giftedness and our tremendous individual need of it. This requires the creation in our minds and hearts of new categorizations of value that transcend the smallness of finances, formal education, and technology. Fung challenged Christians to:

> Think beyond just money terms. God's resources are more than money. In the global family, as the body of Jesus Christ, many of us will bring different gifts. Some will bring and model faithfulness in the context of suffering; and some will model perseverance in the context of poverty and injustice; and some will model godly leadership in their context; and some will model critical theological and missiological reflection beyond the Western paradigm; and some will bring years of experience of commending the Lord Jesus Christ in the context of another world religion. And all of us will contribute together and we will bring a fuller understanding of what it means to be the whole Church bringing the whole Gospel to the whole world.[24]

The *Cape Town Commitment* states:

> We urgently seek a new global partnership rooted in profound mutual love, mutual submission, and dramatic economic sharing without paternalism or unhealthy dependency within the Body of Christ across all continents. And we seek this not only as a demonstration of our unity in the gospel, but also for the sake of the name of Christ and the mission of God in all the world.[25]

So this is the view of global equilibrium in the Church from the perspective of CT2010. It is a view that recognizes both the corporate richness of the body of Jesus Christ and the poverty of isolation. In it, there is no room for the participation in God's mission of a fragmented and fighting Church – 'a divided Church has no message for a divided world'.[26] We must humble

[24] Fung, 'Partnership'.
[25] The Lausanne Movement, 'The Cape Town Commitment'.
[26] The Lausanne Movement, 'The Cape Town Commitment'.

ourselves to the reality of giftedness in Christian brothers and sisters that we did not expect to be rich by developing a more biblical understanding of what is valuable and by acknowledging our own personal poverty. And we must do this all for the sake of the gospel and Christ, our only center.

Cape Town Conversations: Innovative Engagement with the Whole Church

Lastly on the topic of the Church in its wholeness, the breadth of our communion at CT2010, it is imperative that I mention two critical innovations of the Congress that each carry the potential to dramatically impact the communion of the Body of Christ for generations to come. One is the high-tech, sign-of-the-times development of a fully interactive, 'Web 2.0' system of engaging the global Church in the work of Lausanne through the Lausanne Global Conversation. The second innovation, a polar opposite technologically, was the simple and brilliant decision of conducting the bulk of the Congress in table groups.

THE LAUSANNE GLOBAL CONVERSATION

The Lausanne Resource Mobilization Working Group rightly observed that the internet has revolutionized the way Christians access 'information, inspiration and community', a trend, they noted, that is 'accelerating at unprecedented rates'.[27] They wrote:

> With the advent of the 'Web 2.0' sites – sites that offer fluid flow of information, targeted communication, and immediate dialogue via dominant platforms of internet communication – as well as the ever-increasing access to mobile technology worldwide, the continued innovation of internet capabilities can and will dramatically impact the Christ-following ministry in the coming twenty years.[28]

Recognizing both the needs and the opportunities of the times, the Lausanne Movement worked in partnership with *Christianity Today* and World Wide Open to develop and launch the Lausanne Global Conversation. Combining the features of an online social network with the content and focus of the Lausanne Movement, the Global Conversation provided a platform to facilitate members of the global Church sharing and interacting with each other both in preparation for and following CT2010. Through the Global Conversation, the papers written by Congress presenters were made available to all web-connected Christians, who were invited not only to read but to respond, engage the issues, and even create their own content to share with the global Church. The

---

[27] Lausanne Resource Mobilization Working Group. 'Kingdom Stewardship: Equipping Disciples, Mobilizing Resources and Utilizing Technology to Advance God's Mission in the World'. Online: http://conversation.lausanne.org/en/conversations/detail/10459, 2010 [accessed 4 January 2011].

[28] Lausanne Resource Mobilization Working Group.

resulting 'conversation' played a clear role in shaping many of the final presentations at the Congress as well as the *Cape Town Commitment*, a two-part document that serves as a 'call to action arising from the listening process at the Congress'.[29]

More than having a significant impact on the Congress itself, the Global Conversation has provided the Church with a powerful online resource through which the whole Church can conceivably share its collective digital resources with the whole Church for the sake of world evangelization. The potential for the further development of this tool is seemingly without limit and one can only hope that the developers and the Body of Christ in general will invest much in its future.

TABLE GROUPS

It seems so simple. And yet, perhaps no single aspect of the planning and design of CT2010 contributed more to its success than the decision to conduct the bulk of the Congress in the context of small groups of six individuals each, gathered around tables. The mere sight of some 800 tables filling the convention center's main auditorium was breathtaking. At times during the Congress, I found myself stopping to look around the room, trying just to take in the unprecedented thing that God was doing in and through his Church.

As mentioned, table groups consisted of six delegates each, grouped according to which of the eight official Congress languages they preferred. In many cases, an individual table group went quite far in capturing a microcosm of the breadth and diversity of the Body of Christ. My own table group represented six nations and four continents and consisted of two women and four men. Three of us were under the age of 40, and three were from the majority world. Lindsay Olesberg, who was part of the team responsible for intentionally building CT2010 around small groups, noted that the table groups allowed for the global Church to be 'incarnated in each participant's relational experience'.[30] She continued, 'Partnerships rooted in relationship and trust are a key component for the Church's faithfulness and impact in mission. ... CT2010 created an environment to catalyze that'.[31]

At my own table was seasoned missiologist and new friend Knud Jørgensen who, participating in his third Lausanne Congress, was one of many delegates deeply impacted by the use of table groups, which he felt helped to keep the Congress grounded in reflection and relationship. 'To me', said Knud, 'it was a major experience to come so close to five unknown people from different corners of the world. The sharing and reflection in these groups opened many

---

[29] The Lausanne Movement, 'The Cape Town Commitment'.
[30] L. Olesburg, Email to Cody C. Lorance. 1 January 2011.
[31] Olesburg, Email.

eyes to see things from new perspectives. And networks and alliances were created around the tables'.[32]

My personal experience as a table group leader was an unforgettable privilege that I am convinced greatly enhanced my encounter with God and his Church through the Congress. Beyond that, it provided me with a great perspective from which to appreciate and evaluate the effectiveness of such a method in a conference setting. While there were some isolated reports of negative experiences, the feedback regarding the use of table groups was overwhelmingly positive. Two comments were repeated over and over again by delegates that I spoke with. The first was an expressed desire for much more time dedicated to interaction, study, and prayer in the table groups. The second went something like this, 'The table group methodology should serve as an example and model to the global Church of how Christian conferences *should* be done in the future'. Both comments testify to the fact that the use of table groups was widely appreciated.

I have taken this model seriously and have sought to apply the methodology of table groups in my own mission context on multiple occasions since CT2010. One of those occasions was during the main worship service of the Nepali-speaking church that I pastor in the Chicago area. The congregation is unique to say the least. Made up entirely of Bhutanese-Nepali refugees who are all relatively new to the United States, only about 50% of the attendees openly profess faith in Jesus Christ and most of these are new Christians. The others may be classified as 'seekers' from Hindu backgrounds who have become more open to Christ than ever before through our highly contextual presentation of the gospel and Christian discipleship.

That Sunday, I was preaching a message related to three significant global problems that the Lord had impressed upon my heart through Lausanne III – namely, unengaged people groups, human trafficking, and HIV/AIDS. Our congregation of about 70 people was divided into small groups of 5-10 members each. After presenting each problem along with some related Scripture, I asked the groups to discuss whether or not God would have us do anything in response.

What came next was unlike anything I'd ever seen. Christians and seekers passionately engaged each of the issues. Two individuals were identified in our congregation that each had prior experience in Nepal working on issues related to HIV/AIDS and Human Trafficking. An older Hindu man who is slowly opening up to the claims of Christ shared emphatically with his group that we must not neglect the need to confront the underlying evil spiritual beings behind such human brokenness. A young woman and new Christian announced boldly, 'We aren't refugees anymore. God is with us and wants us to do something to reach the unreached!' Our conversations propelled us to write a date on a piece of paper, one year into the future, and post it on the wall

---

[32] K. Jorgensen, Email to Cody C. Lorance. 28 December 2010.

committing with faithful expectancy that God indeed would do something through us to address these issues within a year.

The testimony of the value of table groups is absolutely convincing to me. It will be an indelible part of the legacy of CT2010. But it stands also as another challenge to the global Church – that here is a model that should be imitated in gatherings large and small. The gatherings of the Church are many and varied, but few if any of them ought to be simply performances of a talented minority. If God has distributed his gifts to each one of us, we ought to often pursue increasingly participatory gatherings that allow for a greater sharing of our corporate richness, that facilitate the formation of greater friendships within the family of God, and that encourage greater learning and transformation through collective reflection.

The Core of the Cape Town Communion

> As the most vivid present expression of the kingdom of God, the church is the community of the reconciled who no longer live for themselves, but for the Saviour who loved them and gave himself for them. – The Cape Town Commitment[33]

What Unites Us: The Ephesian Emphasis of Christocentrism

Far from being an epistle that encourages Christians to simply join hands and walk off together into the sunset, Ephesians calls us to a communion built around the Lord Jesus Christ. In her exposition of Ephesians 2, Ruth Padilla DeBorst articulated this well:

> What God in Christ has spoken into being is nothing more and nothing less than the Church, the body of Jesus' followers, the new humanity woven together out of people from different ethnic, linguistic, cultural, and religious strands. … Membership in the household of God is a gift. Gentiles and Jews, slave and free, women and men, old and young, people from the south and north, east and west, people without all their limbs and wits and people with them all belong – thanks to God's reconciling work in Christ.... Christ is the peace without which the entire structure would fall apart. He is the cornerstone![34]

That Ephesians presents a clear emphasis on the wholeness of the Church is indisputable, but from beginning to end what is most striking about Paul's letter is its invariable God-centeredness. This is particularly evident in passages related to the Church. We see that the Ephesians' love for the saints flows out

---

[33] The Lausanne Movement, 'The Cape Town Commitment'.

[34] R. P. DeBorst, 'Bible Exposition: Ephesians 2, Part 2', online: http://conversation.lausanne.org/en/conversations/detail/11326, 19 October 2010 [accessed 1 January 2011].

of their faith in Christ (Eph. 1:15); we have become one body and one new humanity through Christ's cross (Eph. 2:15-16); we are a holy temple in Christ who is the cornerstone (Eph. 2:20-21); we manifest the wisdom of God to the demonic realm because of what Christ has accomplished (Eph. 3:6-11); God is to be glorified in the Church and in Christ (Eph. 3:21); the unity of the body is around one Spirit, one God, and one Lord Jesus Christ (Eph. 4:3-5); our gifts are Christ's gifts (Eph. 4:7); the measure of our unity is the 'measure of the stature of the fullness of Christ' (Eph. 4:13); and Christ is the singular head from which the whole body grows (Eph. 4:15-16).

From this overwhelming testimony of Scripture, we draw the obvious conclusion: our communion in the global body of Christians must be thoroughly Christocentric. Jesus is to be firmly located in the middle of all our relationships in the universal Church; he must be at the center of the interaction between individual disciples, local and regional churches, Christian organizations, networks, denominations, and all kinds of partnerships. If there is a failure in the Christocentrism of our communion, there will inevitably follow failure in our doctrine (Eph. 4:11-16), failure in our commitment to live worthy of the calling we have received (Eph. 4:1-6, 4:17-6:9), and failure in our evangelization of the world (Eph. 3:7-13, 6:15, 6:19). 'What unites us', the *Manila Manifesto* states, 'is our common convictions about Jesus Christ'.[35]

CT2010 has maintained this core. From the opening table group session – which began as we read, 'We preach not ourselves, but Jesus Christ as Lord, and ourselves as your servants for Jesus' sake' (2 Cor. 4:5) – to the final words of the Congress – 'Go in peace. Proclaim the gospel of Jesus Christ! Thanks be to God' – it was at all times clear that the basis of our communion was Jesus Christ. Time will surely prove that much of the legacy of the Third Lausanne Congress will have emerged from this unfaltering Christocentrism.

Cult Leaders among Us: Towards a Sufficient Christocentrism

Pastor Good[36] and I shared much in common. We were both pastors having spent a similar number of years in full-time ministry. We were both Baptists, Lausanne delegates, and men committed especially to reaching a particular cluster of South Asian people groups with the gospel of Jesus Christ. So you can imagine the hurt and surprise I felt when Pastor Good, my new friend and brother in the Lord, looked me in the eye after dinner one night at CT2010 and accused me of inventing and leading a heretical and dangerous cult. Obviously there is a back story to our private conversation, one that I cannot detail here. The essence of it, however, is this: while we likely could have sat down together, carefully read through the *Lausanne Covenant*, the ancient creeds of the Church, and even our own historic Baptist confessions, and found

[35] The Lausanne Movement, 'The Manila Manifesto', online: http://www.lausanne.org/manila-1989/manila-manifesto.html, 1989 [accessed 5 January 2011].
[36] A pseudonym.

agreement on virtually every point, Pastor Good found a number of marginal issues of disagreement to be simply insurmountable. Fellowship and partnership together with me was inconceivable short of absolute theological and liturgical conformity with him.

Sadly, my experience was not the only manifestation of division within the Body of Christ apparent at the Congress. The same old wars over gender roles, the sacraments, spiritual gifts, and more all made their appearances. The debates themselves are never the problem. The problem is when something other than or less than Christ is made to be the center of our communion. We find the temptation towards this to be of two opposite kinds. The first, represented by Pastor Good and alive today in so much of denominational tribalism, is that tendency to place what is theologically marginal at the center – to demand complete conformity in terms of doctrine, liturgy, and methodology. The other, perhaps more subtle, tendency is to place almost nothing at all at the center of our communion and call that vacuum Christ. At the Congress, this attitude was represented as well, chiefly by individuals who affirmed the *Lausanne Covenant* in their application to attend the Congress but, once selected as delegates, openly denied various points of the document. Similarly there are those who advocate the throwing open of the 'gates' of Lausanne to virtually any and every kind of person who professes to be a Christian without regard to their doctrinal convictions. Both extremes represent a failure to keep Christ in the center of our communion.

Now this is a delicate issue to say the least. Most Christians are not on the extremes represented above. Most followers of Christ care as deeply about doctrine as they do the pursuit of unity in the Body of Christ. Many Evangelicals in particular struggle with understanding how to relate to Roman Catholic and Orthodox Christians. What the *Manila Manifesto* stated in 1989 is still true today, 'Some evangelicals are praying, talking, studying Scripture and working with these churches. Others are strongly opposed to any form of dialogue or cooperation with them'.[37]

As we in the Body of Christ continue to wrestle with these critical issues, it is vital that we remember what the Lausanne Movement is not. It is not and never has been an organization designed to convene global ecumenical councils of the Church. I believe that this has been an unfortunate misunderstanding especially prevalent among younger leaders like myself. Rather, Lausanne is a movement inspired and perpetuated by a passion among Christians from throughout the global Church to collaborate together for world evangelization. It is not mere ecumenism that is the goal, but what John H. Armstrong termed 'missional-ecumenism' – a unifying of the Church for the sake of the gospel.[38] Huge swaths of Christians who have little or no interest in evangelism are thus

---

[37] The Lausanne Movement. 'The Manila Manifesto'.

[38] J.H. Armstrong, *Your Church Is Too Small: Why Unity in Christ's Mission Is Vital to the Future of the Church* (Grand Rapids: Zondervan, 2010).

self-excluded as are those who hold to a scripturally deficient gospel. Again, the *Manila Manifesto* is helpful, 'We wish to make it clear ... that common evangelism demands a common commitment to the biblical gospel'.[39]

It is here that CT2010, in continuity with the two previous Lausanne Congresses, has made a tremendous contribution to the cause and Body of Christ. By and large, the spirit of this third Congress was not one of division and hostility but rather of oneness, collaboration, and partnership in Christ for the sake of the gospel. Differences of all kinds were openly and passionately discussed and, with few exceptions, eliminated as excuses to divide. There seemed to be a broad recognition that failure on this front was unacceptable. Calisto Odede, during his riveting exposition of Ephesians 4:17-6:9 at the Congress, provided a sobering example of the kind of 'great missed opportunities' that can result:

> At some point, the king of Swaziland requested the churches to come together so as to baptize him – an activity that would change the whole nation. But the churches could not agree on who ought to baptize the king. And they were not able to come together. Thus the king was not baptized. The opportunity was lost.[40]

I'll not soon forget my own conversation with another pastor from the same region as Pastor Good. With tears shed over those disagreements that have often divided us, we extended the right hand of fellowship to each other, recognizing that our differences were not sufficient grounds to prevent our partnership and collaboration in God's reconciling mission. Rather, we found through the mutual affirmation of the *Lausanne Covenant* that what united us was far greater. We talked late into the night, debating, dreaming, praying, and enjoying Christ as the core of our communion.

This is what CT2010 and the Lausanne Movement as a whole has done for the Church. Through global gatherings and their resulting literature, it has created a powerful platform for and a sound, relevant articulation of our unity in Christ for world evangelization. To date, literally hundreds of gospel partnerships have begun in the global Church because of a mutual affirmation of the *Lausanne Covenant* or the *Manila Manifesto* followed by a face-to-face encounter at a Lausanne sponsored Congress or consultation. I can personally testify to the fact that CT2010 and the resulting *Cape Town Commitment* has already added to that number. Whether it is a female pastor from Latin America or a staunch complementarian from Asia, a fiery Pentecostal from Africa or a somber Lutheran from Europe, a highly contextualized 'Yeshu Bhakta' from India or a passionately traditional Mennonite from the United States, Christians have discovered in the Lausanne Movement a sufficient Christocentric ground

---

[39] The Lausanne Movement. 'The Manila Manifesto'.

[40] C. Odede, 'Bible Exposition: Ephesians 4:17–6:9, Part 2', online: http://conversation.lausanne.org/en/conversations/detail/11554, 23 October 2010 [accessed 6 January, 2011].

for their collaboration in mission, and the Third Lausanne Congress has served powerfully to commend and extend this ground to a new generation.

The Cape Town Commitment: Articulating Our Christocentrism

A Christocentric communion should result in discernable corporate commitments of both belief and action. A lack of such commitment betrays a lack of true Christocentrism, for where Christ is present there must be transformation. Knowing this, the historic gatherings of the Lausanne Movement have always produced documents of profound significance in terms of both their theological affirmations as well as their practical, missional commitments. The *Lausanne Covenant* has stood as the pinnacle of these documents since its writing in 1974, the crowning achievement of a gathering that has been said to have 'saved the unity of evangelicalism'.[41]

Now, out of CT2010, a third great Lausanne document has been produced that stands in harmony with its predecessors, the *Lausanne Covenant* and *Manila Manifesto*, but which engages the burning questions and issues of a new generation. Furthermore, it builds and arguably improves upon the examples of those earlier documents in its representative nature as a truly corporate document, in its skill in marrying theological conviction to practical commitment, and in its value as a confessional and pastoral guide. The *Cape Town Commitment* is the new banner for Lausanne and models for the global Church what the literature of a movement should look like.

A Corporate Document

The *Cape Town Commitment* may be said to be a truly corporate document. It is presented in two parts. The first is entitled, 'For the Lord We Love: Our Confession of Faith'. It consists of an articulation and affirmation of a number of key doctrines including the existence and triune nature of God, the deity and uniqueness of Christ, the inspiration of Scripture and more. The primary work on this section was initiated by a diverse group of theologians from around the world. The longer and second part of the *Commitment*, 'For the World We Serve: Our Call to Action', arose completely out of the content and proceedings of *Cape Town 2010*, the several hundred remote *GlobalLink* sites, the *Lausanne Global Conversation,* and other related sources. This has been called the 'listening process' of the Congress[42] a process that has included a careful and tedious gathering and mining of data from presenters, delegates, observers, and others. The work was entrusted to a small international group of men and women, the Statement Working Group, led by Chris Wright.

---

[41] T. Houston, 'Cooperation in Evangelism and the Lausanne Covenant, online: http://www.strategicnetwork.org/index/php?loc=kb&view=v&id=4651&fto=1701&sfto=lausanne%20covenant&, 1 January 1989 [accessed 5 January 2011].

[42] The Lausanne Movement, 'The Cape Town Commitment'.

Chris Wright, chair of the Lausanne LTWG, has served as the principle architect of the *Commitment* and has testified:

> The *Cape Town Commitment* is not just the memorial of a moment – however significant that moment was, at Cape Town 2010. It is, I think, the conviction of a movement and the voice of a multitude – not only of those who were there at the Congress, but also of those who participated through the Global Link and in the Global Conversation. It distils a vast quantity of input and I am grateful to all who contributed – the team of theologians who began the process, the army of presenters at the Congress, the Cape Town Statement Working Group, and the many unknown friends who emailed helpful comments. We profoundly hope and pray, however, that in this statement we are hearing not just the voice of Cape Town 2010, but to some degree also the voice of our Lord Jesus Christ who walked among us there.[43]

Literature that Facilitates Movement

Most statements of faith are merely that – statements. They are essentially static recitations of theological convictions. In my denomination, they play an important role at the incorporation of a new church into the broader association but are soon shuffled away into a new member's orientation packet or posted to an infrequently visited 'About us' page on the church website. Even in churches where creeds are utilized regularly in the liturgy, they function only to affirm doctrine. They are, by definition, what we believe. They say very little, if anything, about what we should do. The Lausanne Movement has helped the global Church see its need for a different kind of creedal literature – literature that facilitates movement in Christ. The *Cape Town Commitment* has modeled this in three primary ways.

First, the commitment has married doctrinal affirmations with missional commitment through the covenant language of love. We do not simply believe in the Trinity; we love him. We do not simply believe the Bible; we love it. And loving leads to concrete action. So for example, the expression of our love for God the Son – his birth, sinless life, ministry and miracles, death on the cross, resurrection, ascension, and return – leads naturally to committing 'ourselves afresh to bear witness to Jesus Christ and all his teaching in all the world, knowing that we can bear such witness only if we are living in obedience to his teaching ourselves'.[44] This 'love language' facilitates movement by demonstrating that a biblically-based theological foundation *that is loved* is truly a springboard for gospel living.

Secondly, the *Cape Town Commitment* recognizes that movement in Christ requires a laying aside of 'every weight and the sin which clings so closely' (Heb. 12:1) and has thus made confession and repentance a vital part of the

---

[43] C. Wright, Email to Cody C. Lorance, 7 January 2011.

[44] The Lausanne Movement, 'The Cape Town Commitment'.

content of the document. Language of confession, lamentation, and repentance appears more than 25 times in the Commitment and includes lamenting the 'scandal of our shallowness and lack of discipleship' and calling for 'explicit repentance where Christians have participated in ethnic violence, injustice or oppression'.[45] Thus humbled before Christ, the forgiven and unentangled Church can move forward in its mission with freedom and grace.

Finally, the *Commitment* models for the Church the literature of Christocentric movement through its intentional instruction to Christian leaders. It is a kind of modern day, pastoral epistle in that it actually gives clear, specific direction to local church leaders. Pastors, in particular, are encouraged to 'facilitate more open conversation about sexuality', to 'teach and preach the fullness of the biblical gospel', to equip all Christians apologetically and evangelistically, to 'teach biblical truth on ethnic diversity', and more.[46] Such clear instruction shows the way forward, providing a kind of roadmap for our movement in Christ.

The design of the *Cape Town Commitment* is worthy of prayerful study. I believe it stands as one of the great contributions of CT2010. Missiologist and Congress delegate Stanley Green was correct in saying that if embraced by the evangelical community, 'the *Commitment* will reshape that community in ways that auger well for the health and unity of the church and for the advance of God's mission in the world'.[47] Together, the three historic Lausanne documents have shown us that statements of faith need not be mere static recitations of doctrinal beliefs divorced from action, commitment, worship, and discipleship. The *Commitment* may even have eclipsed the *Lausanne Covenant* in its ability to promote movement through theological affirmation and commitment, confession, and instruction.

Proclaiming the Gospel: The Christocentric Impulse

In a message to the delegates of CT2010, Billy Graham exhorted the Congress to 'never forget ... the deepest needs of the human heart have not changed – they need to be reconciled to God'.[48] In his address during the opening ceremonies, Doug Birdsall was clear about the intended focus of Lausanne III: 'God was in Christ reconciling the world to himself. May it ever be before us. It was God's initiative. It is centered in Christ. It is global and cosmic in scope'.[49] Communion that is truly Christ-centered will inevitably be preoccupied with Christ's reconciling work in the world, and a distinctive call to participate in that ministry of reconciliation will always arise from such a communion. If

---

[45] The Lausanne Movement, 'The Cape Town Commitment'.

[46] The Lausanne Movement, 'The Cape Town Commitment'.

[47] S. W. Green, 'Report on Cape Town 2010', *International Journal of Missionary Research* (35:1, 2011), 7-10.

[48] B. Graham, 'Letter to the Delegates of Cape Town 2010', *News and Insights from the Third Lausanne Congress on World Evangelization* (25 October 2010), 4.

[49] D. Birdsall, 'Cape Town 2010 Opening Celebration'.

evangelism does not flow out of a gathering of Christians, that gathering cannot be said to have been Christocentric, for mission and Christocentrism are inextricably linked. Lindsay Brown affirmed this in his message during the closing ceremonies of CT2010, saying, 'Any message which the Church proclaims which does not have the deity, incarnation, death, and resurrection of Jesus Christ at its center is not mission. Our message is unashamedly Christocentric!'[50]

The legacy of CT2010 will include a clear call to proclaim the gospel to the world. Packed into this seemingly simple call, however, is a tremendous amount of study, reflection, discussion, and debate. What is the gospel? What does it mean to proclaim the gospel? What is the world to which we are being sent as Christ's ambassadors? The following paragraphs will be far from sufficient to present a comprehensive account of what the Congress has accomplished in answering these questions. I will settle for presenting a summary of what I believe were a few of the most important contributions of the Congress to the cause of world evangelization.

THE GOSPEL AND OUR MANDATE CLARIFIED

Lindsay Brown shared that one of the greatest aspirations of CT2010 was 'for a ringing affirmation of the uniqueness of Christ and the truth of the biblical gospel and a crystal clear statement on the mission of the Church – all rooted in Scripture'.[51] In terms of clarifying and affirming the gospel, the LTWG made perhaps the most significant contribution in the paper, 'The Whole Church Taking the Whole Gospel to the Whole World'.[52] In it, the gospel in its wholeness is presented as consisting of six overlapping elements, paraphrased below:

The gospel is the historic story of Jesus in whole biblical context.

The gospel is the reality of a new reconciled humanity created in Christ.

The gospel is especially the message of eternal salvation through the cross and resurrection of Christ.

The gospel is that through the Holy Spirit's entering our lives, we can be transformed to become Christ-like.

The gospel is the exposure of evil and falsehood before God's truth; it is the word of truth.

The gospel is that the Triune God is as he is.

This biblically holistic elucidation of the gospel of Jesus Christ is an important help in solving the tension so prevalent in the global Church that exists between those Christians who dedicate themselves primarily to the ministry of social justice and those whose work is focused rather on spiritual conversion. John Piper described this as a kind of battle between two truths.

---

50 Brown, 'Closing Ceremony'.
51 Brown, 'Closing Ceremony'.
52 Lausanne Lausanne Theology Working Group, 'The Whole Church'.

The first, he stated, is as follows: 'When the gospel takes root in our souls it impels us outward to the alleviation of all unjust human suffering in this age'.[53] This, Piper stressed, is true. Secondly, 'When the gospel takes root in our souls it awakens us to the horrible reality of eternal suffering in hell under the wrath of a just and omnipotent God, and it impels us out to rescue the perishing'.[54] Piper argued that this tension could be overcome, and the LTWG made that clear by showing that the gospel, while primarily a message about how God is reconciling the world to himself through the cross of Christ, is also about the complete eradication of evil and the ethical transformation of individuals, families, communities, and societies.

In a particularly weighty moment of the Congress, Piper sought to show the way forward through the tension and towards a balanced and clear articulation of the Church's mission. He pled with the delegates, 'Could the global Church say this: "For Christ's sake, we Christians care about all suffering, especially eternal suffering"?' Resistance to such a statement, Piper argued, signaled that 'either we have a defective view of hell or a defective heart'.[55]

It was not a statement that met with universal acceptance. Nevertheless, it actually captured well the overall sentiment of the delegates who seemed to have grown tired of pitting one emphasis against the other. The debate has not ended, of course, but with the *Cape Town Commitment,* the Lausanne Movement has taken a clear stand and has provided the global Church with a biblically-grounded rallying point:

> The gospel addresses the dire effects of human sin, failure and need. Human beings rebelled against God, rejected God's authority and disobeyed God's word. In this sinful state, we are alienated from God, from one another and from the created order. Sin deserves God's condemnation. Those who refuse to repent and 'do not obey the gospel of our Lord Jesus Christ will be punished with eternal destruction and shut out from the presence of God'. The effects of sin and the power of evil have corrupted every dimension of human personhood (spiritual, physical, intellectual and relational). They have permeated cultural, economic, social, political and religious life through all cultures and all generations of history. They have caused incalculable misery to the human race and damage to God's creation. Against this bleak background, the biblical gospel is indeed very good news. ... We commit ourselves to the integral and dynamic exercise of all dimensions of mission to which God calls his church.

> God commands us to make known to all nations the truth of God's revelation and the gospel of God's saving grace through Jesus Christ, calling all people to repentance, faith, baptism and obedient discipleship.

---

[53] Piper, 'Full Session: Bible Exposition: Ephesians 3'.
[54] Piper, 'Full Session: Bible Exposition: Ephesians 3'.
[55] Piper, 'Full Session: Bible Exposition: Ephesians 3'.

> God commands us to reflect his own character though compassionate care for the needy, and to demonstrate the values and the power of the kingdom of God in striving for justice and peace and in caring for God's creation.[56]

Lindsay Brown powerfully reminded the delegates on the last day of the Congress that 'the gospel of Jesus Christ, the Lamb of God, is the greatest message in the history of the world!'[57] This, the Lausanne community has affirmed, must be understood as true not only for those who do not follow Christ as Lord but also for the millions of people living as prisoners because of the abomination of human trafficking, the countless victims of HIV/AIDS and other global pandemics, those hurt and homeless because of war, genocide, or disaster, and many others wrecked and broken by all manner of sin and evil. For the gospel is always to be understood as good news, and gospel bearers are charged with bringing it contextually to wherever sin and Satan have gripped individuals, families, communities, and societies. Wrote Antoine Rutayisire in his advance paper for the Congress, 'A complete, full gospel will be a gospel that will continually analyze the situation of each community in terms of … [its] alienation [from God, self, others, and nature] and bring a relevant message until change happens'.[58] This, Rutayisire said, makes us ministers of reconciliation 'not just between God and man but also between man and man'.[59]

Critical Concepts as We Move Forward Evangelistically

CT2010 did a great deal to emphasize numerous important considerations for the future mission of the Church. Insightful and timely presentations stimulated vigorous discussion related to apologetics and pluralism, the integrity of the Church, world faiths, the prosperity gospel, media awareness, mission in the workplace, resource stewardship, globalization, urban mission, the next generation, and more. With so much brought to the table, it is not surprising that one of the most common complaints about the Congress was that it simply did not afford enough time for corporate reflection, particularly in the table groups. Indeed every one of these issues demand careful study by the whole Body of Christ as we move forward in our Christocentric mission. However, there are four items which arose from the Congress that deserve special mention – not only because they are absolutely crucial considerations for the Church's future mission but also because they represent some of the most important contributions of the Third Lausanne Congress to world evangelization.

---

[56] The Lausanne Movement, 'The Cape Town Commitment'.

[57] Brown, 'Closing Ceremony – Sermon'.

[58] A. Rutayisire, 'Rediscovering the Gospel of Reconciliation', online: http://conversation.lausanne.org/en/conversations/detail/10867, 2010 [accessed 6 January 2011].

[59] Rutayisire, 'Rediscovering'.

First, the Congress called the Church to prioritize their future mission by concentrating on where the Church is not'.[60] The familiar term of 'unreached people groups' was supplemented by two newer ones – the world's 'missing peoples'[61] and the more technical concept of an 'unengaged, unreached people group'.[62] In either case, the point was the same and the impetus behind the terms was captured in the *Cape Town Commitment:* 'The heart of God longs that all people in all the world should have access to the knowledge of God's love and of his saving work through Jesus Christ. We recognize with grief and shame that there are thousands of people groups around the world for whom such access has not yet been made available through Christian witness'.[63]

Second, the Congress gave a clarion call to the global Church to end biblical poverty. This was expressed in three aspects. First, there is an urgent need for all Christians to resource the task of Bible translation. It was noted that some 2,200 language groups still do not have 'one verse of Scripture and no one is working on them'.[64] Second, with oral learners making up an estimated two-thirds of the world's population, it was stressed that the global Church should become universally engaged in orality ministry, especially through the creation of oral story Bibles in every language and the equipping of vast numbers of effective storytellers.[65] Finally, the distribution and utilization of Scripture was shown to lead to stronger discipleship in the Church and more effective evangelism in the world. CT2010 called on Christian leaders to renew their commitment to integrate the Bible in all areas of their ministries.

Third, the Congress presented to the Body of Christ the reality of the global human diaspora as a two-sided coin in the world missions scene. From one perspective, we see that the 'people on the move' represent perhaps the most powerful mission force in the world today, embodying like nothing else the now oft-repeated phrase, 'mission is from everywhere to everywhere'. The other perspective recognizes that diaspora peoples are indeed a mobile and complicated mission field that must be engaged with the gospel of Jesus Christ. The topic of diaspora missions, said diaspora missiologist Sadiri Joy Tira, created 'quite a buzz in Cape Town'.[66] Tira believes that the Congress marked a historic moment. 'Evangelicals are now embracing diaspora missiology', but he

---

[60] P. Eshleman, 'World Evangelisation in the 21st Century', online: http://conversation.lausanne.org/en/conversations/detail/10522, 7 January 2010 [accessed 6 January 2011].

[61] S. K. Scott, 'Missing Peoples: The Unserved "One-Fourth" World: Especially Buddhists, Hindus & Muslims', online: http://conversation.lausanne.org/en/conversations/detail/10535#article_page_1, 7 May 2010 [accessed 6 January 2011].

[62] Eshleman, 'World Evangelisation'.

[63] The Lausanne Movement, 'The Cape Town Commitment'.

[64] Eshleman, 'World Evangelisation'.

[65] Eshleman, 'World Evangelisation'.

[66] S. J. Tira, 'Dispora Missions at Cape Town 2010' (interview with C. C. Lorance).

explained that there is still a wide gap between the scholars who study diaspora and those Christians who are practically engaged in reaching out to the 'scattered peoples'. Tira stressed that 'academics and practitioners need to get married on the issue' lest we fail to fulfill our Great Commission mandate, and he called on Christian educators to create space in their curricula for equipping younger leaders in diaspora missiology.[67]

Finally, the Congress moved the Church forward in its understanding of contextualization in mission. CT2010 was a key moment for those followers of Christ who pursue contextualization in their mission and discipleship and those who seek to practice their Christian faith incarnationally, as insiders to their own culture. The debate over contextualization has often been dominated by those Christians working among Muslim peoples. While this is certainly an important arena for the topic, it is by no means the only one. Particularly in the work of Antoine Rutayisire, the Congress demonstrated that the pursuit or non-pursuit of contextualization in our mission endeavors has much broader ramifications than simply the speed with which we make converts. For Rutayisire, the most obvious explanation for the 1994 massacre of a million Tutsis in a Rwanda said to be more than 90% Christian was that the gospel message which had been presented 'was not contextualized'.[68] Ethnic, social, spiritual, and educational realities of the context were not engaged. Transformation was largely superficial. Christianity remained a 'colonial importation'.[69] From this, the *Cape Town Commitment* has concluded that the gospel must be 'deeply rooted in the context' if it is to be transformative.[70]

A second key consideration related to contextualization signals a true breakthrough in the ongoing discussion. By far the most common criticism against those who pursue contextualization has been the charge of syncretism. The assumption, propped up by faulty notions often derived from one version or another of a 'contextualization scale', has been that contextualization and syncretism are somehow inextricably linked; that is, one can 'go too far', falling off into heresy, idolatry, and all kinds of related ills. This perspective, however, overlooks the fact that there is no such thing as a 'Christian culture' and that all our Christ-following – whether it be our manner of discipling or mode of evangelizing, our systems of leadership or style of prayer, our calendars or our places of worship – is always contextualized to some single or conglomeration of human culture. The only question is to what extent we are intentional about rooting the gospel in the soil of the context in which we are following and sharing Christ. Syncretism, we find, flows not out of the intentional pursuit of contextualization but rather out of our biblical poverty. Whether the poorly discipled syncretist is intentionally trying to contextualize

[67] Tira, 'Dispora Missions'.

[68] Rutayisire, 'Rediscovering'.

[69] Rutayisire, 'Rediscovering'.

[70] The Lausanne Movement, 'The Cape Town Commitment'.

or not is beside the point. The supposed link between contextualization and syncretism is mythological. This is affirmed by the *Cape Town Commitment* which answers those who would suggest that a special relationship between contextualization and syncretism, "Syncretism … is a danger found among Christians everywhere as we express our faith within our own cultures".[71]

Taking these four issues together (concentrating on where the Church is not, ending biblical poverty, the realities of diaspora, and contextualization), CT2010 has accomplished much in showing the way forward for the global Church in our Christocentric mission. An important result of CT2010 will be for the conversation to continue throughout the whole Church and the gospel in its wholeness to go forth among every people and penetrate every sphere of society.

Conclusion: What the Spirit Is Saying to the Church

The closing ceremonies of CT2010 were in full swing – the final moments of a unique moment in time. I was trying desperately to soak it all in. I begged God to repeat the miracle of Joshua 10, to cause time to slow down, to let us all just abide there with him for a little while longer. I reached into my bag to pull out an extra pair of socks which I then used as handkerchiefs. The tears had started flowing early in the service and showed no signs of drying up. With an empty seat between us, Gloria Katusiime was the only other person at the table. Through the lofty highs and the gut-wrenching lows of that week, God had awakened me to the undeniable fact that this wildly charismatic Ugandan woman was in every meaningful sense my true sister. Silent and prayerful now, she seemed to be standing guard as I did business with the Lord of the universe.

For his part, the Father had rolled all of the Congress and all of my life and all of my brokenness into that single moment. And under the crushing weight of it all, defeat appeared inescapable. But a sermon was preached, some prayers lifted up, Scripture read, and songs sung. There was Holy Communion with the elements literally dancing in procession, a strangely familiar sister keeping watch, a company of saints from every nation, and a still, small voice. And with the final 'Amen', I sighed and settled back in my chair with the unmistakable sense of victory.

Those closing moments of the Third Lausanne Congress were for me a microcosm of the whole. After all, there was the Church in the rich breadth of its diversity, Christocentric in its interaction with the Spirit speaking into the communion. History will surely prove that a great many contributions and thus a strong and godly legacy arose from CT2010, but in the end we were a community of listeners, straining our ears towards the Master and striving to hear what the Spirit of God had to say to the Church. Indeed, he had much to say to all of us. In conclusion, however, I want to offer two particularly ringing

---

[71] The Lausanne Movement, 'The Cape Town Commitment'.

statements that I am convinced represent well what God has said to the global Church through Lausanne III.

First, we who follow Jesus Christ in every nation under heaven have a desperate and abiding need for each other. Ajith Fernando, in his exposition of Ephesians 1, declared, 'When God wants to show the world what his inheritance, what his treasure is, he doesn't talk about the cattle on a thousand hills and things like that. He points to *us* and says, "*There's* my wealth! *There's* my inheritance!"'.[72] A challenge from CT2010 is for the Church wake up from the poverty of Christian isolationism! Ruth Padilla DeBorst poignantly asked the delegates, 'Do we, each of us, envision ourselves as living stones that *must* fit together with others in order to compose God's dwelling place?'[73] God would have us recall the words of Paul who declared that one part of the Body of Christ cannot say to another, 'I have no need of you' (1 Cor. 12:21). Rather, we are to each other indispensible (1 Cor. 12:22). Thus, as we carry out the work of world evangelization, we must not neglect meeting, partnering, collaborating, conversing, praying, worshipping, and walking together, as is the habit of some, but continue to encourage one another, and all the more as we see the Day drawing near (Heb. 10:25).

Second, as Christians, Christ must be the center of all our interactions and relationships with each other. Whether between spouses or siblings, denominations or organizations, our Christocentrism must be sure, clear, and permanent. When this is the case, holistic gospel mission, personal and corporate discipleship, and a sound and sufficient theological common ground will emerge that inspires love and leads to commitment.

CT2010 is now long finished. Whatever work was to be done during that Congress has been completed. Alvaro is back in Mexico. Gloria is in Uganda. Ruth has returned to her ministry of healing in Kigali, and I to my church-planting in Chicago. But it is incumbent upon us all to carry out the work of Lausanne and the legacy of that Third Congress into the everydayness of our mission, to share what we've discovered with as many others in the global Body of Christ as possible, and, above all, to obey what God has said to us.

To be sure, God is indeed at work today. He is reconciling the world to himself through Christ. In one of the most surprising moves of human history, He has called and caught us up into that ministry of reconciliation. At one point in the Congress, Patrick Fung had expressed his heart's prayer 'that out of this Lausanne Congress there will be true, long-lasting, authentic friendships that will inspire us to partner in the body of Jesus Christ for world evangelization – to reconcile the world to God in Christ. Amen!'[74] At times, we feel

---

[72] A. Fernando, 'Bible Exposition: Ephesians 1', online: http://conversation.lausanne.org/en/conversations/detail/11327, 18 October 2010 [accessed 6 January, 2011].

[73] DeBorst, 'Bible Exposition: Ephesians 2'.

[74] Fung, 'Partnership'.

overwhelmed when we look at the world in these darkened days. But even as I write these final lines I cannot help but be reminded of the faces and voices of God's family whom I encountered in Cape Town. I remember that I am not alone.

And that's what Cape Town 2010 was – the launch of a new century of evangelical missions.

Bibliography

Armstrong, J.H. *Your Church Is Too Small: Why Unity in Christ's Mission Is Vital to the Future of the Church*. Grand Rapids: Zondervan, 2010.

Birdsall, D. 'Cape Town 2010 Opening Celebration'. Online: http://conversation.lausanne.org/en/conversations/detail/11322, 17 October 2010 [accessed 27 December 2010].

Birdsall, D. Email to Cody C. Lorance. 9 January 2011.

Brown, L. 'Closing Ceremony – Sermon'. Online: http://conversation.lausanne.org/en/conversations/detail/11646, 24 October 2010 [accessed 27 December 2010].

DeBorst, R. P. 'Bible Exposition: Ephesians 2, Part 2'. Online: http://conversation.lausanne.org/en/conversations/detail/11326, 19 October 2010 [accessed 1 January 2011].

Eshleman, P. 'World Evangelisation in the 21st Century'. Online: http://conversation.lausanne.org/en/conversations/detail/10522, 7 January 2010 [accessed 6 January 2011].

Fernando, A. 'Bible Exposition: Ephesians 1'. Online: http://conversation.lausanne.org/en/conversations/detail/11327, 18 October 2010 [accessed 6 January, 2011].

Fung, P. 'Partnering in the Body of Christ toward a New Global Equilibrium'. Online: http://conversation.lausanne.org/en/conversations/detail/10664, 2010 [accessed 4 January 2011].

______. 'Partnership – Equilibrium vs. Diversity in Unity'. Online: http://conversation.lausanne.org/en/conversations/detail/11611, 24 October 2010 [accessed 4 January 2011].

Graham, B. 'Letter to the Delegates of Cape Town 2010'. News and Insights from the Third Lausanne Congress on World Evangelization (25 October 2010), 4.

Green, S. W. 'Report on Cape Town 2010'. *International Journal of Missionary Research* 35:1 (2011), 7-10.

Houston, T. 'Cooperation in Evangelism and the Lausanne Covenant. Online: http://www.strategicnetwork.org/index/php?loc=kb&view=v&id=4651&fto=1701&sfto=lausanne%20covenant&, 1 January 1989 [accessed 5 January 2011].

Jenkins, P. *The Next Christendom: The Coming of Global Christianity*. Oxford: Oxford University Press, 2002.

Jorgensen, K. Email to Cody C. Lorance. 28 December 2010.

Lausanne Movement. 'Chinese Church Leaders' Exemplary Response Profoundly Impacts Cape Town 2010 Attendees'. Online: http://www.lausanne.org/news-releases/chinese-church-leaders-exemplary-response-profoundly-impacts-cape-town-2010-attendees.html, 20 October 2010 [accessed 9 January 2011].

Lausanne Resource Mobilization Working Group. 'Kingdom Stewardship: Equipping Disciples, Mobilizing Resources and Utilizing Technology to Advance God's Mission in the World'. Online: http://conversation.lausanne.org/en/conversations/detail/10459, 2010 [accessed 4 January 2011].

Lausanne Theology Working Group. 'The Whole Church Taking the Whole Gospel to the Whole World'. Online: http://www.lausanne.org/documents/twg-three-wholes.html, 2010 [accessed 4 January, 2011].

Odede, C. 'Bible Exposition: Ephesians 4:17–6:9, Part 2'. Online: http://conversation.lausanne.org/en/conversations/detail/11554, 23 October 2010 [accessed 6 January, 2011].

Olesburg, L. Email to Cody C. Lorance. 1 January 2011.

Padilla, C. R. L. 'Reflections on Cape Town 2010: Lausanne Congress on World Evangelization'. Online: http://www.micahnetwork.org/en/story/reflections-cape-town-2010-lausanne-congress-world-evangelization, 2010 [accessed 31 December, 2010.

Piper, J. 'Full Session: Bible Exposition: Ephesians 3'. Online: http://conversation.lausanne.org/en/conversations/detail/10970, 20 October 2010 [accessed 30 December 2010].

Ross, Kenneth R. 'The Centenary of Edinburgh 1910: Its Possibilities'. *International Bulletin of Missionary Research* 30:4 (October, 2006), 177-79.

Ruiz, D. 'Partnership: The Global South'. Online: http://conversation.lausanne.org/en/conversations/detail/11607, 24 October 2010 [accessed 4 January 2011].

Rutayisire, A. 'Rediscovering the Gospel of Reconciliation'. Online: http://conversation.lausanne.org/en/conversations/detail/10867, 2010 [accessed 6 January 2011].

Scott, S. K. 'Missing Peoples: The Unserved "One-Fourth" World: Especially Buddhists, Hindus & Muslims'. Online: http://conversation.lausanne.org/en/conversations/detail/10535#article_page_1 , 7 May 2010 [accessed 6 January 2011].

Stafford, T. 'Teeming Diversity: The Third Lausanne Congress Demonstrated That Global Evangelicalism Has Been Transformed'. Online: http://www.christianitytoday.com/ct/2010/december/6.34.html?start=2 , 1 December 2010 [accessed 31 December 2010].

______. 'Who Got Invited to Cape Town and Why: Cape Town 2010 Claims to Represent the Blobal Evangelical Church. How Did They Do It?' Online: http://blog.christianitytoday.com/ctliveblog/archives/2010/10/representing_th.html, 20 October 2010 [accessed 31 December 2010].

The Lausanne Movement. 'The Cape Town Commitment'. Online: http://www.lausanne.org/ctcommitment, 2011 [accessed 6 February 2011].

The Lausanne Movement. 'The Lausanne Covenant'. Online: http://www.lausanne.org/covenant, 1974 [accessed 30 December 2010].

The Lausanne Movement. 'The Manila Manifesto'. Online: http://www.lausanne.org/manila-1989/manila-manifesto.html, 1989 [accessed 5 January 2011].

The Lausanne Movement. 'The Third Lausanne Congress Opens'. Online: http://www.lausanne.org/news-releases/the-third-lausanne-congress-opens.html, 16 October 2010 [accessed 31 December 2010].

The Lausanne Movement. 'Third Lausanne Congress Closes with a Ringing Call to Action'. Online: http://www.lausanne.org/news-releases/congress-closes-with-call-to-action.html, 25 October 2010 [accessed 31 December 2010].

Tira, S. J. 'Dispora Missions at Cape Town 2010'. Interview with C. C. Lorance.

Wright, C. Email to Cody C. Lorance, 7 January 2011.

Evangelicals Return to a Holistic Gospel and Kingdom Mission

The Biggest Trend in Global Mission

Ralph D. Winter

Editors' Note: *Ralph Winter presented this paper at the Korea World Mission Conference in Wheaton, Illinois, in July, 2008. Towards the end of his life Winter reframed his missional thinking in light of renewal in his understanding of the Kingdom of God. In this chapter he explains his approach to mission in light of those developments.*

Introduction

The most important trend in missions today is a recovery from a gospel of merely personal salvation to a restoration of kingdom thinking. Everyone, both Christians and non-Christians, are talking about major world problems. Nowadays, for the first time in 150 years, we see a restoration of emphasis on the gospel of the kingdom, which in the Bible not only means personal salvation but transformation in this world – as in the Lord's prayer, 'Thy will be done on earth'.

To see the roots of this problem we need to go back to the Reformation. In the 16th century contention arose between the Latin speaking Christians and the German speaking Christians.

Confusion in the Reformation

Works alone don't get people to heaven. In Martin Luther's day a man named John Tetzel came through Germany with a big box on a wagon urging people to put money in the box in order to absolve them from divine punishment. He represented a fund raising campaign to help build a cathedral in Rome. His project was not something the Germans were very enthusiastic about. However, for Luther there was an additional problem. Luther's scholarly reaction made clear that giving money – or doing any purely religious good works – will not forgive sin.

On the other hand, faith alone (that is, merely believing in the truth of creedal statements) also doesn't get people to heaven. Luther's alternative was to propose that a heart of faith is what pleases God as can be seen in scripture. However, in English, the use of the word 'believe' can be interpreted to mean merely believing the right doctrines rather than having a heart of faith. Merely mental assent to the correct doctrinal truths never saved anyone. Confusion on this point is still very common. People often think someone's sins are forgiven automatically if that person says he believes merely that it is true that Jesus is the Son of God, and that the blood of Jesus atones for our sins. However, mere intellectual assent to correct doctrines does not save you.

Rather, the Bible plainly says, 'Faith without works is dead' (James 2: 20). For several years Luther condemned the New Testament Book of James. He assumed the second chapter of James denounces heart faith, when it actually denounces mere intellectual assent. Paul agrees with James when he refers to 'the obedience of faith' in Romans 1:5. There Paul brings the heart into the picture when he describes his calling as bringing about the 'obedience of faith' among all peoples. Evangelicals sometimes mistakenly think that the gospel is mere information. However, Peter speaks of people disobeying the gospel which indicates that the gospel of God's kingdom is not merely an invitation to be received but an announcement of an authority to which we must yield and obey.

Apart from this theological confusion, the Reformation as a movement was more a cultural breakaway movement than a case of theological differences. This much stronger force creating the Reformation was the inherent divergence of the Germanic culture from the Latin (Mediterranean) culture. A similar breakaway movement occurred when Paul encouraged Greek believers to develop their own synagogues. A similar breakaway movement occurred when the Latin-speaking Roman Catholic church broke away from the Greek-speaking Orthodox church. In this sense the breakaway of the German-speaking church from the Mediterranean Roman Catholic culture was like the dozens of mission field breakaway movements today, which are attempting to resist a foreign missionary culture. In such cases national believers decide to start a church of their own, which is often very different from the missionary implanted form of Christianity. It is usually true that when a missionary tries to plant his own kind of church the people will eventually breakaway and develop their own kind. This is what happened in the Reformation. In such cases people may take sides and claim that one form is perfect and the other is imperfect Usually both sides are imperfect.

Confusion in Missions Today

Some mission agencies only plant personal-salvation churches. Their interest is in assuring people about going to heaven, and gathering people together to sing about heaven and God's personal blessings. This can be very successful, because it is relatively simple to persuade people around the world to raise their hands in order to get to heaven and to be blessed personally. However, it is more biblical to introduce people to Jesus Christ and urge them to obey Him as their Lord.

Some mission agencies focus on relief and development work. They may help people physically and not lead people to a personal commitment to Christ. What they do is very helpful. But in many cases they have made agreements with governments not to mention Jesus Christ, and without the transforming power of Christ, development work is not very likely to succeed. We need to seek personal transformation, and build on that foundation.

Some mission agencies do both. The biblical record shows that Jesus accompanied His words with works of mercy. Many mission agencies seek both the transformation of individual lives as well as the transformation of society. The older missions rooted in the 19th Century, such as the early Presbyterian missionaries, the early Sudan Interior Mission and the Africa Inland Mission, have made major contributions to the countries where they have worked – universities, medical schools, businesses, technical and agricultural training schools. Mission agencies more recently founded are less likely to sense a responsibility for nation building. They may think that nation building is hopeless or that it is not their responsibility. A great trend today, returning to the 19th Century, is to pursue kingdom mission, which seeks to glorify God by including both personal as well as national transformation.

Confusion in Recent (20th Century) History

Evangelicals in the 19th Century were very influential. In civil government, and in a series of revivals, they not only focused on personal salvation but on the transformation of society. In the USA they founded 100 colleges, and banished slavery. In Korea, missionaries from that era founded universities. In America, the period between the end of the War of 1812 to the beginning of the Civil War was a period of huge transformation. The idea that this world was worth changing was a central emphasis. In China missionaries planted a university in every province of China.

Evangelicals in the 20th century tended to focus on prophecy and eschatology. In the 20th Century, however, most evangelicals did not go to college and felt that there was no use in trying to save the world. For them it was better to focus on personal salvation. For them, getting as many people as possible 'saved' was the most important thing, and was about all they could do. True, personal salvation is, in fact, the most important thing. However, some evangelicals tended to become experts in guessing about the future and the end of history. Eschatology became a very special interest. Since these evangelicals were mainly non-college people, they lacked influence in the public sphere. But, they did what they were able to do. They were active in inner-city missions. Instead of colleges they established 157 Bible Institutes. In their missionary work these evangelicals no longer founded universities but rather Bible schools and seminaries.

Some college-level evangelicals, however, continued to include the idea of changing society. These people even in the 20th Century retained the earlier concern for society but sometimes lost concern for repentance and faith on the part of individuals. The Student Volunteer Movement represented this college level society. The Student Volunteers established 'Yale In China' and thought in terms of university education. Their influence on state and federal governments in the 20th Century gradually diminished.

Thus, *the USA today has inherited from the 20th century a huge and serious polarization.* There are still many arguments about the primacy of evangelism over social action, not realizing that neither deeds without words nor words without deeds are meant to stand alone any more than you can separate faith and works.

Resulting Loss of Glory for God, and Disrespect for Evangelicals

As a result some people wonder, 'Why is there so much evil in the world?' Then ask, 'Is there really a God at all?' Many honest and thinking people today are aware of two things, first, the huge amount of evil in this world – corruption, dishonesty, violence, wars, disease – and, second, they do not see very many Christians fighting against those evils. They also don't believe in Satan. As a result they are led to think that there must not be a God if there is all this hideous evil, or they believe that if there is a God He could not be both powerful and loving.

Thus, *some people wonder why evangelicals are not effective in fighting this world's problems and they even wonder about the validity of the Christian faith.* The absence of any large, strong evangelical mission agencies working against global disease and corruption leads many to feel that the Christian faith does not make any difference in society or that Christians and their God do not care.

Are We on the Eve of a New Era in Christianity and Missions?

But things are changing. As the 20th Century unfolded, one by one within 50 to 90 years every one of the 157 Bible Institutes became colleges or universities. Most evangelicals, *not* gambling or drinking, thus eventually saved enough money to send their children to college, and that way gradually gained greater influence in society. More and more evangelicals by now see reasons to work against evil in this world and in human society, even though others may still feel that such concerns are a diversion from the gospel. Such concerns are, in fact, a change from the simple evangelical personal gospel but they are faithful to the biblical gospel of the kingdom. One sad fact of history is the near total absence of evangelicals in the university world for 50 to 90 years. This is a major reason why the thinking in the university world has become highly secularized and even anti-Christian. Now even Christian colleges and universities around the world are forced to use secular textbooks and secular interpretations of history coming from a secularized university tradition in which they were not involved for most of a century.

But the number of evangelicals worldwide is very large today. There has never been a time when evangelicals had greater ability, influence and responsibility! In the USA the number of evangelicals in public office and in Congress and the Senate is much larger than ever before. Mission agencies have greater resources, potentially, than ever before. God expects more from those who have more to offer and who have received more from Him.

Businessmen are getting involved in mission. Many urgent needs around the world can be filled by honest and good-willed businesses. However, businesses cannot operate when those in need cannot pay. Therefore, many needs can only be filled by mission agencies whose support comes not from those benefited but from good-hearted donors who want to help others.

Local congregations are now often actively sending their own laymen overseas. If a congregation carefully thinks through a long-term plan for a specific place it may accomplish a great deal. However, it is not often that a single congregation, with its limited experience and expertise, can figure things out correctly. A congregation may do good things but not the *most* strategic things. If they want to eradicate diseases that cause terrible suffering to people for example, they also need to help found and support specialized mission agencies. Waiting until people get sick and then treating their illness is not good enough, and is not the same as eradicating a disease pathogen so that people don't get sick in the first place. This is not something lay people going on short trips overseas can accomplish.

New features in existing mission agencies and new features in new mission agencies are necessary. Existing mission agencies that focus exclusively on evangelization and church planting must realize that such efforts alone fail to provide an example of the good works that faith is supposed to produce (Eph. 2:10). Their churches may become merely places of refuge, places where people can concentrate on heaven and personal fulfillment without having to worry about transforming society at all. Newer missions must be concerned about the same wide spectrum of God's concern. God wants His will to be done on earth not just in heaven.

If we do not recover the wide spectrum of God's concern, do we continue in the 20th-century polarization? It *does* seem true that if we cannot reunite words with deeds we will be merely prolonging the tragic polarization which characterized the 20th Century.

How Can God Be Glorified and Evangelicals Respected?

Our mandate is to storm the kingdom of darkness. In Matthew 16:18 Jesus says that He will build his church and the forces of darkness will be unable to resist it. These words of Jesus make clear that for His will to be done on earth, definite action must be taken against evil. And what is needed is not just action against human evil but against deadly germs, and against all the rest of the works of darkness. This is clearly both a spiritual and physical war. Spiritual warfare is commonly thought of as purely a spiritual matter of prayer. However, although Jesus healed by prayer (demonstrating His love), He was also showing us we must be concerned about physical threats like disease. Today we can fight, in God's name, against destructive microbes with all of the knowledge we have gained about microbiology in the last 2,000 years.

Both micro good deeds and macro good deeds are necessary. In the 20th Century to the extent that evangelicals had limited education and wealth they still did all they were able to do. Now we can accept larger challenges and demonstrate God's concern for all problems big or small. Only this way can we properly glorify God and regain respect for evangelicals.

We are saved as individuals. We must serve as teams. A final point here is that big problems usually require not just the work of concerned individuals but groups of organized individuals. Very few young people will become full time ministers, missionaries or mobilizers. Most will be working in some other work, usually in the marketplace. That 'lay' work must *also* be a calling. Some work contributes more vitally to the extension of God's will in this world than other work. We must not assume that the highest paying job is automatically God's will. We are all called to do what we can do that will be the most effective in extending God's will in this world. Almost always this will require a business team or a mission team in order to be effective.

How Can We Keep Our Priorities Straight?

If our mandate is to storm the kingdom of darkness, are there priorities? It seems obvious *that* the highest priority should be to go where that darkness is deepest. That then means clearly to go to those places where Jesus is not yet known. That then means that we are talking now about the thousands of remaining 'Unreached Peoples'.

However, priorities cannot necessarily be dealt with one at a time. Often more than one priority must be acted on simultaneously not in sequence. We need both to save people from sin and from malaria. Every day in Africa alone 45 million people are withdrawn from the *workplace* due to malaria. We can't just save people from sin and ignore malaria which kills four children every sixty seconds. If millions of dollars of aid money is being diverted we can't give first and fight corruption second. In many countries medical schools and nurses training schools have been set up with foreign aid, but the average person cannot pay for such medical services so most of the doctors and nurses so trained leave their own country for jobs in Europe or America. Rural development and rural health must be achieved simultaneously.

Communicable disease is at the top of the priority list of world problems. Nevertheless 90 to 98% of all medical and pharmaceutical activities are focused on treating the sick not on conquering the diseases that make them sick. In America it is still true that 90% of all deaths are *premature* and are due to disease. Where is the Christian mission agency which is focused on the eradication of disease? The Gates foundation is. Within the PCUSA there is now the Presbyterian Institute for the Eradication of Disease. But it is just starting.

Evangelism is the highest priority. But it becomes weak and lacks credibility if it does *not generate committed believers who will tackle the world's problems. A massive shift in that direction is already becoming The Biggest Trend in World Mission.*

The Ebb and Flow of Kingdom Theology

C. René Padilla

Editors' Note: *Noted Latin American evangelical René Padilla provides a prophetic voice for evangelicals by calling us to do more than pay lip-service to holistic mission. In some respects his challenge to engage in integral mission hits directly at the perspectives on mission as evangelism found elsewhere in this book, demonstrating that evangelicals do not all have the same set of priorities and do not work them all out in the same way. This address was delivered at the first annual Ralph D. Winter Lectureship in Pasadena, California, March, 2010.*

The contradiction that oftentimes exists between the Christians' creed and their practical conduct is highlighted in the title of one of Nicolás Berdiaeff's essays, 'The Worthiness of Christianity and the Unworthiness of Christians'. In this way the celebrated Russian thinker attempts to refute the arguments leveled against the truth of the gospel based on the frequent inconsistencies that mark the life of Christians and that are unworthy of the gospel.

As a matter of fact, if the truth of Christianity depended on the fidelity with which Christians have applied it in history, little could be said in its favor. Certainly, the history of the Church abounds in pages that illustrate the power of the gospel for personal and social transformation. Nevertheless, it also abounds in pages that show the ease with which Christians have transformed the gospel of the kingdom of God – the good news of God's reign of justice and *shalom* inaugurated by Jesus Christ – into a religion used in the service of the kingdoms of this world dominated by human interests that go against the purpose of God.

Imperialism and Mission

One of the clearest examples of using Christianity for unworthy purposes is seen in the link between western imperialism and missionary work, both Roman Catholic and Protestant, during the last centuries up until today.

No one can deny that Spain's endeavor to conquer and colonize America in the sixteenth century had a religious dimension. It was meant to be nothing less than the reconstruction of the Sacred Roman Empire in the New World. It was taken for granted that by extending the kingdom ruled by king Fernando and queen Isabel, the kingdom of God would also be extended. And in the name of that supposedly Christian ideal, backed up by the Pope, they committed all kinds of atrocities and crimes against the conquered nations. Sadly, they did not lack the support of theologians, such as Ginés de Sepúlveda, [1]who was more than ready to justify the bloody conquest biblically.

We have to admit that for evangelicals in general, especially in Latin America, it is easy to condemn the close relationship between the Spanish imperialism and Roman Catholic mission to our continent in the years following 1492. And conveniently we tend to ignore the Christian spirit shown by various priests who, risking their own lives, defended the aboriginals. An outstanding example is Bartolomé de Las Casas, from whose courageous prophetic testimony we have much to learn even today.

If those of us in the evangelical camp are willing not to get historically caught up in the sliver in the Roman Catholic eye but to give proper attention to the plank in our own, we need to acknowledge that the drama of an evangelization associated with imperialism also has a Protestant version. In effect, although with different actors and circumstances, the expansion of the United States in the nineteenth century used the same violence as that of the Iberian conquest in the sixteenth century and also found justification for it in the supposed 'manifest destiny' of supernatural origin that accompanied the *conquistadores.* As Ralph D. Winter puts it,

> Missions and 'manifest destiny', as in the earlier European expansion, were closely tied together. Reminiscent of the Crusades, many Americans understood the kingdom of God to include a spiritual and military destiny to seize Texas and California from Mexico, and a little later to exclude the British from the Northwestern by suddenly pushing the Canadian-American border out of the Pacific. Not stopping there, they seized the mission-transformed Sandwich Islands (now Hawaii), Western Samoa, Guam, Puerto Rico and the Philippines...These American 'crusades' were, like the classical Crusades, uneasy mixtures of high-minded religion, low-born politics, and military violence.[2]

Blindfolded by the 'manifest destiny' ideology, the majority of American Protestant church leaders backed up their country's expansionist wars as the God-given instrument for the establishment of an 'empire of justice' favorable to evangelism on a global scale.

It should be added, however, that the concept of manifest destiny was not unique to the United States. Rather, it was a foundational pillar in the colonial

---

[1] See examples of the sophistry of the arguments used in defense of the conquest in Juan Stam, '*Exégesis bíblica en los teólogos de losconquistadores*', *Boletín Teológico*, 24:47-48 (December, 1992).

[2] Ralph D. Winter. 'Three Mission Eras: And the Loss and Recovery of Kingdom Mission, 1800–2000'. In Ralph D. Winter and Steven C. Hawthorne (eds). *Perspectives on the World Christian Movement: A Reader*, 4th ed. (Pasadena: William Carey Library, 2009), 270.

expansion of several European countries especially near the end of the nineteenth century and during the early decades of the twentieth century. For the defenders of manifest destiny, their respective nation had inherited Israel's role as the chosen people of God destined to be a light to the pagan nations. It had both the privilege and the responsibility not only to evangelize but also to colonize the non-Christian nations, thus extending the kingdom of God. Especially during the imperial era, after 1880, it was taken for granted that missionary work was the God-given task of every western colonial country, be it the United States, Britain, France, Belgium, Holland, or whatever the country was that sent the missionaries.

Certainly, this does not mean that the missionary work based in the West was nothing more than the spiritual aspect of colonialism. Such a view would not do justice to the Christian spirit expressed in terms of sacrificial service, made evident by many pages in the history of western missionary work. Besides, it fails to take into account the pressures of the socioeconomic and political conditions under which the missionaries had to work. As David J. Bosch affirms,

> The issue is more serious than just that of demonstrable collusion of mission with the colonial powers. If we were to define it merely in these terms we might easily be persuaded to believe that the colonial traits of western mission belonged only to a particular historical period, that they were merely exterior and could easily be discarded again.... We would then be tempted to treat the issue too narrowly as simply a matter of the relation of mission to colonialism and overlook the fact that this relationship is but an integral part of the much wider and much more serious project of the advance of western technological civilization.[3]

The World Missionary Conference of Edinburgh 1910 and Its Legacy

The World Missionary Conference of Edinburgh took place in June 1910, within the period that the well-known historian Kenneth Scott Latourette has called 'the great century' of Christian missions (1815–1914), a time of full flourishing of manifest destiny and the climax of the idea of progress – an expression of modernity in the West.

Before the Edinburgh Conference, the Ecumenical Missionary Conference had taken place in 1900 at Carnegie Hall in New York, with the surprising participation of around two hundred thousand people and two hundred missionary societies, and with the presence of Mr. William McKinley, President of the United States, who gave the inaugural speech.

The Conference in New York was intended for pastors and ecclesial leaders and its central purpose was to mobilize the church. The Conference in Edinburgh, on the other hand, was a way to project the vision and missionary

[3] Bosch, *Transforming Mission,* 312.

commitment to other Christian countries, especially Great Britain, Germany, France and Belgium. The goal was 'the evangelization of the world in this generation', the motto that the Student Volunteer Movement adopted in 1889 and that, as David Bosch states, 'More than anything else, it epitomized the Protestant missionary optimism of the period: pragmatic, purposeful, activist, impatient, self-confident, single-minded, triumphant'. [4] From the perspective of John Mott, one of the main motivators and promoters of the Edinburgh 1910 Conference, as well as its moderator, this goal was attainable because the church not only had thousands of volunteers ready to take on the task of evangelism, but also the resources were providentially provided by God, including the accomplishments of modern science, financial power and the support of Christian governments. In Bosch's words, from this point of view 'western mission was an undisputed power. Mission stood in the sign of world conquest.' [5]

The year 1910 is memorable in the history of Protestantism not only because of the World Missionary Conference in Edinburgh. It is also memorable because in this year began the publication of *The Fundamentals,* a work of twelve volumes for the purpose of giving 'Testimony to the Truth' (as the subtitle read) from a dispensationalist perspective and to counteract ideas regarded as 'modernist' or 'liberal'. Between 1910 and 1915, this work was widely distributed and it served to feed the fundamentalism/modernism controversy – a controversy that occupied the headlines of religious news in the United States throughout the 1920s and, by reflection, in many other countries.

At the root of it, the polarization between fundamentals and modernists has to do with differences in the way of understanding the kingdom of God and its implications for the Christian mission. Using Ralph Winter's terminology, it is a polarization among those who understand mission as *Church mission* and those who understand it as *Kingdom mission.* For the fundamentalists, the missionary task consists of preaching the gospel in order to expand the church and increasing the number of its members. Strongly influenced by dispensational premillennial eschatology, they believe that the kingdom of God will be established with Christ's return, and that the missionary objective of the present time, before the Second Coming, is the preaching of the gospel to all nations. They reject 'the social gospel' as a modernist theological position, unacceptable because it does not take into account that the only way to solve the social problems is to share the message of salvation through Jesus Christ. This was the position of the majority of cross-cultural missionaries that planted evangelical churches in many countries around the world, including Latin America. It is not surprising that until quite recently the unilateral emphasis on

---

[4] Bosch, *Transforming Mission*, 336. According to George M. Marsden, 'The motto of the Student Volunteer Movement summarized well the spirit of the American Protestantism of the day'. (*Understanding Fundamentalism and Evangelicalism* [Grand Rapids: Eerdmans, 1991], 22).

[5] Bosch. *Transforming Mission*, 338.

the preaching the gospel was one of the most distinctive characteristics of evangelicals around the world.

In contrast to this missiological position, what kingdom mission proposes is that evangelism must be accompanied by action for the sake of social transformation, so that the will of God is fulfilled beyond the church – on the earth as it is in heaven. From a postmillennial or amillennial theological perspective, kingdom mission maintains that the kingdom of God does not belong to the future, nor is it otherworldly; it is a present reality introduced in history by Jesus Christ. In words of Arthur Cushman McGiffert of Union Theological Seminary of New York, a defender of this position quoted by George M. Marsden in *Fundamentalism and American Culture,* the kingdom of God was the central emphasis of Jesus' preaching, 'not a kingdom lying in another world beyond the skies but established here and now', a kingdom that meant 'the control of the lives of [people] and of all their relationships one with another and of all the institutions on which those relationships find expression by the spirit of Jesus Christ who has shown us what God is and who he would have this world be '. According to Marsden, 'these feelings were reiterated countless times throughout the midcentury between 1880 and 1930 '. [6]

For a large sector of the Protestant movement, the Edinburgh 1910 Conference was an indisputable ratification of the fundamentalist or traditionalist approach to the Christian mission – the predominant approach in the evangelical movement continuing until present day especially in the West. In this approach the Christian mission is conceived mainly in geographical terms. It consists of crossing geographic frontiers from the 'Christian west' and into the 'mission fields' of the non-Christian or pagan world, for the purpose of saving souls and planting churches. To speak of mission is to speak of *transcultural evangelism*. The agents of the mission are European or American 'missionaries', with an occasional Australian and South African, the majority of them affiliated with denominational mission societies or interdenominational 'faith missions'. The qualifications to be a missionary vary, but generally (in addition, of course, to an experience of conversion to Jesus Christ) the first requirement is to feel 'called to the mission field'. God's call to be a missionary, as in the case of the call to be a pastor, is regarded as the ultimate call, the highest vocation that a Christian can have to serve God. Of course, it is not for all Christians, but only for a select few.

What is the responsibility of the church according to this traditional paradigm of mission? With the exception of a few churches (especially among Free Brethren, who often send their missionaries without the intervention of missionary societies), the role of the church is reduced to providing personnel and spiritual and economic support for missions. Even the preparation and

---

[6] George M. Marsden. *Fundamentalism and American Culture: The Shaping of Twentieth-Century Evangelicalism, 1870–1925* (Oxford/New York: Oxford University Press, 1980), 50.

training of the missionaries is delegated by the local church to another institution that specializes in that task.

Despite its weakness, this traditional concept of mission that characterizes much of the evangelical missionary movement has inspired many and continues to inspire thousands of transcultural missionaries to cross geographic frontiers for the purpose of sharing the good news about Jesus Christ. As a result, some of the most moving pages of church history have been written and the Christian movement has attained a global reach, with congregations in just about every country in the world. On the other hand, it is important to acknowledge that the identification of the church's mission with transcultural mission – an identification clearly illustrated by the World Missionary Conference of Edinburgh 1910 – has strengthened at least four dichotomies that have negatively affected the church and its mission.

The Dichotomy between Churches that Send and Churches that Receive Missionaries

In this dichotomy, churches that send missionaries are generally from western nations and those that receive missionaries are almost exclusively in countries in Asia, Africa and Latin America. This has been changing in the last decades thanks to the growing numbers of transcultural missionaries sent from the Majority World, including the periphery of the West, Latin America. We should acknowledge, however, that until recently transcultural missions were almost always carried out from a European nation (for example Britain, Scotland, Germany, Switzerland, Holland, Sweden or Norway), or from the United States, Australia or New Zealand. As Andrew Walls puts it, 'with all of the faults, contradictions and ambiguities in the human condition, missionaries were immigrants [from these countries] for the cause of Christ '.[7] The transcultural movement based in Asia, Africa and Latin America is relatively new.

The Dichotomy between the Home and the Mission Field

It is not surprising that the majority of 'career missionaries' (sometimes after many years of service) decide to retire, or their mission society obligates them to do so, in their country of origin, usually in the West.

The Dichotomy between Missionaries Called by God to Serve Him, and Common Ordinary Christians

Ordinary Christians expect to enjoy the benefits of salvation but consider themselves to be exempt from participating in what God wants to do in this world. I suggest that the dichotomy between *clergy* (including pastors) and *laity*

---

[7] Andrew Walls. 'Afterword: Mission in a Five-Hundred Year Context', in Andrew Walls and Cathy Ross (eds), *Mission in the 21st Century: Exploring the Five Marks of Global Mission* (London: Darton, Longman and Todd, Ltd., 2008), 197.

is at the root of the problem of the masses of 'Sunday Christians' that are part of evangelical churches around the world.

THE DICHOTOMY BETWEEN THE LIFE AND THE MISSION OF THE CHURCH.

If in order for a church to be a missionary church it is sufficient that it send a few of its members to far off places to serve in missions, then it is possible for that church to qualify as a missionary church even if it has no significant influence or impact on its own surrounding neighborhood: its life is developed in its local context (at *home*), but its mission is carried out in another setting, preferably in a foreign country (*the mission field*).

All these dichotomies are related to the reduction of mission to transcultural missionary work. The Christian mission is understood primarily as a task carried out by missionaries sent from 'Christian' countries to the mission fields of the world. To put it bluntly, these missionaries fulfill representatively or vicariously the mission of the whole church. Sadly, all these dichotomies are projected on to the international scene.

Integral Mission, a Paradigm Shift in Mission Theology

Against the background that has just been described, there is no doubt that one of the most significant phenomena in today's global evangelical ecclesial scene is the Micah Network, a group of over 330 Christian relief, development and justice organizations from 81 countries. Micah Network was formed in 1999 with the aims to:

1. Build capacity. Strengthen the capacity of participating agencies to make a biblically-shaped response to the needs of the poor and oppressed

2. Encourage integral mission. Speak strongly and effectively regarding the nature of the mission of the Church to proclaim and demonstrate the love of Christ to a world in need

3. Advocate. Prophetically call upon and influence the leaders and decision-makers of societies to 'maintain the rights of the poor and oppressed and rescue the weak and needy .'[8]

The Micah Network makes it quite evident that all over the world, but especially in the Majority World, there is an increasing number of churches and Christian service agencies that do not only talk about mission but are actually involved in integral mission – mission that integrates the proclamation of the kingdom of God and its justice with the demonstration of its presence in history through action carried out by the people of God.

Although this network was not formally organized until 1999, its origin can be traced back to an evangelical movement of global theological reflection within which, under God, the rediscovery of the kingdom of God took place. At least in the case of Latin America, it can easily be proved that this biblical

[8] See www.micahnetwork.org.

concept became the key to the understanding of the biblical basis for the Christian mission. Having started in December 1970, the Latin American Theological Fellowship (FTL its acronym in Spanish) dedicated its second consultation, held in Lima in December 1972, to the topic 'The Kingdom of God and Latin America'. [9] Beginning with that consultation, much of the rich theological production of the FTL would exercise a very strong influence on the articulation of kingdom mission in terms of integral mission not only in Latin America but around the world, especially in the Majority World.

The note of the kingdom of God as the main note to understand both the Christian mission and the role of the church in the great symphony of God's universal purpose was clearly sounded at the First International Congress on World Evangelism held in Lausanne, Switzerland, in 1974. It was heard especially from plenary speakers related to the FTL [10] and from Howard A. Snyder, [11] a plenary speaker with missionary experience in Brazil. It was also very loudly heard through the document entitled 'Theology Implications of Radical Discipleship', [12] written by an *ad hoc* group spontaneously formed after the Congress had started, and signed by about four hundred of the participants, including John Stott. [13] Therein the gospel is defined as 'God's Good News in Jesus Christ. ... Good News of the reign he proclaims and embodies. ... Good News of restoration, of wholeness, and of salvation that is personal, social, global and cosmic'. [14]

For the global evangelical movement, the years following Lausanne 1974 were years characterized by polarization with regards to the Christian mission. One pole is the traditional approach, prevalent especially in the West, with its emphasis on the salvation of souls and the planting of churches through

---

[9] For the proceedings of this consultation see C. René Padilla (ed.), *El Reino de Dios y América Latina* (El Paso, Texas: Mundo Hispano, 1975). On the first decade or so of the FTL, see the *Journal of Latin American Theology* 4:2 (2009). On the development of the integral mission concept since the 1960s, see my chapter 'Integral Mission and its Historical Development' in Tim Cheter (ed.), *Justice, Mercy and Humility* (Carlisle, Cumbria; Paternoster, 2002), 42-58.

[10] See especially C. René Padilla, 'Evangelism and the Word' and Samuel Escobar, 'Evangelism and Man's Search for Freedom, Justice and Fulfillment' in J. D. Douglas (ed.), *Let the Earth Hear His Voice* (Minneapolis: World Wide Publications, 1975), 116-46, 303-26.

[11] See Howard A. Snyder, 'The Church as God's Agent in Evangelism', in J. D. Douglas (ed.), *Let the Earth Hear His Voice*, 327-80. Snyder later expanded his paper and published an excellent book on ecclesiology, *The Community of the King* (Downers Grove: InterVarsity Press, 1977; 2nd rev. ed., 2004).

[12] This document is included in Douglas (ed.), *Let the Earth Hear His Voice*, 1294-96.

[13] According to Rodger C. Bassham, John Stott's 'support of the statement produced by the Radical Discipleship group helped promote the acceptance of the concerns presented by that committee' (*Mission Theology, 1948–1975: Years of Worldwide Creative Tension – Ecumenical, Evangelical and Roman Catholic* [Pasadena: William Carey Library, 1979], 233).

[14] Douglas (ed.), *Let the Earth Hear His Voice*, 1294.

evangelism understood as 'the verbal witness of the Church'. [15] It is closely related to the concept of the kingdom of God as spiritual reality subjectively experienced by Christian believers. As Johnston puts it, 'the kingdom of God is the present inner rule of God in the moral and spiritual dispositions of the soul with its seat in the heart. God does rule as King in the lives of those 'born again''. [16] From this perspective, 'evangelism as the mission of the Church represents the highest vindication of the reconciling work of the Cross and the greatest benefit to the world's poor and oppressed flows from multiple lives made new in Christ Jesus'. [17]

The other pole is the approach focused on integral mission as an expression of the kingdom of God that has *already* entered history through Jesus Christ, although *not yet* in its fullness. It is the approach that took shape especially in the Latin American Theological Fellowship in the 1970s and irrupted through the Radical Discipleship group at the Lausanne Congress in 1974. And we must not forget the important document that, in the same line, emerged from the Consultation, 'The Church in Response to Human Need', that, under the auspices of the World Evangelical Fellowship and with a big contingent of participants from the Majority World, took place in Wheaton, Illinois, in 1983.[18] This document may be regarded as the strongest evangelical statement on integral mission in the last quarter of the twentieth century. Taking as a basis the biblical vision of the kingdom of God as 'the goal of transformation', this document unequivocally affirms that 'evil is not only in the human heart but

---

[15] This is the definition coined by Arthur P. Johnston in his paper on 'The Kingdom in Relation to the Church and the World', in Bruce Nichols (ed.), *In Word and Deed: Evangelism and Social Responsibility* (Exeter, Devon: Paternoster, 1985), 109-33, which the author presented at the Consultation on the Relation Between Evangelism and Social Responsibility (CRESR) held in Grand Rapids, Michigan, in June 1982, under the sponsorship of the Lausanne Commitee for World Evangelism and the World Evangelical Fellowship.

[16] Johnston, 'Kingdom', in *Word and Deed*, 128. How widespread is this understanding of the Kingdom of God in Evangelical circles is made evident by the *NIV Study Bible* comment on Luke 17:12: '*the kingdom of God is within you*. Probably indicating that the kingdom is spiritual and internal (Mt 23:26) rather than physical and external (cf. Jn 18:36)'. Although the rendering *within* is grammatically possible, it should be discarded on two accounts: (a) It makes no sense when one takes into account that Jesus was addressing the Pharisees. How could he say that the kingdom of God was within them? (b) There is no evidence to support the view of the Kingdom of God as 'spiritual and internal'. As Joachim Jeremias has observed, 'Neither in Judaism nor elsewhere in the New Testament do we find the reign of God as something indwelling in men, to be found, say, in the heart; such spiritualistic understanding is ruled out both for Jesus and for the early Christian tradition' (*New Testament Theology: The Proclamation of Jesus* [London: SCM Press, 1971], 101). The NIV comment belongs to the category of what N. T. Wright in another context calls 'retrojections into the first century of a nineteenth-century Romantic ideal of religion in which outward things are bad and inward things good' (*Jesus and the Victory of God* [Minneapolis: Fortress Press, 1996], 290).

[17] Johnston, 'Kingdom', in *Word and Deed*, 111.

[18] The proceedings of this consultation were edited by Vinay Samuel and Chris Sugden in *The Church in Response to Human Need* (Oxford: Regnum, 1987). The document is in pages 254-65.

also in social structures. ... The mission of the church includes both the proclamation of the gospel and its demonstration. We must therefore evangelize, respond to immediate human needs, and press for social transformation.'[19]

This second pole, strongly influenced by evangelical Christians who, on facing in daily life the negative consequences of today's unjust global economic system, have been forced to recognize basic human needs, is the pole that has found expression in the Micah Network. It is the pole that seeks to be faithful to God's demand: 'To act justly and to love mercy and to walk humbly before your God' (Micah 6:8) through a lifestyle characterized by the practice of kingdom mission.

From the perspective of integral mission, transcultural mission is far from exhausting the significance of the mission of the church. Mission may or may not include a crossing of geographical frontiers, but in every case it means primarily a crossing of the frontier between faith and no faith, whether in one's own country ('at home') or in a foreign country (on 'the mission field'), according to the testimony to Jesus Christ as Lord of the whole of life and creation. Every generation of Christians in every place receives the power of the Holy Spirit that makes possible the witness to the gospel 'in Jerusalem, and in all Judea and Samaria, and to the ends of the earth' (Acts 1:8). In other words, every church, wherever it may be, is called to share in God's mission: a mission that is local, regional and world-wide in scope – beginning in its own Jerusalem. In order to cross the frontier between faith and no faith, crossing geographical boundaries is not indispensable; the geographical factor is secondary. Commitment to mission is the very essence of the being of the church; therefore, the church that is not committed to the mission of witnessing to Jesus Christ and thus to crossing the frontier between faith and no faith is no longer the church, but simply a religious club, a group of friends, or a social welfare agency.

When the church is committed to integral mission and to communicating the gospel through everything it is, does, and says, it understands that its goal is not to become large numerically, nor to be rich materially, nor powerful politically. Its purpose is to incarnate the values of the kingdom of God and to witness to God's love and the justice revealed in Jesus Christ, by the power of the Spirit, for the transformation of human life in all its dimensions, both on the individual level and on the community level.

The accomplishment of this purpose presupposes that all the members of the church, without exception, by the very fact of having become a part of the Body of Christ, receive gifts and ministries for the exercise of their priesthood, to which they have been ordained in their baptism. Mission is not the responsibility and privilege of a small group of the faithful who feel 'called to the mission field' (usually in a foreign country), but of all members, since all

---

[19] Samuel and Sugden, *The Church*, 260.

are members of the 'royal priesthood' and as such have been called by God 'that you may declare the praises of him who called you out of darkness into his wonderful light' (1 Pet. 2:9) wherever they may be. As Brian D. McLaren aptly states,

> For Christ, his 'called ones' (which is what the Greek term for 'church' really means) will also be his 'sent ones' [or missionaries]. ... In this line of thinking about the church, we don't recruit people to be customers of our products or consumers of our religious programs; we recruit them to be colleagues in our mission. The church does not exist in order to satisfy the consumer demands of believers; the church exists to equip and mobilize men and women for God's mission in the world.[20]

According to this view, what is the role of the local church in mission? We have already expressed the answer in McLaren's words: 'to equip and mobilize men and women for God's mission in the world' – not exclusively in the church building, which may or may not exist, but in all fields of human life: in the home, in business, in the hospital, in the university, in the office, in the workshop – in conclusion, everywhere, since there is no place that is not within the orbit of the lordship of Jesus Christ.

Understood in these terms, this 'new paradigm for mission' is not so new; it is, rather, the recovery of the biblical concept of mission since, in effect, mission is faithful to the teaching of Scripture to the extent that it is placed at the service of the kingdom of God and his justice. Consequently, it is focused on crossing the frontier between faith and no faith, not only in geographical terms, but in cultural, ethnic, social, economical and political terms, for the purpose of transforming life in all its dimensions, according to God's plan, so that all people and human communities may experience shalom, the abundant life that Christ offers them. As such, integral mission resolves the dichotomies mentioned above.

All Churches Send and All Churches Receive (at Least in Principle)

All churches have something to teach and something to learn from other churches. The road mission follows is not a one-way street. It does not go only from the 'Christian' countries to the pagan countries. It is a two-way street. A good example is seen in the missionary movement from the countries in the South, which are sending a growing number of cross-cultural missionaries even to countries in the North.

[20] Brian D. McClaren, *A New Kind of Christian: A Tale of Two Friends on a Spiritual Journey* (San Francisco: Jossey-Bass, 2001), 156-57.

THE WHOLE WORLD IS A MISSION FIELD, AND EVERY HUMAN NEED IS AN OPPORTUNITY FOR MISSIONARY SERVICE.

The local church is called to demonstrate the reality of the kingdom of God among the kingdoms of this world, not only by what it says, but also by what it is and by what it does in response to the humans needs on every side. Francis de Assisi was right when, as he sent his followers out to proclaim the gospel, he exhorted them to proclaim it by every means at their disposal, and that if it was really necessary they should use words. The proclamation of the gospel includes everything we do moved by the Spirit of Jesus who, when he saw the crowds, 'had compassion on them, because they were harassed and helpless, like sheep without a shepherd' (Matt. 9:36).

EVERY CHRISTIAN IS CALLED TO FOLLOW JESUS CHRIST AND TO BE COMMITTED TO GOD'S MISSION IN THE WORLD

The benefits of salvation are inseparable from a missionary lifestyle, and this implies, among other things, the practice of the universal priesthood of believers in all spheres of human life, according to the gifts and ministries that the Holy Spirit has freely bestowed on his people. It is the responsibility of pastors and teachers to 'prepare God's people for works of service [*diakonia*], so that the body of Christ may be built up' (Eph. 4.12).

MISSION IS LIFE

The Christian life in all its dimensions, on both the individual and the community levels, is the primary witness to the universal lordship of Jesus Christ and the transforming power of the Holy Spirit. Mission is much more than words. It involves the quality of life. It is demonstrated in the life that recovers God's original purpose for the relationship of the human person with his Creator, with his neighbor, and with all of creation.

Conclusion

In conclusion, integral mission is the means designed by God for the church to manifest the presence of the kingdom of God within history, in the midst of the kingdoms of the world and over against every form of imperialism, and to bear witness to God's purpose of love and justice revealed in Jesus Christ, in the power of the Holy Spirit.

A War-Torn Creation

Gregory A. Boyd

Editors' Note: *This article was originally a sermon in a mini-series on spiritual warfare. It represents a minority segment of evangelicals who at the beginning of the 21st century are thinking both in terms of satanic influence on the earth and the responsibility of believers to do what they can to restore creation to its intended state, as an aspect of carrying out God's mission in this world.*

We are talking about spiritual warfare and that warfare permeates the entire creation. We are not talking about human warfare or violence. Paul tells us in Ephesians 6:12 that our struggle as kingdom people is not against flesh and blood, but it is against principalities and powers and rulers and authorities in dark places. If it has flesh and blood, as kingdom people we are commanded to love that person. In fact one of the main ways we do spiritual warfare is by living lives of outrageous, ridiculous love, which is the opposite of violence. So when I use warfare language, it is not about earthly, fleshly violence. Rather, we are talking about spiritual warfare.

Often when people think of spiritual warfare, they immediately think about casting demons out of people. That is one aspect of spiritual warfare, and it is biblical. But that is not the only or even the primary focus of spiritual warfare. Spiritual warfare is a holistic concept. Warfare isn't something that just goes on once in a while. It permeates our lives. It permeates the entire creation. Seeing the world as caught in warfare even at the level of creation, reframes the world in ways that have a practical impact on how we live our lives in kingdom mission.

A passage in Luke serves as a springboard to seeing this world as a war-torn creation. 'One day Jesus said to his disciples, 'Let's go over to the other side of the lake.' So they got into a boat and set out. As they sailed, he fell asleep. A squall came down on the lake, so that the boat was being swamped, and they were in great danger. The disciples went and woke him saying, 'Master, Master, we're going to drown!'' We notice here that there are huge winds, the boat is taking in water, and Jesus is still asleep. The disciples are panicking but Jesus is sleeping in peace. '[Jesus] got up and rebuked the wind and the raging waters; the storm subsided, and all was calm. 'Where is your faith?' he asked his disciples. In fear and amazement they asked one another, 'Who is this? He commands even the winds and the water, and they obey him' (Luke 8:22-25, NIV).

The central problem that I am addressing is this question: If God is all good, all love, and if God created the world, why doesn't the world reflect God's goodness and love? Why is the world such a violent world? Now we can answer that question on a human level, because God gave us free will, we can either love or not love. That one is not that difficult I don't think.

But my question is why doesn't *creation* unambiguously reflect the loving, good character of God? The world we live in is a violent world even at the level of creation. It is a world where we sometimes experience killer earthquakes. Every year it seems, there are earthquakes that kill thousands upon thousands of people. Several years ago, an earthquake in Pakistan killed over a 100,000 people in 7 minutes. Where is the goodness of God revealed in that? And there are hurricanes and tsunamis that wipe out entire cities. Indonesia got hit with a tsunami that left thousands and thousands of people dead, and 10 times that many without homes. Where is the goodness of God revealed in that?

And there are famines and droughts throughout the world, leaving people without adequate food or water, killing hundreds of thousands, perhaps millions. Then of course we have a spectrum of viruses and diseases that we have to fight against: AIDS, Ebola, leprosy, malaria. There have been times in history where large segments of the population were wiped out by the plague. In the middle ages, 30-40% of Europe's population was killed by the plague. How could an all-good all-loving God create a world that has all of these diseases?

And then there are the parasites. One scientist said that parasites are actually humanity's worst enemy. They get in and eat their victim, human or animal, from the inside out. They have a sort of demonic intelligence. They know how to get in there and do the most amount of damage and cause the most amount of misery. One is called the hookworm. I think Satan left his signature on this one. Hookworm infection is a major disease in many countries of the developing world, according to the *International Journal of Epidemiology* (26:6). It latches on to the wall of the intestine and has just the right amount of chemicals in its mouth to keep the blood from clotting. It starves its host of its nutrition. So the infected person, no matter how much they can eat, and in third world countries they often can't get enough to eat anyway, is malnourished, anaemic, and underdeveloped. Then the hookworm replicates itself. When a group from our church went to visit a children's home in Haiti, one of the children they met was a 6 year old girl, and when they put their hand on her stomach, they could feel the worms moving around in her stomach. Where is the goodness of God revealed in that?

Then you have the animal kingdom that is full of carnage. Hyenas attack an antelope, and chunk by chunk, eat it alive. Where is the goodness of God in that? We could recount the various horrors in history, the carnage and waste of life throughout our history. Where is the benevolent God in this?

But what concerns me is that you find that many Christians seem to grant the premise of the objection by many atheists, namely, the premise that God is the one doing all of this. Most Christians seem to believe that nature is right now just the way it is supposed to be, it was created this way. Human beings are a little messed up, but creation is working just fine. And when you hold that view, you have to say God is behind the parasites and the violence and the tsunamis. And then we cannot wonder if people say, 'well if that's the kind of God he is, I'd rather have nothing to do with your God'. Where is the goodness of God reflected in the violence and the carnage that is nature?

I want to give an alternative perspective. It is the perspective that was the dominant view for the first three centuries of church history, up until Augustine. In this view, creation is permeated with spiritual warfare. It is not just human beings who are targets of spiritual warfare, but creation itself has been corrupted, so that creation does not any longer reflect unambiguously the goodness and the glory of God. This is the view C. S. Lewis espoused, as quoted by N.T. Wright in his blog: 'every square inch of space and every split second of time is claimed by God and counter-claimed by Satan'. [1]

Warfare permeates the entire creation. In Luke 8 Jesus rebuked the storm. The word, 'rebuke', is the same Greek word that is always used when Jesus rebuked demons.[2] Nature is permeated by corrupting influences; there is something demonic at work in nature. It doesn't mean that there is a specific demonic power behind every hurricane, tsunami, every parasite and disease. But I am suggesting that nature as we find it now is not identical to nature as God created it to be. It doesn't reflect the glory of God.

Five biblical facts support this position that creation in its present state is not as God intended it to be.

God's Ideal Creation Is a Non-violent Creation

In Genesis 1 God says over and over again, 'it is good', 'it is good', 'it is good'. And part of that goodness is the fact that there was no violence in creation. God said, 'I give you every seed bearing plant on the face of the whole earth and every tree that has fruit with seed in it. They will be yours for food. And to all the beasts of the earth and all the birds of the air and all the creatures that move on the ground--everything that has the breath of life in it – I give every green plant for food' (Genesis 1:29, 30 NIV). God did not say he gave the animals to each other for food. He gave them all the green plants for food. However else that you interpret this chapter, it tells me that it was a non-carnivorous creation. In fact, the Bible tells us that when the kingdom is on earth as it is in heaven, the earth will be rid of violence completely. 'The wolf will live with the lamb,

---

[1] http://www.homileticsonline.com/subscriber/interviews/wright.asp
[2] Paul R. McReynolds, *Word Study Greek-English New Testament with Complete Concordance*, Carol Stream, Ill.: Tyndale House, 1999, 1223-24.

the leopard will lay down with the goat, the calf and the lion and the yearling together' (Isaiah 11:6). Humanity will be reinstated as the rightful rulers of the animal kingdom. When the kingdom is restored, even a little child will be ruler over them (Isaiah 11:6). 'The cow will feed with the bear, their young will lie down together, and the lion will eat straw like the ox. The infant will play near the hole of the cobra, and the young child put his hand into the viper's nest. They will neither harm nor destroy on all my holy mountain' (Isaiah 11:7-9). That 'mountain' is referring to Mount Zion, which is the Old Testament's metaphor for the Kingdom of God.[3] 'For the earth will be full of the knowledge of the Lord as the waters cover the sea' (Isaiah 11:9). The earth will be reconciled to God, animals will be reconciled to animals and peace will reign on earth. The world will then reflect unambiguously the glory of its creator.

Nature Is Cursed

In Genesis 3 we read about a curse, a curse that came to the level of nature. When Adam and Eve rebelled and a curse came upon the world, hostility between serpents and people came about. Pain in childbirth came about at this time and the ground became much harder to work. Thorns and thistles began to grow, and all people will die because of the curse. All of these things seem like they are natural effects. We have difficulty imagining a world without thorns and thistles. However one interprets this passage, it is at least saying that nature is cursed, not operating how it was originally created to operate. 'We know that the whole creation has been groaning as in the pains of childbirth right up to the present time' (Romans 8:22). These are in part the effects of the second law of thermodynamics. We cannot really imagine a world without the second law of thermodynamics. We also see the consequences of the willful reality of sin and its effects on creation. We see much in nature that does reflect God's glory, but we also see a lot that does not.

The two questions are this: (1) In Genesis 3, human beings bring on the curse. What do you do with all of the suffering in the animal kingdom before humans came on the scene? (2) It is clear in Genesis 3 that God brought the curse on the earth. And yet Jesus rebuked the storm as though it was of a demonic origin. So the question is this: Who brings the curse? Is it Satan or God?

To answer these questions, we need to go on to a third biblical fact.

---

[3] See G. Johannes Botterweck and Helmer Ringgren (eds), 'Kabod', *Theological Dictionary of the Old Testament*, Volume 7, 35 [Accessed online 27 December 2010, http://books.google.com/books?id=weqiE1yiPyoC&pg=PA35&lpg=PA35&dq=Zion+Old+Testament+metaphor+for+the+Kingdom+of+God&source=bl&ots=d95yYT2WCx&sig=Syb_1YXYsDhhH6DEyyr-UuefMXc&hl=en&ei=D3QZTdm9OI66sQPR2M2_Ag&sa=X&oi=book_result&ct=result&resnum=8&ved=0CDkQ6AEwBw#v=onepage&q&f=false]

Satan Holds the Power of Death

'Since the children have flesh and blood, he too shared in their humanity so that by his death he might destroy him who holds the power of death-that is, the devil' (Hebrews 2:14). First John 3:8 says that Jesus came into this world to do warfare with the devil, to defeat the devil, and to destroy his works. And one of the works he came to defeat was death. So in Hebrews 2:14 death is a result of Satan's power, and in Genesis 3 death is the result of the curse. Reflecting on these passages together leads to the conclusion that the curse was simply a matter of God removing his protection over human beings and creation so that the evil powers are then free do what they want to do, namely cause destruction and death.

Throughout the Old Testament God was trying to teach Israel the importance of walking with him, saying if they would walk with him, he would protect you from the aggressive nations. But if they did not walk with him, he would lift his hands and let the other nations have their way. The Old Testament writers referred to this as God judging Israel. But God was actually just letting other wicked nations do what they wanted to do. In fact, in Isaiah chapter 10, God punishes Israel by lifting his hand of protection from them, allowing Assyria to come in and defeat Israel. Then God judges Assyria for doing that very thing. Apply this to the garden of Eden and what you get is this, God says to Adam and Eve, guard the garden, walk with me and I will protect you. But if you don't walk with me, you will open up the floodgates and warfare in the heavenly realm will come down to your territory. Humans were meant to be co-rulers with God over this territory, but when the first humans rebelled, like a vacuum the warfare of the heavenly realms was sucked in and humanity surrendered its God-given dominion over the earth (Genesis 1:28) to the rebels in the heavenly realms.

Disease Has Demonic Origins

Acts 10:38 says that Jesus 'went around doing good and healing all who were under the power of the devil, because God was with him'. Apparently everyone he healed was under the power of the devil because of their sickness or infirmity. In the Gospels Jesus always regarded illness, sickness and disease as either the direct or indirect result of satanic oppression. He always treated illness and suffering as a result of this world being in an oppressed state. Never once does Jesus come upon somebody with an affliction and say well, this is the mysterious will of God. Or, this is just the natural law of cause and effect, and unfortunately it happens to go bad for you. Rather than passively accepting these conditions, he does something to correct the situation because creation was never supposed to be this way. A scientist could explain these afflictions by natural laws, but that should tell us that the natural laws operating right now are not operating exactly the way God intended them to. So now 'natural laws' can produce things like leukemia and cancer – not that there is a specific demon behind every occurrence of disease, but there is a corruption in nature.

All Creation Is Corrupted and Needs Saving

Colossians 1:19, 20 says 'God was pleased to have all his fullness dwell in him, and through him to reconcile to himself all things, whether things on earth or things in heaven, by making peace through his blood, shed on the cross' – all things on heaven, all things on earth. Not only humans are estranged from God – all thing need to be reconciled. It is not just humans that are prone to violence it is all things. Every square inch of this cosmos has been permeated with this warfare, which is why nothing operates exactly the way it is supposed to operate. This world is corrupted and messed up. We are physically messed up, some of us are mentally messed up, and we are all to some extent spiritually messed up because we are born in this polluted incubator. Living a godly life does not come natural for any of us. We have a propensity and inclination that works against us. We can still see the glory and image of God in people sometimes. But it is off a bit, it has been corrupted.

What the Holy Spirit is doing in our life is readjusting it and the same thing is true of all creation. We see the glory of God and the beauty of God in creation. But we also see much that does not look like it was intended to look. God never intended a creation in which there are 330 million people who don't have access to clean water. That wasn't part of God's perfect design. He never intended a creation in which 30,000 people die each day of starvation or of diseases related to starvation. He never intended a creation where 20 million people have died of AIDs and another 25 million are infected right now. He never intended a creation in which 100,000 people are killed in a 7 second interval. He never intended a creation with tsunamis and hurricanes that wipe out entire cities. Nor did God intend for babies to die at birth, or for mothers to die giving birth.

The good news is that it won't always be like this. Paul says in Romans 8 that creation's groaning isn't just groaning in pain. It is also groaning in hope, because it is giving birth to something new, and the thing it is giving birth to is called the kingdom of God. We are right now in this in-between epoch. We are deciding how we are going to be birthed into eternity. For the purpose of this probationary epoch we have free will. That's why humans can inflict evil on people. But when this age comes to an end, the promise of God is that there will be a new heaven and a new earth. The principalities will be destroyed and the earth will look like God wanted it to. And in that world, there will not be any tsunamis or parasites, the wolf shall lay down with the lamb and the bear with the cow. When Jesus rebuked the storm, he gave a foretaste of what is going to come – an eschatological sign. A time is coming when all kinds of wrong things in this world are going to be rebuked and the creation will reflect the beauty and love of its Creator.

What Does This Mean to Us?

Don't Look for the Hand of God in Natural Disasters

Yes, we can find a few places in the Bible where God used natural ("unnatural"?) disasters to teach Israel lessons. But no legitimate hermeneutic would lead us to think we can extrapolate from those incidents to explain all earthquakes and natural disasters. The arguments presented here are evidence against that. In Luke 13:4 Jesus referred to the natural disaster of a tower falling on a group of people. Jesus says, do you think for a moment that they were worse sinners than all the others living in Jerusalem? Jesus' point was that those in his audience were all sinners and what they should worry about is their relationship with God.

We should not attempt to read the will of God or the hand of God in catastrophes in nature. Because when we start doing that, we start discerning the character of God in those disasters, and then we start attributing to God that which should be attributed to Satan. There are a lot of people who will say, if that's what God is like I don't think I can believe in that kind of God.

If you want to know what God looks like, don't look at the hookworm, don't look at the parasites, don't look at the earthquakes. Look at Jesus dying on Calvary for the very people that crucified him. That's what God looks like.

Live with a Warfare Mindset

There is a world of difference between living life on vacation and living life like you are in a war. When you are on vacation, you pamper yourself, you want as little inconvenience as possible for yourself. And we all need that once in a while. But when you are in a battle, the important thing is to do what your commanding officer tells you to do. People either live like they are on vacation or they live like they are in a war. Perhaps only one out of a thousand people live like they are in a war. In America, we call it the American dream to pamper ourselves, get as many toys as we can, get as big a house and car as we can. If the world was a wonderful place I would be all for it. But the world is not a wonderful place. We are in a battle. Maybe 999 people out of a thousand don't know it, but God's people are supposed to know it. And that knowledge needs to affect how we live, how we spend our money and how we use our talents. The question is not 'can I afford it', the question is 'what does God want'? A warfare mindset is not a vacation mindset.

Fight the Evil Effects of Nature

We are doing spiritual warfare when we fight disease. This is more than just prayer. Anything we do to push back the harmful effects of nature is a step toward reclaiming nature, toward rebuking the curse. Funding famine relief is spiritual warfare. Supporting organizations that bring relief to those who are suffering from a drought is doing spiritual warfare. Teaching people better farming and irrigation skills can be spiritual warfare. When scientists do scientific engineering to develop improved crops they are doing spiritual warfare. When they investigate new ways to sanitize water, they are doing spiritual warfare. When they discover ways to fight diseases and discover their origins, that is spiritual warfare. Anything we do to fight poverty and hunger is spiritual warfare. Having mercy on animals is a form of spiritual warfare. Anything we do to reflect God's ideal for creation is a form of spiritual warfare. By these and other means we are fighting back against the curse of death that is not God's will. In fact, every positive thing we do for the earth (including recycling!) is a form of spiritual warfare. Many evangelical Christians may see this as a 'liberal' agenda, but care for creation was our first command: 'Fill the earth and subdue it. Rule over the fish of the sea and the birds of the air and over every living creature that moves on the ground' (Genesis 1:28).

A New Era of Mission Is upon Us[1]

Robert Priest

Editors' Note: *Where are Evangelicals headed? Given the directions already noted in the rest of the book, this chapter offers a broadly based and carefully articulated response.*

In the late 1950's my parents were part of a team of missionary linguists arriving in Bolivia with Wycliffe Bible Translators. A brief 30 years later Wycliffe announced that the Scriptures (or at least the New Testament) had been translated into every Bolivian language spoken by a couple hundred people or more. Wycliffe withdrew its members from this 'field'. Their task was finished.

According to a typology of Protestant mission history articulated by Ralph Winter, my parents were part of the 'third era' of Protestant mission. The first era, exemplified by William Carey, called for missionaries to establish the church outside of Christendom, which they did on the islands of the South Pacific and the coasts of Asia and Africa. The second era, exemplified by Hudson Taylor, strove to expand missionary efforts geographically 'inland' and to 'regions beyond' where the church was not yet present. The third era, exemplified by William Cameron Townsend, focused on 'unreached peoples' and strove to bring the gospel, the Scriptures, and the church into every ethno-linguistic group where they were not yet present.

As 'third era' missionaries successfully complete their task of initial evangelism, Bible translation, and church planting among 'unreached peoples' in major swaths of the world (such as Bolivia), many 'third era' missionaries understand the task of mission to have been completed, leaving a shrinking portion of the world still necessitating mission. And indeed this model of mission has often framed mission as a task that can be 'finished' within specific time frames, allowing for us to anticipate 'closure' of the missionary task in the near future. Others, of course, understand mission in broader terms.

Toward the end of his life Ralph Winter proposed that although the important task of third-era mission would not be completely finished for some decades, much of contemporary mission today is better thought of as part of a fourth 'Kingdom Era' where mission is understood in more holistic terms and

[1] I would like to thank my colleagues James Plueddemann, Craig Ott, Harold Netland, and Richard Cook for providing critical feedback on an earlier version of this paper.

in relation to communities where churches do already exist. Winter rewrote his classic article, 'Three Mission Eras', to include this fourth era; but prior to publication, in October of 2006, he convened a gathering of mission leaders for feedback.[2] A number of missiologists who were deeply committed to the 'third era' paradigm, were highly critical of his 'Kingdom Era',[3] and persuaded Winter to withdraw his proposal that we are entering such a fourth era.[4] This was, in my opinion, a mistake on Winter's part.

As an empirical matter, Winter was correct to stress that the majority of what is now being done by evangelical Christians in the name of mission is not best understood in terms of an initial transmission of the gospel to 'unreached people groups.' Unfortunately his exposition of a 'fourth era' vacillated between empirical description and theological advocacy, with his theological advocacy foregrounded and articulated in somewhat idiosyncratic ways. That is, his theological exposition of fourth era mission did not reliably reflect the theological thinking of many people involved in the new patterns of mission Winter described – and thus may not have been the most helpful way to describe this era. Furthermore, by framing the discussion in theological terms, this allowed critics to respond primarily at a theological level, rather than having to first analyze the actual contours and dynamics of new trends in mission.[5]

In this paper I attempt to outline descriptively how mission in the present era diverges from earlier patterns, patterns present for example at the time of Edinburgh 1910. My exposition is not intended to closely mirror that of Ralph Winter, although in many respects it is congruent with his.

Edinburgh 1910 assumed a world divided between those geographic spaces where Christianity was present and other spaces where Christianity was absent, or largely so. Mission involved sending missionaries from Christian regions to non-Christian regions. The task of these missionaries? To evangelize and establish churches among people where Christian churches did not yet exist.

In this era Christianity had high prestige in missionary sending lands, with missionaries celebrated as heroes. Even westerners who were not evangelical often supported the missionary enterprise because of its perceived congruence with western colonial interests and with civilizational, religious, and racial evolutionary hierarchies which western elites embraced.

In much of the non-Christian world, under the power of colonial governments or of treaties forced through by western powers, a protected space had been created for westerners to enter regions that were not Christian and to

---

[2] David Hesselgrave. 'A Tribute to Dr. Ralph D. Winter', *Occasional Bulletin* 22:3 (2009), 4.

[3] See for example, David Hesselgrave. 'A Prolegomena to Understanding and Evaluating Dr. Ralph Winter's 'Fourth Era Kingdom Mission', *Occasional Bulletin* 21:3 (2008), 1-4 and Christopher Little, 'Assessing the 'Fourth Era'', *Occasional Bulletin* 22:1 (2009), 5.

[4] Hesselgrave. 'A Tribute,' 5.

[5] Again see Hesselgrave, 'A Prolegomena,' 1-4.

exercise the role of full-time missionaries – full-time religious professionals advocating for religious conversion. While missionaries frequently provided medical care or established educational institutions, these were often thought of as ancillary or instrumental contributors to the core mission of establishing Christianity where it did not yet exist.

With improved medical care and political protection, missionaries could increasingly expect a life-long career, just as pastors did. This was an era stressing the professionalization of missionary service. Seminaries added mission chairs, and a variety of other missionary training institutions were birthed, including notably Hartford Seminary's Kennedy School of Missions – where top linguists, comparative religionists, and anthropologists were soon offering PhD education in service of mission.

One hundred years later, the world looks rather different. Racial, colonial, and civilizational hierarchies whose rightness was formerly taken for granted have now been discredited as evil. Christianity's earlier links to power, especially as mediated through such hierarchies, now appears problematic. Popular representations of missionaries (such as in James Michener's *Hawaii*, Peter Matthiessen's *At Play in the Fields of the Lord*, or Barbara Kingsolver's *The Poisonwood Bible*) now present the career missionary, not as admirable hero, but as paternalistic, ethnocentric, bigoted anti-hero.

Geographic spaces formerly presumed to be Christian have witnessed either a remarkable decline in Christian allegiance, such as in Western Europe, or at least a changing environment where missionary Christianity is widely disrespected (the USA). By contrast, many of the geographic spaces formerly defined as mission fields are now centers of Christian presence.

The Christian missionary enterprise has itself changed significantly. The 1910 concept of a mission field as a geographic or ethno-linguistic space where Christianity is absent applies to a much smaller percentage of the world today. And these remaining 'unreached' regions of the world such as in Afghanistan, for example, are fundamentally different from what Bolivia or Kenya were back when they were first being 'reached'. The remaining 'unreached' regions of the world, with few exceptions, do not allow the presence of full-time foreign religious professionals devoting themselves to the task of religious conversion. Furthermore, today there are no power structures forcibly creating protected space for such missionaries in these regions. These regions do not give missionary visas. This does not mean that such regions cease to be a focus of missionary concern, but that the older model and identity of residential full-time missionary advocate for religious change is not viable for these regions. Either one tries to play this role while lying about it and pretending to be something else, or one accepts another full-time role which is valued (such as development worker) as a handmaid to witness. But in this case the older model and identity of full-time missionary to the unreached is simply not being lived. This does not mean that there are no longer full-time career missionaries, only that they now live primarily in spaces where Christianity is already present and usually serve in partnership with local Christians. This includes both spaces that formerly were not thought of as mission fields (such as Western Europe), and other spaces, now old mission fields, but where Christianity currently is present and may even be numerically strong. And of course this career missionary force now comes from South Korea, China, Costa Rica, Peru, or Nigeria as well as from Europe or North America.

Shifts in missionary location have coincided with shifts in understandings of mission. Rather than thinking of Christian mission primarily in terms of a geographic extension of Christianity into regions where Christianity is absent, mission today is increasingly understood by evangelicals as needed even in regions where Christian churches exist. Under 'third era' mission thinking, mission agencies (such as the Christian and Missionary Alliance or Wycliffe Bible Translators) began withdrawing from Peru once the Bible was translated and churches were established in each ethno-linguistic group. But the fact that Quechua churches existed in Peru, did not mean that every Quechua community had a viable Christian presence and witness. And thus evangelical Peruvians formed their own missionary organization *(Misión Amen)* and became 'missionaries' to extend the gospel throughout Peru. Peruvian power structures were sometimes hostile to their evangelical witness. But when Peruvian missionaries partner with long-term foreign missionaries or with visiting groups of short-term missionaries in acts of social service, they discover that doors to ministry and public witness are opened, and that their own credibility and evangelistic influence are enhanced. That is, even in old mission fields with significant numbers of Christians, those Christians often live under marked economic and social constraints in commending the gospel to their own communities, and find that partnerships with foreigners from abroad are often pivotal to effective missional public presence and witness. Partnership is core to mission today. A majority of North Americans today who serve as foreign missionaries do so in strategic partnerships with indigenous Christians, partnerships where foreign missionaries and local Christians strive synergistically through word and deed to commend the gospel to others who are not yet Christian.

The trajectory of much mission activity today involves global movement, not from spaces where there are Christians to spaces where there are not, but movement from spaces where there are Christians and churches that have extensive material resources to other spaces where there are significant numbers of Christians and churches that live under circumstances of material poverty and social constraint. A high proportion of mission today involves the synergy of global partnerships across such marked socio-economic divides, partnerships mobilized on behalf of human need and of Christian witness and discipleship. The vast majority of mission trips, for example, travel from resourced regions of the world (such as America, Europe, Korea or Singapore) to the regions of the world where significant numbers of Christians exist but under circumstances of poverty and material constraint (such as Uganda or

Guatemala). Scholars have calculated that as much as a third of all US Christian dollars channeled abroad on behalf of 'mission' is mediated through mission trips.[6] Across the world of Africa or Latin America, 'holistic ministry' or 'integral mission' has become central to ministry patterns and to gospel witness – even among Pentecostal megachurches.[7] And it is often through relations with American (or European or Korean) congregations, mission teams, Christian foundations, and missionary organizations that strategic material, cultural, and symbolic resources are mobilized on behalf of human need and gospel witness. And for Americans involved in mission, it is strategic partnerships with Christians in destination sites that are pivotal to effective gospel witness in those sites. In this model of mission, the foreigner is not the sole or even central agent of missional witness, but nonetheless contributes strategically to a joint witness where local Christians and churches are missionally central.

Under older 'Christendom' or 'parish' habits of thinking, people within the geographic orbit of parish or Christendom were not thought of as the object of mission. But as elderly missionaries reared on 'Christendom' habits of thinking (such as Lesslie Newbigin) returned home from 'the mission field', they were sometimes startled to perceive that their home country was itself a mission field requiring missional attention. In today's understanding of mission, there are no geographic spaces, no societies, where mission is not needed. Earlier models had sometimes contrasted evangelism (what is done in home spaces) with mission (what is done in another culture). Evangelism was seen as simple and straightforward, with training for evangelism perhaps featuring mastery of Kennedy's 'Evangelism Explosion' approach, or Campus Crusade's 'Four Spiritual Laws'. Mission, by contrast, required profound missiological preparation to engage people and their cultures. But increasingly there is a widespread recognition that even evangelism in home spaces faces overwhelming challenges and requires profound missiological underpinnings. Those wishing to commend the gospel in post-Christian Europe or North America face many of the same overwhelming missiological challenges that missionaries in foreign lands have faced. By conceptualizing the task as missional, and not simply as evangelistic, missional leaders are highlighting the cultural contextual realities which must be strategically engaged for effective witness, and calling for witness through integral mission involving word and deed.

Again, 'third era' missiologists often drew stark contrasts between the task of mission and the task of discipleship. Contemporary patterns highlight the

---

[6] Robert Wuthnow, *Boundless Faith: The Global Outreach of American Churches* (Berkeley, CA: University of California Press, 2009), 180 and Robert J. Priest, Douglas Wilson, and Adelle Johnson. 'U.S. Megachurches and New Patterns of Global Mission', *International Bulletin of Missionary Research* 34:2 (2010), 98.

[7] Donald Miller and Tetsunao Yamamori. *Global Pentecostalism: The New Face of Christian Social Engagement* (Berkeley: University of California Press, 2007).

theme of Christian faithfulness and discipleship being itself oriented missionally. Instead of a contrast between a relatively few professional missionaries focused on mission (with others simply giving and praying), the trend is to stress that all believers must live as Christians within their diverse social arenas in ways which favorably impact the public witness of the church in the world. And with the constraints of geography on social action and communication dissipating under globalization, even North Americans with full-time jobs in the US discover that participating in strategic mission partnership initiatives in distant regions is now possible.

Under 'third era' thinking, mission emphasized expanded geographic or linguistic transmission of a religious message, with the need for a larger quantity of religious proclamations. By contrast, missional effort today is centrally preoccupied with the quality, credibility and authenticity of Christian witness, whether in Rwanda, America, or Afghanistan. Older missionary linkages with racial and colonial projects are now understood as having compromised the credibility of Christian witness. We live in a world where wider discourses systematically construct Christianity in negative terms, not all of it undeserved, and this conditions the settings in which missional witness occurs today.

In North America and Europe powerful secularizing impulses stigmatize and sanction public expressions of Christian faith, exerting constant pressure on believers to privatize their faith. Three Christian responses to such pressure are common. One response is to keep religious faith private, unvoiced except within the religious frame of an already Christian worshipping community. This of course is a recipe for Christian decline. A second response is to go public in political modes of engagement – with public Christian presence framed as political conflict over values and where Christians try to 'take back the culture', 'win the culture wars', etc. This of course feeds into negative views of Christianity as unlovingly adversarial to others and as having hegemonic aspirations which disrespect others and their rights. Old memories of Christendom power structures now discredited are triggered. Such a predominantly political public presence on the part of Christians is damaging to Christian witness.[8]A third response is to seek for modes of Christian action which are both public and which positively commend the gospel to others. Acts of love and shalom, enacted publically in the name of Christ, are understood to do this. To live sacrificially for others *in Jesus' name*, focusing on poverty, disease, AIDS orphans, sex trafficking, environmental damage detrimental to health and well-being, not only fulfills biblical commands to love and serve others but does so in ways that are widely perceived as commendable.

Many North Americans live and work in settings which limit and sanction religious expression and identity – hampering their ability to bear public

---

[8] James Davison Hunter, *To Change the World: The Irony, Tragedy, and Possibility of Christianity in the Late Modern World* (New York: Oxford University Press, 2010).

witness to others. But when a nurse, for example, sacrificially gives up her vacation, a vacation her colleagues use for travel to all-inclusive resorts in the Caribbean, and instead participates with her church on a medical mission trip to Haiti, she is able to tell about her trip in her work setting, may be given supplies to help out, and will often have an opportunity to report on the trip in her hospital newsletter. This allows her to foreground her Christian identity and motivation and to 'let her light shine before others' who 'see her good works' and who recognize that her commendable action is grounded in relationship with God. Such positive public Christian presence opens doors for witness. Again, when one group of university students uses spring break to travel to Tijuana to go to the beach to get drunk and get laid, girls gone wild, guys gone predatory – and another group of university students uses spring break to go to Tijuana and sacrificially serve the poor in the slums in partnership with a local church, the contrast redounds favorably on the second group. Or when a megachurch pastor such as Rick Warren develops a passion for addressing AIDS and poverty in Rwanda, this contributes to his having an enhanced platform for public visible witness in America. Newspapers across America routinely describe mission trips favorably, mission trips focusing on everything from 'children at risk' to providing distant villagers with safe sources of water. That is, such mission trips not only potentially strengthen the public witness of partnering churches in receiving communities, but they provide a form of public witness in the home community as well.

Again, when Intervarsity Christian Fellowship attempts to evangelize university campuses, they find older paradigms of evangelistic outreach to be less effective than a campaign focused on sex trafficking. By publically working towards the good of vulnerable girls and women being sinned against, this latter campaign helps produce a framework of authenticity and positive witness, counteracting negative stereotypes of Christian patriarchy and misogyny, for example, while morally impressing and disarming even secular feminists. Within the framework of such a 'sex trafficking' focus, Intervarsity chapters find an enhanced moral respect and credibility which wins them open doors for verbally sharing their faith with others in a witness no longer easily dismissed as inauthentic.

Contemporary mission by evangelicals prioritizes holistic ministry or integral mission, not in an effort to substitute secular projects of social engagement for the Christian task of gospel communication, but out of a deep conviction that such patterns of positive public Christian presence are essential for credible Christian witness.

While Winter frames the fourth era of mission as the 'Kingdom Era', I prefer 'Missional Era'. Although some in this era do frame ministry in 'kingdom' terms, others do not. The term 'kingdom' is sometimes understood in ways not centrally focused on commending the gospel to unbelievers, whereas the term 'missional' better retains this as a central motivation. Furthermore, in my view the term 'kingdom' does not differentiate sufficiently between the political mode of engagement and the missional mode. The political mode of engagement has often used a kingdom language to express a desire for dominion, conquest, or 'taking over' of the culture. James Davison Hunter has powerfully demonstrated the prevalence of such an approach, and its negative consequences for Christian witness, in his recent book *To Change the World: The Irony, Tragedy, and Possibility of Christianity in the Late Modern World.* The missional impulse which I see exemplified in much contemporary mission is rather a thirst for a faithful public Christian presence which is non-hegemonic in nature but which strives to visibly and winsomely commend the beauty of the gospel to others.

Earlier eras of mission conceptualized the missionary, the full-time professional religious worker, as the sole or central agent of mission. Others participated by giving and by praying, but their core work lives were disconnected from the sacred task of mission, something understood as actually carried out by a small elite. In contemporary understandings, the task of living missionally is thought to belong to all believers, not merely religious professionals. Furthermore there is a pervasive recognition that missional presence is best accomplished through the full body of Christ, and that lay Christians living out their various vocational commitments in ways which establish a visible Christian presence is a critical component of authentic witness. Religious professionals are extremely limited, by contrast, in the social arenas they have access to and in the extent to which their lives are likely to be perceived as potentially paradigmatic for others. Instead of professional religious workers with seminary training pretending to be businessmen in order to be allowed to have social presence (perhaps justified in terms of 'tentmaking'), now there is a vigorous world of Christian businessmen striving to faithfully live out their calling globally as businessmen, but in ways which instantiate a positive and public missional Christian presence in business arenas. New trends in mission do not emphasize that helping the poor or teaching English are purely instrumental in service of gospel communication. Purely instrumental efforts are felt to undercut positive witness. But nor are these goods and vocations divorced from Christian witness, a substitute for the good of gospel witness. Rather there is a deep desire to bring the two together in a way which serves goods anyone can recognize to be good, but which is done in the name of Christ – such that the climate for verbal gospel witness is enhanced.

The contemporary missional era encompasses a wide variety of initiatives and impulses (short-term missions, business as mission, ministry to children at risk, efforts at church-based racial reconciliation, relief and development, environmental concerns) which fit the description above. Youth ministries, megachurch initiatives, the efforts of Christian donor foundations, relief and development agencies, church-to-church partnerships, initiatives to address sex trafficking, the activities of many older mission agencies, and efforts by church leaders attempting to engage contemporary American culture missionally, may all use a language of mission and/or of missional to describe their own aspirations and entrepreneurial efforts to have a positive public Christian presence and witness around the globe.

In earlier eras young people were recruited to become career missionaries under relatively clear ideas about what a missionary career might entail. But today, while tens of thousands of seminarians in America plan and prepare for pastoral careers with a relatively clear sense of what a pastoral career might look like, it is no longer the case that missionary recruits or recruiters have a clear sense of what a missionary career might look like which begins in 2011. Certainly a wide variety of specialized careers (in medicine, business, development work, teaching English) lend themselves to global presence even in regions which would not permit the presence of a Christian religious professional. And such specialized careers, if genuinely lived out with a sense of vocational excellence, allow for a credible and authentic Christian presence and witness in regions where gospel witness by religious professionals is limited. Of course Filipino or Latin American evangelicals may enter the same social spaces through service sector jobs, providing house help or child care, for example, and also endeavouring to live out a Christian presence and witness. This is one pattern of mission, with such persons not living the life of professional missionaries, professional religious workers, but nonetheless consciously using their work or vocational calling as a setting for missional presence and witness.

Others will more explicitly claim the title, role, and support base of professional missionary. But these will usually serve in settings where Christian churches exist and where partnership is central. Many of the roles played in such settings are, for foreigners, transitional roles. That is, the foreigner may temporarily fill a ministry role that will eventually be filled by someone who is a cultural and linguistic insider. Part of what this means, given the growth and increasing maturity of Christianity in diverse regions, is that most missionary positions today cannot be conceptualized as stable long-term positions or roles that will be filled over the course of a life-time. Candidates thus are inclined to commit to missionary service for relatively brief periods of not more than a few years. Otherwise they must be willing to envision and commit to an uncertain career of shifting roles, and with an uncertain support base for such shifting future possible roles. Mission agencies, supporting churches, and even missionary candidates in the present era, seldom envision a clear idea of what a given missionary's role will be for the next 30 or 40 years. This is directly a reflection of the social dynamics now present in global Christianity. So while it is easy for seminarians today to envision a stable long-term role as pastor, it is not so easy to envision what a stable long-term role of missionary will be.

There is one emerging role for contemporary missionaries which is likely to be needed for decades, and this is the role of broker. That is, in a world of global partnerships on behalf of Christian mission, a world where geography is less constraining on communication and travel, the role of mediators and brokers who can facilitate missional partnerships and initiatives, strategic resource sharing, and cultural understanding across marked cultural and socio-economic divides becomes increasingly important.[9] Missionaries with gifting and training in this area, able to strategically help the broader church missionally engage a wide variety of communities through word and deed, will fulfill a role likely to be present for decades to come.

As a missiology professor, it is important to me that a strong focus be retained on reaching 'unreached peoples' and on the verbal communication of the gospel. Furthermore I believe there are strategic long-term roles in the contemporary era for career missionaries, religious professionals with missiological training, who will play strategic roles in facilitating the collaborative task of global mission. But I am convinced that the insistence on restricting the scope of mission to 'unreached peoples' understood in 'third era' terms, and on restricting the agent of mission to professional missionaries, is neither biblically justified nor helpful to our own discipline. There are a wide variety of people (megachurch mission pastors, youth ministers, development personnel, businessmen, medical personnel, or local pastors) who long to live out their vocations in missional ways, striving to commend the gospel through deed and word to a wide variety of peoples across the world who need to be confronted with an authentic Christian witness. If missiologists and professional missionaries can bring the knowledge and understandings of missiology into close connection with the settings of missional action which these people strive for, while also helping them recognize, and prioritize, mission to categories of persons that are most distant from a credible gospel witness, we can provide correctives and strengthening to their task, and simultaneously make ourselves less marginal to the vast variety of Christians and vocations God is using today to commend his message to others around the world.

Bibliography

Hesselgrave, David. 'A Prolegomena to Understanding and Evaluating Dr. Ralph Winter's 'Fourth Era Kingdom Mission''. *Occasional Bulletin* 21:3 (2008), 1-4.

Hesselgrave, David. 'A Tribute to Dr. Ralph D. Winter'. *Occasional Bulletin* 22:3 (2009), 1-5, 8.

Hiebert, Paul. 'The Missionary as Mediator of Global Theologizing'. In Craig Ott and Harold Netland (eds). *Global Theology: Belief and Practice in an Era of World Christianity*. Grand Rapids: Baker Academic, 2006, 288-308.

Hunter, James Davison. *To Change the World: The Irony, Tragedy, and Possibility of Christianity in the Late Modern World*. New York: Oxford University Press, 2010.

---

[9] Another person who has articulated the changing role of missionaries today as that of 'mediator' is Paul Hiebert. See Paul Hiebert, 'The Missionary as Mediator of Global Theologizing' in Craig Ott and Harold Netland (eds), *Global Theology: Belief and Practice in an Era of World Christianity*, (Grand Rapids: Baker Academic, 2006), 297-301.

Little, Christopher. 'Assessing the 'Fourth Era''. *Occasional Bulletin* 22:1 (2009), 5.

Miller, Donald and Tetsunao Yamamori. *Global Pentecostalism: The New Face of Christian Social Engagement.* Berkeley: University of California Press, 2007.

Priest, Robert J., Douglas Wilson, and Adelle Johnson. 'U.S. Megachurches and New Patterns of Global Mission'. *International Bulletin of Missionary Research* 34:2 (2010), 97-103.

Winter, Ralph D. 'Three Mission Eras: And the Loss and Recovery of Kingdom Mission.' In Ralph D. Winter and Steven C. Hawthorne (eds). *Perspectives on the World Christian Movement: A Reader*, 4th edition. Pasadena: William Carey Library, 1999, 263-78.

Wuthnow, Robert. *Boundless Faith: The Global Outreach of American Churches.* Berkeley: University of California Press, 2009.

INDEX

CONTRIBUTORS

A. Scott Moreau, Professor of Intercultural Studies and Missions at Wheaton College. He is Editor of Evangelical Missions Quarterly and General Editor of the Encountering Mission series (Baker Books).

David Taylor, Research Director, Global Network of Mission Structures; Co-Organizer of the Tokyo 2010 Consultation; Member of the Global Network of Mission Structures Task Force.

Greg Parsons, Global Director, US Center for World Mission

Ezra Sargunam, Bishop of the Evangelical Church in India and an Indian challaji (disciple) of Donald McGavran.

Andrew Swamidoss, Dean of the India Graduate School of Missiology.

Yvonne Wood Huneycutt, Perspectives Instructor and Global Perspectives Consultant.

Alan R. Johnson, Assemblies of God Missionary to Thailand .

Moussa Bongoyok, Field Dean, William Carey International University, Assistant Professor of Islamic Studies, Biola University, Former Academic Dean, Bangui Evangelical School of Theology.

Timothy K. Park, Director of Korean Studies and Associate Professor of Asian Mission at Fuller Graduate School of Intercultural Studies; President of East-West Center for Missions Research and Development; Head Chairman of Asia Missions Association.

Yalin Xin, Research Fellow, Center for the Study of World Christian Revitalization Movements, Asbury Theological Seminary; Senior Editor, William Carey International Development Journal.

Robert A. Blincoe, US Director of Frontiers; author of Ethnic Realities and the Church: Lessons from Kurdistan.

Jim Haney, has served as Director of the Globla Research Department of the International Mission Board since 1999. Prior to that he served as a church planter in West Africa.

Yong Cho, Co-organizer of Tokyo 2010 Consultation; Director of the Global Network of Mission Structures.

Kevin S. Higgins, Executive Director, Global Teams.

Enoch Wan, President, Evangelical Missiological Society; Director, Doctor of Missiology Program, Western Seminary; Vice President, Great Commission International.

Cody C. Lorance, Senior Pastor and Church Planting Leader for Trinity International Baptist Mission (Carol Stream, IL) and a church planting strategist with the North American Mission Board of the Southern Baptist Convention currently serving in the Chicago metro area among diasporas. Cody also serves as a Catalyst for the Global Diasporas Network.

Ralph D. Winter, Founder, US Center for World Mission.

René Padilla, President, Micah Network; Emeritus President of the Kairos Foundation; General Secretary of the Latin American Theological Fellowship from 1983 to 1992.

Gregory A. Boyd, Senior Pastor, Woodland Hills Church in St. Paul, Minnesota; Founder, Christus Victor Ministries.

Robert J. Priest, Professor of Mission and Anthropology and Director of the PhD Program in Intercultural Studies Trinity Evangelical Divinity School.

REGNUM EDINBURGH 2010 SERIES
Series Listing

David A. Kerr, Kenneth R. Ross (eds.)
Edinburgh 2010
Mission Then and Now
2009 / 978-1-870345-73-6 / xiv + 343pp (paperback)
2009 / 978-1-870345-76-7 / xiv + 343pp (hardback)

No one can hope to fully understand the modern Christian missionary movement without engaging substantially with the World Missionary Conference, held at Edinburgh in 1910. As the centenary of the Conference approaches, the time is ripe to examine its meaning in light of the past century and the questions facing Christian witness today. This book is the first to systematically examine the eight Commissions which reported to Edinburgh 1910 and gave the conference much of its substance and enduring value. It will deepen and extend the reflection being stimulated by the upcoming centenary and will kindle the missionary imagination for 2010 and beyond.

Daryl M. Balia, Kirsteen Kim (eds.)
Edinburgh 2010
Witnessing to Christ Today
2010 / 978-1-870345-77-4 / xiv +301pp

This volume, the second in the Edinburgh 2010 series, includes reports of the nine main study groups working on different themes for the celebration of the centenary of the World Missionary Conference, Edinburgh 1910. Their collaborative work brings together perspectives that are as inclusive as possible of contemporary world Christianity and helps readers to grasp what it means in different contexts to be 'witnessing to Christ today'.

Claudia Währisch-Oblau, Fidon Mwombeki (eds.)
Mission Continues
Global Impulses for the 21st Century
2010 / 978-1-870345-82-8 / 271pp

In May 2009, 35 theologians from Asia, Africa and Europe met in Wuppertal, Germany, for a consultation on mission theology organized by the United Evangelical Mission: Communion of 35 Churches in Three Continents. The aim was to participate in the 100th anniversary of the Edinburgh conference through a study process and reflect on the challenges for mission in the 21st century. This book brings together these papers written by experienced practitioners from around the world.

Brian Woolnough and Wonsuk Ma (Eds)
Holistic Mission
God's plan for God's people 2010 / 978-1-870345-85-9

Holistic mission, or integral mission, implies God is concerned with the whole person, the whole community, body, mind and spirit. This book discusses the meaning of the holistic gospel, how it has developed, and implications for the the church. . It takes a global, eclectic approach, with 19 writers, all of whom have much experience in, and commitment to, holistic mission. It addresses critically and honestly one of the most exciting, and challenging, issues facing the church today. To be part of God's plan for God's people, the church must take holistic mission to the world.

Kirsteen Kim and Andrew Anderson (Eds)
Mission Today and Tomorrow
2011/978-1-870345-91-0

The centenary of the historic and influential World Missionary Conference held in Edinburgh 1910 presented a unique opportunity for the whole church worldwide to come together in celebration, reflection and recommitment to witnessing to Christ today. Edinburgh 2010 also engaged in serious study and reflection on the current state of world mission and the challenges facing all those who seek to witness Christ today. The results of this research was presented and debated within the context of Christian fellowship and worship at the conference in June 2010. This record of that conference is intended to give the background to that Call, to share the spirit of the conference, and to stimulate informed and focused participation in God's mission in Christ for the world's salvation.

Tormod Engelsviken, Erling Lundeby and Dagfinn Solheim (Eds)
The Church Going Glocal
Mission and Globalisation 2011/978-1-870345-93-4

This book provides thought-provoking and inspiring reading for all concerned with mission in the 21st century. I have been challenged by its contributors to re-think our Gospel ministries in our new local contexts marked by globalisation and migration. With its biblical foundation, its missiological reflection and interaction with contemporary society I warmly recommend this volume for study and pray that it will renew our passion for the Gospel and compassion for people.

REGNUM Studies in Global Christianity

(Previously GLOBAL THEOLOGICAL VOICES series)

Series Listing

David Emmanuuel Singh (ed.)
Jesus and the Cross
Reflections of Christians from Islamic Contexts
2008 / 978-1-870345-65-1 / x + 226pp

The Cross reminds us that the sins of the world are not borne through the exercise of power but through Jesus Christ's submission to the will of the Father. The papers in this volume are organised in three parts: scriptural, contextual and theological. The central question being addressed is: how do Christians living in contexts, where Islam is a majority or minority religion, experience, express or think of the Cross? This is, therefore, an exercise in listening. As the contexts from where these engagements arise are varied, the papers in drawing scriptural, contextual and theological reflections offer a cross-section of Christian thinking about Jesus and the Cross.

David Emmanuuel Singh (ed.)
Jesus and the Incarnation
Reflections of Christians from Islamic Contexts
2011/978-1-870345-90-3

In the dialogue of Christians with Muslims nothing is more fundamental than the Cross, the Incarnation and the Resurrection of Jesus. This book contains voices of Christians living in various 'Islamic contexts' and reflecting on the Incarnation of Jesus. The aim of these reflections is constructive and the hope is that the papers weaved around the notion of 'the Word' will not only promote dialogue among Christians on the roles of the Person and the Book, but, also, create a positive environment for their conversations with Muslim neighbours.

Sung-wook Hong
Naming God in Korea
The Case of Protestant Christianity
2008 / 978-1-870345-66-8 / xiv + 170pp

Since Christianity was introduced to Korea more than a century ago, one of the most controversial issue has been the Korean term for the Christian 'God'. This issue is not merely about naming the Christian God in Korean language, but it relates to the question of theological contextualization—the relationship between the gospel and culture—and the question of Korean Christian identity. This book examines the theological contextualization of the concept of 'God' in the contemporary Korean context and applies the translatability of Christianity to that context. It also demonstrates the nature of the gospel in relation to cultures, i.e., the universality of the gospel expressed in all human cultures.

Hubert van Beek (ed.)

Revisioning Christian Unity

The Global Christian Forum

2009 / 978-1-870345-74-3 / xx + 288pp

This book contains the records of the Global Christian Forum gathering held in Limuru near Nairobi, Kenya, on 6 – 9 November 2007 as well as the papers presented at that historic event. Also included are a summary of the Global Christian Forum process from its inception until the 2007 gathering and the reports of the evaluation of the process that was carried out in 2008.

Paul Hang-Sik Cho

Eschatology and Ecology

Experiences of the Korean Church

2010 / 978-1-870345-75-0/ 260pp (approx)

This book raises the question of why Korean people, and Korean Protestant Christians in particular, pay so little attention (in theory or practice) to ecological issues. The author argues that there is an important connection (or elective affinity) between this lack of attention and the other-worldly eschatology that is so dominant within Korean Protestant Christianity. Dispensational premillennialism, originally imported by American missionaries, resonated with traditional religious beliefs in Korea and soon came to dominate much of Korean Protestantism. This book argues that this, of all forms of millennialism, is the most damaging to ecological concerns.

Dietrich Werner, David Esterline, Namsoon Kang, Joshva Raja (eds.)

The Handbook of Theological Education in World Christianity

Theological Perspectives, Ecumenical Trends, Regional Surveys

2010 / 978-1-870345-80-4/ 759pp

This major reference work is the first ever comprehensive study of Theological Education in Christianity of its kind. With contributions from over 90 international scholars and church leaders, it aims to be easily accessible across denominational, cultural, educational, and geographic boundaries. The Handbook will aid international dialogue and networking among theological educators, institutions, and agencies. The major objectives of the text are (1) to provide introductory surveys on selected issues and themes in global theological education; (2) to provide regional surveys on key developments, achievements, and challenges in theological education; (3) to provide an overview of theological education for each of the major denominational / confessional traditions; and (4) to provide a reference section with an up-to-date list of the regional associations of theological institutions and other resources.

David Emmanuel Singh & Bernard C Farr (eds.)

Christianity and Education

Shaping of Christian Context in Thinking

2010 / 978-1-870345-81-1/ 244pp (approx)

Christianity and Education is a collection of papers published in *Transformation: An International Journal of Holistic Mission Studies* over a period of 15 years. It brings to life some of the papers that lay buried in shelves and in disparate volumes of *Transformation,* under a single volume for theological libraries, students and teachers. The articles here represent a spectrum of Christian thinking addressing issues of institutional development for theological education, theological studies in the context of global mission, contextually aware/informed education, and academies which deliver such education, methodologies and personal reflections.

J.Andrew Kirk

Civilisations in Conflict?

Islam, the West and Christian Faith 2011- 978-1-870345-71-2

Samuel Huntington's thesis, which argues that there appear to be aspects of Islam that could be on a collision course with the politics and values of Western societies, has provoked much controversy. The purpose of this study is to offer a particular response to Huntington's thesis by making a comparison between the origins of Islam and Christianity; the two religions that can be said to have shaped, in contrasting ways, the history of the Western world. The early history of each faith continues to have a profound impact on the way in which their respective followers have interpreted the relationship between faith and political life. The book draws significant, critical and creative conclusions from the analysis for contemporary intercultural understanding, and in particular for the debate about the justification of violence for political and religious ends.

REGNUM STUDIES IN MISSION
Series Listing

Kwame Bediako

Theology and Identity

The Impact of Culture upon Christian Thought in the Second Century and in Modern Africa

1992 / 1-870345-10-X / xviii + 508pp

The author examines the question of Christian identity in the context of the Graeco–Roman culture of the early Roman Empire. He then addresses the modern African predicament of quests for identity and integration.

Christopher Sugden

Seeking the Asian Face of Jesus

The Practice and Theology of Christian Social Witness in Indonesia and India 1974–1996

1997 / 1-870345-26-6 / xx + 496pp

This study focuses on contemporary holistic mission with the poor in India and Indonesia combined with the call to transformation of all life in Christ with micro-credit enterprise schemes. 'The literature on contextual theology now has a new standard to rise to' – Lamin Sanneh (Yale University, USA).

Hwa Yung

Mangoes or Bananas?

The Quest for an Authentic Asian Christian Theology

1997 / 1-870345-25-8 / xii + 274pp

Asian Christian thought remains largely captive to Greek dualism and Enlightenment rationalism because of the overwhelming dominance of Western culture. Authentic contextual Christian theologies will emerge within Asian Christianity with a dual recovery of confidence in culture and the gospel.

Keith E. Eitel

Paradigm Wars

The Southern Baptist International Mission Board Faces the Third Millennium

1999 / 1-870345-12-6 / x + 140pp

The International Mission Board of the Southern Baptist Convention is the largest denominational mission agency in North America. This volume chronicles the historic and contemporary forces that led to the IMB's recent extensive reorganization, providing the most comprehensive case study to date of a historic mission agency restructuring to continue its mission purpose into the twenty-first century more effectively.

Samuel Jayakumar

Dalit Consciousness and Christian Conversion

Historical Resources for a Contemporary Debate

1999 / 81-7214-497-0 / xxiv + 434pp

(Published jointly with ISPCK)

The main focus of this historical study is social change and transformation among the Dalit Christian communities in India. Historiography tests the evidence in the light of the conclusions of the modern Dalit liberation theologians.

Vinay Samuel and Christopher Sugden (eds.)

Mission as Transformation

A Theology of the Whole Gospel

1999 / 0870345133/ 522pp

This book brings together in one volume twenty five years of biblical reflection on mission practice with the poor from around the world. The approach of holistic mission, which integrates proclamation, evangelism, church planting and social transformation seamlessly as a whole, has been adopted since 1983 by most evangelical development agencies, most indigenous mission agencies and many Pentecostal churches. This volume helps anyone understand how evangelicals, struggling to unite evangelism and social action, found their way in the last twenty five years to the biblical view of mission in which God calls all human beings to love God and their neighbour; never creating a separation between the two.

Christopher Sugden

Gospel, Culture and Transformation

2000 / 1-870345-32-0 / viii + 152pp

A Reprint, with a New Introduction, of Part Two of Seeking the Asian Face of Jesus

Gospel, Culture and Transformation explores the practice of mission especially in relation to transforming cultures and communities. - 'Transformation is to enable God's vision of society to be actualised in all relationships: social, economic and spiritual, so that God's will may be reflected in human society and his love experienced by all communities, especially the poor.'

Bernhard Ott

Beyond Fragmentation: Integrating Mission and Theological Education

A Critical Assessment of some Recent Developments in Evangelical Theological Education

2001 / 1-870345-14-2 / xxviii + 382pp

Beyond Fragmentation is an enquiry into the development of Mission Studies in evangelical theological education in Germany and German-speaking Switzerland between 1960 and 1995. The author undertakes a detailed examination of the paradigm shifts which have taken place in recent years in both the theology of mission and the understanding of theological education.

Gideon Githiga

The Church as the Bulwark against Authoritarianism

Development of Church and State Relations in Kenya, with Particular Reference to the Years after Political Independence 1963-1992

2002 / 1-870345-38-x / xviii + 218pp

'All who care for love, peace and unity in Kenyan society will want to read this careful history by Bishop Githiga of how Kenyan Christians, drawing on the Bible, have sought to share the love of God, bring his peace and build up the unity of the nation, often in the face of great difficulties and opposition.' Canon Dr Chris Sugden, Oxford Centre for Mission Studies.

Myung Sung-Hoon, Hong Young-Gi (eds.)

Charis and Charisma

David Yonggi Cho and the Growth of Yoido Full Gospel Church

2003 / 1-870345-45-2 / xxii + 218pp

This book discusses the factors responsible for the growth of the world's largest church. It expounds the role of the Holy Spirit, the leadership, prayer, preaching, cell groups and creativity in promoting church growth. It focuses on God's grace (charis) and inspiring leadership (charisma) as the two essential factors and the book's purpose is to present a model for church growth worldwide.

Samuel Jayakumar

Mission Reader

Historical Models for Wholistic Mission in the Indian Context

2003 / 1-870345-42-8 / x + 250pp

(Published jointly with ISPCK)

This book is written from an evangelical point of view revalidating and reaffirming the Christian commitment to wholistic mission. The roots of the 'wholistic mission' combining 'evangelism and social concerns' are to be located in the history and tradition of Christian evangelism in the past; and the civilizing purpose of evangelism is compatible with modernity as an instrument in nation building.

Bob Robinson

Christians Meeting Hindus

An Analysis and Theological Critique of the Hindu-Christian Encounter in India

2004 / 1-870345-39-8 / xviii + 392pp

This book focuses on the Hindu-Christian encounter, especially the intentional meeting called dialogue, mainly during the last four decades of the twentieth century, and specifically in India itself.

Gene Early

Leadership Expectations

How Executive Expectations are Created and Used in a Non-Profit Setting

2005 / 1-870345-30-4 / xxiv + 276pp

The author creates an Expectation Enactment Analysis to study the role of the Chancellor of the University of the Nations-Kona, Hawaii. This study is grounded in the field of managerial work, jobs, and behaviour and draws on symbolic interactionism, role theory, role identity theory and enactment theory. The result is a conceptual framework for developing an understanding of managerial roles.

Tharcisse Gatwa

The Churches and Ethnic Ideology in the Rwandan Crises 1900-1994

2005 / 1-870345-24-X / approx 300pp

Since the early years of the twentieth century Christianity has become a new factor in Rwandan society. This book investigates the role Christian churches played in the formulation and development of the racial ideology that culminated in the 1994 genocide.

Julie Ma

Mission Possible

Biblical Strategies for Reaching the Lost

2005 / 1-870345-37-1 / xvi + 142pp

This is a missiology book for the church which liberates missiology from the specialists for the benefit of every believer. It also serves as a textbook that is simple and friendly, and yet solid in biblical interpretation. This book links the biblical teaching to the actual and contemporary missiological settings with examples, making the Bible come alive to the reader.

Allan Anderson, Edmond Tang (eds.)

Asian and Pentecostal

The Charismatic Face of Christianity in Asia

2005 / 1-870345-43-6 / xiv + 596pp

(Published jointly with APTS Press)

This book provides a thematic discussion and pioneering case studies on the history and development of Pentecostal and Charismatic churches in the countries of South Asia, South East Asia and East Asia.

I. Mark Beaumont

Christology in Dialogue with Muslims

A Critical Analysis of Christian Presentations of Christ for Muslims from the Ninth and Twentieth Centuries

2005 / 1-870345-46-0 / xxvi + 228pp

This book analyses Christian presentations of Christ for Muslims in the most creative periods of Christian-Muslim dialogue, the first half of the ninth century and the second half of the twentieth century. In these two periods, Christians made serious attempts to present their faith in Christ in terms that take into account Muslim perceptions of him, with a view to bridging the gap between Muslim and Christian convictions.

Thomas Czövek,

Three Seasons of Charismatic Leadership

A Literary-Critical and Theological Interpretation of the Narrative of Saul, David and Solomon

2006 / 978-1-870345484 / 272pp

This book investigates the charismatic leadership of Saul, David and Solomon. It suggests that charismatic leaders emerge in crisis situations in order to resolve the crisis by the charisma granted by God. Czovek argues that Saul proved himself as a charismatic leader as long as he acted resolutely and independently from his mentor Samuel. In the author's eyes, Saul's failure to establish himself as a charismatic leader is caused by his inability to step out from Samuel's shadow.

Jemima Atieno Oluoch

The Christian Political Theology of Dr. John Henry Okullu

2006 / 1-870345-51-7 / xx + 137pp

This book reconstructs the Christian political theology of Bishop John Henry Okullu, DD, through establishing what motivated him and the biblical basis for his socio-political activities. It also attempts to reconstruct the socio-political environment that nurtured Dr Okullu's prophetic ministry.

Richard Burgess

Nigeria's Christian Revolution

The Civil War Revival and Its Pentecostal Progeny (1967-2006)

2008 / 978-1-870345-63-7 / xxii + 347pp

This book describes the revival that occurred among the Igbo people of Eastern Nigeria and the new Pentecostal churches it generated, and documents the changes that have occurred as the movement has responded to global flows and local demands. As such, it explores the nature of revivalist and Pentecostal experience, but does so against the backdrop of local socio-political and economic developments, such as decolonisation and civil war, as well as broader processes, such as modernisation and globalisation.

David Emmanuel Singh & Bernard C Farr (eds.)

Christianity and Cultures

Shaping Christian Thinking in Context

2008 / 978-1-870345-69-9 / x + 260pp

This volume marks an important milestone, the 25th anniversary of the Oxford Centre for Mission Studies (OCMS). The papers here have been exclusively sourced from Transformation, a quarterly journal of OCMS, and seek to provide a tripartite view of Christianity's engagement with cultures by focusing on the question: how is Christian thinking being formed or reformed through its interaction with the varied contexts it encounters? The subject matters include different strands of theological-missiological thinking, socio-political engagements and forms of family relationships in interaction with the host cultures.

Tormod Engelsviken, Ernst Harbakk, Rolv Olsen, Thor Strandenæs (eds.)

Mission to the World

Communicating the Gospel in the 21st Century:
Essays in Honour of Knud Jørgensen

2008 / 978-1-870345-64-4 / 472pp

Knud Jørgensen is Director of Areopagos and Associate Professor of Missiology at MF Norwegian School of Theology. This book reflects on the main areas of Jørgensen's commitment to mission. At the same time it focuses on the main frontier of mission, the world, the content of mission, the Gospel, the fact that the Gospel has to be communicated, and the context of contemporary mission in the 21st century.

Al Tizon

Transformation after Lausanne

Radical Evangelical Mission in Global-Local Perspective

2008 / 978-1-870345-68-2 / xx + 281pp

After Lausanne '74, a worldwide network of radical evangelical mission theologians and practitioners use the notion of "Mission as Transformation" to integrate evangelism and social concern together, thus lifting theological voices from the Two Thirds World to places of prominence. This book documents the definitive gatherings, theological tensions, and social forces within and without evangelicalism that led up to Mission as Transformation. And it does so through a global-local grid that points the way toward greater holistic mission in the 21st century.

Bambang Budijanto

Values and Participation

Development in Rural Indonesia

2009 / 978-1-870345-70-5 / x + 237pp

Socio-religious values and socio-economic development are inter-dependant, inter-related and are constantly changing in the context of macro political structures, economic policy, religious organizations and globalization; and micro influences such as local affinities, identity, politics, leadership and beliefs. The three Lopait communities in Central Java, Indonesia provide an excellent model of the rich and complex negotiations and interactions among all the above factors. The book argues that the comprehensive approach in understanding the socio-religious values of each local community is essential to accurately describing their respective identity which will help institutions and agencies, both governmental and non-governmental, to relate to these communities with dignity and respect.

Young-hoon Lee

The Holy Spirit Movement in Korea

Its Historical and Theological Development

2009 / 978-1-870345-67-5 / x + 174pp

This book traces the historical and theological development of the Holy Spirit Movement in Korea through six successive periods (from 1900 to the present time). These periods are characterized by repentance and revival (1900-20), persecution and suffering under Japanese occupation (1920-40), confusion and division (1940-60), explosive revival in which the Pentecostal movement played a major role in the rapid growth of Korean churches (1960-80), the movement reaching out to all denominations (1980-2000), and the new context demanding the Holy Spirit movement to open new horizons in its mission engagement (2000-). The volume also discusses the relationship between this movement and other religions such as shamanism, and looks forward to further engagement with issues of concern in wider society.

Alan R. Johnson

Leadership in a Slum

A Bangkok Case Study

2009 / 978-1-870345-71-2 xx + 238pp

This book looks at leadership in the social context of a slum in Bangkok from an angle different from traditional studies which measure well educated Thais on leadership scales derived in the West. Using both systematic data collection and participant observation, it develops a culturally preferred model as well as a set of models based in Thai concepts that reflect on-the-ground realities. This work challenges the dominance of the patron-client rubric for understanding all forms of Thai leadership and offers a view for understanding leadership rooted in local social systems, contrary to approaches that assume the universal applicability of leadership research findings across all cultural settings. It concludes by looking at the implications of the anthropological approach for those who are involved in leadership training in Thai settings and beyond.

Titre Ande

Leadership and Authority

Bula Matari and Life - Community Ecclesiology in Congo

2010 / 978-1-870345-72-9 xvii + 189pp

This book proposes that Christian theology in Africa can make significant developments if a critical understanding of the socio-political context in contemporary Africa is taken seriously. The Christian leadership in post-colonial Africa has cloned its understanding and use of authority on the Bula Matari model, which was issued from the brutality of colonialism and political absolutism in post-colonial Africa. This model has caused many problems in churches, including dysfunction, conflicts, divisions and a lack of prophetic ministry. Titre proposes a Life-Community ecclesiology for liberating authority, where leadership is a function, not a status, and 'apostolic succession' belongs to all the people of God.

Frank Kwesi Adams

Odwira and the Gospel

A Study of the Asante Odwira Festival and its Significance for Christianity in Ghana

2010 /978-1-870345-59-0

The study of the Odwira festival is the key to the understanding of Asante religious and political life in Ghana. The book explores the nature of the Odwira festival longitudinally - in pre-colonial, colonial and post-independence Ghana - and examines the Odwira ideology and its implications for understanding the Asante self-identity. The book also discusses how some elements of faith portrayed in the Odwira festival could provide a framework for Christianity to engage with Asante culture at a greater depth. Theological themes in Asante belief that have emerged from this study include the theology of sacrament, ecclesiology, eschatology, Christology and a complex concept of time. The author argues that Asante cultural identity lies at the heart of the process by which the Asante Christian faith is carried forward.

Bruce Carlton

Strategy Coordinator

Changing the Course of Southern Baptist Missions

2010 / 978-1-870345-78-1 xvii + 268pp

In 1976, the Southern Baptist Convention adopted its Bold New Thrusts in Foreign Missions with the overarching goal of sharing the gospel with every person in the world by the year 2000. The formation of Cooperative Services International (CSI) in 1985 and the assigning of the first non-residential missionary (NRM) in 1987 demonstrated the Foreign Mission Board's (now International Mission Board) commitment to take the gospel message to countries that restricted traditional missionary presence and to people groups identified as having little or no access to the gospel. Carlton traces the historical development along with an analysis of the key components of the paradigm and its significant impact on Southern Baptists' missiology.

Julie Ma & Wonsuk Ma

Mission in the Spirit:

Towards a Pentecostal/Charismatic Missiology

2010 / 978-1-870345-84-2 xx + 312pp

The book explores the unique contribution of Pentecostal/Charismatic mission from the beginning of the twentieth century. The first part considers the theological basis of Pentecostal/Charismatic mission thinking and practice. Special attention is paid to the Old Testament, which has been regularly overlooked by the modern Pentecostal/Charismatic movements. The second part discusses major mission topics with contributions and challenges unique to Pentecostal/Charismatic mission. The book concludes with a reflection on the future of this powerful missionary movement. As the authors served as Korean missionaries in Asia, often their missionary experiences in Asia are reflected in their discussions.

S. Hun Kim & Wonsuk Ma (eds.)

Korean Diaspora and Christian Mission

2011-978-1-870345-89-7

As a 'divine conspiracy' for Missio Dei, the global phenomenon of people on the move has shown itself to be invaluable. In 2004 two significant documents concerning Diaspora were introduced, one by the Filipino International Network and the other by the Lausanne Committee for World Evangelization. These have created awareness of the importance of people on the move for Christian mission. Since then, Korean Diaspora has conducted similar research among Korean missions, resulting in this book. It is unique as the first volume researching Korean missions in Diasporic contexts, appraising and evaluating these missions with practical illustrations, and drawing on a wide diversity of researchers.

GENERAL REGNUM TITLES

Vinay Samuel, Chris Sugden (eds.)
The Church in Response to Human Need
1987 / 1870345045 / xii+268pp

Philip Sampson, Vinay Samuel, Chris Sugden (eds.)
Faith and Modernity
Essays in modernity and post-modernity
1994 / 1870345177 / 352pp

Klaus Fiedler
The Story of Faith Missions
1994 / 0745926878 / 428pp

Douglas Peterson
Not by Might nor by Power
A Pentecostal Theology of Social Concern in Latin America
1996 / 1870345207 / xvi+260pp

David Gitari
In Season and Out of Season
Sermons to a Nation
1996 / 1870345118 / 155pp

David. W. Virtue
A Vision of Hope
The Story of Samuel Habib
1996 / 1870345169 / xiv+137pp

Everett A Wilson
Strategy of the Spirit
J.Philip Hogan and the Growth of the Assemblies of God Worldwide, 1960 - 1990
1997 /1870345231/214

Murray Dempster, Byron Klaus, Douglas Petersen (eds.)
The Globalization of Pentecostalism
A Religion Made to Travel
1999 / 1870345290 / xvii+406pp

Peter Johnson, Chris Sugden (eds.)
Markets, Fair Trade and the Kingdom of God
Essays to Celebrate Traidcraft's 21st Birthday
2001 / 1870345193 / xii+155pp

Robert Hillman, Coral Chamberlain, Linda Harding
Healing & Wholeness
Reflections on the Healing Ministry
2002 / 978-1- 870345-35- 4 / xvii+283pp

David Bussau, Russell Mask
Christian Microenterprise Development
An Introduction
2003 / 1870345282 / xiii+142pp

David Singh
Sainthood and Revelatory Discourse
An Examination of the Basis for the Authority of Bayan in Mahdawi Islam
2003 / 8172147285 / xxiv+485pp

For the up-to-date listing of the Regnum books see www.ocms.ac.uk/regnum

regnum

Regnum Books International

Regnum is an Imprint of The Oxford Centre for Mission Studies
St. Philip and St. James Church
Woodstock Road
Oxford, OX2 6HR
Web: www.ocms.ac.uk/regnum